W9-AOJ-551

MAIN CURRENTS IN AMERICAN THOUGHT

Main Currents in American Thought

AN INTERPRETATION OF AMERICAN LITERATURE

FROM THE BEGINNINGS TO 1920

Vernon Louis Parrington

VOLUME ONE · 1620-1800

The Colonial Mind

VOLUME TWO · 1800-1860

The Romantic Revolution in America

VOLUME THREE · 1860-1920

The Beginnings of Critical Realism
in America

HARCOURT, BRACE AND COMPANY, NEW YORK

TO THE MEMORY

OF

J. ALLEN SMITH

SCHOLAR TEACHER DEMOCRAT GENTLEMAN

Omnium Amicus erat
qui
Justiciam ament.

FOREWORD

It is with a certain feeling of temerity that I offer the present study of a field of American letters which has been pretty largely neglected. That feeling springs from no sense of the slightness of the materials treated of, or their remoteness from present-day interests. To one who has dwelt for any length of time amidst the polemics of colonial debate, a conviction of the greatness of the issues and the intellectual honesty and masculine vigor of the disputants, comes home with compelling force. The subjects with which they dealt are old-fashioned only in manner and dress; at heart they were much the same themes with which we are engaged, and with which our children will be engaged after us. The feeling springs rather from a sense of the complexity and many-sidedness of the materials, with their ramifications into theology and politics and economics, and with backgrounds that conduct to remote origins in European systems of thought; and it is quickened by the realization that the interpretation here offered, runs in many points counter to that frequently given. The point of view from which I have endeavored to evaluate the materials, is liberal rather than conservative, Jeffersonian rather than Federalistic; and very likely in my search I have found what I went forth to find, as others have discovered what they were seeking. Unfortunately the *mens aequa et clara* is the rarest of attributes, and dead partisanships have a disconcerting way of coming to life again in the pages of their historians. That the vigorous passions and prejudices of the times I have dealt with may have found an echo in my judgments is, perhaps, to be expected; whether they have distorted my interpretation and vitiated my analysis is not for me to determine.

Of the present volume portions of Book One have already appeared in a much abbreviated form in the *Cambridge History of American Literature*, and certain passages of Book Three have appeared in *Selections from the Connecticut Wits*, of the *American Authors Series;* and I am indebted to the courtesy of G. P. Putnam's Sons and of Harcourt, Brace and Company for the privilege of reprinting them here. My obligations

to many students are too great to be adequately acknowledged in
a few words; they appear at large in the footnotes. I find myself
especially indebted to the critical historians who for the past score
of years have been working with such fruitful results in the Revolutionary and Constitutional periods of our development. Without
the assistance of their searching investigations the difficulties in
the way of understanding those complex times would have proved
insuperable. To the sane and acute scholarship of my friend and
colleague, Prof. Edward McMahon, and to the generous counsel
and encouragement of the late Prof. J. Allen Smith, I am under
particular obligations; but in those instances in which I may
unwittingly have gone astray, the fault is mine. In a study dealing with so long a period of time and with such diverse and difficult
fields, I can scarcely hope to have escaped the many traps laid for
the unwary. Perhaps I should add that the seeming neglect, in
the present volume, of southern backgrounds, has resulted from
the desire to postpone the detailed consideration of the mind of
the South to a later volume.

V. L. P.

Seattle, January 1, 1926

INTRODUCTION

I HAVE undertaken to give some account of the genesis and development in American letters of certain germinal ideas that have come to be reckoned traditionally American—how they came into being here, how they were opposed, and what influence they have exerted in determining the form and scope of our characteristic ideals and institutions. In pursuing such a task, I have chosen to follow the broad path of our political, economic, and social development, rather than the narrower belletristic; and the main divisions of the study have been fixed by forces that are anterior to literary schools and movements, creating the body of ideas from which literary culture eventually springs. The present volume carries the account from early beginnings in Puritan New England to the triumph of Jefferson and back-country agrarianism. Volume II concerns itself with the creative influence in America of French romantic theories, the rise of capitalism, and the transition from an agricultural to an industrial order; and Volume III will concern itself with the beginnings of dissatisfaction with the regnant middle class, and the several movements of criticism inspired by its reputed shortcomings.

Such a study will necessarily deal much with intellectual backgrounds, and especially with those diverse systems of European thought that from generation to generation have domesticated themselves in America, and through cross-fertilization with native aspirations and indigenous growths, have resulted in a body of ideals that we reckon definitively American. In broad outline those germinal contributions were the bequests successively of English Independency, of French romantic theory, of the industrial revolution and *laissez faire*, of nineteenth-century science, and of Continental theories of collectivism. Transplanted to American soil, these vigorous seedlings from old-world nurseries took root and flourished in such spots as proved congenial, stimulating American thought, suggesting programs for fresh Utopian ventures, providing an intellectual sanction for new experiments in government. Profoundly liberalizing in their influence, they gave impulse and form to our native idealisms, and contrib-

iii

uted largely to the outcome of our social experience. The child of two continents, America can be explained in its significant traits by neither alone.

In the present volume, I have examined with some care the bequests of seventeenth and eighteenth-century Europe to the colonial settlements, and in particular the transplanting to America of old-world liberalisms. In the main those liberalisms derived from two primary sources, English Independency and French romantic theory, supplemented by certain contributions from English Whiggery. From the first came the revolutionary doctrine of natural rights, clarified by a notable succession of thinkers from Roger Williams to John Locke, a doctrine that destroyed the philosophical sanction of divine right, substituted for the traditional absolutism the conception of a democratic church in a democratic state, and found exemplification in the commonwealths of Rhode Island and Connecticut. But unfortunately the liberal doctrine of natural rights was entangled in New England with an absolutist theology that conceived of human nature as inherently evil, that postulated a divine sovereignty absolute and arbitrary, and projected caste divisions into eternity—a body of dogmas that it needed two hundred years' experience in America to disintegrate. From this clash between a liberal political philosophy and a reactionary theology, between English Independency and English Presbyterianism, sprang the broad features of the struggle that largely determined the course of development in early New England, with which Book One is concerned.

Book Two deals with new beginnings from the raw materials of European immigrants, in other colonies than New England, who came hither singly and unorganized, and took immediate imprint from the new environment, creating during the eighteenth century the great body of yeomanry that was to determine in large measure the fate of America for a hundred years or more. It was to these scattered and undistinguished colonials that French romantic theory was brought by a group of intellectuals in the later years of the century, a philosophy so congenial to a decentralized society that it seemed to provide an authoritative sanction for the clarifying ideals of a republican order, based on the principle of local home rule, toward which colonial experience was driving. Exploring the equalitarian premises of the doctrine of natural rights, it amplified the emerging democratic theory by substituting for the Puritan conception of human nature as vicious, the conception of human nature as potentially excellent and capable of indefinite development. It asserted that the present evils of society are the consequence of vicious institutions rather than of depraved human nature; and that as free men and equals it is the right and duty of citizens to re-create social and political institutions to the end that they shall further social justice, encouraging the good in men rather than perverting them to evil. Romantic theory went further and provided a new economics and a new sociology. Since the great desideratum is man in a state of nature, it follows, according to the Physiocratic school, that the farmer is the ideal citizen, and agriculture the common and single source of wealth; and that in consequence the state should hold the tillers of the soil in special regard, shaping the public policy with a primary view to their interests. And since social custom is anterior to statutory laws, since the individual precedes the state, government must be circumscribed in its powers and scope by common agreement, and held strictly to its sole concern, the care of the social well-being. The political state, rightly conceived, must be reckoned no other than a great public-service corporation, with government as its responsible agent.

But while French romantic theory was spreading widely through the backwoods of America, providing an intellectual justification for the native agrarianism, another philosophy, derived from English liberalism of the later eighteenth century, was taking possession of the commercial towns. Realistic and material rather than romantic and Utopian, it was implicitly hostile to all the major premises and ideals of the French school. It conceived of human nature neither as good nor bad, but as acquisitive; and it proposed to erect a new social and political philosophy in accordance with the needs of a capitalistic order. It was concerned with exploitation and the rights of trade, rather than with justice and the rights of man. Its aspirations were expressed in the principle of *laissez faire*, and in elaborating this cardinal doctrine it reduced the citizen to the narrow dimensions of the economic man, concerned only with buying in the cheapest market and selling in the dearest. It would reduce the political state to the rôle of policeman, to keep the peace. With humanitarian and social interests, the state must not intermeddle—such functions lie outside its legitimate sphere. An expression of the aspirations of trading and speculating classes, it professed to believe that economic law—by which term it glorified the spontaneous play of the acquisitive instinct—was competent to regulate men in society, and that if freedom of trade were achieved, all lesser and secondary freedoms would follow.

In the light of such over-seas bequests to the American venture, the choice of materials for the present volume is predetermined. The line of liberalism in colonial America runs through Roger Williams, Benjamin Franklin, and Thomas Jefferson. The first transported to the new world the plentiful liberalisms of a great movement and a great century; the second gathered up the sum of native liberalisms that had emerged spontaneously from a decentralized society; and the third enriched these native liberalisms with borrowings from the late seventeenth-century natural-rights school and from French romantic theory, engrafting them upon the vigorous American stock. Over against these protagonists of liberalism must be set the complementary figures of John Cotton, Jonathan Edwards, and Alexander Hamilton, men whose grandiose dreams envisaged different ends for America and who followed different paths. The Carolinian Seeker and the Jacobean theocrat, the colonial democrat and the colonial Calvinist, the Physiocratic republican and the capitalistic financier, embody in concrete form the diverse tendencies of primitive America; and around these major figures lesser ones will group themselves, parties to the great struggle of those early years, the eventual outcome of which was the rejection of the principles of monarchy and aristocracy, and the venturing upon an experiment in republicanism continental in scope.

That our colonial literature seems to many readers meager and uninteresting, that it is commonly squeezed into the skimpiest of chapters in our handbooks of American literature, is due, I think, to an exaggerated regard for esthetic values. Our literary historians have labored under too heavy a handicap of the genteel tradition—to borrow Professor Santayana's happy phrase—to enter sympathetically into a world of masculine intellects and material struggles. They have sought daintier fare than polemics, and in consequence mediocre verse has obscured political speculation, and poetasters have shouldered aside vigorous creative thinkers. The colonial period is meager and lean only to those whose "disedged appetites" find no savor in old-fashioned beef and puddings.   The seventeenth century in America as well as in England was a *saeculum theologicum*, and the eighteenth century was a *saeculum politicum*.   No other path leads so directly and intimately into the heart of those old days as the thorny path of their theological and political controversies; and if one will resolutely pick his way amongst the thorns, he will have his reward in coming close to the men who debated earnestly over the plans and specifications of the Utopia that was to be erected in the free spaces of America, and who however wanting they may have been in the lesser arts, were no mean architects and craftsmen for the business at hand.   The foundations of a later America were laid in vigorous polemics, and the rough stone was plentifully mortared with idealism.   To enter once more into the spirit of those fine old idealisms, and to learn that the promise of the future has lain always in the keeping of liberal minds that were never discouraged from their dreams, is scarcely a profitless undertaking, nor without meaning to those who like Merlin pursue the light of their hopes where it flickers above the treacherous marshlands.

CONTENTS

CONTENTS

Part II

The Twilight of the Oligarchy—1660–1720

BOOK II: THE COLONIAL MIND

CONTENTS

PART II

The Awakening of the American Mind—1763-1783

BOOK III: LIBERALISM AND THE CONSTITUTION

PART I

The Agrarian Defeat—1783–1787

PART II

Political Democracy Gets under Way—1787–1800

CONTENTS

BOOK ONE: LIBERALISM AND PURITANISM

BOOK ONE

LIBERALISM AND PURITANISM

COMMON report has long made out Puritan New England to have
been the native seat and germinal source of such ideals and institutions as have come to be regarded as traditionally American. Any
critical study of the American mind, therefore, may conveniently
seek its beginnings in the colonies clustered about Massachusetts
Bay, and will inquire into the causes of the pronounced singularity
of temper and purpose that marked off the New England settlements from those to the south, creating a distinctive New England
character, and disciplining it for later conquests that were to set
a stamp on American life. The course of its somewhat singular
development would seem from the first to have been determined
by an interweaving of idealism and economics—by the substantial
body of thought and customs and institutions brought from the
old home, slowly modified by new ways of life developing under
the silent pressure of a freer environment. Of these new ways,
the first in creative influence was probably the freehold tenure of
landholdings, put in effect at the beginning and retained un-
modified for generations; and the second was the development of a
mercantile spirit that resulted from the sterility of the Massachusetts soil, which encouraged the ambitious to seek wealth in
more profitable ways than tilling barren acres. From these
sources emerged the two chief classes of New England: the yeomanry, a body of democratic freeholders who constituted the
rank and file of the people, and the gentry, a group of capable.
merchants who dominated the commonwealth from early days to
the rise of industrialism. And it was the interweaving of the aims
and purposes of these acquisitive yeomen and gentry—harmonious
for the most part on the surface, yet driving in different directions—with the ideal of a theocracy and the inhibitions of
Puritan dogma, that constitutes the pattern of life to be dealt
with here. The Puritan and the Yankee were the two halves
of the New England whole, and to overlook or underestimate

3

the contributions of either to the common life is grossly to misinterpret the spirit and character of primitive New England. The Puritan was a contribution of the old world, created by the rugged idealism of the English Reformation; the Yankee was a product of native conditions, created by a practical economics.

PART ONE: THE PURITAN HERITAGE
1620-1660

CHAPTER I

ENGLISH BACKGROUNDS

I

THE body of thought brought to America by the immigrant Puritans, and which gave a special cast to the New England mind, may be summed in a phrase as Carolinian liberalism. It was the confused bequest of a hundred years of English idealism, struggling with the knotty problems of a complex society in transition from the old static feudal order to the modern capitalistic; and it took a particular form and received a narrow ideology from the current ecclesiastical disputes concerning the nature and governance of the true church. It was exclusively a product of the Reformation, unleavened by the spirit of the Renaissance. But though English Puritanism was wholly theological in its immediate origins, it gathered about it in the century and a half of its militant career all the forces of unrest fermenting in England. Economics and politics joined hands with theology; the center of gravity of the total movement tended to sink lower in the social scale; and in the end all England was involved in the great struggle.

In its deeper purpose Puritanism was a frank challenge of the traditional social solidarity of English institutional life by an emergent individualism, and far-reaching social readjustments followed inevitably in its train. If the evolution of modern society is conceived of as falling into two broad phases, the disintegration of a corporate feudal order into unregimented individual members of society, and the struggles of those free individuals to regroup themselves in new social commonwealths, the historical significance of English Puritanism may perhaps become clear: it was one of the disruptive forces that disintegrated the traditional solidarity of church and state by creating a revolutionary philosophy of individual rights that purposed to free the individual, both as Christian and subject, from subjection to a fixed corporate status.

5

The sixteenth century had announced the great doctrine of the priesthood of all believers, and the seventeenth century was engaged in adapting the forms of social and political institutions to that revolutionary principle. It was concerned to discover a new system of social organization that should adjust equitably the rights of the individual to the needs of the political state and to society. To that end the whole theory of the origin and functions of the political state must come in for review, and a new conception of the rights of the individual subject-citizen must be evolved.

This is the sufficient explanation of the close interweaving of theology and politics that marked the broadening movement of English Puritanism. Unless one keeps in mind the social forces that found it convenient to array themselves in Puritan garb, the clear meaning of it all will be lost in the fogs of Biblical disputation, and some of the ablest men the English race has ever bred will be reduced to crabbed theologians involved in tenuous subtleties and disputing endlessly over absurd dogmas. But tenacious disputants though they certainly were, pursuing their subtleties into the last refuge and cranny of logic, those Puritan dogmatists were very far from being vain practitioners of eccentricity. It is the manner and dress and not the matter of their argument that is strange; and if we will resolutely translate the old phrases into modern equivalents, if we will put aside the theology and fasten attention on the politics and the economics of the struggle, we shall have less difficulty in discovering that the new principle for which those old Puritans were groping was the later familiar doctrine of natural rights; and the final end and outcome of their concern for a more equitable relation of the individual to society, was the principle of a democratic commonwealth, established in the conception of political equalitarianism. Here are liberalisms in plenty to reward the search for the inner core of Puritanism. There was gunpowder packed away in Luther's doctrine of the priesthood of all believers, and the explosion that resulted made tremendous breaches in the walls of a seemingly impregnable feudalism. An intellectual like Roger Williams, who had thought his way resolutely to the logical outcome of the reforming principles, could not fail to be reckoned a firebrand by his generation. The doctrine of "thorough" was dangerously revolutionary.

If the economics of England had not been in a state of flux during the century following the accession of Elizabeth, the Puritan movement would not have moved forward by successive stages to the explosion of the Civil War. But because, as later in France, a rising economic order was restive under the restrictions of an outworn order, the Puritan protest found capable allies at hand, and supported by the money and arms of the commercial interests, it passed under the control of the latter and set about the great business of making England over in accordance with the new plans and specifications. On the whole it is no mistake to regard the Puritan revolution as primarily a rebellion of the capable middle class, whose growing trade interests demanded a larger measure of freedom than a paternal king and a landed aristocracy were willing to grant; and its significant contributions to the modern world were the two systems it did so much to further: the system of capitalism and the system of parliamentary government. From the Puritan conception of the stewardship of talents came a new ethic of work that provided a sanction for middle-class exploitation, by supplanting the medieval principle of production for consumption with the capitalistic principle of production for profit; and from the conception of the dignity of the individual came the sanction for the self-pride of the merchant that sustained him in his encounters with a domineering aristocracy. A prosperous merchant who accounted himself a son of God and who was persuaded that he was fighting for a freer England was no mean foe to be awed by the rustlings of a Cavalier. The London burgesses were the backbone of Puritanism in the days before the movement passed into the extremer form of Independency and was taken over by the sectarian radicals; and the Presbyterian middle-phase of Puritanism spread widely amongst the middle class throughout central and southern England. But in unloosing the traditional social bonds Puritanism awakened aspirations that in the end proved hostile to the middle-class program. It created bitter partisan divisions; it set the social underling and the aristocrat apart from the middle-class core, and created those major political parties that have since carried on the parliamentary struggle. Inevitably it sharpened class alignments, and the reactions of those alignments vitally affected the development of New England. The struggles in Massachusetts can scarcely be understood unless they are set against the greater struggles then going forward in England.

The three parties that emerged from the theological disputes, Anglican, Presbyterian, and Independent, followed, in the main, broad social cleavages and corresponded roughly to the later political divisions of Tory, Whig, and Democrat. The first stoutly upheld the absolutist principle in church and state. It stood for Bishop and King. Numbering probably a large majority of the English people, and led by the hereditary masters of England, it was dominated by the feudal spirit of corporate unity. It believed that social order, the loyal subjection of subject to ruler, was possible only through a coalescence of church and state. The subject-citizen was born into the one as he was born into the other, and owed allegiance both to his spiritual and temporal overlords. Authority, whether in church or state, was of divine origin, and Bishop and King were the Lord's anointed, answerable for their stewardship only to God. The second party was a compromise between aristocracy and democracy. It substituted the principle of elective stewardship for divine right. Rejecting the absolutism of the hierarchy, it turned to the system newly brought over from Geneva, a system that retained the principle of a state church, but which yielded control of the parish to the eldership, a select body of the best and wisest chosen by the laity, with final authority in doctrine and discipline vested in the synod. It drew its support largely from the London burgesses, but with a considerable following of country gentlemen. As the party developed it tended to merge with the nascent capitalism, restricted the doctrine of natural rights to property rights, and prepared the way for the later Whiggery of Pitt, or capitalistic imperialism. The third party was more or less consciously democratic in spirit and purpose, the expression of the newly-awakened aspirations of the social underling. Numbers of rebellious individualists appeared who wanted to be ruled neither by bishop nor elder, but who preferred to club with the like-minded and set up an independent church on a local, self-governing basis. They took literally the command of Paul, "Come out from among them, and be ye separate, saith the Lord, and touch not the unclean thing." That only was the true church, they asserted, which withdrew from all communion with sinners and rejected the authority of a sinful state; and so they called themselves Separatists.

Separatism, quite evidently, was the extreme left wing of the total Puritan movement, concerned to explore all the logical deductions from the revolutionary premise of the Reformation. It was the final expression of the disintegrating gospel of individualism implicit in the doctrine of the priesthood of all believers. Its unworldly sincerity was as uncompromising as its unworldly scripturism. Not finding sanction for them in the Bible, it rejected the established ecclesiastical authorities, and laid rude hands on the garments of Mother Church. Counsels of social expediency were accounted as dust in the balance against the explicit commandment of the Lord to separate from the sins of the world; and clinging to the text of the Scripture the Separatist was led straight to the conception of a Christian democracy. If the true church was a Congregation of the Saints, and if the Saints were equal in the sight of God, why should not the principle of equality prevail in the rule of the congregation? And if it were a brotherhood in Christ, owning allegiance to the King of Kings, by what Scriptural right did profane authorities exercise control over the tender consciences of the brethren? The autonomy of the congregation was a fruitful conception, certain to appeal to vigorous natures; and out of the loins of Separatism came a numerous and often ungainly progeny that greatly scandalized the conservative Carolinian: Anabaptist, Digger, Fifth-Monarchy man, Quaker, Seeker, Congregationalist—to name only a few—each following his particular path to his divinely sanctioned Utopia, regardless of social ties, denying the worth of social conformity. Imperious individualists, the Separatists were certain to prove an offense to all respectable folk, who demanded in the name of common sense that they be put down.

It was the doctrines of Separatism, quite as much as the principle of the independency of the congregation, that aroused the fierce antagonism of Presbyterians equally with Anglicans. In the main those doctrines did not derive from John Calvin; they go back rather to Wittenberg than to Geneva, to the principles of Luther and certain German sects. The Anabaptist and the Digger, clearly, were of German descent and of somewhat ancient lineage, offspring of late medieval communism and other primitive enthusiasms. The Quaker was a mystic, sprung from the New Testament, who denied the Scriptural validity of a Hebraized Calvinism and a hireling priesthood, and accepted the Holy Spirit as the sole guide to his feet. The Seeker, on the other hand, who may perhaps be regarded as the completest expression of Puritan radicalism, was an open-minded questioner who professed to have found no satisfactory answer to his inquiry concerning the nature of the true church, and was awaiting further light. The Seekers were individuals rather than a sect, few in numbers yet greatly influential, men like Roger Williams, Sir Harry Vane, Cromwell, and perhaps Milton, outstanding figures of a great age, who embodied the final results of Puritan idealism before it was submerged by the Restoration.

During the long years of rule by divine right under the first Stuarts, the Anglicans held the Puritan unrest in strict control. Nevertheless a hundred years of debate and changing economic conditions had rendered the attempt to erect in England a counterpart of the French centralized state, no better than an anachronism. The Presbyterian opposition grew rapidly in numbers and prestige, and the early years of the Long Parliament marked the culmination of Presbyterian power. The bishops were overthrown and the elders were in a fair way to seize control of England. But unfortunately for Presbyterian hopes, the radical sects thrown up out of the war clashed with the moderates and finally broke with them; whereupon followed the "root and branch" revolution that had been long preparing. The left-wing Independents secured control of the army and set about the work of erecting a government that should be a real commonwealth of free citizens. The voice of the underling, for the first time in English history, was listened to in the national councils, for the excellent reason that his sword was drawn to enforce his demands. But they were too small a minority to leaven the sodden mass of a people long subject to absolutist rule. The psychology of custom was against them. They could strike down their armed enemies in the field, but they could not liberate the minds of men unfit to be free. Militant Puritanism was overthrown and its idealisms became the jest of every drunken tapster in London. But fortunately, not before its political principles, long obscured by theology, were sufficiently clarified to be laid open to the common understanding of Englishmen. Out of the debates around the camp fires of the army had come a new philosophy that rested on the principle that the individual, both as Christian and citizen, derives from nature certain inalienable rights which every church and every state is bound to respect. This far-reaching doctrine of natural rights, to the formulation of which many thinkers had contributed and which received later its classic form from the pen of Locke, was the suggestive contribution of Puritanism to political theory, with the aid of which later liberals were to carry forward the struggle.

II

The far-reaching liberalisms implicit in the rejection of a hierarchical organization of the church were to discover no allies in the major premises of the system of theology accepted generally by the English Puritans, and by them transported to New England. Calvinism was no friend of equalitarianism. It was rooted too deeply in the Old Testament for that, was too rigidly aristocratic. It saw too little good in human nature to trust the multitude of the unregenerate; and this lack of faith was to entail grave consequences upon the development of New England. That the immigrant Puritans brought in their intellectual luggage the system of Calvin rather than of Luther must be reckoned a misfortune, out of which flowed many of the bickerings and much of the intolerance that left a stain on the pages of early New England history.

Two divergent systems of theology, it will be remembered, were spreading through northern Europe during the years of the Reformation, systems that inevitably differentiated in consequence of certain variations of emphasis in the teachings of Luther and Calvin. Both thinkers accepted the adequacy of the Scriptures to all temporal needs, but Luther was at once more mystical and more practical than Calvin, deriving his inspiration chiefly from the New Testament, discovering the creative source of the Christian life in the spiritual union of the soul with Christ, and inclining to tolerance of differences of opinion amongst believers; whereas Calvin was ardently Hebraic, exalting righteousness above love, seeking the law in the Old Testament and laying emphasis on an authoritarian system. The one was implicitly individualistic, the other hierarchical in creative influence. The teachings of Luther, erected on the major principle of justification by faith, conducted straight to political liberty, and he refused to compromise or turn away from pursuing the direct path. If one accepts the doctrine of the priesthood of all believers, one can scarcely refrain from following Luther in his conception of Christian liberty. If the mystical union of the soul with Christ has superseded all lesser loyalties by a higher and more sacred, the enjoyment of spiritual freedom must be reckoned the inalienable right of every child of God. Neither the political state nor the official hierarchy can justly coerce the individual conscience. "One thing and one thing only," said Luther in his *Treatise on Christian Liberty*, "is necessary for Christian life, righteousness and liberty." And from this he deduced the conclusion that "neither pope nor bishop nor any other man has the right to impose a single syllable of law upon a Christian man without his consent; and if he does, it is done in the spirit of tyranny." [1] Clearly, this is the spirit of uncompromising individualism that would eventually espouse the principle of democracy in church and state; and it was their native sympathy with such liberalism that led the radical Separatists to turn more naturally to Luther than to Calvin. Many of the differences that set Roger Williams so greatly apart from the New England brethren must be traced to the Lutheran origins of his thinking.

There was scant room in the rigid system of John Calvin for such Christian liberty. The Genevan thinker was a logician rather than a philosopher, a rigorous system-maker and dogmatist who knotted every argument and tied every strand securely into its fellow, till there was no escape from the net unless one broke through the mesh. To the formalist who demanded an exact system, and to the timid who feared free speculation, the logical consistency of Calvinism made irresistible appeal; and this perhaps suffices to explain its extraordinary hold on the rank and file of middle-class English Presbyterians. More original minds might break with it—men like Richard Hooker and Roger Williams and Vane and Milton—but academic thinkers and schoolmen, men whom the free spaces of thought frightened and who felt safe only behind secure fences, theologians like John Cotton and his fellows, made a virtue of necessity and fell to declaiming on the excellence of those chains wherewith they were bound. How narrow and cold was their prison they seem never to have realized; but that fact only aggravated the misfortunes that New England was to suffer from the spiritual guidance of such teachers. In seeking for an explanation of the unhappy union of a reactionary theology and a revolutionary political theory,

[1] See "The Babylonian Captivity," in *Works*, Vol. II, p. 233 (Philadelphia, 1915).

Harriet Beecher Stowe suggested in *Poganuc People* that the Puritan immigrants were the children of two different centuries; that from the sixteenth century they got their theology, and from the seventeenth their politics, with the result that an older absolutist dogma snuggled down side by side in their minds with a later democratic conception of the state and society. In England the potential hostility between Calvinist dogma and individual freedom was perceived by the more liberal Separatists, but in America it was not till the rise of the Revolutionary disputes of the next century that Calvinism was discovered to be the foe of democratic liberalism and was finally rejected. It is a fruitful suggestion, and in its major contention that the liberalisms implicit in the Puritan revolution were ill served by a reactionary theology, it is certainly in harmony with the facts.

That Calvinism in its primary assumptions was a composite of oriental despotism and sixteenth-century monarchism, modified by the medieval conception of a city-state, is clear enough today to anyone who will take the trouble to translate dogma into political terms. In recasting the framework of the old theology, Calvin accepted as a sovereign conception the idea of God as arbitrary and absolute will—an august *Rex regum* whose authority is universal and unconditioned; and this conception he invested with Hebraic borrowings from the Old Testament. The principle of absolutism, indeed, he could scarcely have escaped. It came down to him through the Roman Empire and the Roman Church, from the ancient oriental despotisms, and it was interwoven with all the institutions and social forms against which the Reformation was a protest. But unhappily, instead of questioning the principle, he provided a new sanction for it and broadened its sway, by investing it with divine authority and erecting upon it a whole cosmology. That the ancient Hebrew thinkers, in seeking to give concrete form to their speculations on the nature of Jehovah, should have made use of the political ideas of primitive Israel, that they should have used all the wealth of oriental imagery in describing the regal attributes of their God, was inevitable. They knew only oriental potentates, and so Jehovah became a greater Ptolemy, with Cherubim and Seraphim, Angels and Principalities and Powers, duly ranked about the heavenly throne. So saturated with monarchical and caste ideas is the Old Testament, that it is almost impossible today to put the old phrasing out of mind, and

we talk as naturally of the Kingdom of God as did the men of
that older world who knew no other political phraseology. Calvin
rejected the individualism of Luther and followed in the footsteps
of older thinkers like Duns Scotus. The monarchical principle was
everywhere gaining ground in Europe. He had a lawyer's love of
law, and law reposed in the absolute will of the prince. Hebraize
this fact, erect a cosmology upon it, and we have the vital principle of Calvinism.

From this cosmic absolutism, that conceived of God as the
stable Will sustaining the universe, binding together what otherwise would fly asunder, two important corollaries were derived:
the universality of the moral law, and the necessity of divine
judgment. From the former flowed that curious association of
God's will with natural causes which induced Cotton Mather,
when suffering from toothache, to inquire what sin he had committed with his teeth, and which left no free spaces or non-moral
impulses in the lives of men. From the latter flowed the doctrine
of theological determinism. If time is embedded in the eternity
of God's mind, if to Him past and future are here and now, fore-
knowledge is an inevitable divine attribute, and predestination is
only a finite way of expressing God's understanding of how human
fate works itself out. Ally this doctrine of determinism with the
Biblical account of the fall of man, and the doctrine of the elect
becomes the theological complement of the class prejudices of the
times. Bred up in the current aristocratic contempt for the sodden
mass of the people, Calvinist theologians easily came to regard
them as stupid, sensual, veritable children of Adam, born to sin
and heirs of damnation. Only the elect shall be saved. That there
was a remnant in Israel whom God had chosen, Isaiah had long
before pointed out; and the doctrine of the remnant was confirmed
for Calvinism by the sinful herd whose daily actions testified to
their lost estate.

According to such a theology, the individual clearly is in no
effective sense a free soul. There is no room for the conception of
human perfectibility. The heritage of natural freedom was long
since cast away by the common forefather; and because of the
pre-natal sin which this act entailed on all mankind, the natural
man is shut away eternally from communion with God. He is no
better than an oriental serf at the mercy of a Sovereign Will that
is implacable, inscrutable, the ruler of a universe predetermined

in all its parts and members from the foundation of the earth. Except for the saving grace of divine election, which no human righteousness can purchase, all must go down to the everlasting damnation that awaits the sons of Adam. In the eyes of such a philosophy it is sheer impertinence to talk of the dignity and worth of the individual soul. Men are no other than the worms of the dust. The boon of eternal life is not included in God's enumeration of natural rights; it is a special grant from the Lord of the universe who is pleased to smile on whom he is pleased to smile. In the hard words of Paul, "Therefore hath he mercy on whom he will have mercy, and whom he will he hardeneth." And those on whom he hath had mercy are his Saints, and they are gathered into his church, as the free city-states had risen out of the muck of medieval despotism. They are the stewards of his righteousness and are called to the great work of rulership on earth that God's will may be done and righteousness may prevail over iniquity.

It was an ambitious program, and so long as the Presbyterian party maintained its ascendency in England it endeavored to thrust its Calvinism down every throat, no matter how unwelcome; but with the passing of power from its hands, and the growth of a common-sense spirit of toleration, Calvinistic dogma lost its authority and the minds of Englishmen turned to more humane philosophies. In New England, on the other hand, by virtue of a rigid suppression of free inquiry, Calvinism long lingered out a harsh existence, grotesque and illiberal to the last. In banishing the Antinomians and Separatists and Quakers, the Massachusetts magistrates cast out the spirit of liberalism from the household of the Saints.

CHAPTER II

THE TRANSPLANTING OF IDEAS

I

THE Great Migration, it will be remembered, fell in the time of
the Laudean reaction, when the Presbyterian Utopia seemed
remote and the hopes of the Puritan dreamers were fallen low.
The Boston leaders quitted England ten years before Charles
summoned the Long Parliament, and twelve before the royal
standard was unfurled at Nottingham. The armed struggle for
supremacy was far below the horizon, and the outlandish philosophies that later sectaries were to propagate so diligently were as
yet little known in the land. The generous grain of liberal thought
was still in the milk, its fruitful doctrines unripened. The immigrant gentlemen who came to Massachusetts Bay were Puritan
Anglicans who professed a hearty love for the mother church and
were no friends to the principle of Separatism. They were potential Presbyterians who rejected alike the Arminianism of Laud
and the autocracy of the bishops. It is reasonable to suppose
that as strict Calvinists, trained in the ordinances as well as in the
doctrine of the French theologian, they came hither with the
conscious purpose of setting up the complete Genevan discipline
in the new world. If such was their plan—and certainly before
their coming over they seem not to have entertained any thoughts
of Separatism—it received a check from the Plymouth influence
and the Puritan experiment was turned aside from the path of its
natural development.

It was a somewhat curious misadventure that was to entail
unforeseen consequences. Except in matters of doctrine Pilgrim
and Puritan consorted ill together. Their social antecedents were
as unlike as their views on political and religious institutions. The
intellectual leaders of Plymouth—whatever may be said of the
London adventurers who joined the Holland group—had been
nurtured in Elizabethan radicalism. They were Brownist-Sepa-
ratists of plebeian origins, who had arrived at their conception of
the true church from a close study of Biblical texts, with perhaps

16

some admixture of Anabaptist influence, nearly a generation before the Stuarts came with their divine-right theory. During their years on the continent they lived remote from the current of events in England, and under the guidance of the tolerant Robinson they had been disciplined in the theory and practice of primitive Congregationalism. On their removal to America they brought with them a consciously democratic church order, that met their simple needs and had taken shape from the experience of daily life. This democratic model of church government was spontaneously supplemented by the plantation covenant of civil government drawn up aboard ship, which was to serve as the organic law of the new commonwealth. Two cardinal principles—which at bottom were one—thus found their way to New England in the *Mayflower*· the principle of a democratic church and the principle of a democratic state. When ten years later the Boston leaders were faced with the problem of erecting a social order, they accepted the Plymouth model of Congregationalism, but rejected the plantation covenant. They saw no need for the latter as they were already provided with an organic law. The charter which Winthrop was insistent upon bringing with them out of England was asserted to be the constitution of the commonwealth and, meticulously interpreted, was to determine largely the form and scope of the new political state. It was construed to grant a legal sanction to government; but as the charter of a Carolinian trading company it quite naturally restricted authority to the managing heads, and granted powers to its directors that were useful in managing trade ventures but might easily become intolerable if interpreted as the organic law of a commonwealth. With such enlargement of powers the directors of the corporation would constitute a political oligarchy. There was a striking difference, certainly, between the covenant of Plymouth and the charter-constitution of Massachusetts Bay, and a political philosopher could readily enough have foreseen the course that events would take in the Puritan commonwealth, given the men and the ideals in control.

II

THE PURITAN PRESBYTERIAN

To make clear what was involved in the attempt to adapt the Plymouth model of church government to the charter commonwealth, it is necessary to consider somewhat particularly the body of prejudice and principle brought to the new world aboard the *Lady Arbella*, as the Puritan contribution to New England. The capable leaders who created the early institutions of Massachusetts Bay colony were Jacobean Englishmen of middle station, halfway between the aristocrat and the burgess, with certain salient characteristics of both. Fashioned by a caste society, they transported to the little commonwealth an abundant heritage of class prejudice. They aspired to be reckoned gentlemen and to live in the new world as they had lived in the old, in a half feudal state, surrounded by many servants and with numerous dependents. They honored rank, were sticklers for precedence, respected class distinctions, demanded the hereditary rights of the gentry. They had been bred up in a static order where gentlemen ruled and the people obeyed, and they could not think in terms of the Plymouth plantation covenant, subscribed by all heads of families. To the modern reader of his journal there is something almost childish in Winthrop's insistence on public deference to his official position and his grief when the halberd-bearers refused to provide the usual formality to his little progresses. But if they aspired to be rated as gentlemen, there was much also of the burgess nature in them. They were potential capitalists, eager to accumulate ample landholdings, keen to drive a bargain, given to trade and with as sharp an eye to the main chance as any London merchant. The community of goods that marked the early days of Plymouth they disliked so greatly as to account it almost sinful. In the infancy of the settlement they entered upon an active mercantile life, building their ships for the West Indian trade, joining in the fisheries off the Newfoundland coast, venturing far in pursuit of gain. Active, capable men, excellent administrators rather than speculative thinkers, stewards of the public interests as well as their own, they would take it ill to have their matured plans interfered with by busybodies and incompetents. Their own counsel sufficed them and they wanted no help from outsiders.

Endow such men with religious zeal; let them regard themselves as particular repositories of righteousness; give them a free hand to work out their program unhampered by rival policies; provide them with a handbook elaborated in complete detail by a master system-maker; and the result was certain. Their Utopia must be a close-knit church-state, with authority reserved to the aristocracy of Christian talent. It is needless to inquire whether a definite conception of a theocracy was in their minds before their coming over; some such order was clearly implicit in their religious fervor, their Hebraic theology, their Genevan discipline, their aristocratic prejudices.   They might nominally accept the Plymouth model of church-government, but they would meddle with democracy in church and state no more than necessity compelled. Circumstances, as well as their own promptings, would counsel quite an opposite course.   They were engaged in a difficult and perilous undertaking, begirt by wilderness enemies, and fearful of hostile interference by the home authorities.   If the venture were to survive, a drift towards centralization of power was as natural as it was inevitable.   The common security would not suffer any dispersion of forces or domestic bickerings over authority.   Dissatisfied members must be held in subjection and dangerous swarmings from the mother-hive must be prevented.   The principle of Separatism was too disruptive to insure cohesive solidarity; the parts must be welded into a protective whole; and for such business what ideal was more efficient than a theocracy with Jehovah substituted for King Charles—not openly and seditiously, but quietly, in the hearts of the people.   The historian need not wander far in search of the origin of the theocratic principle; it is to be found in the self-interest of the lay and clerical leaders. Ambitious men could not have devised a fitter means to weld together the two groups of magistrates and ministers, and endow their charter prerogatives with divine sanction.   The Stuarts were bunglers at the business in comparison with Winthrop and Cotton. But if they worked the metal to such shape as they chose we must not forget that it had been well heated in the smithy of John Calvin. Overlook that fact and the theocracy becomes incredible.

There are perhaps sufficient grounds to assume that some plan of minority control was worked out before the migration took place. The preliminary discussions in England had been long and the terms of the charter were carefully seen to. By its provisions the right of franchise rested with the freemen of the corporation, in number about a hundred and ten. Of the total body of freemen it was known that only a small group would undertake the venture; probably fewer than a score came over with the emigrants, and through removals and death the number was speedily reduced to about a dozen. This handful of freemen constituted the court, and chose the governor, deputy governor, and the assistants or

magistrates. These latter were to number eighteen according to
the charter provision; but with more offices than eligible candidates, the number was necessarily reduced, and six assistants with
the governor came to be reckoned a quorum of the court with
sovereign powers.[1] It was a patriarchal undertaking, and to
Carolinian gentlemen there was nothing unusual or unjust in a
handful of leaders exercising plenary powers over the lives and
fortunes of two thousand members of the commonwealth. If the
charter could not have been construed as granting such powers, it
is reasonable to assume that they would not have entered upon
the business. The lay leaders were practical men. They had
ventured their estates in the hope of bettering their condition,
both spiritual and material, and with their personal fortunes at
stake they were in no mind to intrust the fate of the undertaking
to other hands than their own. They loved power quite as much
as did the ungodly, and accounting themselves God's stewards
they reckoned it sin not to use it in his name. As Puritans they
would not keep a weather eye on the majority will. God did not
speak in the Scriptures through majority votes; his chosen were a
minority, the remnant in Israel.

A further sanction was at hand. If these Hebraized Englishmen
created a close corporation and ruled magisterially, if the order
in the new church-state was inquisitorial and stern, it was in strict
conformity with the teachings and example of Calvin. Men deeply
read in the *Institutes*, familiar with the Genevan Ordinances and
the practices of the Consistory, were not likely to discover in them
any lessons in democratic toleration. Righteousness may be fearfully relentless, and John Calvin had been a tyrant on principle.
Iron-willed and masterful, he had risen to power in the turbulent
city-state of Geneva in sixteenth-century fashion. A few splotches
of blood on the white garments of the Church did not greatly
trouble him. He was never squeamish about ways and means of
furthering the Lord's work. He violated the right of refuge to
bring to the stake the pantheistic Unitarian Servetus, and he
thanked God when the bungling of the executioner prolonged the
sufferings of certain others of his victims. The Genevan discipline
was rigorous, and the clerical inquisitors were more relentless than
the lay. The tyrannies that have been freely charged upon the
New England oligarchy are easily explained in the light of the

[1] See James Truslow Adams, *The Founding of New England*, Chapter VI.

Calvinistic Ordinances. There were no whippings or banishments or hangings in early Pennsylvania where Quaker and Lutheran dwelt together in peace if not in fellowship. But they were New Testament men and not out of the Old, like the Saints in Massachusetts Bay. They worshiped a God of love rather than a God of wrath.

Granted the conception on which the theocratic experiment went forward, namely, that Jehovah was the sole lawgiver and the Bible the sufficient statute-book; granted also that these priests and magistrates were stewards of God's will; and the centralization of power in the commonwealth becomes invested with a higher sanction than the terms of the charter. It was an oligarchy of Christian grace. The minister was the trained and consecrated interpreter of the divine law, and the magistrate was its trained and consecrated administrator; and both were chosen by free election of the Saints. If unfortunately the Saints were few and the sinners many, was not that a special reason for safeguarding the Ark of the Covenant from the touch of profane hands? Hence all legislative experiments by annually elected deputies, no matter how exactly those experiments might fall in with the wishes of the majority, were sternly frowned upon or skillfully nullified. Not only were such popular enactments, it was held, too often prompted by the carnal desires of the natural man, but they were no better than an insult to God, as implying the insufficiency of the Scriptures to every temporal need. Unregenerate and sinful men must have no share in God's work. The Saints must not have their hands tied by majority votes. This explains, quite as much as mere love of power, the persistent hostility of the leaders to every democratic tendency. Such institutions as grew up spontaneously out of the necessities of the situation, were sharply hedged about by restrictions. The town meeting, which was extra-legal under the charter, was safeguarded by limiting the right of voting to freemen, except in a few trivial matters; and the more popular deputies, who inclined to become self-willed, were forced to accept the principle of magisterial veto on their actions. When a law was passed, it was purposely left vague as to penalties, in order to give a free hand to the judges to punish as they wished; and it was not till 1641, after much insistence from the representatives of the people, that Ward's Body of Liberties was finally adopted.

Later critics of Puritanism discover in the theocratic experiment of Massachusetts Bay a preposterous attempt to turn back the pages of history, and refashion Englishmen after an ungainly Hebraic pattern. But to the leaders of that experiment it seemed rather a Utopian venture to create in the new world a nobler social order than elsewhere existed. Whether such a society was either possible or desirable, has long since become only an academic question; what is more suggestive is the fact that in spite of some bitterness on the part of a small minority, the stewardship of an oligarchy remained the accepted principle of government in Massachusetts Bay until the vacating of the charter in 1684. That it lingered out so long a life is a testimony to the skillful opportunism of the leaders. They early adopted a strategic policy which the British ministry foolishly refused to adopt a hundred years later; they cautiously undermined any potential disaffection by admitting the wealthiest and most influential to the rights of freemen, thus allying the ambitious and capable members of society with the ruling group, and laying the foundations of a provincial aristocracy, which in the course of time would secularize the government and substitute an economic for a theocratic basis of authority. The loss of the charter only hastened what in the nature of things must have come about eventually.

III

CERTAIN MISTAKES

Skillful as were the theocratic rulers and logical as was their course, it seems plain in the light of later developments that they fell into certain grave mistakes at the very beginning of their work that were to hamper them seriously in after days. Those mistakes were the adoption of the covenant-principle of church organization borrowed from Plymouth, that started the new churches on the road to Congregationalism, and the granting of the land in fee-simple to non-freemen, that was to create an independent yeomanry. Of the two the second was far graver, for it threw the economics of the developing commonwealth on the side of local home rule and provided a substantial foundation for the erection of a democratic opposition to the oligarchy. If the plantation system of Virginia, or the Patroon system of New York, had been adopted, the covenanted church would naturally

have followed the path of Genevan Presbyterianism in harmony
with the desires of the leaders, and the democratic opposition
both in church and state must have been starved into submission.
But with the system of small holdings and the development of a
vigorous yeomanry, the eventual development of Congregationalism into a federated group of self-governing churches was predetermined more rigidly than by any logic of John Calvin. The
defeat of the Presbyterian program of the theocrats was implicit
in a decentralized land system.

The decision of the Salem church in 1629 to adopt the Plymouth
model, and the acceptance of that decision by later churches in
Massachusetts Bay, has been abundantly commented upon, but
the significance of it has been somewhat inadequately explored.[2]
Very likely it was a deep hatred of episcopal rule that opened the
mind of Endicott and his fellows to the reasoning of Dr. Fuller of
Plymouth, and persuaded them to take this first step towards
Separatism; nevertheless as disciples of Calvin, desirous of establishing a Bible commonwealth, they must soon discover that a
system centrifugal in tendency and decentralizing in spirit, unless
closely restrained, was certain to lead them far from the Canaan
of their hopes. Separatism was the negation of a state church,
and the rule of the congregation was the negation of an official
creed and ecclesiastical unity. If Congregationalism were suffered
to develop its democratic potentialities, the leaders must eventually find themselves in like position with Laud, with schismatics
disturbing the orthodox harmony and rending the church from
within. The authorities early began to feel, what the Anglican
Lechford pointed out in 1641, that the system was dangerously
democratic, and the principle of centralizing conformity was set
to work. The spirit of Calvin's Consistory was invoked. Under
the guise of brotherly counsel, or church fellowship, the principle
of consociation was developed, a principle that opened a convenient
door to official coercion. Brotherly counsel that comes armed
with the weapon of excommunication, that points its argument
with the threat of banishment or hanging, is certainly not the
pure spirit of Christian fellowship that Congregational historians
have chosen to see in the principle of consociation. The most
ardent apologist has hard work in discovering the democratic

[2] See Williston Walker, *A History of the Congregational Churches in the United
States*, Chapter IV.

principle of Congregationalism in the theocratic application of the methods of the Genevan Consistory. The early churches of the theocracy were Presbyterian in spirit and rule, in spite of the official promulgation of the covenant-principle in the Cambridge Platform. Certainly real Separatists like Roger Williams, who suffered from too much brotherly counsel and did not want a Christian fellowship imposed by magistrates, were under no illusions in regard to the coercive spirit that lay behind the principle of consociation.

More open and above board were the successive statutes that effectively nullified the principle of Separatism by erecting an official state church. The law of 1631, restricting the franchise to church members, and the law of 1635, making attendance at church compulsory on all, were followed in 1636 by a law requiring the approval of the magistrates and elders before a new church could be set up, and in 1638 by the institution of a system of state support for the ministry. The principle of the covenant was being pretty effectively whittled away. Equally Presbyterian was the movement for the establishment of a definitive state creed. In consequence of the Antinomian schism effected by the eloquent tongue of Mistress Anne Hutchinson, the first general synod was convened at Newtown in 1637, which sat for four and twenty days and drew up a list of eighty-two heretical opinions, "some blasphemous, others erroneous, and all unsafe," together with "nine unwholesome expressions," which were alleged to be disturbing the peace of the community. Whereupon the synod broke up, the members congratulating themselves "that matters had been carried on so peaceably and concluded so comfortably in all love." How much Christian love was awakened by such brotherly counsels in the heart of Mistress Hutchinson, who was banished and later slain by the Indians, is not revealed, but her sin was made of record as a warning to other schismatics. It was this: "He hath let me distinguish between the voice of my beloved and the voice of Moses," which being interpreted, meant an appeal from the Old Testament to the New, from Mosaic authority to the inner light.

With the promulgation of the Cambridge Platform by the synod of 1646–47, and the acceptance of the Westminster Confession of Faith, the work of creating the organism and creed of an authoritative state-church was completed. According to Williston Walker, the Cambridge Platform "pictures with great clearness

the abiding principles of Congregationalism"—the covenant
origin of the local church, the autonomy of the congregation, the
sole authority of the Bible, and the fellowship of the churches.[3]
But it needs the sharp eyes of an apologetic historian to discover
the spirit of democratic Congregationalism in a discipline that
sanctions the power of the state to intervene in ecclesiastical
matters and requires the magistrate to enforce uniformity in
creed and worship. "Idolatry, Blasphemy, Heresy, Venting
corrupt and pernicious opinions, are to be restrayned and punished
by civil authority," the Platform states. "If any church one or
more shall grow schismaticall, rending it self from the communion
of other churches, or shall walke incorrigibly or obstinately in any
corrupt way of their own, contrary to the rule of the word; in
such case, the Magistrate is to put forth his coercive power, as the
matter shall require." If such be Congregationalism, how greatly
have the later churches departed from the primitive faith! To
the layman, wanting in insight, it would seem rather to be stark
Calvinism, that reveals how completely the coercive spirit of the
Ordinances and Consistory of the French theologian had come to
dominate the theocratic mind of New England. The reluctant
adoption of the Cambridge Platform by the suspicious deputies
was the grim prelude to Baptist whippings and Quaker baitings,
and the setting-in of the dark days of militant intolerance. "Yourselves pretend liberty of conscience," wrote Roger Williams in 1670,
"but alas! it is but self, the great god self, only to yourselves."[4]

But while the covenant principle was thus being effectively
whittled away by the theocratic leaders, another principle, likewise of Plymouth origin, was silently working to the overthrow
of the theocratic power. Following the example of the Pilgrims
the several towns apportioned their lands in fee to their members;
and if so acute a political thinker as Daniel Webster is to be
trusted, it was from the creative influence of freehold tenure that
the political institutions of New England became later democratized. As a disciple of James Harrington, accepting the doctrine
of economic determinism as it had been elaborated in the *Oceana*,
Webster traced the spontaneous rise of republicanism in New
England to the wide diffusion of property; and in the light of his
economic interpretation the harsh intolerance of the Cambridge

[3] *Ibid.*, p. 162.
[4] *Narragansett Club Publications*, Vol. VI, p. 133.

Platform is seen to be only the aberration of a passing bigotry. In his anniversary speech at Plymouth he said:

> Their situation demanded a parceling out and division of the lands, and it may be fairly said, that this necessary act *fixed the future frame and form of their government.* The character of their political institutions was determined by the fundamental laws respecting property. . . . The property was all freehold . . . alienation of the land was every way facilitated, even to the subjecting of it to every species of debt. The establishment of public registries, and the simplicity of our forms of conveyance, have greatly facilitated the change of real estate from one proprietor to another. The consequence of all these causes has been, a great subdivision of the soil, and a great equality of condition; the true basis, most certainly, of a popular government. "If the people," says Harrington, "hold three parts in four of the territory, it is plain there can neither be any single person nor nobility able to dispute the government with them; in this case, therefore, *except force be interposed,* they govern themselves." [5]

With such a clue it is easier to understand how the liberalisms implicit in Plymouth Congregationalism—its theory of compact in church and state—should find support from an independent yeomanry and eventually rise against the oligarchical rule. The new world would ultimately throw off the old-world repressions and explore the reaches of those generous idealisms that were the bequest of English Separatism. The fathers were engaged in an impossible undertaking. Sanctuaries were close at hand for all dissenters from the theocracy, in Connecticut for the Congregationalists, in Rhode Island for the Separatists, along the Maine frontier for the rebellious individualist. Seated securely in these regions beyond the reach of the Massachusetts magistrates, the diverse liberalisms that were being stifled by the oligarchy prospered and brought forth after their kind. Differentiation in the provinces was the natural counterpart of coercive conformity at the capital; and from very early days New England divided into three diverse groups journeying to their Utopias by different roads. Massachusetts Bay, Connecticut, and Rhode Island, were variant answers to the question of what might be expected to result from the domestication in a free environment of the inchoate idealisms of English Puritanism. How they differentiated themselves from the norm, and why, will perhaps become clearer from an examination of the diverse philosophies of their intellectual leaders.

[5] *Works,* Vol. I, pp. 35–36.

CHAPTER III
THE CHIEF STEWARDS OF THEOCRACY

I

MASTER JOHN COTTON
Priest

THE most authoritative representative in New England of the ideal of priestly stewardship was the excellent John Cotton, first teacher to the church at Boston. While pastor of the church of St. Botolph, in old Boston, he had dreamed of a Utopia of the Saints, unharassed by tyrannous prelates; and while sweetening his mouth with a morsel of Calvin, as he was fond of doing, no doubt he turned over in his mind the plans and specifications of that Utopia. "When God wrappes us in his ordinances," he said in his sermon to Winthrop's company on the eve of its departure from England, "and warmes us with the life and power of them as with wings, there is the land of Promise." Left behind by the departing brethren, he lingered for a while in an England that was every day becoming colder for such as dreamed of other Canaans than Laud's, until urged by many invitations, at the age of forty-six he followed overseas to devote his remaining life to the great work being done there. For more than a score of years he labored faithfully, and the New England which the emigrant generation bequeathed to its sons bore upon it the marks of John Cotton's shaping hand more clearly than those of any other minister.

It is not easy today to judge fairly the life and work of John Cotton. No adequate biography has been written, and his dreams and aspirations lie forgotten in the grave of lost causes and forsaken faiths. But to the Boston freemen of his own day, Master John Cotton was a very great man. Of excellent family and sound university training, he was both a notable theologian and a courteous gentleman. "Twelve hours in a day he commonly studied, and would call that a *scholar's* day," his grandson reported of him. From the hour when he entered Trinity College, Cambridge, at the age of thirteen, to his death in 1652, he was a bookman, and in sheer bulk of acquisition probably no man of his time outdid him.

In Cotton Mather's judgment he was "a most *universal scholar*, and a *living system* of the liberal arts, and a *walking library*." His intellectual equipment was so highly regarded that many excellent persons "believed that God would not suffer Mr. Cotton to err"; and that "if ever there be any considerable blow given to the Devil's kingdom," Master Cotton was the man for the business. No other New England champion was so renowned for "beating out the truth in controversie"; and when he turned to the work of answering Roger Williams, the latter exclaimed: "I rejoice it hath pleased [God] to appoint so able, and excellent, and conscionable an Instrument to bolt the Truth to the bran." But though he was bred in Elizabethan days and entered college in the year when Shakespeare's *Henry IV* and Jonson's *Every Man in his Humour* first appeared on the stage, there is no touch of Renaissance splendor in his crabbed style and ascetic reasoning. That was early washed out of him by the rising tide of Hebraism which was slowly submerging the England of poets and playwrights.

But however much he loved cloistered scholarship, the immediate source of his great influence was the spoken rather than the written word. By the universal testimony of his generation he was "a soul-melting preacher," whose reasoned eloquence swayed congregations trained to solid argumentative discourse. When he ascended the pulpit on Sundays and lecture days, he spoke as a prophet in Israel; and on occasions of public ceremonial, or when dissensions arose touching the polity of church or state, he was summoned by the magistrates to convince with his logic and persuade with his eloquence. The strong-minded Anne Hutchinson was but one of many who chose exile in New England rather than lose the edification of Mr. Cotton's preaching. Good men were drawn to him by his sweetness of temper, and evil men were overawed by his venerable aspect. He seems to have been an altogether lovable person, with white hair framing a face that must have been nobly chiseled, gentle-voiced, courteous, tactful, by nature "a tolerant man" who placidly bore with a dissentient and gladly discovered a friend in an antagonist. If his quiet yielding before opposition suggests that he may have been given to opportunism, or his fondness for intellectual subtleties drew from his grandson the comment "a most excellent casuist," we must not too hastily conclude that he served the cause of truth less devotedly than the cause of party.

For a score of years before his coming over, his position in the rising Puritan party had been honorable. Few among the dissenting ministers were better known, none more esteemed. He had shone as an intellectual light at the university, he had long been pastor of one of the loveliest churches in England, he counted among his friends some of the ablest contemporary Englishmen. To Cromwell he was one "whom I love and honour in the Lord"; to Lord Say and Sele, to the Earl of Warwick, the Earl of Lincoln, and a notable company of Puritan gentlemen, he was a trusted friend and lieutenant; to thousands of the substantial burgesses who were drawing together to form the new Puritan-Whig party, he was "a fixed and conscionable light." That such a leader should have been received with thanksgiving by the Boston congregation was to be expected; that he should have taken high place at once among the members of the Massachusetts oligarchy was equally to be expected. Thenceforth his busy career was no more than a reflection of the ambitions of the theocracy.

Unfortunately his daily contact with narrow-minded and intolerant men gave an unhappy bias to his later career. Cotton seems to have been something of a Puritan intellectual, with an open-minded curiosity that made him receptive to new ideas and tempted him to play with doctrines that were intolerable to his bigoted associates. It was possibly this native sympathy with free speculation that drew him into the camp of Mistress Hutchinson with her doctrine of the inner light. When the schism became serious, dividing the commonwealth into warring camps, Cotton seems to have become frightened and broke with the Boston Antinomians. In this matter he came near to being a shuffler. The Hutchinson trial with its resulting banishments was the turning point of his career in America as it was a crisis in the history of early New England. He was not a man to persecute and harry, nor was he one to stand in isolated opposition to associates whom he respected, and he allowed himself to be coerced by narrower-minded men like Endicott and Dudley. After 1637 the better nature of John Cotton was submerged by the rising intolerance, and "the most tolerant, as he was the ablest of the Massachusetts divines," was brought so low as to defend the meanest and cruelest acts of the oligarchy. He descended to disgraceful casuistry in defense of the first whippings of the Quakers, and he urged the death penalty upon King Philip's son and the enslavement of the remnant of

Philip's tribe, against the plea of John Eliot that "to sell soules for mony seemeth to me a dangerous merchandize." The sins of the oligarchy rest in large measure on the head of John Cotton, and the judgment of the most recent historian of New England must stand:

> With a broader mind and wider vision than any of the other clergy of the colony, he had not the courage to stand alone, beyond a certain point, against their unanimity in intolerance. The higher promptings of his nature were crushed by the united voice of the priesthood, as Winthrop's had been so short a time before, and the noblest of the colony's leaders, lay and clerical, from that time tended to sink to the lower level of their fellows.[1]

An apologist—and whoever has felt the charm of John Cotton's personality easily becomes an apologist—will perhaps find some grounds of excuse for his later conduct. He was in an unhappy position. He was ill at ease in his mind, and his frequent tacking in the face of adverse winds was characteristic of the intellectual who sees all sides of a question. He heartily approved of the theocratic ends that his associates were seeking, and his influential position made him the defender of acts which his better nature must have disapproved. The historian, however, will seek a more adequate explanation in the roots of his environment. The idealism of John Cotton was the fruit of his training, and his theocratic dreams were conditioned by the facts that he was both a Calvinist and a Carolinian gentleman. The fusion of these two influences resulted in the unique political theory of an ethical aristocracy, consecrated to moral stewardship in the state. A lifelong student of Calvin's *Institutes*, he found there a system of social organization that responded to every demand of the theologian and the aristocrat. The very texture and pattern of Cotton's political philosophy is exemplified in such a passage as this, over which he must have brooded much:

> When these three forms of government of which philosophers treat, are considered in themselves, I, for my part, am far from denying that the form which greatly surpasses the other is aristocracy, either pure or modified by popular government; not indeed in itself, but because it very rarely happens that kings so rule themselves as never to dissent from what is just and right, or are possessed of so much acuteness and prudence as always to see correctly. Owing therefore to the vices or defects of men, it is safer and more tolerable when several bear rule, that they may thus

1 James Truslow Adams, *The Founding of New England*, p. 170.

mutually assist, instruct, and admonish each other, and should any be disposed to go too far, the others are censors and masters to curb his excess. This has already been proved by experience, and confirmed also by the authority of the Lord himself, when he established an aristocracy bordering on popular government among the Israelites, keeping them under that as the best form, until He exhibited an image of the Messiah in David.[2]

As a Carolinian gentleman, this was as far as Cotton would go on the path of liberalism. The elders were responsible to God for the spiritual well-being of the people, and the state must aid and not hinder them in their leadership. The doctrine of unlimited popular sovereignty was for him no other than a thistle in the garden of the Lord. The desire for liberty he regarded as the sinful prompting of the natural man, a denial of the righteous authority of God's chosen rulers. If democracy were indeed the best form of government, was it not strange that divine wisdom should have failed to discover the fact? In the history of the chosen people nowhere does God approve the democratic as the best form, but the theocratic; was He now to be set right by sinful men who courted popularity by appealing to the selfishness of depraved hearts? To the scripturist the logic of his argument was convincing:

It is better that the commonwealth be fashioned to the setting forth of God's house, which is his church: than to accommodate the church frame to the civill state. Democracy, I do not conceyve that ever God did ordeyne as a fit government eyther for church or commonwealth. If the people be governors, who shall be governed? As for monarchy, and aristocracy, they are both of them clearly approoved, and directed in scripture, yet so as referreth the soveraigntie to himselfe, and setteth up Theocracy in both, as the best forme of government in the commonwealth, as well as in the church.[3]

If John Cotton, like other Carolinian gentlemen, was a confirmed aristocrat, he was at the same time a social revolutionary, who would substitute an aristocracy of the Saints for the landed aristocracy, and refashion society upon ethical rather than economic lines. At what time the ideal of a Presbyterian Bible commonwealth took shape in his mind, it is impossible to determine; but it was a natural outcome of his most cherished beliefs. A

[2] *Institutes*, Book IV, Chapter XX, Paragraph 8.
[3] "Letter to Lord Say and Sele," in Hutchinson, *History of Massachusetts Bay Colony*, Vol. I, p. 497.

devout scripturist, he accepted the Bible as a rule of universal
application, perfect and final. The sufficiency of the Scriptures
to all social needs was axiomatic with him; "the more any law
smells of man the more unprofitable," he asserted in his draft of
laws offered for acceptance by the commonwealth; and at another
time he exclaimed, "*Scripturae plenitudinem adoro*." He chose
exile rather than yield to what he regarded as the unscriptural
practices of Laud, and now that he was come to a new land where
a fresh beginning was to be made, was it not his Christian duty to
"endeavour after a *theocracy*, as near as might be, to that which
was the glory of Israel, the 'peculiar people'"? The old Common
Law must be superseded by the Mosaic dispensation; the citizen
of the commonwealth must become the subject of Jehovah; the
sovereignty of temporal authorities must serve the higher sovereignty of God.

Holding to such views the duty devolving upon him was plain:
to assist the magistrates in checking the dangerous drift towards
a democratic organization of church and state, which the new
environment encouraged; and to defend the theocratic ideal
against all critics. The first he sought to accomplish by creating
a more perfect theocratic machinery. As we catch glimpses of
him moving tactfully back and forth through the brisk little
scenes, he seems always to have a finger in some magisterial
affair. Three months after his arrival in Boston he preached a
sermon, the purport of which Winthrop noted in his *Journal:*

> After much deliberation and serious advice the Lord directed the
> teacher Mr. Cotton, to make clear by the scripture, that the minister's
> maintenance, as well as all other charges of the church, should be defrayed
> out of a stock, or treasury, which was to be raised out of the weekly con-
> tribution: which accordingly was agreed upon.[4]

In his first election sermon, preached in the May following, he
joined issue with the democratic spirit of the deputies, by supporting a principle which was flagrantly oligarchical:

> That a magistrate ought not to be turned into the condition of a private
> man without just cause, & to be publicly convict, no more than the
> magistrates may turn a private man out of his freehold, etc., without like
> public trial, etc.[4a]

Unrebuffed by the rejection of this curious doctrine of the
freehold tenure of magistrates, Cotton made a more ambitious

[4] Vol. I, p. 116. [4a] *Ibid.*, Vol. I, p. 125.

attempt to theocratize the state, when at the October court of
1636, in response to the persistent pressure for a fundamental law,
he presented his code for adoption by the commonwealth, the
scriptural origin of which is revealed in the title, "Model of Moses
his Judicials." Cotton Mather tells of this venture in constitution
making, in the following glowing but inaccurate words:

> On Mr. Cotton's arrival he found the whole country in a perplexed & a
> divided state, as to their *civill constitution*. . . . It was then requested of
> Mr. *Cotton* that he would, from the laws wherewith God governed his
> ancient people, form an *abstract* of such as were of a moral and a lasting
> equity; which he performed as acceptably as judiciously. But inasmuch
> as very much of an *Athenian democracy* was in the mould of the govern-
> ment, by the royal charter. . . . Mr. Cotton effectually recommended
> it unto them that none should be *electors*, nor *elected* therein, except such
> as were *visible subjects* of our Lord Jesus Christ, personally *confederated*
> in our churches. In these, and many other ways, he propounded unto
> them an endeavour after a theocracy, as near as might be, to that which
> was the glory of Israel, the "peculiar people." [5]

Cotton's code was rejected in favor of one, somewhat less
Hebraic, prepared by Nathaniel Ward, but he continued to be the
chief guide and mentor to the magistrates in political as well as
theological matters, and his theocratic philosophy determined in
large measure the policy of the oligarchy. To found an Hebraic
state in which political rights should be subordinate to religious
conformity, in which the magistrates should be chosen from a
narrow group, with authority beyond the reach of the popular
will, and with the ministers serving as court of last resort to interpret the divine law to the citizen-subjects of Jehovah—this was
the great ambition of John Cotton; and the untiring zeal and
learned scriptural authority which he dedicated to that ambition
justify us in regarding him as the greatest of the New England
theocrats. In the categories of the Puritan philosophy of ethical
stewardship there was no recognition of the profane doctrine of
natural rights. Freedom was the prerogative of righteousness;
the well-being of society required that the sinner should remain
subject to the Saint. Nowhere does he lay down this principle
more unmistakably than in an important state paper:

[5] *Magnalia*, Vol. I, p. 265. Compare with this Cotton's own words: "The law,
which your Lordship instanceth (in that none shall be chosen to magistracy amongst
us, but a church member) was made and enacted before I came into the country;
but I have hitherto wanted sufficient light to plead against it" (Hutchinson,
History of Massachusetts Bay Colony, Vol. I, p. 498).

Now if it be a divine truth, that none are to be trusted with public permanent authority but godly men, who are fit materials for church membership, then from the same grounds it will appear, that none are so fit to be trusted with the liberties of the commonwealth as church members. For, the liberties of this commonwealth are such, as require men of faithful integrity to God and the state, to preserve the same. . . . Now . . . these liberties are such as carry along much power with them, either to establish or subvert the commonwealth, and therewith the church, which power, if it be committed to men according to their godliness . . . then, in case worldly men should prove the major part, as soon they might do, they would readily set over us magistrates like themselves, such as might . . . turn the edge of all authority and laws against the church and the members thereof, the maintenance of whose peace is the chief end which God aimed at in the institution of magistracy.[6]

This, quite evidently, is the negation of democracy, and it has been freely charged against his reputation by later critics. But in fairness it must be added, that it is equally the negation of the principle of hereditary aristocracy; and to reject the latter was a severer test of his integrity than to deny the former. He wanted neither a democracy nor an aristocracy to control the church-state. "Hereditary honors both nature and scripture doth acknowledge," he argued cautiously in reply to "Certain Proposals made by Lord Say, Lord Brooke, and other Persons of quality, as conditions of their removing to New-England." "Two distinct ranks we willingly acknowledge . . . the one of them called Princes, or Nobles, or Elders (amongst whom gentlemen have their place), the other the people." To the former he willingly accorded the right of rulership so long as they were of approved godliness, faithful to their stewardship. But "if God should not delight to furnish some of their posterity with gifts fit for magistracy, we should expose them rather to reproach and prejudice, and the commonwealth with them, than exalt them to honor, if we should call them forth, when God doth not, to public authority." It must be set down in John Cotton's accounts that he discouraged the transplanting of English aristocracy to the soil of Massachusetts.

There remains to consider how he conducted himself in another weighty matter that was laid upon his shoulders—the defense of the New England polity against old-world critics. Congregationalism had been somewhat caustically handled by the English

[6] Hutchinson, *History of Massachusetts Bay Colony*, Vol. I, Appendix 2.

Presbyterians, as smacking both of democracy and Separatism; and John Cotton was called to justify to them the apparent innovations. His most notable work in this field was his celebrated volume, *The Way of the Congregational Churches Cleared*, a treatise crammed, in the language of a contemporary admirer, with "most practical Soul-searching, Soul-saving, and Soul-solacing Divinitie"; "not Magisterially laid down, but friendly debated by Scripture, and argumentatively disputed out to the utmost inch of Ground." Into the subtleties of this learned work we need not enter; its main thesis alone need detain us, and that thesis was an implied denial of the democratic tendencies of the "New England way." Cotton was greatly concerned over the charge of Joseph Baillie, a vigorous Scotch Presbyterian, that Congregationalism was only a different form of lower-class Brownism, "a native branch of Anabaptism"; and that in resting ecclesiastical sovereignty upon "the particular, visible Church of the Congregation," it was Separatist in principle as well as in practice. The charge was true, but John Cotton was too thoroughly a Jacobean gentleman to concede it; dishonor would come upon the New England churches, he believed, if it were conceded. So he was driven to casuistry: "No marvall, if Independents take it ill to bee called Brownists. . . . He separated from Churches and Saints: we, onely from the world, and that which is of the world"; and then to a categorical denial, "for New England there is no such church of the Separation at all that I know of." [7] From this it was a natural step to a downright rejection of the democratic principle of Congregationalism:

> Neither is it the Scope of my whole Book, to give the people a share in the Government of the Church. . . . Nay, further, there be that blame the Book for the other Extreme, That it placeth the Government of the Church not at all in the hands of the People, but of the Presbyterie.[8]

The same note of disingenuous casuistry runs through his well-known controversy with Roger Williams over the question of toleration. In seeking to parry the thrust that the Saints, after quitting England to escape persecution, had themselves turned persecutors, he argued: "There is a vast difference between men's inventions and God's institutions; we fled from men's inventions, to which we else should have been compelled; we compel none to men's inventions." From which it followed, that "if the worship

[7] See *Narragansett Club Publications*, Vol. II, p. 203.
[8] *Ibid.*, Part II, p. 15.

be lawful in itself, the magistrate compelling him to come to it, compelleth him not to sin, but the sin is in his own will that needs to be compelled to a Christian duty." [9] The brethren of Massachusetts were not singular in believing that they were very near to God and privy to His will; nor were the dissenters to their policy singular in their skepticism concerning such infallibility; and when skepticism blows its cold breath upon it, the logic of John Cotton turns to ashes. Not freedom to follow the ways of sin, but freedom to follow the law of God as he expounded that law—such was Cotton's restriction upon the "natural liberties" of the subject of Jehovah. Let there be freedom of conscience if it be under no error, but not otherwise; for if freedom be permitted to sinful error, how shall the will of God and John Cotton prevail upon earth?

After the battle has been fought and lost it is easy to see the strategic mistakes; but it is not so easy to keep one's head in the thick of the struggle. As John Cotton looked overseas at the social revolution then threatening to submerge, not only Presbyterianism, but the very social order in which he had been nurtured; as he considered the logical implications of the strange, heretical doctrines that were bandied about in pamphlet and sermon, he was put almost in a panic. The solid foundations of church and state were threatened by mischievous men, not only in England but in the new Canaan which had cost so much in prayer and sacrifice; should he keep silent while, in the name of toleration, the gunpowder was being put in place for the work of destruction? Even today we can feel the anxious concern of John Cotton's mind in such a vibrant passage as this:

I confesse we . . . have cause to admire, and adore the wisdome, and dreadfull Justice of God herein, That seeing Mr. *Williams* hath been now as a branch cut off from the Church of *Salem* these many yeares, he should bring forth no spirituall good fruit: and that in such a season, when the Spirit of Error is let loose to deceive so many thousand soules of our English Nation: So that now their hearts are become as Tinder, ready to catch and kindle at every sparke of false light. Even so, O Father, because thy good pleasure is such, to let loose this Spirit of Error in the mouth of this Backslider, in the very houre and power of darknesse: for these are the dayes of vengeance: when the Antinomians deny the whole law; the Anti-sabbatarians deny the Morality of the fourth Commandement; the Papists deny the Negative part of the second Commandement. It is a

[9] See Hutchinson, *Papers*, Vol. II, pp. 131 ff.; quoted in Adams, *Founding of New England*, p. 261.

wofull opportunitie that God hath left Mr. *Williams* to, now to step in. . . . For, take away (as Mr. *Williams* doth) all instituted worship of God, as Churches, Pastors, Teachers, Elders, Deacons, Members, Publick Ministery of the Word, Covenant, Seales of the Covenant (Baptisme, and the Lords Supper), the Censures of the Church, and the like, what is then left of all the institutions, and Ordinances of God, which the Lord established in the second Commandement, against the Institutions, Images and Inventions of men in his worship.[10]

How easy it is for good men, in presence of the new and strange, to draw back in timid reaction; and failing to understand, or fearing for their prestige, to charge upon the new and strange a host of evils that exist only in their panic imaginations! In this great matter of toleration of conscience, it is quite clear today that the eyes of the troubled theocrat, "so *piercing* and *heavenly* (in other and precious Truths of God)"—as Roger Williams acknowledged—were for the moment sadly "over-clouded and bloud-shotten." For this the age was more to blame than the man. It was no fault of John Cotton's that he was the child of a generation reared under the shadow of absolutism, fearful of underling aggression, unable to comprehend the excellence inhering in the democratic faith. He reasoned according to his light; and if he rather too easily persuaded himself that the light which shined to him was the single divine light, he proved himself thereby an orthodox Puritan if not a catholic thinker. It is a pity that the priest in his later years overcame the intellectual, nevertheless the epitaph carved on his headstone does no violence to truth:

JOHANNES COTTONUS
Cujus Ultima Laus est,
Quod fuerit inter Nov-Anglos Primus.

To have been accounted by his fellows first among the notable company of Puritan emigrants was no slight testimony to the sterling qualities of Master John Cotton.

[10] "Master John Cottons Answer to Master Roger Williams," in *Narragansett Club Publications*, Vol. II, pp. 22–23.

II

JOHN WINTHROP

Magistrate

If John Cotton embodied the ideal and polity of the theocratic ministry, John Winthrop represented the ideal and polity of the theocratic magistracy. Rulership in the new church-state, while nominally the function of lay officers, in reality was quite as much ecclesiastical as political. The civil authorities were chosen by a narrow body of orthodox electors with a single view to theocratic ends. To the traditional conception of magistracy, in which the gentlemen of the Migration had been reared, was now added a special function, the care of the church, "the maintenance of whose peace," John Cotton asserted, "is the chief end which God aimed at in the institution of magistracy." The career of John Winthrop in Massachusetts must be judged, therefore, from this two-fold point of view. He was not exclusively, or chiefly, a civil governor, but a magistrate-elder; and his political conduct was determined by this dual character of his office. Unless one keeps in mind the theocratic framework of the early Massachusetts commonwealth, one cannot understand the limitations of his authority, or judge his conduct intelligently.

John Winthrop was a skillful executive upon whose shoulders largely rested the success or failure of the undertaking during the difficult early years. But he was very much more than that; he was a Puritan steward of temporal affairs, who accepted his stewardship as a sacred duty lying upon his conscience. A cultivated gentleman, "browghte Up amonge boockes & learned men," with a tender and sympathetic nature—inclining overmuch to mildness, as he confessed apologetically—by every right he belongs with that notable group of Puritans, with Eliot and Vane and Hutchinson and Milton, in whom the moral earnestness of Hebraism was tempered to humaner issues by a generous culture. There was in him not a little fruitful sap of Elizabethan poetry to quicken his thought, lifting him out of the petty world of Jacobean lawyer and landed gentleman, and opening his eyes to a vision of the future significance of the great venture to which he dedicated his later years. Grave and dignified, he looks out at us from his portrait with a certain stoic calm not untouched with sadness, as if this life had proved a serious business, filled with responsibilities and weighty matters, and darkened by sorrow and disappointment. The pagan *joie de vivre* of Elizabethan times is gone, and in its stead is a serious intelligence that must grapple with realities and shape them to its will.

He had lived amply in England before his removal, with much that was feudal lingering in the habits of his patriarchal household; and in the little village of Boston he kept twenty male servants, some of them heads of families. A decay of fortune had come upon him during his last years on the family estate, and the hope of recouping his losses may have been an additional reason for venturing to remove to the new world. In his *Considerations for J. W.* he explains that "he cannot live in the same place and calling (as before) and so, if he should refuse this opportunity, *that talent which God hath bestowed upon him for publick service were like to be buried.*" Something to the same purpose is suggested in another passage, which touches upon the economic disturbances of the time, with the attendant extravagance and ostentation of the new rich:

> This Land growes weary of her Inhabitants. . . . We are growne to that height of Intemperance in all excesse of Riott, as noe man's estate allmost will suffice to keepe saile with his æqualls. . . . The ffountains of Learning & Religion are soe corrupted as—men straine at knatts & swallowe camells, use all severity for mainetaynance of cappes & other accomplyments, but suffer all ruffianlike fashions & disorder to passe uncontrolled.[11]

Writing to his wife Margaret in 1629, he gave expression to apprehensions that were very likely quickened by his own failure to keep pace with his neighbors:

> My dear wife, I am veryly persuaded, God will bringe some heavye Affliction upon this lande & that speedylye. . . . The Lorde hath admonished, threatened, corrected, & astonished us, yet we growe worse & worse, so as his Spirit will not always strive with us, we must needs give way to his furye at last.[12]

But material considerations alone scarcely suffice to explain the motives of one who wrote: "It were happy for many if their parents had left them only such a legacy as our modern spirit of poetry makes his motto, *Ut nec habeant, nec careant, nec curent.*"

[11] *Life and Letters of John Winthrop*, Vol. I, p. 310.
[12] *Ibid.*, Vol. I, p. 296.

Such consolation—that the Christian should possess nothing, desire nothing, trouble about nothing—may have been only the refuge of the stoic from the impending loss of material possessions; but the conscious discipline in ascetic Hebraism which was to change the Jacobean gentleman into a militant Puritan had already created a temper to which such stoic abnegation must appeal. Winthrop's diary, running from his fourteenth to his thirty-second year, is a homely record in self-discipline, not unlike Bunyan's *Grace Abounding*. It is introspective and tediously moralizing, but it reveals how long and arduous was the training before he felt confident that he was "improved in all the points of experimental Godliness."

But Winthrop was the child of a great age before he was born into the fellowship of the Saints; and when we come upon the natural man beneath the theological wrappings, we discover a many-sided, rich and sympathetic human nature. He had gone to school to the English Bible, and the noble Hebrew poetry stirred the poetic imagination that was his Elizabethan birthright. Like so many of his fellow Puritans he delighted in the Book of Canticles, and the rich oriental imagery flowed easily from his pen. In one of his last letters before he quitted the old home, he took leave of a friend in these words:

It is time to conclude, but I know not how to leave you, yet since I must, I will put my beloved into his arms, who loves him best, & is a faithful keeper of all that is committed to him. Now, Thou, the hope of Israel, and the sure help of all that come to thee, knit the hearts of thy servants to thyself in faith and purity. Draw us with the sweetness of thine odours, that we may run after thee—Allure us, and speak kindly to thy servants, that thou mayest possess us as thine own, in the kindness of youth, and the love of marriage—Seal us up, by that holy spirit of promise, that we may not fear to trust in thee—Carry us into thy garden, that we may eat and be filled with those pleasures, which the world knows not—Let us hear that sweet voice of thine, my love, my dove, my undefiled—Spread thy skirt over us, and cover our deformity—Make us sick with thy love—Let us sleep in thine arms, and awake in thy kingdom—The souls of thy servants, thus united to thee, make us one in the bonds of brotherly affection—let not distance weaken it, nor time waste it, nor changes dissolve it, nor self-love eat it out; but when all means of other communion shall fail, let us delight to pray for each other: and so let thy unworthy servant prosper in the love of his friends, as he truly loves thy good servants . . . and wishes true happiness to them and to all theirs—Amen.[13]

[13] *Life and Letters*, Vol. I, pp. 397–398.

When his heart was touched Winthrop's tenderness flowed out in a wealth of affectionate sympathy, that lends a rich and lovely cadence to his English prose. To a sister who had suffered the loss of her husband, he wrote:

Go on cheerfully (my good sister), let experience add more confidence still to your patience. Peace shall come. There will be a bed to rest in, large and easy enough for you both. It is preparing in the lodging appointed for you in your Father's house. He that vouchsafed to wipe the sweat from his disciple's feet, will not disdain to wipe the tears from those tender affectionate eyes. Because you have been one of his mourners in the house of tribulation, you shall drink of the cup of joy, and be clothed with the garment of gladness, in the kingdom of his glory. The former things, and evil, will soon be passed; but the good to come shall neither end nor change.[14]

At another time, writing to his son of the death of his father, Adam Winthrop, he said:

He hath finished his course; and is gathered to his people in peace, as the ripe corn into the barn. He thought long for the day of his dissolution and welcomed it most gladly. Thus is he gone before; and we must go after in our time: This advantage he hath of us—he shall not see the evil which we may meet with ere we go hence. Happy those who stand in good terms with God and their own conscience: they shall not fear evil tidings; and in all changes they shall be the same.[15]

A lovable man was John Winthrop, richly endowed and admirably disciplined, gracious in manner, persuasive in speech, generous in action—in all England there could scarcely have been found a leader better equipped for the work in hand, when at the age of forty-three he became head of the emigrant church-state, which by reason of its charter and the removal of the corporation to New England, was become effectively an independent commonwealth, free to shape its domestic polity as seemed best. During the score of years that remained to him, he was the guiding spirit of the Massachusetts settlements, impressing his will upon others by sheer force of character. It was inevitable that in so strange and unprecedented an experiment, undertaken in an environment so unfamiliar, serious and often bitter divisions would arise touching the fundamental principles of government. In the frequent discussions Winthrop bore a leading part; he marshaled his arguments with the skill of a lawyer; he separated the broad principle

[14] *Ibid.*, Vol. I, p. 288. [15] *Ibid.*, Vol. I, p. 170.

from the special circumstance; and in the end he usually carried the assent of his fellow counselors to his proposals. His social and political philosophy, in consequence, greatly influenced the development of Massachusetts Bay during the early years when its institutions and polity were taking shape, and throws much light on the spirit and purpose of that development.

Winthrop's political bias was unconsciously shaped by his experience, of which the determining fact was the principle and practice of Jacobean magistracy. As an English squire he had long served as magistrate, and this experience he brought to New England as a legacy from an autocratic past. In that old world the magistrate exercised a patriarchal police power well-nigh absolute, sanctioned by ancient custom, upheld by the church, and acquiesced in by subjects well trained in subordination. Transported to New England and adapted to theocratic ends, the principle of magistracy was both augmented in power and ennobled in conception. To the police power over things temporal was added a police power over things spiritual. In the Bible commonwealth the legislative function was regarded as of minor importance. The law being already set down in the Scriptures, the chief authority in the commonwealth naturally rested with the magistrates who were responsible for its strict fulfillment. As stewards intrusted with a divine stewardship, they exercised absolute legislative and judicial powers; in their councils the ministers were summoned to participate, but no others. It was the duty of the magistrates to debate and determine, and the duty of the people to obey.

To a modern this is no other than sheer absolutism, but it was deeply embedded in Calvinistic theory and practice, and was justified by the Puritan principle of special talents. God calls to the post of duty those best fitted to serve. As a devout follower of Calvin, Winthrop must have often pondered upon the passages in the *Institutes* which set forth the nature of magistracy and the duties of the magistrate, and in particular this: "If they remember that they are the vicegerents of God, it behooves them to watch with all care, diligence, and industry, that they may exhibit a kind of image of the Divine Providence, guardianship, goodness, benevolence, and justice." [16] To a devout Jacobean like Winthrop, this patriarchal conception of stewardship would appear as a

[16] Book IV, Chapter XX, Paragraph 6.

noble ideal, worthy of a Christian. The potential absolutism implied would scarcely trouble one who had grown up in a society where absolute authority was interwoven with everyday life. The Christian magistrate was still a magistrate, but with the great difference that his hands must be kept clean and his conscience clear. This nobler spirit of Calvinistic stewardship is revealed in Winthrop's *Modell of Christian Charity*, written on shipboard during the voyage out. A sense of profound responsibility devolving upon the leaders imparts dignity to the thought: they must bear and forbear, knitting themselves together in a common purpose, and seeing that "the care of the public" should "oversway all private interests." And this "care of the public," remained in theory if not always in practice, the guiding principle of Winthrop's official activities.

The bearing of this doctrine of magistracy upon the early movement of democracy in Massachusetts is not far to seek. If magistracy was a duty laid upon those of fit talents, they would serve God ill who should turn a willing ear to popular protests against magisterial policy. On this point Winthrop was adamant. He would have no meddling on the part of those who had not been called. When it was attempted to bring him to account before the congregation for an unpopular judicial decision, he denied the competency of the congregation in such matters, and then as he often did in cases of doubt, he made a "little book" in which he elaborated the thesis, "That a Church hath not Power to call any Civill Magistrate to give Account of his Juditiall proceedings in any Court of Civill Justice: and what the Church may doe in such Causes." [17] The shoemaker should stick to his last, Winthrop believed, and he would suffer no interference by the congregation with his duties as magistrate. On another occasion when difficulties had arisen in certain negotiations with the Connecticut settlements, he noted in his journal:

These and the like miscarriages in point of correspondency were conceived to arise from these two errors in their government: 1. They chose divers *scores* men, who had no learning nor judgment which might fit them for those affairs, though otherwise men holy and religious. 2. By occasion hereof, the main burden for managing of state business fell upon one or other of their ministers, (as the phrase and style of these letters will clearly discover), who, though they were men of singular wisdom and

[17] The heads of argument are given in *Life and Letters*, Vol. II, pp. 211–214.

godliness, yet stepping out of their course, their actions wanted that blessing which otherwise might have been expected.[18]

The political philosophy which underlay Winthrop's theory and practice of magistracy, was a Puritan modification of the commonly accepted English theory of a "mixt aristocratie." He had been trained in the law but was little given to speculative thought. There is evidence that he read somewhat in the fast accumulating political literature of the times, but little indication that his reading modified his theory or influenced his conduct. He was an administrator rather than a philosopher, and from the fragmentary records that have survived it is difficult to piece together a consistent political theory. As a magistrate under the dominance of the English Common Law, he seems to have accepted the constitutional theory of Coke, who sought to interpose the customary and ancient law of the land between the growing absolutism of the Crown, and the increasing importunity of the Commons, with sovereignty inhering in the judiciary. As a Puritan, however, he superimposed the law of Moses on the law of the land, and by ignoring the King on the one hand, and denying power to the representatives of the people on the other, he created the framework of a magisterial theocracy.

The two chief sources to which we must turn for his political views, in addition to his letters and journals, are: *A Replye to the Answ: Made to the Discourse about the Neg: Vote*, and *Arbitrary Governmt Described: & the Governmt of the Massachusetts Vindicated from that Aspersion*, both of which have been preserved in the form of heads of argument.[19] The principle that underlies these skeleton arguments is the theory of a state held static by exact constitutional arrangements. King and people represent the great supplementary functions of constitutional government, sovereignty and liberty; both are necessary in a well ordered society, and neither may encroach upon the other. This Winthrop regarded as the vital principle of the English constitution, which had been embodied in the government of Massachusetts.

The Government of the Massachusetts consists of Magistrates & Freemen: in the one is placed the Auth'ye, in the other the Lib'tye of the Com: W: either hath power to Acte, both alone, & both togither, yet by a distinct power, the one of Lib'tye, the other of Auth'ye: the Freemen

[18] *Ibid.*, Vol. II, p. 236.
[19] Both are given in the appendix to Vol. II of the *Life and Letters*.

Acte alone in all occurrences out of Court: & both Acte togither in the
Gen'll Court: yet all limited by certaine Rules, bothe in the greater &
smaller affaires: so as the Governm't is Regular in a mixt Aristocratie,
& no wayes Arbitrary.[20]

In settled times and places this nice balance between sovereignty
and liberty is maintained by use and wont; but in periods of
disturbance, such as then existed in England, and in new experiments, such as marked the setting up of the commonwealth of
Massachusetts, there was certain to be much pulling and straining
between these antagonistic principles; and his refusal to accept
this fact, and his stubborn insistence on transferring to New
England the old English static order, brought on Winthrop's head
many of the difficulties that greatly troubled his administration.
Both in the old world and the new, the principle of liberty was
encroaching on feudal authority. With the rise of the middle
class, many Englishmen, and particularly the colonial New Englanders, were fast outgrowing the old paternalisms, and coming
to regard them as no other than tyranny. The freemen of the
Massachusetts towns were restive under the strict rule of the
magistrate-elders, and a growing party of democratic deputies
was eager to try its hand at government. All such democratic
pretensions Winthrop held in contempt, although he was at pains
to deny the arbitrary nature of magisterial rule.

Some of the deputies had seriously conceived, that the magistrates
affected an arbitrary government. . . . For prevention whereof they
judged it not unlawful to use even *extrema remedia*, as if *salus populi*
had been now the transcendent rule to walk by, and that magistracy must
be no other, in effect, than a ministerial office, and all authority, both
legislative, consultative, and judicial, must be exercised by the people in
their body representative.[21]

If government were regular it could not be arbitrary—this was
Winthrop's brief reply to the deputies. In his arguments he
deliberately avoided the difficult question of sovereignty; in part,
no doubt, because of the delicate situation resulting from fear of
royal interference, but chiefly because he was unwilling to bring
into jeopardy the unlimited powers of magistracy. That he
denied sovereignty to the people is abundantly clear from his
actions, as well as from specific comment. By the law of the
corporation, namely, the written terms of the charter, authority

[20] *Ibid.*, Vol. II, p. 454.   [21] *Journal*, Vol. II, p. 240.

was vested in a limited body of freemen; and he saw no reason in expediency or otherwise to extend that authority. Thus he argued, "it is well proved & concluded by a late Juditious writer, in a booke newly come over, intituled an Answ: to Dr Ferne, that thoughe all Lawes, that are sup'structive, may be altered by the representative bodye of the Com:w: yet they have not power to alter anythinge w'ch is fundamental." [22] What delimitations were to be drawn between "superstructive" and "fundamental," he was not careful to make clear; but it is certain that he regarded as fundamental not only the charter terms and the British constitution but the will of God. Doubtful as this last may seem to students of political science, and difficult to determine, it was neither doubtful nor difficult to Winthrop and his fellow magistrates and ministers. The Mosaic law was specific. Back of the citizen-legislator was the subject of Jehovah, and he was politically free only to do the will of God. There must be divine sanction for all human law; lacking such sanction all majority votes and legislative enactments were null and void. Sovereignty inheres finally in God, and it is by his fundamental law that all superstructive laws and institutions must be judged.

In theocratic philosophy, therefore, the magistrate became no other than God's vicegerent, with authority beyond popular limitation or control. No English squire presumed to exercise the magisterial powers which Winthrop and his associates quietly usurped. Among other innovations they early claimed the right of veto on the acts of the deputies, and in reply to the dissatisfaction voiced at such arbitrary encroachment, Winthrop argued that the magisterial veto was no infringement on the liberties of the people, but was a means to "preserve them, if by any occasion they should be in danger: I cannot liken it better to anythinge than the brake of a windmill: w'ch hathe no power, to move the runninge worke: but it is of speciall use, to stoppe any violent motion, w'ch in some extraordinary tempest might endanger the wholl fabricke." [23] The convenient weapon of divine sanction Winthrop did not scruple to use at need. Thus when a petition was presented for the repeal of a law which arbitrarily decreased the number of deputies, he denied the lawfulness of the procedure:

[22] *Ibid.*, Vol. II, p. 438.
[23] *Discourse about the Neg: Vote, Life and Letters,* Vol. II, p. 434.

When the people have chosen men to be their rulers, now to combine together . . . in a public petition to have an order repealed . . . savors of resisting an ordinance of God. For the people, having deputed others, have no right to make or alter laws themselves, but are to be subject.[24]

The old English right of petition, in short, was not a right in theocratic Massachusetts, and any unauthorized joining together of citizens for political purposes was a conspiracy against the will of God. The practical result of this doctrine of magisterial vicegerency was that a small group of freemen set up an unlimited oligarchy over some four or five thousand of their fellow Englishmen, even going so far as to advance the novel doctrine of a freehold tenure of power.

Winthrop's extreme jealousy of popular power cannot be explained away by the doctrine of stewardship. Hooker of Hartford had no such distrust of the people, but he was not a gentleman, like Winthrop, and had not grown up with an aristocratic contempt for democracy. The preposterousness of democratic aspiration was a stock jest among English gentlemen, and in seeking to refute the arguments of the deputies for greater popular power Winthrop did little more than give a Hebraic twist to his aristocratic prejudices:

Where the chief Ordinary power & administration thereof is in the people, there is a Democratie . . . the Deputies are the Democraticall p'te of o'r Governm't. Now if we should change from a mixt Aristocratie to a meere Democratie: first we should have no warr'nt in scripture for it: there was no such Governm't in Israell. 2: we should heerby voluntaryly abase o'rselves, & deprive o'rselves of that dignitye, w'ch the providence of God hath putt upon us: w'ch is a manifest breach of the 5th Com't: for a Democratie is, among most Civill nations accounted the meanest & worst of all formes of Governm't: & therefore in writers, it is branded w'th Reproachfull Epithets as Bellua multorū capitū, a monster, &c: & Historyes doe recorde, that it hath been allwayes of least continuance & fullest of trouble.[25]

In an often quoted letter to Thomas Hooker, then engaged in erecting a democratic commonwealth in Connecticut, Winthrop diplomatically moderated his terms and put the aristocratic doctrine in more attractive form. "I expostulated about the unwarrantableness & unsafeness of referring all matter of counsel or judicature to the body of the people, *quia* the best is always the least, & of that best part the wiser part is always the lesser." [26]

[24] *Journal.*   [25] *Life and Letters*, Vol. II, p. 430.   [26] *Ibid.*, Vol. II, p. 237.

But he must have agreed heartily with another English gentleman, who writing to Winthrop under date of July 9, 1640, remarked pithily:

I say agayne noe wise man shoud be soe folish as to live whear every man is master, & masters must not correct theyr servants: Where wise men propound & fooles determine, as it was sayde of the citties of Greece. [27]

As the responsible steward of God's plan for New England, Winthrop would not flatter the people by pretending to the doctrine of *vox populi, vox dei*. The multitude he regarded as factious, overswayed by expediency and self-interest, incapable of governing wisely. Law, by its nature, was ethical, the expression of God's absolute and just will; and this law, the magistrates were called of God to enforce.

From this conception of the absolute nature of law, came the famous discussion of liberty and authority, known as the "little speech," which is the most highly praised of Winthrop's utterances. In a certain police-court matter that had loosed the class prejudices of all parties, he had held against the popular feeling, and was impeached before the general court. Upon his acquittal he rose and addressed the court in words which he afterwards set down in his journal. No other episode in his varied career reveals so well the admirable poise of the man—the dignity, the self-control, the fair-mindedness, despite an attack that hurt him to the quick.

For the other point concerning liberty, I observe a great mistake in the country about that. There is a twofold liberty, natural (I mean as our nature is now corrupt) and civil or federal. The first is common to man with beasts and other creatures. By this, man, as he stands in relation to man simply, hath liberty to do what he lists; it is a liberty to evil as well as to good. This liberty is incompatible and inconsistent with authority, and cannot endure the least restraint of the most just authority. The exercise and maintaining of this liberty makes men grow more evil, and in time to be worse than brute beasts: *omnes sumus licentia deteriores*. This is that great enemy of truth and peace, that wild beast, which all the ordinances of God are bent against, to restrain and subdue it. The other kind of liberty I call civil or federal; and it may also be termed moral, in reference to the covenant between God and man, in the moral law, and the politic covenants and constitutions amongst men themselves. This liberty is the proper end and object of authority, and cannot subsist without it; and it is a liberty to that only which is good, just, and honest. This liberty you are to stand for, with the hazard (not only of your goods,

[27] *Letter of Lord Say and Sele*, in *ibid.*, Vol. II, p. 426.

but) of your lives, if need be. Whatsoever crosseth this, is not authority, but a distemper thereof. This liberty is maintained and exercised in a subjection to authority; it is of the same kind of liberty wherewith Christ hath made us free. . . . On the other side, ye know who they are that complain of this yoke and say, let us break their bands, etc., we will not have this man to rule over us. Even so, brethren, it will be between you and your magistrates. If you stand for your natural corrupt liberties, and will do what is good in your own eyes, you will not endure the least weight of authority, but will murmur, and oppose, and be always striving to shake off that yoke; and if you will be satisfied to enjoy such civil and lawful liberties, such as Christ allows you, then will you quietly and cheerfully submit unto that authority which is set over you, in all the administrations of it, for your good. Wherein, if we fail at any time, we hope we shall be willing (by God's assistance) to hearken to good advice from any of you, or in any other way of God; so shall your liberties be preserved, in upholding the honor and power of authority amongst you.[23]

The doctrine of aristocratic stewardship has never been more skillfully presented. It is John Cotton's reply to Roger Williams, translated into political terms; the philosophy of natural rights whittled down to a covenant between God and man. It rests on the assumption of an absolute law, superior to expediency. But may not honest men disagree as to what constitutes the good, just, and honest? and may not godly authority imperceptibly slide over into plain tyranny? Although the Saints may have professed themselves satisfied with Winthrop's doctrine, the pages of early Massachusetts history bear ample record of the dissatisfaction of the sinners. Most of the difficulties experienced by Winthrop in his administration of the commonwealth had their root in this assumption of arbitrary power, the immediate outcome of which was a spontaneous development of incipient democracy. How far such an assumption of divine custodianship may lead a generous man from the path of justice, appears in his summing up of the case against Mistress Anne Hutchinson, who because she insisted upon her own interpretation of the good, just, and honest, was adjudged "A woman not only difficult in her opinions, but also of an intemperate spirit." "The ground work of her revelations is the immediate revelation of the spirit, and not by the ministry of the Lord . . . and this hath been the ground of all these tumults and troubles; and I would that those were all cut off that trouble us." The kernel of the offense for which Mistress Hutchinson was banished, is then laid bare: "We see not that any should have

[23] *History of New England*, Vol. II, pp. 279–282.

authority to set up any other exercise beside what authority hath already set up." [29]

In this arbitrary judgment of Winthrop's—the natural fruit of the tree of theocratic stewardship—the "little speech" discovers its suitable commentary. Urged on by his bigoted associates, the kind-hearted governor descended to their level, and began the unhappy business of playing the tyrant under pretense of scourging God's enemies. The lords-brethren served notice upon all dissenters that henceforth there must be no dissent in New England. The admirable courage of Mistress Hutchinson availed no more against the magisterial interpretation of the good, just, and honest, than the boldness of Roger Williams before her; or later, the zeal of the Baptists who were sent away by Endicott; or later, still, the piety of the Quakers, who were whipped at the cart-tail and hanged, men and women both. The policy of the political stewardship of the best and wisest never had fuller trial, with abler or more conscientious agents, than in Massachusetts Bay; and its failure was complete. Such progress as Massachusetts made towards freedom and tolerance was gained in the teeth of theocratic opposition; New England democracy owes no debt to her godly magistrates.

Bred up in a half-feudal world, the leaders of the Migration remained patriarchal in their social philosophy, unable to adapt old prejudices to new conditions. Human motives are curiously mixed, human actions rarely consistent; and if the shortcomings of John Winthrop show blacker by contrast with the excellence of the ideal which he professed, the fault must be charged against his time and associates and not against his manly, generous nature. Most English gentlemen of his day were steeped in a sodden Toryism, yet he earnestly desired to be a faithful steward of church and state. If as a gentleman he held firmly to the privilege of rulership, as a Christian he endeavored to rule honorably and in the fear of the Lord. If he followed the beaten path and tried to shape the great experiment by the traditional principles of his class; if his zeal at times led him into indisputable tyrannies; it was because he was led away from the light, not because he sought selfish ends. Godliness has its own special temptations, and it would be ungenerous to bear ill-will against so lovable a man.

[29] Hutchinson, *History of Massachusetts Bay Colony*, Vol. II, pp. 482–520.

CHAPTER IV

THE CONTRIBUTIONS OF INDEPENDENCY

I

OTHER ideals than those of Winthrop and Cotton, fruitful or feculent according to the special bias of whoever judges them, came out of England in the teeming days of the Puritan revolution to agitate the little settlements. A Hebraized theocracy could not satisfy the aspirations of advanced English liberals who were exploring all the avenues to freedom, and who, now that the old feudal bonds were loosening, were projecting a more generous basis for the reorganization of society. The democratic elements were beginning to make their voices heard in England; the doctrine of the priesthood of all believers was bearing fruit in the minds of obscure Independents; and the eventual outcome would be the shouldering aside of a snug Presbyterian order, and the clarification of a program for a democratic commonwealth. In those excellent words commonweal and commonwealth—words much on men's tongues in the creative later years of the Puritan revolution—was fittingly summed up the political ideal of Independency. English liberalism had come to believe that social conformity, established in the practice of coercion, with its monarchical state and hierarchical church, must give way to an order founded in good will, that conceived of the political state as a public-service corporation, concerned solely with the *res publica*, or public thing, careful of the well-being of all, allowing special rights or grants to none. The state, it was coming to be argued freely, rightly understood, was no other than society organized to further the great end of the commonweal; no longer must it remain a private preserve for gentlemen to hunt over.

But before that should come about a great battle must be fought, in New England as well as in old England. The principle of individual freedom must first be established securely in the public mind, and to that business the party of Independents devoted its energies. In the theory and practice of Independency two fundamental rights were implied: the right of the individual

51

to determine his own belief, uncoerced by external authority; and the right to join freely with his fellows in the institutional expression and spread of such belief. In order to realize the first, it was a necessary preliminary to establish the right of free inquiry on a firm constitutional basis—the principle that the state shall safeguard the citizen in the exercise of such right, and not hinder or thwart him; and in order to realize the second, it was necessary to establish in social practice a much more fiercely disputed principle, namely, the right to proselytize, to spread one's views freely, to endeavor to make them prevail over contrary views. Certainly neither right would be freely granted; they must be won in the teeth of supposedly divine sanctions to conformity. However intimately the two are related, it is over the second that the long fierce battle has been waged in modern history. Liberalism faces no severer test than in its attitude towards the right of unpopular minority propaganda. The broad principle of toleration of differences, so vital to a democratic society, searches out and lays bare every insincerity of liberal professions. The will to power is so universal in appeal, it is so quick to attack every threatening nonconformity, that no other social right has traveled so arduous a road, or lags so far in the rear of the liberal advance. The principle of religious toleration that was involved in the movement of Independency was the ecclesiastical form of a struggle, which, shifting later to the field of politics and then to economics, is still raging about us. The long battle is still far from being won. In few countries today do more than a small minority regard the principle of toleration otherwise than as a social luxury to be indulged in only when times are settled.

It was in the nature of things that a clash should soon come in Massachusetts Bay. There Independency would certainly be looked upon as no better than a weed from the devil's wilderness, and in the name of God and the theocracy it would be trampled under foot. Liberalism and the Cambridge Platform would no more mix than oil and water. But the more immediate and narrower question of religious toleration was only incidental to the broader divergencies that lay in antagonistic principles of church and state, and that brought on the clash. A general engagement was preparing between the principles of Presbyterianism and Independency, and the real issue at stake was the future form of society in New England—whether it was to be aristocratic or democratic. The free environment was a strong stimulus to idealists who looked upon the new field as a heaven-sent opportunity for their own special Utopias to take root, and who would bitterly resent any intrusion by a rival. Commonwealth building is a great adventure, and the Independents with their carefully elaborated plans would not sit quietly by and permit the Saints to preëmpt the land for their inhospitable theocracy without a struggle. In such a contest the more liberal party was fortunate in its leaders. Thomas Hooker and Roger Williams were men of creative ability, of inflexible purpose, of fine idealism, the ablest amongst the entire group of Puritan immigrants, in whom the great principles of Independency found worthy stewards; and the long struggle they carried on, each in his own way, with the theocratic leaders of Massachusetts was to affect profoundly the later development of New England. In the end the Presbyterianism of Boston was to surrender to the Congregationalism of Hartford. From Connecticut and Rhode Island, it must be recalled, rather than from the Bay colony, came those democratic principles and institutions that were to spread widely in later years, and create the New England that after generations have liked to remember.

II

THOMAS HOOKER

Puritan Liberal

Among the Englishmen who came to Massachusetts were some to whom the "New England way" seemed to promise a democratic organization of the church, and who looked with disapproval upon the Presbyterizing policy of the oligarchy. Of this number the congregations of Newtown, Dorchester, and Watertown were noteworthy for the quiet determination with which they seceded from the theocratic commonwealth, and set up for themselves in the Connecticut wilderness. Their leaders were liberals who believed that everything should be done decently and in order, but who were determined that the outcome of such decent orderliness should be a free church in a free state; and so while Roger Williams was engaged in erecting the democracy of Rhode Island, Thomas Hooker was as busily engaged in erecting the democracy of Hartford.

Concerning the "grave and judicious Hooker" surprisingly little is known, in spite of the important work that he did and the influence that he wielded during a masterful life. He was evidently a man regardless of fame, who took small pains to publish his virtues for the edification of posterity; what record he left behind bears evidence of being the expression of a man to whom desire for celebrity was nothing in comparison with the needs of his Master's work. Unlike his fellow ministers he was not much given to making books. The works that bore the name of Thomas Hooker on the title-page were put through the press usually by other hands than his, and were taken from shorthand notes. His great contribution, *A Survey of the Summe of Church Discipline*, published anonymously and in an imperfect form, was written against his will in consequence of his having been drafted for the service by his fellow ministers. In removing from Newtown he cut himself off from the group of diarists who diligently recorded the happenings of the day, and so failed of being portrayed and praised by divers busy pens. Lacking exacter information, we are forced to rely mainly upon such hearsay reports as have come down to us, pieced out by Puritan tradition; and these reports make Thomas Hooker to have been a strong and resourceful man, a better democrat than his fellow ministers, the father of New England Congregationalism as it later came to be when the Presbyterianizing tendency was checked—a practical leader who rejected equally the reactionary theocracy of John Cotton, and the leveling radicalism of Roger Williams.

For the pronounced democratic sympathies of this "light of the western churches"—a sympathy quite unusual in his day and world—some grounds will be discovered in his commonplace origin. Unlike John Cotton, who had a "descent from honourable progenitors," Hooker was sprung from a plain yeoman family that had made no stir in the world. His native hamlet, Marfield in Leicestershire, numbered no more than six houses, tucked away in a secluded countryside. His schooling was got by the aid of scholarships: at Market-Bosworth and later at Cambridge, where he entered as sizar, which meant among other things that he was waiter on tables in the Hall. When he was settled in a forty-pound living at Esher, in Surrey, he married a "waiting-woman" to the wife of his patron; and when he died, after a laborious life spent in the cause of righteousness, he left an estate appraised at

846 pounds, 15 shillings, exclusive of his books, more than half of which modest sum was represented by the Hartford homestead.[1] Which scanty information is sufficient to tell us that Thomas Hooker was a simple man in worldly ambitions as well as in origin, not given to climbing or feathering his own nest, with none of the great associates or aristocratic ties of Winthrop and Ward and Cotton, a churchman more inclined to the ways of Independency than to Presbyterianism.

In his professional work he was rather the pastor than the teacher, caring more for experimental religion than for theological disputation.   He was an embodiment of the moral fervor of the Reformation that protested against the scandal of "dumb priests." He seems to have been the most stimulating preacher of early New England, and it was as a lecturer that he had made a name for himself before he was driven from his English charge by Laud. The lecturer was a characteristic Puritan innovation, much hated by the Anglicans.   Translated into a modern equivalent, it meant an agitator who used the pulpit to spread the new gospel of free judgment in religious matters, and other gospels displeasing to absolutism.   That such men were not liked by Charles and his Archbishop goes without saying; they were "the people's creatures" —a certain Tory churchman complained to the King—and "blew the bellows of their sedition."   Such being the case it seemed but common prudence to muzzle them, and as early as 1622 James laid down an orthodox program, forbidding any of lesser rank than "a bishop or dean [to] presume to preach in any popular auditory on the deep points of predestination, election, reprobation, or of the universality, efficacy, irresistibility of God's grace," and re- stricting Sunday afternoon sermons to such innocuous themes as the "Catechism, Creed, or Ten Commandments."[2]   It was an endeavor to stop men's thinking by putting the crown of martyr- dom on the lovers of truth.   To forbid the Puritan to talk of such things, to shut up the Word of God from him, was to blow the bellows of his sedition indeed.

That Thomas Hooker was not a man to be muzzled must have been clear to all who knew his stubborn English will.   In his homely vigor he was not unlike Hugh Latimer, direct and vigorous in speech and action, not easily turned aside from the path of duty,

---

[1] See Walker, *Thomas Hooker, Preacher, Founder, Democrat.*
[2] *Ibid.*, pp. 40–44.

possessing much of the old bishop's courage in dealing with great men and their follies. He knew a fool and a tyrant in high places, and was bold to call them by their true names. "He was a person," said Cotton Mather, "who while doing his Master's work, would put a king in his pocket." He was the more dangerous because he had put his own temper under strict governance—"For though he were a man of cholerick disposition, and had a mighty vigour and fervour of spirit . . . yet he had ordinarily as much govern-ment of his choler as a man has of a mastiff dog in a chain; he 'could let out his dog, and pull in his dog, as he pleased.'"

So ardent a temperament, joined to remarkable powers of oratory, gave to Thomas Hooker very unusual popular influence, some measure of which is revealed in a letter of a certain sycophant of the court party, who wrote to Laud's tool, Chancellor Duck, under date of May 20, 1629, as follows:

All men's eares are now filled with ye obstreperous clamours of his followers against my Lord . . . as a man endeavouring to suppress good preaching and advance Popery. All would be here very calme and quiet if he [Hooker] might depart. . . . If he be suspended its the resolution of his friends and himselfe to settle his abode in Essex, and maintenance is promised him in plentifull manner for the fruition of his private conference, which hath already more impeached the peace of our church than his publique ministry. His genius will still haunte all the pulpits in ye coun-try, where any of his scholers may be admitted to preach. . . . There be divers young ministers about us . . . that spend their time in conference with him; and return home and preach what he hath brewed. . . . Our people's pallats grow so out of tast yt noe food contents them but of Mr. Hooker's dressing. I have lived in Essex to see many changes, and have seene the people idolizing many new ministers and lecturers, but this man surpasses them all for learning and some other considerable partes and . . . gains more and far greater followers than all before him. . . . If my Lord tender his owne future peace . . . let him connive at Mr. Hooker's departure.[3]

Clearly the England of Laud with its pursuivants and tattling tongues of "dumb ministers"—who might well be jealous of his eloquence—was no fit place for the activities of Thomas Hooker. Even though he should be suspended, he would still be reckoned dangerous to prerogative with his private conferences and his following of young ministers. So he was driven overseas into Holland, whence after a few years' experience with the Archbishop's spies, and dislike of the Presbyterian system there practiced, he

3 *Ibid.*, pp. 45–46.

set forth for America where he arrived on the same boat with John Cotton and Samuel Stone, and was inducted as pastor of the church at Newtown which had been awaiting his coming over. Shortly thereafter began the open dissatisfaction of the Cambridge congregation with the policy of the oligarchy, which resulted three years later in the removal of Hooker and his church to Hartford. The causes of this removal—an event that profoundly agitated the colony—have been much discussed, but they have never been cleared of what may have been an intentional vagueness. Possibly, as Hubbard suggests, there were jealousies between Hooker and Cotton, Winthrop, and Haynes, which it would have been unseemly to expose in open court;[4] but the likelier explanation would seem to lie in the incompatibility of political views, which at bottom was a division on the question of aristocracy or democracy in church and state. The Cambridge men seem to have disliked the oligarchic rule of the magistrates; they doubtless sympathized with the popular party and may have encouraged the counter aggressions of the deputies, whose assertiveness fills so much space in Winthrop's journal and betokens his concern. It is likely that there was more dissatisfaction than got into journals, either private or official; and it is equally likely that Thomas Hooker was a prime force in quickening the democatic unrest. "After Mr. Hooker's coming over," said Hubbard in an often quoted passage, "it was observed that many of the freemen grew to be very jealous of their liberties." Nevertheless, Hooker was not a contentious person, to spread a clamor through the commonwealth and endanger the success of the plantation. He believed that "Time, Place, Outward Decency and Comelinesse" were desirable in the management of public affairs; and so instead of descending to sharp dispute with men whom he respected and loved even though he disagreed with them in political views, he chose to remove quietly out of their jurisdiction, making as little cause for embroilment as possible.

After all, the most illuminating commentary upon the causes of the removal is the spirit of the institutions set up in the new

[4] The testimony of Roger Williams seems to imply as much: "Mr. Haynes, Governor of Connecticut, though he pronounced sentence of my long banishment against me, at Cambridge, then Newtown, yet said to me . . . 'I think, Mr. Williams, I must now confess to you, that the most wise God hath provided and cut out this part of His world for a refuge and receptacle for all sorts of consciences. I am now under a cloud, and my brother Hooker, with the Bay, as you have been, we have removed from them thus far, and yet they are not satisfied.'" (*Letter to Major Mason* [1670], in *Narragansett Club Publications*, Vol. VI, p. 133 ff.)

settlement. While we need not go so far as to assert, with the historians of Connecticut, that "the birthplace of American democracy is Hartford," we must recognize in the Fundamental Orders adopted by the General Assembly, January 14, 1639, a plan of popular government so broadly democratic as to entitle it to be called "the first written constitution of modern democracy." [5] Concerning the important part played by Hooker in this work there can be no doubt. His influence was commanding, and the sneer of old Samuel Peters—"Hooker reigned twelve years high-priest over Hertford"—scarcely overstates the fact. And this great influence was thrown persistently in favor of democratic procedure in church and state. He definitely rejected the Boston practice of magisterial autocracy. In opposition to Winthrop, who asserted, "Whatsoever sentence the magistrate gives, the judgment is the Lord's, though he do it not by any rule prescribed by civil authority," Hooker argued:

That in the matter which is referred to the judge, the sentence should lie in his breast, or be left to his discretion, according to which he should go, I am afraid it is a course which wants both safety and warrant. I must confess, I ever looked at it as a way which leads directly to tyranny, and so to confusion, and must plainly profess, if it was in my liberty, I should choose neither to live nor leave my posterity under such a government.[6]

At another time, replying to Winthrop's justification of oligarchic rule on the ground that "the best part is always the least, and of that best part the wiser is always the lesser," Hooker frankly rested his case for democracy on the good sense of the people as a whole:

It is also a truth that counsel should be sought from counsellors; but the question yet is, who should those be. Reserving smaller matters which fall in occasionally in common course, to a lower counsel, in matters of greater importance which concerns the common good, a general counsel chosen by all, I conceive, under favour, most suitable to rule and most safe for relief of the whole.[7]

Before the General Court, on May 31, 1638, eight months before the Fundamental Orders were adopted, Hooker preached a remarkable sermon on popular sovereignty. Taking for his text

[5] Borgeaud, *The Rise of Modern Democracy*, p. 123.
[6] Quoted in J. T. Adams, *The Founding of New England*, p. 194.
[7] Walker, *Thomas Hooker, etc.*, p. 122.

Deut. 1:13—the passage on which John Eliot later erected his fantastic Utopia—he elaborated the thesis that "the foundation of authority is laid, firstly, in the free consent of the people," and therefore that "the choice of public magistrates belongs unto the people by God's own allowance," and "they who have the power to appoint officers and magistrates, it is in their power also, to set the bounds and limitations of the power and place unto which they call them." [8] This was Hooker's reply to the oligarchic policy of the Bay in limiting the number of freemen in order to maintain the supremacy of the magistrates; and it throws light on the comment written out of England in the spring of 1636, to John Wilson, that "there is great division of judgment in matters of religion amongst good ministers & people which moved Mr. Hoker to remove"; and that "you are so strict in admission of members to your church, that more than halfe are out of your church in all your congregations, & that Mr. Hoker befor he went away preached against yt (as one reports who hard him)." [9] In the new commonwealth there was neither a property qualification nor a religious test limiting the right of franchise; the admission of freemen was reckoned a political matter and left to the several township democracies. The reaction against the oligarchic policy of Massachusetts Bay carried far.

If we had Hooker's sermon in full we should know much more about his political theory; yet even from the meager and tantalizing notes that have been preserved, we can deduce fairly certainly the major principles of his philosophy. Three creative ideas seem to have determined his thinking: the compact theory of the state, the doctrine of popular sovereignty, and the conception of the state as a public-service corporation, strictly responsible to the will of the majority—ideas that Roger Williams elaborated in detail and during many years of service reduced to a working system in the commonwealth of Rhode Island. That Hooker should have grasped so firmly the essentials of the new democratic theory will surprise no one who is acquainted with the political speculations of English Independency. They were all implicit in the new theory of church and state that such thinkers as Williams and Vane and Milton were clarifying, and since the days of Robert Browne they had been familiar in one form or another to the young Puritan radicals at the universities. The compact idea, which held

[8] *Ibid.*, p. 125.   [9] *Ibid.*, p. 88.

in solution the doctrine of natural rights, had established itself firmly in New England with the coming of the Pilgrims. The Mayflower compact and the church covenant provided the basis for the social organization of Plymouth; and the covenant idea had taken so strong a hold on the popular mind of Massachusetts Bay that the astute leaders of the oligarchy were quick to see the advantage of investing the charter, in the popular imagination, with the sanctity of the compact idea; and by a subtle process of idealizing, they transmuted the charter of a trading company into a fundamental organic law, that was reckoned an adequate written constitution to safeguard the rights of the people. It was a clever political move, but it seems not to have satisfied Thomas Hooker, who was too liberal in his views to accept the shadow for the substance. As a left-wing Independent he would have a real compact, and a popular fundamental law to safeguard the liberties of the people; and he saw to it that the new commonwealth was broadly based on the common will, rather than narrowly on the rule of the gentry. The democractic order of Connecticut was English Independency transplanted to the new world.

To Hooker New England Congregationalism owes as great a debt as does New England democracy. The last great work he undertook was a defense of the New England way against the criticism of the English Presbyterians. He was to prove a powerful advocate, for not only was he intellectually equipped to write a knotty book in answer to other knotty books, but unlike Cotton and Davenport and Mather, he was wholly in sympathy with Congregationalism, and had no mind to conceal or equivocate concerning its democratic tendencies. He would write no apology, but a frank and vigorous defense. His church polity, as elaborated in his *Survey of the Summe of Church Discipline*, is professedly Hebraic. "Ecclesiastical Policy," he asserts baldly, "is a skill of ordering the affairs of Christ's house, according to the pattern of his word," and he then proceeds to postulate the principle of absolutism by accepting a divine sovereign will. But this divine sovereignty was a blow struck at all temporal absolutisms, for it spoke through no vicegerent of pope, bishop, presbytery or magistrate, but only through the voice of the individual subject. It is the priesthood of all believers. "The *Supreme* and *Monarchicall* power resides onely in our Saviour, can onely be given and attributed to him, and to none other." There remained, then, the difficult business of determining how the sovereign will of Christ is to be wrought on earth, and into this Hooker delved with such convincing thoroughness that, in his own words, "no man that hath supped on Logick, hath a forehead to gainsay" his conclusions. He was bold in innovation—"a cause is not the lesse true, because of late discovered"; but after quieting "the stomachs of such, whose expectations are not answered in any opinion, unless it be moldy with age," he proceeds to explain the true nature of church organization thus:

But whether all Ecclesiasticall power be impaled, impropriated, and rightly taken in to the Presbytery alone: Or that the people of the Particular Churches should come in for a share, according to their places and proportions; This is left as the subject of the inquiry of this age, and that which occasions great thought of heart of all hands: Great thoughts of hearts in the Presbytery, as being very loth to part with that so chief privilege, and of which they have taken possession so many years. Great Thoughts of heart amongst the Churches, how they may clear their right, and claim it in such pious sobriety and moderation, as becomes the Saints: being unwilling to loose their cause and comfort, meerly upon a *nihil dicit:* or forever to be deprived of so precious a legacy, as they conceive this is, though it hath been withheld from them, by the tyranny of the Pope, and prescription of times. Nor can they conceive it lesse, then a heedlesse betraying of their speciall liberties, and not selling but casting away their inheritance, and right, by a careless silence, when the course of providence, as the juncture of times now present themselves, allows them a writt *Ad melius inquirendum.* . . . These are the times when people shall be fitted for such priviledges, fit I say to obtain them, and fit to use them. . . . And whereas it hath been charged upon the people, that through their ignorance and unskilfulnesse, they are not able to wield such priviledges, and therefore not fit to share in any such power, The Lord hath promised: To take away the vail from all faces in the mountain, the *weak* shall be as David, and David as an Angel of God.[10]

The church of Visible Saints confederating together to walk in the fellowship of the faith . . . is *Totum essentiale.* . . . Election of the People rightly ordered by the rule of Christ, gives the essentials to an Officer, or leaves the impression of a true outward Call, and so an Office-power upon a Pastor . . . *there is a communicating of Power* by Voluntary Subjection when, though there be *no Office-power, formaliter* in the people, yet they willingly yeelding themselves to be ruled by another, desiring and calling of him to take that rule; he accepting of what they yeeld, possessing that right which they put upon him, by free consent; *hence ariseth* this Relation and authority of Office-rule.[11]

[10] *Survey of the Summe of Church Discipline*, Introduction.
[11] *Ibid.*, Part II, pp. 66, 72.

It is crabbed prose, not altogether worthy of a man who kept the thorns crackling under the pot when he stood face to face with his congregation, and though we may feel inclined to accept the challenge of a certain old Puritan, and "lay a *caveat* against the author's sweet and solid handling" of his matter, we shall be little inclined to lay a *caveat* against his doctrine. Here is no casuistry like John Cotton's, denying Congregationalism while ostensibly defending it; but a frank acceptance of the supreme power of the people. "The Lord hath promised to take away the veil from all faces"—in this faith Thomas Hooker walked all his days, and what he could himself do to remove the veil from the faces of the common people, he did heartily as unto the Lord, thereby proving his right to be remembered among the early stewards of our American democracy.

III

ROGER WILLIAMS

Seeker

The gods, it would seem, were pleased to have their jest with Roger Williams by sending him to earth before his time. In manner and speech a seventeenth-century Puritan controversialist, in intellectual interests he was contemporary with successive generations of prophets from his own days to ours. His hospitable mind anticipated a surprising number of the idealisms of the future. As a transcendental mystic he was a forerunner of Emerson and the Concord school, discovering an indwelling God of love in a world of material things; as a speculative Seeker he was a forerunner of Channing and the Unitarians, discovering the hope of a more liberal society in the practice of the open mind; as a political philosopher he was a forerunner of Paine and the French romantic school, discovering the end of government in concern for the *res publica*, and the cohesive social tie in the principle of good will. Democrat and Christian, the generation to which he belongs is not yet born, and all his life he remained a stranger amongst men. Things natural and right to John Cotton were no better than anachronisms to him. He lived and dreamed in a future he was not to see, impatient to bring to men a heaven they were unready for. And because they were unready they could not understand the grounds of his hope, and not understanding they were puzzled and angry and cast him out to dream his dreams in the wilderness. There was abundant reason for his banishment. A child of light, he came bringing not peace but the sword. A humane and liberal spirit, he was groping for a social order more generous than any theocracy—that should satisfy the aspirations of men for a catholic fellowship, greater than sect or church, village or nation, embracing all races and creeds, bringing together the sundered societies of men in a common spirit of good will.

Roger Williams was the most provocative figure thrown upon the Massachusetts shores by the upheaval in England, the one original thinker amongst a number of capable social architects. An intellectual barometer, fluctuating with every change in the rising storm of revolution, he came transporting hither the new and disturbant doctrines of the Leveler, loosing wild foxes with fire-brands to ravage the snug fields of the Presbyterian Utopia. He was the "*first rebel* against the divine *church-order* established in the wilderness," as Cotton Mather rightly reported. But he was very much more than that; he was a rebel against all the stupidities that interposed a barrier betwixt men and the fellowship of their dreams. Those who found such stupidities serviceable to their ends, naturally disliked Roger Williams and believed they were serving God by undoing his work. There is a naïve passage in the *Magnalia* that suggests how incomprehensible to the theocratic mind was this stormy petrel that came out of England to flutter and clamor about Boston and Salem, until he was driven forth to find such resting place as he might, there to bring forth after his kind.

In the year 1654, a certain windmill in the Low Countries, whirling round with extraordinary violence, by reason of a violent storm then blowing, the stone at length by its rapid motion became so intensely hot as to fire the mill, from whence the flames, being dispersed by the high winds, did set a whole Town on fire. But I can tell my reader that, above twenty years before this, there was a whole country in America like to be set on fire by the rapid motion of a Windmill in the head of one particular man. [12]

And John Cotton, worsted in his bout with his brilliant antagonist, and perhaps frightened at the latter's free speculation, found such satisfaction as he could in epithets. Roger Williams was an "evill-worker"; his "head runneth round"; "it would weary a sober

[12] *Magnalia*, Vol. II, p. 495.

minde to pursue such windy fancies," such "offensive and disturbant doctrines"; when "a man is delivered up to Satan . . .
no marvell if he cast forth fire-brands, and arrows, and mortall-
things"; "it is such a transcendent light, as putteth out all the
lights in the world besides."

The open facts of Roger Williams' life are known to everybody.
Born in the year 1603,[13] he became a protégé of the great Coke, was
educated at Cambridge, and destined for the law, but forsook it
for the ministry. He was well advanced in his studies and coming
to conclusions that must have disturbed his conservative friends,
at the time of the Great Migration. Beginning as an Anglican,
then turning Separatist, then Baptist, and finally Seeker,[14] he is
perhaps more adequately described as a Puritan intellectual who
became a Christian freethinker, more concerned with social commonwealths than with theological dogmas. He passed rapidly
through successive phases of current thought to end as a Leveler.
Before quitting England he had embraced the principle of Separatism, and on his first coming over he refused the teachership of the
Boston church—the position given to Cotton two years later—
because it had not broken wholly with Anglicanism. He went to
the more liberal Salem, where his inconvenient questioning of land
titles and his views on the charter brought him into conflict with
the Boston authorities. Refusing to be silenced he was banished
and made his way to Rhode Island—"sorely tossed for one fourteen
weeks, in a bitter winter season, not knowing what bread or bed
did mean"—there to found a commonwealth on democratic principles.

Yet how inadequately do such meager facts reveal the deeper
sources of his militancy! He lived in the realm of ideas, of inquiry
and discussion; and his actions were creatively determined by
principles the bases of which he examined with critical insight.
Instead of being a weather vane, blown about by every wind of
doctrine, he was an adventurous pioneer, surveying the new fields

[13] For the date, see *Rhode Island Historical Society*, Vol. VIII, p. 156; *Narragansett
Club Publications*, Vol. VI, p. 599.

[14] The Seekers were thus described by a contemporary English pen: "Many have
wrangled so long about the Church that at last they have quite lost it, and go
under the name of *Expecters* and *Seekers*, and do deny that there is any Church, or
any true minister, or any ordinances; some of them affirm the Church to be in the
wilderness, and they are seeking for it there; others say that it is in the smoke of the
Temple, and that they are groping for it there—where I leave them praying to
God." (Paget, *Heresiography;* quoted in Masson, *Life of Milton*, Vol. III, p. 153.)

of thought laid open by the Reformation, and marking out the several spheres of church and state in the ordering of a true commonwealth. He was the incarnation of Protestant individualism, seeking new social ties to take the place of those that were loosening; and as a child of a great age of political speculation his religion issued in political theory rather than in theological dogma. Like other Separatist-Levelers he had penetrated to the foundations of the New Testament and had taken to heart the revolutionary ideals that underlie its teachings. It was the spirit of love that served as teacher to him; love that exalted the meanest to equality with the highest in the divine republic of Jesus, and gave an exalted sanction to the conception of a Christian commonwealth. He regarded his fellow men literally as the children of God and brothers in Christ; and from this primary conception of the fatherhood of God and the brotherhood of man, he deduced his political philosophy. Like Channing two hundred years later, he sought to adjust his social program to the determining fact that human worth knows neither Jew nor Gentile, rank nor caste; and following the example of his Master he went forth into a hostile world, seeking to make it over.

With this spirit of Christian fellowship, warm and human and lovable, repudiating all coercion, there was joined an eager mysticism—a yearning for intimate personal union with Christ as symbolized in the parable of the vine and the branches, a union as close as that of the bride and her husband. Running through his writings is a recurrent echo of the Hebrew love-song that Puritan thought suffused with a glowing mysticism: "I am my beloved's and my beloved is mine: he feedeth among the lilies. . . . I will rise now, and go about the city in the streets, and in the broad ways I will seek him whom my soul loveth." But when he went out into the broad ways of Carolinian England, seeking the rose of Sharon and the lily of the valley, he discovered only abominations. The lover was tempted by false kisses; the Golden Image was set up in the high places, and the voice of authority commanded to bow down to it. And so as a Christian mystic Roger Williams became a Separatist, and set his mind upon the new world as a land where the lover might dwell with his bride. Yet upon his arrival there he found the churches still "implicitly National," and "yet asleep in respect of abundant ignorance and negligence, and consequently grosse abominations and pollutions of Worship, in which the choicest servants of God, and most faithfull Witnesses of many truths have lived in more or lesse, yea in maine and fundamental points, ever since the Apostasie." Which "abominations and pollutions of Worship," he now proposed to sweep away altogether.[15] It was not an easy program, nor one entered upon lightly. Better than most, Roger Williams understood how closely interwoven were the threads of church and state. Separatism, with its necessary corollary of toleration, could not be unraveled from Carolinian society without loosening the whole social fabric. It was a political question even more than ecclesiastical; and it could justify itself only in the light of a total political philosophy. No other man in New England comprehended so fully the difficulties involved in the problem, as Roger Williams, or examined them so thoroughly; and out of his long speculations emerged a theory of the commonwealth that must be reckoned the richest contribution of Puritanism to American political thought.

The just renown of Roger Williams has too long been obscured by ecclesiastical historians, who in emphasizing his defense of the principle of toleration have overlooked the fact that religious toleration was only a necessary deduction from the major principles of his political theory, and that he was concerned with matters far more fundamental than the negative virtue of non-interference in the domain of individual faith. He was primarily a political philosopher rather than a theologian—one of the acutest and most searching of his generation of Englishmen, the teacher of Vane and Cromwell and Milton, a forerunner of Locke and the natural-rights school, one of the notable democratic thinkers that the English race has produced. Much of his life was devoted to the problem of discovering a new basis for social reorganization, and his intellectual progress was marked by an abundant wreckage of

---

[15] The Biblical authority for Separatism Williams found in both general and specific injunctions. The former, in the second commandment, in the third chapter of Daniel, in the seventeenth and eighteenth chapters of Revelation—the "wine of her fornication" being the ceremonial and ordinances of the English church—and in the Song of Solomon. The latter were: Revelation, 18:4: "And I heard another voice from heaven, saying, Come out of her, my people, that ye be not partakers of her sins. . . ."; Isaiah, 53:11: "Depart ye, depart ye, go ye out from thence, touch not the unclean thing; go ye out in the midst of her; be ye clean, that bear the vessels of the Lord"; II Corinthians, 6:17: "Wherefore come out from among them, and be ye separate, saith the Lord, and touch not the unclean thing; and I will receive you." On these texts he based his argument with Cotton for the total separation of the New England churches. (See *Narragansett Club Publications*, Vol. I, p. 300.)

obsolete theory and hoary fiction that strewed his path. He was a
social innovator on principle, and he left no system unchallenged;
each must justify itself in reason and expediency or be put aside.
Broadly the development of his thought falls into three stages: the
substitution of the compact theory of the state for the divine-
right theory; the rejection of the suppositious compact of the earlier
school and the fictitious abstract state—still postulated by many
thinkers—and the substitution of a realistic conception of the
political state as the sovereign repository of the social will, and
the government—or agent of the state—as the practical instrument
of society to effect its desired ends; and finally, the difficult problem
of creating the necessary machinery of a democratic commonwealth, as the exigencies of the Rhode Island experiment required.
Throughout, the inspiration of his thinking was social rather than
narrowly political or theological, and the creative source would
seem to have been the middle ages with their fruitful principle
of men in a given society enrolling themselves voluntarily as
members of bodies corporate, finding in such corporate ties a
sufficient and all-embracing social bond.[16]

In his substitution of the compact theory for divine right,
Williams was brought face to face with the fundamental assumption of the Massachusetts theocracy, based on numerous passages
of Scripture, that the political state is established and sanctioned
by the God of the Hebrews—an assumption that was freely used
to justify the engrossing of authority by the magistracy. As a
theologian he critically examined the Scriptural authorities, and
while conceding the divine source of government in general, he was
careful to cut away all autocratic deductions from the Pauline
assertion that "the powers that be are ordained of God." "Government and order in families, towns, etc., is an ordinance of the
Most High, Rom. 13, for the peace and good of mankind"[17] he admitted; but he agreed with Richard Hooker in discovering this
order of government to be no other than natural law. The state
is divine in origin because it is natural, and what is natural is of
God. The Hebraic commonwealth had been established immediately in an ordinance of Jehovah, but Christ and his disciples

[16] For much of the material made use of here, I am indebted to *The Political
Theory of Roger Williams*, a dissertation by Dr. James E. Ernst of the University of
Washington.
[17] "Letter to the Town Clerk of Providence," in *Narragansett Club Publications*,
Vol. VI, p. 401.

regarded the state and God as distinct authorities, not to be confused—"Render, therefore, unto Caesar the things which are Caesar's; and unto God the things that are God's." The conclusion at which he arrived, then, from the merging of divine ordinances and natural law, was expressed in a doctrine that sets apart the individual citizen in all his spiritual and intellectual rights, from the subject of the commonwealth, and provides the basis for his principle of toleration. "A Civill Government is an ordinance of God, to conserve the Civill peace of the people, so farre as concerns their Bodies and Goods," and no farther.[18] From this position he never retreated.

Every lawful Magistrate whether succeeding or elective, is not only the Minister of God, but the Minister or servant of the people also (what people or nation soever they be all the world over), and that Minister or Magistrate goes beyond his commission who intermeddles with that which cannot be given him in commission from the people. . . .[19]

Having thus reduced the divine-right field within narrow limits and translated it into an abstraction, he preëmpts all the ground of practical politics for his compact theory. In accord with a long line of liberal thinkers running back through Richard Hooker to Augustine and the earlier Roman school, he accepted the major deductions from the compact theory of the state: that government is a man-made institution, that it rests on consent, and that it is founded on the assumed equality of the subjects. He had only to translate these abstractions into concrete terms, and apply them realistically, to create a new and vital theory. The covenant idea of church organization had long been familiar to Separatists. To this the Pilgrims had added the Mayflower compact and Thomas Hooker had drawn up the Connecticut compact. Government resting on consent and authorized by written agreement was then no untried novelty when Roger Williams began his long speculations on the nature and functions of the political state. With Hobbes he traced the origin of the state to social necessity. The condition of nature is a condition of anarchy—a war of all against all; and for mutual protection the state takes its rise. "The World otherwise would be like a sea, wherein Men, like Fishes, would hunt and devoure each other, and the greater devoure the lesse." [20]

18. "The Bloudy Tenent," in *Narragansett Club Publications*, Vol. III, p. 349.
19 "The Bloudy Tenent Yet More Bloody," in *Narragansett Club Publications*, Vol. IV, p. 187.
20 "The Bloudy Tenent," in *Narragansett Club Publications*, Vol. III, p. 398.

But unlike the fiction assumed by Hobbes and Locke, this was no supposititious contract between ruler and ruled in prehistoric times, but present and actual, entered into between the several members of a free community for their common governance; nor on the other hand, like Burke's irrevocable compact, was it an unyielding constitution or fundamental law; but flexible, responsive to changing conditions, continually modified to meet present needs. It is no other than a mutual agreement, arrived at frankly by discussion and compromise, to live together in a political union, organizing the life of the commonwealth in accordance with nature, reason, justice, and expediency.

From this conception of the flexible nature of compact law came the sharp delimitation between state and government that he was at pains to make clear, and that constitutes a significant phase of his theory. Having rejected in his thinking the fictitious abstract state, the repository of an equally fictitious abstract sovereignty, he located sovereignty in the total body of citizens embraced within the community consciousness, acting in a political capacity. The state is society organized, government is the state functioning—it is the political machinery devised by the sovereign people to effect definite ends. And since the single end and purpose for which the body of citizens erect the state is the furtherance of the communal well-being, the government becomes a convenient instrument to serve the common weal, responsible to the sovereign people and strictly limited by the terms of the social agreement. "The Sovereign power of all civill Authority," he asserted, "is founded in the consent of the People that every Commonwealth hath radically and fundamentally. The very Common-weales, Bodies of People . . . have fundamentally in themselves the Root of Power, to set up what Government and Governors they shall agree upon." [21] Since governments are but "Derivatives and Agents immediately derived and employed as eyes and hands and instruments," the state or sovereign people can make their "own severall Lawes and Agreements . . . according to their severall Natures, Dispositions and Constitutions, and their Common peace and wellfare." [22] Final appeal is to "the Bar of the People or Commonweal, where all may personally meet, as in some Commonweales of small number, or in greater by their Representatives"—a system that

[21] See *Narragansett Club Publications*, Vol. III, pp. 214, 355, 366.
[22] "The Bloudy Tenent Yet More Bloody," in *ibid.*, Vol. IV, p. 487.

suits with the "Nature, Conditions and circumstances of the
People," according to the "Circumstances of time and place." [23]
In a well-known passage he puts the matter more compactly, thus:

> From this *Grant* I infer . . . that the *Soveraigne, originall,* and *founda-*
> *tion of civill power* lies in the *People.* . . . And if so, that a People may
> erect and establish what *forme* of *Government* seemes to them most meete
> for their *civill condition:* It is evident that such *Governments* as are by them
> erected and established, have no more *power*, nor for no longer time, then
> the *civill power* or people consenting and agreeing shall betrust them with.
> This is cleere not only in *Reason*, but in the experience of all *commonweales,*
> where the people are not deprived of their naturall freedom by the power of
> Tyrants.[24]

The state, then, is society working consciously through experience and reason, to secure for the individual citizen the largest
measure of freedom and well-being. It is armed with a potential
power of coercion, but only to secure justice. In such a state
government can subsist only by making proselytes to sound
reason, by compromise and arbitration, and not by force. But if
sovereignty inheres in the majority will, what securities remain for
individual and minority rights? What fields lie apart from the
inquisition of the majority, and by what agencies shall the engrossing of power be thwarted? The replies to such questions, so fundamental to every democratic program, he discovers in a variety
of principles; to the former in an adaptation of the spirit of medieval society that restricted political functions by social usage, and
to the latter by the application of local home rule, the initiative
and the referendum, and the recall. In the large field he ascribes
to social custom, he was a follower of Luther and a forerunner of
French romantic thinkers. His creative conception was an adaptation of the medieval theory of the corporation, or group of persons
voluntarily joining for specific purposes under the law; and this
idea he applies to the vexed question of the relation of church and
state. The legal status of the church, he argued, is identical with
that of a trading company; it is a corporate body with corporate
rights, and the several members enjoy all the freedoms and privileges that inhere in them by law and nature in their civil capacity.
The character of its membership and the content of its creed are
of no different concern to the civil magistrates than those of any

---

[23] "The Bloudy Tenent," in *ibid.*, Vol. III, p. 248.
[24] *Ibid.*, Vol. III, p. 248.

other corporation. "The state religion of the world," he asserted, "is a Politic invention of men to maintain the civil state." [25] Elaborated at greater length, his thesis is this:

The *Church* or company of *worshippers* (whether true or false) is like unto a . . . *Corporation, Society,* or *Company* . . . in *London;* which Companies may hold their *Courts,* keep their *Records,* hold *disputations;* and in matters concerning their *Societie,* may dissent, divide, breake into *Schismes* and *Factions,* sue and implead each other at the *Law,* yea wholly breake up and dissolve into pieces and nothing, and yet the *peace* of the *Citie* not be in the least measure impaired or disturbed; because the *essence* or being of the *Citie,* and so the *well-being* and *peace* thereof is essentially distinct from those particular *Societies;* the *Citie-Courts, Citie-Lawes, Citie-punishments* distinct from theirs. The *Citie* was before them, and stands absolute and intire, when such a *Corporation* or *Societie* is taken down.[26]

Having thus effectively secularized the church on its institutional side, he laid down twelve theses, of which these reach to the heart of the matter:

(1) *God* requireth not an *uniformity* of *Religion* to be *inacted* and *inforced* in any *civill state;* which inforced *uniformity* (sooner or later) is the greatest occasion of *civill Warre, ravishing* of *conscience, persecution* of *Christ Jesus* in his servants, and of the *hypocrisie* and destruction of millions of souls. (2) It is the will and command of *God,* that . . . a *permission* of the most *Paganish, Jewish, Turkish,* or *Antichristian consciences* and *worships,* bee granted to *all* men in all *Nations* and *Countries:* and they are onely to bee *fought* against with that *Sword* which is onely (in *Soule matters) able* to *conquer,* to wit, the *Sword* of *Gods Spirit,* the *Word* of *God.* (3) True *civility* and *Christianity* may both flourish in a *state* or *Kingdome,* notwithstanding the *permission* of divers and contrary *consciences,* either of *Jew* or *Gentile.*[27]

Abhorrent as such doctrine was to the Massachusetts theocrats, Roger Williams did not cease to press it home to their minds and consciences. "I know and am persuaded," he wrote Winthrop on July 21, 1637, "that your misguidings are great and lamentable, and the further you pass in your way, the further you wander, and the end of one vexation will be but the beginning of another, till conscience be permitted (though erroneous) to be free amongst you." [28] It was not toleration in the narrow sense of benevolent

[25] "The Bloudy Tenent Yet More Bloudy," in *ibid.,* Vol. IV, p. 222.
[26] "The Bloudy Tenent," in *ibid.,* Vol. III, p. 76.
[27] Preface to "The Bloudy Tenent," in *ibid.,* Vol. III, p. 3.
[28] *Narragansett Club Publications,* Vol. VI, p. 51.

non-interference by an authority that refrained from exercising its reserved right, that Roger Williams was interested in; it was rather religious liberty as a fundamental right, that had never been surrendered to the civil power, that lay beyond its jurisdiction and was in no way answerable to it, that he upheld in his great work *The Bloudy Tenent of Persecution for Cause of Conscience;* and the long dispute with John Cotton was, in its deeper significance, a dispute between two schools of political theory and two experiments in commonwealth building. In that notable debate aristocracy and democracy joined issues, and the vital question of the rights and liberties of the individual citizen in the political state for the first time was critically examined in America.

From the foregoing analysis of his political theory it should be clear that Roger Williams was a confirmed individualist who carried to its logical conclusion the Reformation principle of the right of private inquiry. Only Vane and Milton of his generation of Englishmen went so far along that path. He had seen the liberalisms involved in Luther's premises submerged by the rising nationalism which ambitious princes found useful for selfish ends; and he had seen the policy of the Massachusetts magistrates driving boldly in the same direction. That Rhode Island should not repeat the old unhappy mistake of coercive absolutism, was a matter therefore of vital concern to him. A great experiment in democracy was to be tried, and to that experiment he devoted his life. Into the form and structure of the new commonwealth went the best thought of English Independency. It was founded on the principles of "liberty and equality, both in land and government," [29] and established in the sovereignty of the people. That government should not engross its powers, the compact entered into provided for frequent elections, a single-chambered legislature, joint and individual initiative of laws, compulsory referendum, the right of recall of all laws including the constitution, and appeal to arbitration. A rigid constitution, augmenting in authority with age and veneration, Roger Williams feared as acutely as did Paine or Jefferson. To vest sovereignty in the courts through the right of review and interpretation was repugnant to his whole political theory. The fundamental law could be interpreted only by the power that created it originally, namely,

[29] "Letter to the Town of Providence," in *Narragansett Club Publications,* Vol. VI, p. 263.

the sovereign people acting in a political capacity. Within the larger framework of the state the several towns retained the right of home rule in local matters. They were corporations, erected like the church in the spirit of medieval corporate law, competent to rule themselves, yet not infringing on the sovereignty that granted them their powers. In short, to adapt the words of a modern student, the state of Rhode Island as erected by Roger Williams in accordance with the principles of his political philosophy, was "nothing so much as a great public-service corporation." [30] Or, as another student has put it, "If democracy . . . in its ultimate meaning be held to imply not only a government in which the preponderant share of power resides in the hands of the people, but a society based on the principles of political and religious freedom, Rhode Island beyond any other of the American Colonies is entitled to be called democratic." [31]

It was a hazardous experiment to undertake in an age when the ark of the democratic covenant found few places of refuge. Its friends were only a handful and its enemies many and powerful, and had it not been for a group of defenders in Parliament, the Rhode Island venture would have been brought to a speedy end. English Independency saved for America what English Presbyterianism would have destroyed. To Sir Harry Vane Rhode Island owes a debt of gratitude second only to that due Roger Williams. But though its godly neighbors were not permitted to destroy Rhode Island, they were free to slander and spread evil reports, and so thoroughly did they do their work that for upwards of two hundred years the little commonwealth was commonly spoken of in such terms as Rogues Island and the State of Confusion; not indeed, till it left off following agrarian and Populistic gods, till it had ceased to be democratic, did it become wholly respectable. It was not so much the reputed turbulence of Rhode Island that was disapproved by the Boston magistrates; but rather the disturbing example of a colony at their very doors, which, in denying the right of the godly to police society, gave encouragement to evil-disposed persons in their own sober commonwealth. Every democracy, they believed, was so notoriously mad and lawless— as both sacred and profane authorities had sufficiently demonstrated—that the Boston oligarchy never forgave Parliament for

[30] Duguit, *Law in the Modern State*, p. 51.
[31] Gooch, *History of Democratic Ideas*, p. 80.

refusing them permission to establish a mandatory over their self-willed neighbors.

It was to prevent such meddling that Roger Williams had been at pains to secure a Parliamentary charter; and he saw to it that the charter terms should not restrict the democratic liberties. His faith in the sobriety and good sense of the people of Rhode Island was never shaken. In spite of many difficulties that grew out of the sharp individualism of vigorous characters, the colony proved to be a good place to dwell for those who were content to share the common rights and privileges. In a letter to Vane, written in 1654, the founder apologizes for some of the things reported of them, but the apology does not detract from the just pride with which he contemplated the solid achievements of the Rhode Island experiment:

Possibly a sweet cup hath rendered many of us wanton. We have long drunk of the cup of as great liberties as any people we can hear of under the whole heaven. We have not only been long free (together with all New England) from the iron yolk of wolfish bishops, and their popish ceremonies . . . but we have sitten quiet and dry from the streams of blood spilt by that war in our native Country. We have not felt the new chains of Presbyterian tyrants, nor in this colony have we been consumed with the over-zealous fire of the (so called) godly christian magistrates. Sir, we have not known what an excise means; we have almost forgotten what tithes are, yea, or taxes either, to church or commonwealth. We could name other special privileges, ingredients of our sweet cup, which your great wisdom knows to be very powerful (except more than ordinary watchfulness) to render the best of men wanton and forgetful.[32]

England gave her best when she sent us Roger Williams. A great thinker and a bold innovator, the repository of the generous liberalisms of a vigorous age, he brought with him the fine wheat of long years of English tillage to sow in the American wilderness. How much America owes to him is perhaps, after all the intervening years, not adequately realized; the shadow of Massachusetts Bay still too much obscures the large proportions of one who was certainly the most generous, most open-minded, most lovable, of the Puritan emigrants—the truest Christian amongst many who sincerely desired to be Christian. He believed in men and in their native justice, and he spent his life freely in the cause of humanity. Neither race nor creed sundered him from his fellows; the Indian was his brother equally with the Englishman. He was a Leveler be-

CONTRIBUTIONS OF INDEPENDENCY

cause he was convinced that society with its caste institutions dealt unjustly with the common man; he was a democrat because he believed that the end and object of the political state was the common well-being; he was an iconoclast because he was convinced that the time had come when a new social order must be erected on the decay of the old. *"Liberavi animam meam,"* he said with just pride; "I have not hid within my. breast my *souls* belief." "It was more than forty years after his exile that he lived here," wrote Cotton Mather, "and in many thinges acquitted himself so laudably, that many juditious persons judged him to have the root of the matter in him, during the long winter of this retirement." Since those words were written increasing numbers of "juditious persons" have come to agree with the reluctant judgment of Cotton Mather, and are verily persuaded that Master Roger Williams "had the root of the matter in him." In his own day he was accounted an enemy of society, and the commonwealth of Massachusetts has never rescinded the decree of banishment issued against him; yet like so many unshackled thinkers, he was a seeker after a better order, friend to a nobler and more humane society. If he transported to America the democratic aspirations of English Independency, it is perhaps well to recall the price that was exacted of him for his service:

Let the reader fancy him in 1640, a man of thirty-four, of bold and stout jaws, but with the richest and softest eyes, gazing out over the Bay of his dwelling, a spiritual Crusoe, the excommunicated even of Hugh Peters, and the most extreme and outcast soul in all America.[33]

[33] Masson, *Life of Milton*, Vol. II, p. 563.

CHAPTER V

OTHER DREAMERS IN ISRAEL

I

NATHANIEL WARD

Elizabethan Puritan

THE most caustic pen of early New England was wielded by the lawyer-minister and wit, Nathaniel Ward of Ipswich, author of the crotchety little book, *The Simple Cobler of Aggawam*, and chief compiler of the celebrated *Body of Liberties*. He is a strange figure to encounter in the raw little settlements. To come into his presence is to feel oneself carried back to an earlier age, when the courtly wits were weaving their silken terms into gorgeous tapestries. Born about the year 1578, he was only five years younger than Ben Jonson. Highly educated and intimate with the best society of England and the continent, he was well advanced in middle life when he set foot in the new world, and in his late sixties when he wrote *The Simple Cobler*. Far more strikingly than any of his emigrant brethren he belonged in taste and temperament to the later Elizabethan world, which lingered on into the reigns of James and Charles, zealously cultivating its quaint garden of letters, playing with inkhorn terms, and easing its cares with clever conceits. Faithful disciple of Calvin though he was, he was something of a courtier as well, with a rich sap of intelligence, which, fermented by much thought and travel in many lands, made him the raciest of wits, and doubtless the most delightful of companions over a respectable Puritan bottle. "I have only Two comforts to Live upon," Increase Mather reported him as saying. "The one is in the Perfections of Christ; The other is in The Imperfections of all Christians."

The Simple Cobler of Aggawam is certainly the brightest bit of Renaissance English penned in America—an Elizabethan clipped garden set down in a wilderness of theology. It deserves to be far better known than it is, not only for its "convenient condiments" of speech that will tickle the palate of an epicure, but for its quaint exposition of the muddled state of England in the year 1645. Like a belated Euphuist, Nathaniel Ward delighted in fantastic words.

> If I affect termes [he confessed, by way of apology] it is my feeblenesse; my friends that know me, thinke I doe not: I confesse, I see I have here and there taken a few finish stitches, which may haply please a few Velvet eares; but I cannot now well pull them out, unlesse I should seame-rend all. It seems it is a fashion with you to sugar your papers with Carnation phrases, and spangle your speeches with new quodled words. . . . I honour them with my heart, that can expresse more than ordinary matter in ordinary words; it is a pleasing eloquence; them more, that study wisely and soberly to inhance their native language. . . . Affected termes are unaffecting things to solid hearers; yet I hold him prudent, that in these fastidious times, will helpe disedged appetites with convenient condiments, and bangled ears, with pretty quicke pluckes.[1]

The casual reader is chiefly impressed by the quaint satire of the book, with its caustic comment on women's fashions—the "foolefangles" of "nugiperous Gentledames," who "transclout" themselves into "gant bar-geese, ill-shapen-shotten-shell-fish"; and it is such bits that are commonly picked out for reprinting in the anthologies. But the real significance of the work lies elsewhere. *The Simple Cobler* is an old man's plea for accommodation of differences. It is bitter with intolerance of toleration; it is torn between an old loyalty to King Charles whom Ward knew and loved—"my long Idolatry towards you," as he confesses sadly—and a new loyalty to Parliament; and it is sobered by a strong concern over the desperate condition of England, which required looking to speedily, he believed, if the realm were not to be torn past all mending. On both sides there was abundant "misprision of Treason," which properly considered, he held to be no other than a "misprision of Reason"; and it was in the hope of summoning reason back to the national councils that the Cobbler offered his humble suggestions for the consideration of Englishmen.

Ward had been a lawyer before he turned to the ministry, and he seems to have impressed himself upon his fellow emigrants chiefly as a "subtile statesman." In his own way he was a political philosopher, little given like Roger Williams to exploring theory and examining principles, but applying rather a shrewd common sense to the problems of the times. He was convinced that old ways no longer sufficed; that prerogative and liberty could not much longer strain and pull against each other without rending the

[1] *The Simple Cobler*, edition of 1843, pp. 89–90.

whole fabric of the commonwealth; and the kernel of the book lies in a new theory of constitutional government for England which he offers as a convenient way out of the difficulties. Ward recognized that new interests were challenging the long sway of King and Tories; and as the antagonisms of rival interests strengthened, the insufficiency of the traditional use and wont to maintain a due balance of power was daily becoming more apparent. Hence had resulted confusion, and out of the confusion, civil war. From these patent facts Ward had convinced himself that there must be an overhauling of the fundamental law of England: the twilight zones must be explored and charted; the several rights and privileges of King, Lords, and Commons, must be sharply delimited; and thus every party in the government be brought to understand the exact bounds of its sphere. Neither King nor Commons would then encroach upon the other, and royal prerogative and popular will no longer dwell at sword's point with each other. What was needed, in short, was a written constitution, carefully arrived at by common consent, the terms of which should be just to all. Hitherto God "hath taken order, that ill prerogatives, gotten by the Sword, should in time be fetched home by the Dagger, if nothing else will doe it: Yet I trust there is both day and means to intervent this bargaine."

To preserve a just balance between rival interests in the state, and to hold all parties to their responsibility to God, were then the two problems to which Nathaniel Ward addressed himself, and the manner and terms of his argument are sufficiently revealed in the following passages:

Authority must have power to make and keep people honest; People, honesty to obey Authority; both a Joynt-Councell to keep both safe. Morall Lawes, Royall Prerogatives, Popular Liberties, are not of Mans making or giving, but Gods: Man is but to measure them out by Gods Rule: which if mans wisdome cannot reach, Mans experience must mend: And these Essentialls, must not be Ephorized or Tribuned by one or a few Mens discretion, but lineally sanctioned by Supreme Councels. In *pro-re-nascent* occurrences, which cannot be foreseen; Diets, Parliaments, Senates, or accountable Commissions, must have power to consult and execute against intersilient dangers and flagitious crimes prohibited by the light of Nature: yet it were good if States would let People know so much beforehand, by some safe woven *manifesto*, that grosse Delinquents may tell no tales of Anchors and Buoyes, nor palliate their presumptions with pretense of ignorance. I know no difference in these Essentialls, between Monarchies, Aristocracies, or Democracies. . . . And in all, the best Standard to measure Prerogatives, is the Ploughstaffe; to measure Liberties, the Scepter: if the tearms were a little altered into Loyall Prerogatives and Royall Liberties, then we should be sure to have Royall Kings and Loyall Subjects. . . .

He is a good King that undoes not his Subjects by any one of his un-limited Prerogatives: and they are a good People, that undoe not their Prince, by any one of their unbounded Liberties, be they the very least. I am sure either may, and I am sure neither would be trusted, how good soever. Stories tell us in effect, though nor in termes, that over-risen Kings, have been the next evills to the world, unto fallen Angels; and that over-franchised people, are devills with smooth snaffles in their mouthes. A King that lives by Law, lives by love: and he that lives above Law, shall live under hatred doe what he can. Slavery and knavery goe as seldome asunder, as Tyranny and Cruelty. I have a long while thought it very possible, in a time of Peace . . . for disert Statesmen, to cut an exquisite thred between Kings Prerogatives, and Subjects Liberties of all sorts, so as *Caesar* might have his due, and People their share, without such sharpe disputes. Good Casuists would case it, and case it, part it, and part it; now it, and then it, punctually.[2]

Nathaniel Ward was no democrat like Hooker and therefore no Congregationalist. "I am neither Presbyterian, nor plebsbyterian, but an Interpendent," he said of himself. But his "Interpend-ency" would seem to have been only an individualistic form of Presbyterianism. For the radical Sectaries who were rising out of the turmoil of revolution, he had the contempt of a thorough-bred Jacobean gentleman; and for their newfangled notion of religious toleration and their fetish of popular liberties—founded and nourished he believed in sentimentalism—he would substitute the solid reality of absolute truth, the faithful friend and coadjutor of which he professed himself to be. "Justice and Equity were before time, and will be after it"; and he regarded it as folly to try to circumvent them. He would have no great altering of the fundamental arrangements of society, such as Independents like Roger Williams were seeking. The solidarity of church and state was an anciently accepted principle, far safer to trust in, he believed, than the vagaries of unhistorical sects.

Experience will teach Churches and Christians, that it is farre better to live in a State united, though a little Corrupt, then in a State, whereof some Part is incorrupt, and all the rest divided. . . . The Scripture saith, there is nothing makes free but Truth, and Truth saith, there is no Truth but One. . . . He that is willing to tolerate any Religion, or discrepant way of Religion, besides his own, unless it be in matters

[2] *Ibid.*, pp. 54–55.

meerly indifferent, either doubts of his own, or is not sincere in it. . . .
He that is willing to tolerate any unsound opinion, that his own may also
be tolerated, though never so sound, will for a need hang Gods Bible at the
Devils girdle.[3]

As an honest Christian and a loyal subject he would honor both
the divine and temporal authorities; nevertheless, in order that
the law of God and the law of the land might be known of all and
march together, he would have the exact terms of the constitution
written out by "disert statesmen" in time of peace, and published
broadly, in Massachusetts as well as in England. And so when
he was commissioned to draw up a body of liberties for the new
commonwealth, he found the task congenial. As a lawyer he
seems to have been concerned at the non-legal methods of the
magistrates in dispensing judgment, so repugnant to the spirit
of the Common Law; and in the election sermon of 1641, that he
was invited to preach, he "advanced several things that savored
more of liberty, than some of the magistrates were prepared to
approve." [4]   But it was the lawyer protesting against court
methods that spoke out, not the liberal concerned with broader
liberties. In a letter to Winthrop, December 22, 1639, dealing with
the body of laws, he questioned, "Whether it will not be of ill
consequence to send the Court business to the common consideration of the Freemen," adding:

I fear it will too much exauctorate the power of that Court to prostrate
matters in that manner, I suspect both Commonwealth and Churches
have discended to lowe already. I see the spirits of the people runne
high, and what they gett they hould. They may not be denied their
proper and lawfull liberties, but a question whether it be of God to interest
the inferiour sort in that which should be reserved *inter optimates penes
quos est sancire leges* [*i. e.* to the aristocracy with whom rests the power to
establish the law].[5]

The celebrated *Body of Liberties* was presented three years after
The Simple Cobler was written, and in spite of his frankly aristocratic bias, Nathaniel Ward did a real service to Massachusetts
by incorporating into the law of the commonwealth many of the
old English safeguards of person and property, in some instances
advancing beyond current English practice. Yet true to his
Hebraic leanings, and in harmony with the spirit of the theocracy,

---

[3] *Ibid.*, pp. 8, 10.   [4] *Ibid.*, Introduction.
[5] Dean, *Memoir of the Rev. Nathaniel Ward*, pp. 56–57

he added certain brutalities drawn from the Mosaic code that
were soon to drop away.

There is something refreshing in the extraordinary frankness of
this old Puritan of the days of Elizabeth. He was no demagogue,
but a stout upholder of authority, who accepted the rule of caste
and the law of an eye for an eye. The militant severity of his
judgments, and the caustic wit of his comments, suggest somewhat
startlingly how long and bitter would be the struggle in New
England before the spirit of liberalism should find wide acceptance there. Gentlemen of the immigrant generation were set in
their ways, and none more inflexibly than Nathaniel Ward. He was
too old to adjust himself to new conditions, a fact which he recognized by returning to England to die, leaving behind as a warning
certain pithy quatrains of which this is one:

> The upper world shall Rule,
> While Stars will run their race:
> The nether world obey
> While People keep their place.

II

JOHN ELIOT

A Theocratic Utopia

At the session of the General Court holden at Boston, May 22,
1661, it was ordered:

> This Court taking notice of a booke entituled Christian Commonwealth,
> written . . . by Mr. John Eliot of Roxbury in New England, which . . .
> is justly offensive and in speciall relating to kingly Gouvernment in Eng-
> land, the which the said Mr. Eliot hath also freely and fully acknowledged
> to this Court. It is therefore ordered by this Court and the Authority
> thereof, that the said Booke be totally suppressed and the Authors ac-
> knowledgement recorded; and that all persons whatsoever in this jurisdic-
> tion that have any of the said Bookes in theire Custody shall on theire
> perrills within fowerteene dayes after publication hereof either cancel or
> deface or deliver them unto the next Magistrate or to the Secretary,
> whereby all farther divulment and improovement of the said offensive
> Booke may be prevented.[6]

The little book over which such a pother was made by the New
England magistrates in the days when they were under the censo-
rious eye of the newly restored Stuart government was the single

[6] *Massachusetts Historical Society Publications*, Vol. IX, Third Series, p. 128.

venture in the field of political speculation by the excellent John
Eliot, apostle to the Indians. It was a slender volume, written
about 1650, although not printed till 1659; but within the narrow
compass of twenty-one pages this dreamer in Israel has sketched
the outlines of an ideal Christian commonwealth. It was a day
and a world of idealists, and so John Eliot paused in the midst of
his missionary labors to fashion a brick for the building of that
temple which the Puritans of the Protectorate were dreaming of.
The idols had been broken by the hammer of Cromwell; the malev-
olent powers of this world were brought low; it remained now only
for the people of God to enter into a solemn covenant to establish a
commonwealth after the true divine model. That no mistake
should be made in so important a matter, John Eliot was moved
to send out of the American wilderness the plan of a Christian
Utopia, sanctioned by the Mosaic example and buttressed at
every point by chapter and verse, which he offered to the godly
Puritans of England as a suitable guide to their feet.

Naked theocracy is nowhere else so uncompromisingly de-
lineated as in the pages of *The Christian Commonwealth*. At the
basis of Eliot's political speculations were the two germinal conceptions which animated his theocratic brethren generally: the
conception that Christ is King of Kings before whom all earthly
authority must bow, and the conception that the Scripture alone
reveals the law of God. So long as the Stuarts were ruling at St.
James's speculative theocrats found it expedient to gloss their
principles with nice distinctions between temporal and spiritual
overlords; but with monarchy overthrown, they came out boldly
and urged the English people to put away all profane institutions.
"*Scripturae plentitudinem adoro*," John Cotton had exclaimed;
and to the same purpose John Eliot laid down the thesis:

> There is undoubtedly a forme of civil Government instituted by God
> himself in the holy Scriptures; whereby any Nation may enjoy all the
> ends and effects of Government in the best manner, were they but per-
> swaded to make trial of it. We should derogate from the sufficiency and
> perfection of the Scriptures, if we should deny it.
> The prayers, the expectation, and faith of the Saints in the Prophecies
> and Promises of holy Scripture, are daily sounding in the ears of the Lord,
> for the downfall of Anti-christ, and with him all humane Powers, Polities,
> Dominions, and Governments; and in the room thereof, we wait for the
> coming of the Kingdom of the Lord Jesus, who by his Divine Wisdom,
> Power, Government and Laws, given us . . . in the holy Scriptures, will

reign over all the Nations of the earth in his due time: I mean the Lord Jesus will bring down all people, to be ruled by the Institutions, Laws, and Directions of the Word of God, not only in Church-Government and Administrations, but also in the Government and Administration of all affairs in the Common wealth. And then Christ reigneth, when all things among men, are done by the direction of the word of his mouth: his Kingdom is then come amongst us, when his will is done on earth, as it is done in heaven, where no Humane or Angelical Policy or Wisdom doth guide anything, but all is done by Divine direction (Ps. 103:20); and so it shall be on earth, when and where Christ reigneth.

Much is spoken of the rightful Heir of the Crown of England, and of the unjustice of casting out the right Heir; but Christ is the onely right Heir of the Crown of England (Ps. 2:8) and of all other Nations also (Rev. 11:15).

That which the Lord now calleth England to attend is not to search humane Politics and Platformes of Government, contrived by the wisdom of man; but as the Lord hath carried on their works for them, so they ought to go unto the Lord, and enquire at the Word of his mouth, what Platforme of Government he hath therein commanded and prescribed.

From his Scriptural premises Eliot deduced a system of government that is altogether remarkable, not only for its rejection of the Separatist theory of natural rights, but for its naïve simplicity. Since the law has been declared once for all, perfect and final, there is no need for a legislative branch of government; and since Christ is sole ruler and king, there is no place for a profane head of the state; it remains only for the Christian theorist to provide a competent magisterial system to hear causes and adjudicate differences. Society is concerned wholly with duties and not at all with rights; government, therefore, begins and ends with the magistrate. In order to secure a suitable magistracy, Eliot proposed to divide society into groups of tens, fifties, hundreds and thousands, each of which should choose its rulers, who in turn should choose their representatives to the higher councils; and so there was evolved an ascending series of magistrates until the supreme council of the nation was reached, the decisions of which should be final.

The duties of all the Rulers of the civil part of the Kingdom of Christ, are as followeth: . . . to govern the people in the orderly and seasonable practice of all the Commanders of God, in actions liable to Political observations whether of piety and love to God, or of justice and love to man with peace.

Far removed as *The Christian Commonwealth* was from the democratic political theory of the Army radicals, or the practical

constitutionalism of Nathaniel Ward, it was the logical culmination of all theocratic programs. The ideal of social unity, of
relentless conformity, according to which the rebel is a social outcast to be silenced at any cost, dominates this godly Utopia as
mercilessly as it dominated the policy of Laud. In setting up King
Jesus for King Charles, there was to be no easing of the yoke upon
rebellious spirits; and in binding society upon the letter of the
Scripture there was to be no consideration for the aspirations of
the unregenerate. It is not pleasant to consider what the Saints
would have made of New England if their will had prevailed.
Curious as this little work is—testifying rather to the sincerity of
Eliot's Hebraism than to his political intelligence or his knowledge
of men—it is characteristic of the idealist who consecrated his life
to the Indian mission. How little disturbed he was by the per-
versities and limitations of everyday fact, is revealed in the policy
which he laid down for his Indian converts:

And this Vow I did solemnly make unto the Lord concerning them;
that they being a people without any forme of Government and now to
chuse; I would endeavour with all my might, to bring them to embrace
such Government, both civil and Ecclesiastical, as the Lord hath commanded in the holy Scriptures; and to deduce all their Lawes from the
holy Scriptures, that so they may be the Lord's people, ruled by him alone
in all things.

Which vow, considering the state of the Indian tribes to whom it
was to apply, may serve to throw light upon the reason for the
scant success of the Saints in their dealings with the red-men.

PART TWO: THE TWILIGHT OF THE OLIGARCHY
1660–1720

IT is not pleasant to linger in the drab later years of a century
that in its prime had known able men and accomplished notable
things. A world that accepted Michael Wigglesworth for its
poet, and accounted Cotton Mather its most distinguished man of
letters, had certainly backslidden in the ways of culture. The
final harvest of the theocracy must be reckoned somewhat scanty.
English Independency had been the robust and rebellious child
of a great age; New England Puritanism was the stunted offspring
of a petty environment. With the passing of the emigrant generation, a narrow provincialism settled upon the commonwealth of
Massachusetts Bay. Not a single notable book appeared; scarcely
a single generous figure emerged from the primitive background.
A thin soil and the law of Moses created a capable but ungainly
race, prosaic and niggardly. Their very speech lost much of the
native English beauty that had come down from medieval times.
The clean and expressive idiom that Bunyan caught from the
lips of English villagers, with its echoes of a more spontaneous life
before the Puritan middle class had substituted asceticism for
beauty, grew thinner and more meager, its bright homespun dyes
subdued to a dun butternut. The town records which in the first
years had been set down in dignified and adequate phrase became
increasingly crabbed and illiterate, laboriously composed by plain
men to whom spelling had become a lost art. The horizons of
life in New England were contracting to a narrow round of chores
and sermons. "When I first saw the Lieut. Governor," Sewall
remarked of Stoughton, "He was Carting Ears of Corn from the
Uper Barn." The picture suggests the pastoral note, but it suggests
much else as well.

Against this incursion of the provincial the church was the
single force to be counted on to do battle. The ministers did their
best, but it needed abler men than were available to counteract
the growing formalism of the times. They might lament that
their admonitions fell on unheeding ears, that they preached in

vain to a "sermon-proof, gospel-glutted generation"; but the blame must attach in part to the formalism of their appeals. The straw was over-threshed. The common provincialism infected the pulpit as well as the pew, and the creative vigor of the ministry steadily declined. The ground was being prepared for superstition and bigotry. As the belief spread through the New England villages that the end of the world would fall on the end of the century, men's thoughts naturally ran much on the demonology that is a logical consequence of the Hebraic dualism, and the most intelligent saw no reason to doubt that "the Evening Wolves will be much abroad, when we are near the Evening of the World." The psychology was being prepared for the witch-mania of Salem, and Cotton Mather was only echoing the common belief when he cried, "An Army of Devils is horribly broke in upon the place which is the *Centre*, and after a sort, the First-born of our *English Settlements*." [1] In this matter, as in so many others, the ministers were no better than their congregations; they were blind leaders of the blind, and they lent their sanction to the intolerance of the mass judgment. In an environment so stifling, with every unfamiliar idea likely to be seized upon as evidence of the devil's wiles, there was no room for free speculation. A generation under the terror of witchcraft was given over to stark reaction. The Salem outbreak was the logical outcome of the long policy of repression, that had hanged Quakers and destroyed independent thought, in its attempt to imprison the natural man in a strait-jacket of Puritan righteousness. Emotions long repressed sometimes find sinister outlets, and the witchcraft madness was only a dramatic aftermath of a generation of repressions and inhibitions. [2]

It was during these unhappy years that power finally slipped from the hands of the oligarchy. With the charter gone, a Royal Governor presiding over the Council, and a property qualification instead of a religious test for suffrage, the old order was broken past mending. The members of the oligarchy still hoped against hope, and under the governorship of Phips they made heroic attempts to bolster up the cause; but the Quebec expedition was so badly muddled as to bring the commonwealth to the verge of ruin, and the Governor and Council wrote to England that God had "spit in our

[1] *Wonders of the Invisible World*, p. 14.
[2] See Lucien Price, "Witchcraft, Then and Now," in *The Nation*, Vol. CXV, No. 2987.

faces."[3] Whether or not that was a correct analysis of the divine reaction to the Quebec fiasco is of no importance today; a good many New Englanders, it would seem, doubted it, and under the pressure of high taxes, a depreciated currency and a great debt, they made their dissatisfaction heard at the royal court. When the English government at last "resolved to settle the Countrey," the end of the oligarchy was come. The cautious amongst them were for throwing the whole responsibility on the Lord: "the foundations being gone, what can the righteous do?" argued Judge Sewall with shrewd worldly-wisdom. But the ministers would make no compromise with Baal. The tongues of false prophets might seduce the people, but they stood for the old order, fighting a losing fight with righteous zeal. On June 1, 1702, Sewall noted in his diary that he had "much adoe to persuade Mr. Willard to dine with me," the pastor being in a sulk because the civil representatives had taken precedence over the ministers in the procession for proclaiming Queen Anne. But in the end even "good Mr. Willard" was forced to acknowledge that his loyalty was given to a lost cause.

[3] J. T. Adams, *The Founding of New England*, p. 442.

CHAPTER I

SAMUEL SEWALL

Yankee

By good fortune an intimate record of daily life in old New England has been preserved in abundant detail. The diary of Samuel Sewall not only narrates the homely activities of Boston in the evening of the theocracy, *antiquis moribus, prisca fide*, but it unconsciously reveals the transformation of the English Puritan into the New England Yankee. The sober Boston citizens who on the Sabbath droned Windsor and York tunes, and took notes of long sermons, on week-days plied their gospel of thrift with notable success. They loved the meetinghouse as their fathers had loved it, but they were the sons and grandsons of tradesmen, and true to their English instincts they set about erecting a provincial mercantile society, dominated by the ideals of the little capitalist. Of this rising world of mercantilism, Samuel Sewall was a worthy representative. A Puritan magistrate and village capitalist, he made full use of his opportunities to worship God, to thrive and to rise. As the older ideal of theocratic stewardship is revealed in the career of John Winthrop, the newer practice of incipient capitalism is revealed in the life of Samuel Sewall.

The *Diary* is a fascinating book, with its petty gossip interwoven with matters of public concern, and its brisk activities set in a black border of innumerable funerals: the one among all the books of the time that is still quick with life after these two hundred years and more. In its meager entries we can trace the change that was coming to Massachusetts in the transition from a theocracy to a royal colony; and we can feel the strong emotions which that change aroused. The dry facts of history take on flesh and blood; forgotten names become living men walking the streets of Boston or arguing in the Council Chamber; Samuel Sewall himself becomes more real to us than our own contemporaries. He was the veritable embodiment of his serious, prudential Massachusetts, reflecting its changing fortunes with painstaking fidelity. In that petty world of conventional piety and shrewd self-interest, the kind-hearted Judge bustled about, a sermon in one hand to soothe the doubts of the troubled, and a bit of chocolate in the other to comfort the bedridden—as honest and friendly and prosaic a soul as Massachusetts ever bred. If one wishes to understand the first native New England generation, one cannot do better than linger over the daily jottings of this lawyer-tradesman, who knew his Calvin far better than his Coke, and who while busily adding new acres to his holdings strove to keep the younger generation uncontaminated by wigs and revels and other godless things, by the sweet ravishment of the psalms, in the singing of which the voice of the Judge was lifted up with pathetic earnestness.

For many years after his death fame dealt more than generously with Samuel Sewall. The prosperity that came to him during his earthly pilgrimage long provided for his memory, and made of him a greater figure than either nature or good fortune created. Who does not know Whittier's tribute?

> Stately and slow, with thoughtful air,
> His black cap hiding his whitened hair,
> Walks the Judge of the Great Assise,
> Samuel Sewall, the good and wise.
> His face with lines of firmness wrought,
> He wears the look of a man unbought,
> Who swears to his hurt and changes not;
> Yet touched and softened nevertheless
> With the grace of Christian gentleness;
> The face that a child would climb to kiss;
> True and tender and brave and just,
> That man might honor and woman trust.

And a hundred and forty-eight years after the cold January day when all that was mortal of him was "honorably Inter'd" in the Sewall tomb whither so many of his family had gone before,[1] a brilliant student of early American letters gave fresh currency to the stately Sewall of tradition. "He was a man built, every way, after a large pattern. By his great wealth, his great offices, his learning, his strong sense, his wit, his warm human sympathy, his fearlessness, his magnanimity, he was a visible potentate among men in those days."[2]

That was before the diary was published and the lay figure of

---

[1] Two of his three wives and eleven of his fourteen children he had buried.

[2] Tyler, *History of American Literature during the Colonial Period*, Chapter XIII, Part IV.

tradition vanished in presence of the real man. We know Samuel Sewall now and see him as he was. That he was a great man it is impossible to make out; but that he was a small man by no means follows. Behind the formal trappings of magistrate and councilor, we discover a capable, middle-class soul, honest, simple-hearted, serving himself yet not unmindful of his fellow townsmen, an excellent neighbor and citizen, to whom the strongest appeal of life was the economic. Like those kindred spirits, Defoe and Franklin, the dominant inspiration of his life was prudential, as befitted the descendant of generations of tradesmen. "Mr. Henry Sewall, my great Grandfather," wrote the Judge in old age, "was a Linen Draper in the City of Coventry in Great Britain. He acquired a great Estate, was a prudent Man, and was more than once chosen Mayor of the City." [3] In turning Puritan the English burgess did not change his nature, and Samuel Sewall was true to his breeding in fashioning his life upon that of his great grandfather. To acquire wealth and honors, to occupy a dignified position among his fellows, was the dominant ambition of his life. With excellent thrift he fixed his young affections upon the only child of a wealthy merchant, the richest heiress in the colony; no penniless "waiting-woman," for Samuel Sewall, such as had contented the unworldly Thomas Hooker. He understood how desirable it is to put money in one's purse; so he made a great alliance and proved himself a shrewd husbandman as well as a kind husband. [4] From commerce and land speculation and money lending and the perquisites of many offices, he accumulated steadily until his wealth entitled him to be regarded as one of the first citizens of Massachusetts. He did not forget his prudence even in his generosities, but set down carefully in his diary what his benefactions cost, that there might be no mistake when he came to make his reckoning with the Lord. He knew his rights and upheld them stoutly; and in the petty quarrels and litigations in which he found himself involved, he stuck to the letter of the law and usually won his point. He did not misuse his official position to feather his own nest, but what might be got legally from public office he took care to get.

With abundant wealth the path of preferment was easy to him.

[3] *Diary*, in *Massachusetts Historical Society Collections*, Fifth Series, Vol. I, p. xi.
[4] Compare his haggling over the terms of settlement upon a later proposed marriage; see *Diary*, Vol. III, p. 205.

From his election to the privileges of a freeman in 1678, at the age of twenty-six, to the end of a long life, he was continuously engaged in public affairs. He sought office and was not backward in pushing his claims upon a desirable post; [5] and by careful attention to business rather than by exceptional parts, he rose to a place of very great influence in the commonwealth. Like a competent man of affairs, he was prompt in meeting engagements—"am, I think, the most constant attender of Councils," he remarked of himself approvingly. He carried out to the letter the early advice given him: "Mr. Reyner . . . Advised me not to keep overmuch within, but goe among men, and that thereby I should advantage myself." [6] Capable, industrious, public-spirited, he led a busy and useful life that justified more than commonly the responsibilities which came to him. His qualities might be middle-class, but they were sterling and worthy of honor. It was a fortunate star that led him out of Tory England, where he would never have been more than a prosperous tradesman, to the new world where kindred spirits were erecting a commonwealth after his own heart.[7]

Nevertheless with all his excellent qualities Samuel Sewall was not a great or original nature. The evidence is convincing that he was a capable executive and administrator rather than a creative thinker or forceful leader; a Puritan embodiment of Defoe's merchant ideal; an example of the man who rises to civic honors by simple business virtues. He was at home in the narrow round of routine, but for bold speculation he reveals the incapacity of the practical soul. His intellectual interests were few; his ready curiosity was that of the uncreative mind, concerning itself with persons

[5] See *Diary*, Vol. III, p. 168.
[6] *Diary*, Vol. I, p. 32.
[7] The following is part of an obituary notice by his son:

In 1684, He was chosen a Magistrate of the *Massachusetts* Colony. . . . In 1692, He was appointed by King William and Queen Mary in their Royal Charter, one of the first Council for their Majesties in this Province, into which He was annually chosen and sat till 1725, when He resign'd his Election, having outlived all the others nominated in that Fundamental Constitution. In 1692 He was made one of the Judges, and in 1718, Chief Justice of our Superior Courts of Judicature thro' the Province, in which He sat till 1728, when his Infirmities growing on Him, He resign'd that Place also. In 1715, He was made Judge of Probates for this County of *Suffolk*, and continued in that Office till 1728, when He laid it down; it being the last Publick Post wherein He served and honoured his Country. *Diary*, Vol. III, pp. 409-410. In addition to the above, he was at times an overseer of Harvard College, censor of the press, and captain of the Ancient and Honourable Artillery Company; a frequent moderator of Boston town meeting, member of innumerable committees on church, parish and commonwealth matters, and adviser at large to whoever was in difficulties.

and happenings rather than with ideas. To say that Sewall possessed either an economic or political philosophy would be too generous an interpretation of his opinions. The views which he upheld vigorously were little more than prejudices. Of the several economic questions which engaged the attention of the Council during his years of service, the most insistent was the question of issuing bills of credit to supplement the scanty currency. There was the usual class alignment, the wealthy opposing the issues, and the poor generally favoring them. The position of Sewall was clear. He vigorously opposed every issue, from the conviction that the only honest money was hard money, even going so far as to prefer barter to bills.[8] Nowhere does he reveal any intelligent grasp of the economics of the problem, nor was he aware that his judgment might have been influenced by his private interests as a money lender.

In his political views he was equally unconcerned with broad principles. He seems to have been wholly unread in political theory, and like his fellow magistrates he never examined fundamentals. He accepted without question the right of the godly to police society, and he would have no meddling with affairs of state by tavern and fireside politicians. As a member of the oligarchy he naturally approved oligarchic rule. Although he would turn to the democracy for support against the Lords of Trade, when the latter were moving to overturn the theocracy, he put no trust in the political wisdom of the common people. He was as magisterial as John Winthrop in his belief in the principle of the stewardship of the elders. Stability of government was the prime essential; there must be no criticism of government by private individuals or by newspapers. On an occasion when Dudley's administration had been sharply attacked in a London paper, a copy of which had been brought over and talked about, there was a great pother in Council. Although Sewall was not willing to defend Dudley, he was troubled.

At last the Council voted, it tended to the disturbance of the Government. Lt. Govr. and Council order'd me to Reprimand Mr. Dummer. . . . I told him how intolerable it was for privat persons to print Reflections and Censures on the highest Acts of Government. . . . Twas ill done of them who printed it in London, and twas ill done by them that carried it on here.[9]

[8] See *Diary*, Vol. II, p. 366; Vol. III, pp. 87 and 345.
[9] *Diary*, Vol. III, pp. 84–85.

His characteristic attitude then comes out in the phrase: "I said
. . . I was for upholding Government whether in or out of it."
Samuel Sewall was no rebel against authority. But if he was
firm in support of the *de facto* government, he was insistent that
it should be honest. He protested to Governor Dudley against
padding the muster pay-rolls [10] and he dissented strongly against
introducing the current English practice of buying commissions
in the army.[11] The scandalous corruption of English politics must
not be permitted to sully the government of Massachusetts.

Sewall enjoyed in his lifetime the repute of a scholar. He was
Latinist enough to justify his Harvard degree of Master of Arts;
he read a good deal, and wrote and published books. But he seems
to have cared nothing for pure literature, and was unacquainted
with the English classics. His intellectual interest was in things
either occult or inconsequential. Biblical prophecy was his favorite study, and his most ambitious work, *Phaenomena Quaedam
Apocalyptica*, essayed to prove that America was to be the final
"rendezvous of Gog and Magog." Although long a magistrate
and judge of the highest court, he was not a lawyer. He received
no preliminary training in the law, and there are few indications
in the *Diary* that he read the literature of the profession. His
indifference seems to have given concern to his friends, for on
January 13, 1696, four years after he had been chosen judge, he
noted:

When were there at first, Mr. Danforth bad me look on the Cup-
board's head for a book; I told him I saw there a Law-book, Wingate on
the Common Law. He said he would lend it me, I should speak to Amsden
to call for it; and if he died, he would give it me. Again when took leave
after prayer, He said he lent me that Book not to wrap up but to read, and
if misliked it, should tell him of it.[12]

Primitive New England did not take kindly to lawyers, and in
administering a patriarchal justice by rule of thumb, Sewall was
like other New England magistrates. Neither did it take kindly
to the spirit of free speculation, and in his potterings over occult-
isms he was confessing the sterility of intellectual interests.

If the kind-hearted Judge lacked capacity for bold and liberal
thought, he lacked capacity as well for emotional fervor. He was
quite without imagination. Despite his honest concern for his
soul, and his sincere desire for the advancement of God's kingdom

[10] *Diary*, Vol. II, p. 228.   [11] *Ibid.*, p. 214   [12] *Diary*, Vol. I, p. 419.

in New England, Sewall did not possess a deeply religious nature. In his religious life he was the same prudent, plodding soul, that stowed away in his strong-box deeds to ample possessions during his pilgrimage through this vale of tears. The natural man was strong in his two hundred and odd pounds of flesh, and the religious mysticism that lurked in the heart of primitive Puritanism found no response in his phlegmatic soul. He was no Seeker, like Roger Williams, to be driven by a passionate fervor along untried paths; nor was he a philosopher, like John Wise, to concern himself with broad ecclesiastical principles. Instead, there is more than a hint of the tradesman's conception of religion—one has only to understand the profitableness of salvation to be led to invest in it. His religion must be orthodox; no untried methods or gambler's chances; a good business man will scrutinize title-deeds with due care, and the title-deeds to salvation are of the first importance. How characteristic are the following entries in the diary:

Sabbath, March 2d. I Pray'd in the Family, that might have an interest in God, Signed, Sealed and Delivered, and that all that tended to make it sure, might be perfected.
Febr. 6. [1718] This morning . . . I had a sweet and very affectionat Meditation Concerning the Lord Jesus; Nothing was to be objected against his Person, Parentage, Relations, Estate, House, Home! Why did I not resolutely, presently close with Him! And I cry'd mightily to God that He would help me so to doe!
23. 5. [1721] Mr. Prince preaches the Lecture, from Gen. 22. 18 . . . A very seasonable Discourse. One Fly was discovered in his Ointment: He asserted that the 1000. years Rev. 20. stood for Three Hundred and Sixty Thousand years; taking every day of the 1000. years for a year: as 365. days i.e. years. *Apage has nugas!* ["Away with this nonsense!"] [13]

No higher criticism for Samuel Sewall. If we quibble over the plain words of Scripture, how shall we be certain of the terms of the contract?

A man so cautious by nature, and with so large a stake in the existing order, could not fail to be a conservative, content with a world that justified itself by the prosperity which it brought him, and which it would bring to others, he doubted not, if they governed their conduct with equal prudence. He desired no innovations in church or state; established forms answered his needs and filled the measure of his ideal. The existing system was approved by all the respectable people of the community; there was every-

13 *Diary*, Vol. I, p. 312; Vol. III, p. 165; Vol. III, pp. 281–282.

thing to gain in upholding it, and likelihood of loss in suffering power to pass into the hands of a royal governor or of the ignorant poor. And so, determined by complex motives, by habit, by class ties, by economic interest, and by honest liking, Samuel Sewall went with the stream of conventional orthodoxy, strong for the old theocratic principles, seeing no need for readjustments to meet changing conditions. The true principles of church and state had been laid down by the fathers, to which the common acceptance by the best people gave final sanction.

It is characteristic of the prosperous bourgeoisie, and the old Judge walked the streets of Boston, or sat in his pew, or took his place on the bench, as stubborn and unimaginative a conservative as any of his fellows. If his persistent opposition to change, whether in the matter of wigs, or Christmas keeping, or creed, or politics, was due in part to a phlegmatic love of use and wont, it was prompted also by an instinctive fear of innovation. The world doubtless is imperfect, but it answers to God's will and we understand its ways and can draw our contracts with open eyes. Whereas change, however desirable it may seem theoretically, entails too many disturbing uncertainties. Very likely it was this subconscious concern for his material interests that so often made the simple-minded Judge an unintelligent opponent of all popular movements looking to a freer and more liberal society. When his native kindliness was touched he spoke out frankly. His anti-slavery tract (*The Selling of Joseph*), slight in extent and somewhat overpraised by historians, was not only much in advance of his time, but it contains one sentence that should not be forgotten, "There is no proportion between twenty pieces of silver and liberty." Equally significant was his stand against capital punishment for counterfeiting.[14] Such acts as the following must also be set down to his credit: "I essay'd June 22 [1716], to prevent Indians and Negros being Rated with Horses and Hogs; but could not prevail." [15] His native sense of justice was as strong as his kindliness. Who does not know of his confession in regard to the witchcraft persecutions—an act that set all Boston tongues wagging. When he was convinced that he had made a grievous and sorrowful mistake, he rose in the congregation while the minister read his public acknowledgment of that mistake, and his repentance for his share in the unhappy business. Thereafter

[14] See *Diary*, Vol. III, p. 277. [15] *Ibid.*, p. 87.

in commemoration he kept an annual day of prayer and fasting. We can forgive him much for that honest and manly act.

To the end of his life Sewall refused to go forward with the changing times, and his voluntary assumption of the office of *praefectura morum* laid him under a heavy responsibility to see that the primitive ways were upheld.   He was magisterial in rebuke and few transgressors of the strict New England code escaped a censure.   One would like to have James Franklin's private opinion of the sharp-eyed old Judge.   To Franklin and other members of the Hell-fire Club—young fellows keenly interested in domesticating the new wit literature in homespun Boston, openly skeptical, inclining to Arianism and even to deism—he must have seemed a prosy old reactionary, upholding a decadent orthodoxy and an obsolete social order.   No doubt many a sharp jibe was aimed at his back, for there were many to whom the older ways began to seem preposterous.   It may very well have been that those who committed a certain prank which Sewall records may have had him in mind.

Aug. 3. [1717] . . . 'Tis sad it should be so, but a virulent Libel was starch'd on the Three Doors of the Meeting House, containing the following Words:

TO ALL TRUE-HEARTED CHRISTIANS

Good people, within this House, this very day,
A Canting Crew will meet to fast, and pray.
Just as a miser fasts with greedy mind to spare;
So the glutton fasts, to eat a greater share.
But the sower-headed Presbyterians fast to seem more holy,
And their Canting Ministers to punish sinfull foley.[16]

Happily there is another and pleasanter side to the character of Samuel Sewall, and one that looked forward to the future instead of backward to the past.   Despite the harshness of the Puritan creed and the bigotry of Puritan rule, the fields and meadows of New England, that sent a breath of the countryside through the crooked streets of Boston, were a wholesome influence in the lives of men and women.   Magistrate and money-lender though he was, Samuel Sewall was a countryman and farmer also, a judge of milch cows and fat porkers as well as criminals, a lover of robins and flowers and fruitful orchards, one who sat his horse well, and when on circuit often drew up at a rail-fence to discuss the crops

[16] *Diary*, Vol. III, pp. 116–117.   Note the use of the word Presbyterian in these lines.

with some gossipy farmer. Above all, a lover of men, the most neighborly soul in the world, mingling freely with all classes, and although quite properly proud of a visit from the Governor or other great person, never above chatting with the carpenter, or doing a kindness to an old nurse. It was the friendly heart of the man that prompted so many little errands of helpfulness; and if sermons and tracts and good advice flowed from him like a spring freshet, if he was magisterial in petty rebuke, such little oddities of the man and the time did not detract from his sympathy or lessen his helpfulness. Men stood in awe of Cotton Mather, and children must have run from him, but neither awe nor fear threw their shadow across Sewall's path. We can make too much of the countless funerals that dot his pages, with their thrifty reckoning of gloves and scarfs and rings that were the queer perquisites of pallbearers. It was not an unwholesome world despite the smell of mortality that exudes from the old records, or the terrors of little children smitten with the fear of hell; and the homely round of Samuel Sewall's activities was very far from unwholesome.

It was his neighborliness that made him so representative of the leveling tendencies of a provincial village life—an easy comradeship with men of all conditions, unknown to the rigid class divisions of the old world. Going one day to visit the Jews' burial place at Mile-End, while on a visit to London, he invited the sexton to a pot of beer and a quiet chat, remarking in friendly fashion, "wisht might meet in Heaven: He answered, and drink a Glass of Beer together, which we were then doing." [17] His English friends would scarcely have understood that homely little scene, so natural to the colonial. Sewall is the first Yankee who reveals the native kindliness of the New England village. He was zealous to do good and to deal generously with others, because he had been generously dealt by. Growing more human with the ripening years, yet instinctively conservative, stubbornly intent on managing his own affairs in his own way and by his own agents, provincial to the core and strong in local pride, he reveals the special bent of the New England character, as it unconsciously differentiated itself from its English original. Not American as yet like Franklin, and no longer wholly English like Winthrop, far from democratic and yet no Tory, he was the progenitor of a practical race that was to spread the gospel of economic individualism across the continent.

[17] *Diary*, Vol. I, p. 301.

CHAPTER II

THE MATHER DYNASTY

I

FOR one who is not a loving student of the unamiable bickerings that clutter the records of early New England, and who does not read them by the gentle light of filial loyalty, it would seem presumptuous to venture into the thorny fields tilled by the Mathers. He is certain to get well scratched, and not at all certain to return with any fruit gathered. The rancors of dead partisanships beset him on every side, and the gossip of old wives' tales fills his ears. He will encounter many a slanderous hearsay, and the authentic documents to which he would naturally turn are often inaccessible, and always inhospitable. The countless tracts, for the most part inconsequential, that issued in an unbroken stream from the tireless Mather pens, consuming all the italics in the printer's case, constitute a veritable *cheval-de-frise* to protect their authors' literary reputations from any Philistine attack; and behind that bristling barricade they have long bidden defiance to casual invasion. Only a siege can reduce their stronghold and bring them forth into the clear light of day.

Two generations of Harvard scholarship have essayed the undertaking, but there is still wanting the detached critic who will set the Mathers against an adequate historical background, and appraise them objectively in relation to their times. The Harvard contributions are excellent in their way, but a consciousness of dealing with Harvard worthies would seem to have laid the writers under certain inhibitions. Exposition too easily slides into apologetics. The latest study [1] is a somewhat meticulous defense. It is an extraordinarily painstaking document, that has added to our knowledge of Increase Mather's life and work, but it was unhappily conceived in the dark of the moon, a season congenial to strange quirks of fancy. Some tangle it has cleared away, but fresh obstacles have been added by the intrusion of a thesis to be defended. In consequence, the interpretation of motives is

[1] Kenneth B. Murdock, *Increase Mather*, 1925.

98

colored by special pleading, and the very necessary inquiry into the sources of those virulent antagonisms that sprang up full-armed in the minister's every footprint is put aside as ungermane to a biography. It is an unfortunate assumption for it puts aside much that is crucial. The rehabilitation becomes too easy and complete. It proves too much. It would have us believe that in spite of all the smoke that gathered about Increase Mather's militant pilgrimage through life, there was never any fire of his kindling; that in spite of all the puddles through which the priestly politician splashed to reach his ends, no spot or stain ever smutched his gown. The contention may be sound, but it puts credulity to the strain, and unless one has something of a Mather stomach for marvels, one is likely to indulge in the luxury of doubt.

II

The Mathers were a singularly provocative family, capable, ambitious, certain to have a finger in every pie baking in the theocratic oven. From the emigrant Richard with the great voice, chief architect of the Cambridge Platform, to the provincial Cotton, the family combativeness and love of publicity put their marks on New England history. Of the three generations, certainly Increase Mather was the most generously endowed with capacity for leadership; an able man, practical and assertive, liking to be in the forefront of affairs, not wanting his light hidden under a bushel. An arch-conservative, he justified his ways to his conscience by the excellence of the heritage he strove to conserve. A formalist, he satisfied his intellectual curiosity by extolling the sufficiency of the creed of the fathers. He closed the windows of his mind against the winds of new doctrine, and bounded the fields of speculative inquiry by orthodox fences. He was of the succession of John Cotton rather than Thomas Hooker, a priestly theocrat, though never a shuffler like Cotton, less troubled by free inquiry, less by the intellectual. All his life he was inhibited from bold speculation by his personal loyalties and interests. As a beneficiary of things as they were, certain to lose in prestige and power with any relaxing of the theocracy, it would be asking too much of human nature to expect him to question the sufficiency of the established system of which he was the most distinguished representative. Not to have approved it would have been to repudiate his habitual way of thinking, his deepest prejudices, his strongest convictions. He had been molded and shaped by the theocracy; it was the very marrow of his bones; as well demand that pig iron turn molten again after it comes from the matrix. The ore of which he was fashioned was excellent, but once molded it was rigid; there would be no return to fluidity. And so determined by every impact of environment, by every appeal of loyalty, and by a very natural ambition, Increase Mather became a stout upholder of the traditional order, a staunch old Puritan Tory of the theocratic line. How could any promptings of liberalism find nourishment in such a mind? [2] Why should one expect to find in the works of such a man the seeds of new systems of thought or more generous institutions? He was the outstanding figure of the theocracy in the days of its overthrow, but intellectually he was not worthy to unloose the shoe-strings of Roger Williams.

In his professional capacity, Increase Mather was the priest rather than the theologian, a pastor of the flock, an expounder of the creed, rather than a seeker after new light. As a minister his mind was circumscribed by the thinking of John Calvin. He learned nothing from Luther, and was bitterly hostile to those phases of Independency that embodied the more generous Lutheran principles. No man was by temperament better fitted to embrace the coercive spirit of the Genevan discipline. Strong-willed and ascetic, he discovered in discipline the chief end for which the children of Adam are created. A profound admirer of the close-knit Genevan system, he was a Presbyterian in spirit, a man after Calvin's own heart, who clung to the old coercions in an age that was seeking to throw them off. If he counseled innovation it was in the way of strengthening ministerial authority, never in the way of liberalizing either creed or practice. It was the Congregationalism of the Cambridge Platform, and not that of early Plymouth, that he upheld; and to strengthen that order he turned earnestly to the practical work of Presbyterianizing. He was the prime mover in summoning the synod of 1679–80, requested by the Court to consider amongst other things what "may appear necessary for the preventing schisms, haeresies, prophaneness, & the establishment of the churches in one faith & order of the gospell," [3] and the chief suggestions of the body, of which he was the conspicuous leader, were a return to a stricter discipline, and a strengthening

[2] Compare Murdock, *Increase Mather*, pp. 394–395.
[3] Quoted in W. Walker, *A History of Congregational Churches, etc.*, p. 187.

of the passage in the Savoy Confession of faith—adopted by the synod—by borrowings from the Westminster Confession, which "more positively set forth the authority of the state in doctrinal questions." [4]

In 1691, while in London, Mather had been active in the work of uniting the Presbyterian and Congregational churches of England, under articles that would seem to have been more Presbyterian than Congregational; and in 1705, following the curiously spiteful controversy over the Brattle Street Church he joined vigorously in the proposed work of rejuvenating the New England system by engrafting further shoots from the Presbyterian stock. One of these grafts from the London agreement—the principle of licensing ministerial candidates by the association of ministers, thereby effectively preventing the intrusion of undesired members —established itself on the Congregational system; but another— the principle of associational control of the several churches—was blighted by the attack of John Wise.[5] What this desired consolidation of power in the hands of the ministers implied, is suggested by the terms of the Cambridge Platform, which asserted that "the work & duty of the people is expressed in the phrase of obeying their Elders," and that they may not "speak in church, before they have leave from the elders: nor continue so doing, when they require silence, nor may they oppose nor contradict the judgment or sentence of the Elders, without sufficient & weighty cause." [6] Recalling that the elders of a church had been reduced in number to the single minister, one may perhaps venture to suggest that a man ardently working to strengthen the hands of the ministerial oligarchy by further Presbyterianizing was no friend to Separatist-Congregationalism, nor one in whom the spirit of humility would work any lessening of the authority of the Lord's stewards.[7]

In his conception of toleration Mather followed naturally in the footsteps of John Cotton. He would tolerate all views that

[4] *Ibid.*, p. 190. His biographer has overlooked the significance of this. See Murdock, *Increase Mather*, p. 151.

[5] His biographer has somewhat slurred his account of the "Proposals." See p. 282. But his justification is worth noting: "If the original brand of Puritan piety was worth saving, and Mather believed it was, an oligarchic church government was the only means of securing it in an age when men were inclined to change their religious ideas as they changed their thought on other affairs."

[6] W. Walker, *A History of the Congregational Churches, etc.*, p. 205.

[7] Compare Murdock, *Increase Mather*, pp. 361-363.

were not in error, but his criteria of truth were so far from catholic as to lead him into constant and vehement attack upon other sects. As a responsible leader he was careful to clothe his attacks with generous professions; but he never stepped forward to uphold the right of free thought, or to dissuade his brethren from heresy-baiting. His biographer is greatly impressed by the minister's professions, and takes them at somewhat more than face value, forgetting the ancient saying that by the fruits of men's lives they shall be known. Casuistry is useful for purposes of defense, and a skillful apologist can explain away much; but the spirit of tolera-tion revealed in the following passages was certainly no child of liberalism:

The "Anabaptists" had given trouble in New England. They had installed as minister a man excommunicated from the Congregational church, and, when their meeting-house was closed to them, they per-sisted in assembling publicly before its barred doors rather than worship unmolested in a private house, To Mather these were attacks upon the true faith, and manifest disturbances of the civil peace. Naturally there is some acidity in his strictures on the "blasted Error" of "Antipedobap-tism." . . . He denounces Baptists roundly enough, points to their kinship with the turbulent Anabaptists in Europe, and writes: "Are they not generally of a bad Spirit? Bitter enemies to the Lords most eminent Servants? yea, to the faithfull Ambassadors, spitting the cruel venome of Asps against them."

He then concludes: "Nor is the modern reader likely to disagree" with the apology by President Oakes, who wrote in an introduction to Mather's screed:

It is sufficiently known to those that know the Author, that he is none of the Ishmaels of the times, that have their hand against every man and love to be taking a Dog by the Ears . . . or to be dabling in the waters of strife. . . . They that know his Doctrine and manner of life, cannot but know that the life of his Spirit is in the things of practical Divinity, and the great Design of his ministry is to promote the power and practice of piety in the greatest instances. . . . I dare undertake . . . his design . . . is not to traduce . . . those that are otherwise minded, or expose them to severities & sufferings on the bare account of their opinion.[8]

From these curious passages the unsympathetic realist is likely to draw the conclusions that the spirit of mutual admiration came to early birth in New England, and that it makes a vast difference

[8] Murdock, *Increase Mather*, pp. 138-139.

whose ox is gored. Something of the same casuistry is employed
to explain away Increase Mather's unhappy part in the witchcraft mess.[9] The whole matter is involved and rendered difficult
by guilty consciences and the need to save reputations, and perhaps the facts are not to be got at; yet it is only another instance
to show how quickly candor flies out at the window when a Mather
comes in at the door. One may make much or little of the son's
statement that Increase grew more tolerant in his later years; it
would seem at best to have been only the difference between black
and dark gray. A dominating man does not take kindly to differences of counsel. Increase Mather was a stout upholder of the
law and order in the shaping of which he had a hand, but he looked
with no friendly eye on the architects of a different order; and the
bitterness of his later years was the natural consequence of a
strong, proud, ambitious man, thwarted in his dearest projects.

If he contributed nothing to a more liberal theology or church
organization, it is idle to expect him to have contributed to political
speculation. As a leader of the theocracy he meddled much in
practical politics, but it would seem that he was quite unread in
the political philosophers and wholly ignorant of major principles.
The great English liberals of Commonwealth times and later left
him untouched. He bought and read many books, but almost
none of a political nature.[10] Hobbes, Harrington, Sidney, Milton,
Filmer, Locke, were as much out of his intellectual ken as were
the speculations of Roger Williams. Interest in political theory
had ceased in Massachusetts with the banishment of the great
Independent, and the principles of liberal thinkers like Harrington
and Milton would have awakened little sympathy in so stalwart a
theocrat as Increase Mather. He was a practical man, an administrator and mentor, a stern *castigator morum* to the commonwealth, and as a college president he had been trained in a school
little notable for its sympathetic consideration of the views of sub-
ordinates. He got on ill with his Harvard tutors, and one of the
unseemliest squabbles of his later years grew out of the bitterness
sowed between a "strong" administrator and his teaching staff.[11]
A man accounted less pious, concerned with ends more patently
worldly, might well be reckoned dictatorial and domineering; but

[9] See pp. 294–295, where he seeks unsuccessfully to refute the position taken by
J. T. Adams.
[10] See Murdock, *Increase Mather*, pp. 125–127.
[11] "The Brattle-Street Church Controversy," for which see *ibid.*, pp. 258 ff.

Puritan righteousness, perhaps, is not to be judged by profane standards, nor the same severity of judgment applied to politicians laboring in the theocratic vineyard, that is applied to the common breed.

Perhaps the happiest years of Increase Mather's arduous life were those spent in London as agent of the theocratic party to secure such terms as he could for the settlement of New England. It was a congenial task and a congenial field. His love of diplomacy and his fondness for England were both gratified. He mingled there on terms of equality with the intellectual leaders of English Nonconformity, and matched his wit with men high in station. He proved himself a skillful manager, but the threads were too tangled for any Puritan diplomat to smoothe out, and he fell short of his hopes. The terms of the charter as finally drafted satisfied few of the Boston theocrats, and his nomination of Sir William Phipps for Governor was certainly ill-judged. Sir William had been converted to the true faith by Increase himself and was reckoned by him a chosen vessel of the Lord; but he turned out to be no better than a cracked pot, and with the coming of Dudley the political influence of Increase Mather was finally broken. He was maneuvered out of his position as president of Harvard and later suffered the mortification of seeing the post fall into the hands of Leverett, the old tutor now become an influential politician, with whom he had been bitterly at outs. "Doubtless there is not any government in the world," he wrote, "that has been laid under greater obligations by a greater man than this government has been by me. Nevertheless I have received more discouragement in the work of the Lord, by those in government, than by all the men in the world besides. Let not my children put too much confidence in men." [12] It is not pleasant to be ousted from one's position by politicians, and if one is certain that the slight intended for the servant falls on the Master, it is scarcely to be borne. If waves of black pessimism swept over him in those unhappy later years when his ambitions were hopelessly frustrated, there was provocation enough. He had outlived his age and the ablest of the native-born theocrats had become a byword and a mocking amongst the profane of Boston.

Not a great man, as the world reckons greatness, Increase Mather may scarcely be accounted a great Puritan. As a theo-

[12] *Ibid.*, pp. 373–4, note.

logian he was wanting in speculative vigor, and as a pastor he was wanting in self-denying love. It is not necessary to set him over against Roger Williams or Jonathan Edwards or William Ellery Channing, to reveal his intellectual and spiritual shortcomings. One has only to place him beside so rugged and honest a Puritan as Samuel Hopkins, who in true Christian humility, utterly regardless of his own fame, gave his life to theology and the care of the poor and the outcast, to realize how conventional a soul was Increase Mather, how incurious intellectually, how ambitious and self-seeking. Men loved Samuel Hopkins even though they might vigorously reject his doctrine, as they loved Roger Williams and Ellery Channing; but few seem to have loved Increase Mather. One might respect his abilities, but he was too austerely forbidding to like, too overbearing to awaken the spirit of good will. Ideas in the abstract held no interest for him. His biographer has happily recalled Mather's forgotten interest in scientific inquiry, and for this slight relief from the intolerable drab of his life-story one may be grateful. Yet one must not build too high on an insubstantial foundation. In the England that Mather loved, and toward which he was strongly drawn—hoping that opportunity would offer for a pulpit there—pottering over natural philosophy had become a mark of distinction, and a man so envious of repute would have wished to approve himself to those whom he admired. Though he lived in Boston he would not have it thought that he was provincial.

Of the miscellaneous literary output that flowed from his pen in an abundant stream, little need be said. It is of concern only to minute historians of the local. That he was master of an excellent prose style, clear and straightforward, is sufficiently evident; if his matter had been so good, his legitimate fame would have been far greater. The work on which his reputation largely rests is *An Essay for the Recording of Illustrious Providences*, printed at Boston and London in 1684, and twice reissued in the nineteenth century under the title *Remarkable Providences*. It is an amusing book of old wives' tales, not singular at all for the times, but characteristic rather; an expression of the naïveté that crops out in Winthrop's *History of New England*, and other writings of the emigrant generation, but now become a fashion amongst the lesser lights of the Royal Academy and English Nonconformists. It suited to a nicety the Mather love of marvels, and Increase constituted himself a generous repository of all the chimney-corner tales of the countryside. To call such a book "a scientific and historical recording of phenomena observed in New England," as his biographer has done, is to gall the back of a thesis with hard riding.[13] In one chapter only does Mather suggest the spirit of scientific inquiry; four out of the twelve deal with witchcraft and kindred topics; and the rest are made up of such instances of divine providence as great fish jumping out of the sea into the boats of starving sailors adrift, of the freaks played by lightning and tornadoes, and of God's punishments on wicked Quakers. At the time it was a harmless enough book, but in the light of after developments it was scarcely so harmless. The emphasis laid upon witchcraft was an unfortunate, if unconsidered, influence in preparing the psychology of New England for the Salem outbreak, and the minister later reaped a bitter harvest from it.

"Not many years ago," he wrote in the preface to *Illustrious Providences*, "I *lost* (and that's an afflictive *loss* indeed!) several moneths from study by sickness. Let every God-fearing reader joyn with me in prayer, that I may be enabled to redeem the time, and (in all ways wherein I am capable) to serve my generation." That Increase Mather sincerely desired to serve his generation according to his lights, none may deny. His labors were appalling, his reputation was great, and when he died the light of the old churches went out. The spirit of Presbyterianism went to its grave in New England, and not till a hundred years later did the new light—which was no other than primitive English Independency—shine out in the life and work of William Ellery Channing. After two centuries Unitarianism recovered for the Massachusetts churches the spirit of early Separatism that had been lost since the days of the Cambridge Platform. Channing finally uprooted the vine that Increase Mather had so laboriously tended.

III

Of the unpopularity that gathered about the name of Mather after the fall of the theocracy, the larger portion fell to the lot of the son, the eccentricities of whose character made him peculiarly vulnerable to attack. In his youth the spoiled child of Boston, in middle life he was petulant and irritable, inclined to sulk when

[13] *Ibid.*, p. 170.

his will was crossed. In the career of no other New England
Puritan is the inquisitorial pettiness of the Genevan system of
theology and discipline revealed so disagreeably. The heroic qualities of an earlier age had atrophied in an atmosphere of formalism, and Boston Calvinism of the year 1690 had become a grotesque
caricature of a system that in its vigor had defied the power of
Rome and laid kingdoms at its feet. Embodied in Cotton Mather
it was garrulous, meddlesome, scolding, an echo of dead voices,
a shadow of forgotten realities. The common provincialism had
laid its blight upon it. The horizons of the New England imagination grew narrow, and Puritan anthropomorphism unconsciously
reduced the God of the Hebrew prophets to the compass of a
village priest, clothed in stock and gown, and endowed with the
intellect of a parish beadle. In the egocentric universe wherein
Cotton Mather lived and labored the cosmos had shrunk to the
narrow bounds of a Puritan commonwealth, whereof Boston was
the capital and the prosperity of the North Church the special
and particular object of divine concern. The mind of Increase
Mather had been enlarged by contact with English life; the mind
of the son was dwarfed by a village world.

Cotton Mather is an attractive subject for the psychoanalyst.
Intensely emotional, high-strung and nervous, he was oversexed
and overwrought, subject to ecstatic exaltations and, especially
during his celibate years, given to seeing visions. In the carefully
edited *Diary* which he left for the edification of his natural and
spiritual children, at the beginning of his twenty-third year, is an
apologetic entry—"*Cum Relego, Scripsisse Pudet!*"—that Professor Wendell has put into English thus:

A strange and memorable thing. After outpourings of prayer, with
the utmost fervor and fasting, there appeared an Angel, whose face shone
like the noonday sun. His features were as those of a man, and beardless;
his head was encircled by a splendid tiara; on his shoulders were wings;
his garments were white and shining; his robe reached to his ankles; and
about his loins was a belt not unlike the girdles of the peoples of the East.
And this Angel said that he was sent by the Lord Jesus to bear a clear
answer to the prayers of a certain youth, and to bear back his words in
reply. Many things this Angel said which it is not fit should be set down
here. But among other things not to be forgotten he declared that the
fate of this youth should be to find full expression for what in him was
best; . . . And in particular this Angel spoke of the influence his branches
should have, and of the books this youth should write and publish, not
only in America but in Europe. And he added certain special prophecies

of the great works this youth should do for the Church of Christ in the revolutions that are now at hand. Lord Jesus! What is the meaning of this marvel? From the wiles of the Devil, I beseech thee, deliver and defend Thy most unworthy servant.[14]

The passage throws a good deal of light on the psychology of Cotton Mather. Such visions were clearly the result of abnormal stimuli, acting on a neurotic temperament. From both sides of his family he inherited a tense nervous system that was aggravated by precocity and an unnatural regimen. The inevitable result was a hothouse plant of Puritan forcing. His religious exaltation flowered from the root of egoism. His vanity was cosmic. He esteemed himself a beacon set on a hill, a divine torch which the very hand of God had lighted. The success or failure of God's plan for New England, he believed, rested on his shoulders; and with such heavy responsibilities devolved upon him he was driven, hot-haste, by the prick of urgency. The king's business requireth haste. The work of the Lord cannot wait upon sluggards. "O then *To work* as fast as you can," he wrote in *The Magnalia*, "and of soul-work and church-work as much as ever you can. Say to all *Hindrances. . .* 'You'll excuse me if I ask you to be short with me, for my work is great and my time is but little.'" And so with an amazing activity that was little short of neurosis, he gave himself over to the great business of managing the affairs of New England in accordance with God's will.

In undertaking so difficult a job, he frequently came into conflict with other interpreters of God's plan for New England, and partisan venom gathered about him wherever he passed. Tact was never a Mather virtue, and Cotton made two enemies to his father's one. His quarrels trod on each other's heels, and a downright vindictiveness breathes through his private records of them. He railed at whoever disagreed with him, and imputed silly or malignant motives. The pages of his diary are filled with epithets that he flung privately at his enemies; one marvels that so many in the little town of Boston could be singled out as "strangely and fiercely possessed of the Devil." Robert Calef, whose *More Wonders of the Invisible World* was an inconvenient reply to his *Wonders of the Invisible World*, was set down as "a very wicked sort of a Sadducee in this Town, raking together a crue of Libels . . . an abominable Bundle of Lies, written on purpose, with a

---

[14] *Cotton Mather, Puritan Priest*, p. 64.

Quil under a special Energy and Management of Satan, to damnify my precious Opportunities of Glorifying my Lord Jesus Christ." [15] When an anti-Mather group of Cambridge men set up the Brattle Street Church, and invited Benjamin Colman, who had received Presbyterian ordination in England, by way of reply to the Mather group, to become their pastor, Cotton wrote in his diary:

A Company of Head-strong Men in the Town, the cheef of whom, are full of malignity to the Holy Waye of our Churches, have built in this Town, another Meeting-house.   To delude many better-meaning Men in their own Company, and the Churches in the Neighbourhood, they past a Vote . . . that they would not vary from the Practice of these Churches, except in one little Particular. . . . But a young Man, born and bred here, and hence gone for England, is now returned hither, at their Invitation, equip'd with an *Ordination*, to qualify him, for all that is intended.

On his "returning and arriving here, these fallacious People" gave themselves over, in short, to "Their violent and impetuous Lusts, to carry on the Apostasy," and Cotton Mather prayed God to make him an instrument to defeat the "Designs that Satan may have in the Enterprise." [16] Similar passages of extravagant abuse of men so wicked as to disagree with him flowed from his pen in copious abundance.   Although he constantly prayed that his daily life might be "a trembling walk with God," he was clearly a difficult fellow to get on with; and in the opinion of many he was justly described by a contemporary, as a "malecontent priest," consumed with an "Hereditary rancour" that made him "everlastingly opposite" to every will but his own.

The diary of Cotton Mather is a treasure-trove to the abnormal psychologist.   The thing would be inconceivable if the record were not in print.   What a crooked and diseased mind lay back of those eyes that were forever spying out occasions to magnify self!   He grovels in proud self-abasement.   He distorts the most obvious reality.   His mind is clogged with the strangest miscellany of truth and marvel.   He labors to acquire the possessions of a scholar, but he listens to old wives' tales with greedy avidity.   In all his mental processes the solidest fact falls into fantastic perspective.   He was earnest to do good, he labored to put into effect hundreds of "Good devices," but he walked always in his own shadow.   His egoism blots out charity and even the divine mercy.

[15] *Diary*, Vol. I, p. 271.   [16] *Ibid.*, pp. 325–326.

Consider his account of an "execution sermon" preached to a name-
less girl condemned for killing her natural child, and the light it
throws on both minister and congregation:

The Execution of the miserable Malefactor, was ordered for to have
been the last Week, upon the Lecture of another. I wondred then what
would become of my *Particular* Faith, of her condition being so ordered in
the Providence of God, that it should furnish me, with a *special Opportunity* to glorify Him. While I was entirely resigning to the wisdome of
Heaven all such Matters, the Judges, wholly without my seeking, altered
and allow'd her Execution to fall on the Day of *my Lecture.* The *General
Court* then sitting, ordered the Lecture to bee held in a larger and a
stronger House, than that *old* one, where 'tis usually kept. For my own
part, I was weak, and faint, and spent; but I humbly gave myself up to
the *Spirit* of my Heavenly Lord and Hee assured mee, that Hee would
send His good Angel to strengthen mee. The greatest Assembly, ever in
this Countrey preach'd unto, was now come together; It may bee four or
five thousand Souls. I could not gett unto the *Pulpit,* but by climbing
over *Pues* and *Heads:* and there the Spirit of my dearest Lord came upon
mee. I preached with a more than ordinary Assistance, and enlarged, and
uttered the most awakening Things, for near two hours together. My
Strength and Voice failed not; but when it was near failing, a silent Look
to Heaven strangely renew'd it. In the whole I found Prayer answered
and Hope exceeded, and Faith encouraged, and the Lord using *mee,* the
vilest in all that great Assembly, to glorify Him. Oh! what shall I render
to the Lord! [17]

Straightway thereafter, he rendered the Lord another characteristic service. No sooner was the girl hanged—for whose safe-
keeping no good angel seems to have been available after the
minister had bespoken his—than he hastened to the printer to
arrange for printing the sermon, and "annexed thereunto, an
History of Criminals executed in this Land, and effectually, an
Account of their dying Speeches, and of my own Discourses with
them in their last Hours. . . . I entitled the Book, PILLARS OF
SALT." Clearly this was the time to peddle his wares, when all
Boston was talking of the great event; and with a nose for publicity
as keen as Defoe's, he flung together a jumble of material, and
trusted to its timeliness to sell. Some such origin, no doubt,
accounts for a good many of the small library of titles that bore
his name, an output that seems to have justified the angelic
prophecy of "the books this youth should write and publish."
With a very lust for printer's ink, he padded his bibliography like

[17] *Diary,* Vol. I, p. 279.

a college professor seeking promotion; but in spite of all the prayers poured out in behalf of them, they would seem for the most part to have been little more than tuppenny tracts, stuffed with a sodden morality, that not even an angel could make literature of.

Holding so strong a conviction of apostleship, Cotton Mather would certainly play the politician, and quite as certainly blunder and go wrong. Far more than his father he was a bookman, who believed that all knowledge was shut up between pigskin covers. He was as lacking in worldly wisdom as a child, and in his ecstatic contemplation of the marvels wrought by God in primitive New England he never discovered that that older world had passed away. Another age was rising, with other ideals than ecclesiastical, which the three thousand books in his library told him nothing about. He was an anachronism in his own day. Living in an earlier age, when the hierarchy was in its prime, he would have been carried far on the tide of theocratic prestige; a generation later, when lay-power had definitely superseded clerical, he would have taken his place as a stout defender of Tory ways. But at the moment when a critical realignment of parties was under way in Massachusetts; when the villagers were becoming democratized and the gentry toryized; when even the clergy were dividing—Cotton Mather was a general without an army. He was a primitive Puritan in a Boston that was fast becoming Yankee, and his love for the theocracy grew stronger with every defeat.

The judgment of after times finds little in his political activities to approve and much to condemn. After all allowances are made the fact remains that he was a leader of reaction; and no protestations can obscure the motive of personal ambition. His own prestige was involved with that of the theocracy. It was due to the traditional authority of the ministry that he enjoyed the distinction of being a "Person, whom the Eye and the Talk of the People is very much upon," and any lessening of that authority would hurt him cruelly in his vanity. This remains the sufficient explanation of his varied political activities in the course of which he trimmed his sails to different winds. He first essayed a frontal attack on the secular power, but suffering a personal slight, he shifted and struck in the dark at an exposed flank; and finally, receiving only further mortification, he made overtures of peace and found his way back to the tables of the great. It was against the administration of the wily and unscrupulous Dudley that he waged his bitterest warfare. Failing to make headway by open hostility, he seized upon a current trade scandal, poured out his grievances in an anonymous pamphlet sent to London to be published, and awaited the result. It was a slashing attack, done in the tone of a lover of the ancient rights and privileges of New England, and it must have cut Dudley to the quick. A quotation or two will suffice to reveal the nature of the charges:

But, when the President [Dudley] was pleased, out of an Active and Passive Principle, to tell our Countreymen, in open Council, *That the People in* New-England *were all Slaves; and that the* only *Difference between Them and Slaves, was their not being* Bought *and Sold: And that they must not think the Privileges* of Englishmen *would follow them to the end of the World.* I say, when the People heard this, they lookt upon themselves in a manner Lost. . . .
All the People here are Bought and Sold, betwixt the Governour and his son Paul. . . .
This is the *Third Time* that he has been Trusted with Power from the *Crown* in *America*, and he has constantly Abus'd it, to the Dishonour of the Government, and almost Ruin of the People he was sent to Govern.[18]

There was enough truth in the charges to make them serious, but the spleen was quite too evident. The author was at once discovered and Cotton Mather suffered a vigorous counter-attack that damaged a reputation already undermined. Perhaps even worse was the social slight put upon him by those in government. What it cost him to be left out of the invitations of the great he reveals in the *Diary:*

2 d. 7m. [September] Friday. [1709] The other Ministers of the Neighbourhood, are this Day feasting with our wicked Governour; I have, by my provoking Plainness and Freedom, in telling this *Ahab* of his wickedness, procured myself to be left out of his Invitations. I rejoiced in my Liberty from the Temptations, with which they were encumbred, while they were *eating of his Dainties* and durst not reprove him. And, considering the Power and Malice of my Enemies, I thought it proper of me, to be this day Fasting, in Secret, before the Lord.

Ten years later there is a different story to tell. The minister has left the opposition bench and gone over to the government. A note in Sewall's diary tells the tale:

18 *A Memorial of the Present Deplorable State of New-England . . . by the Male-Administration of their Present Governour, Joseph Dudley, Esq., and his Son Paul,* London, 1707, in *Massachusetts Historical Society Collections*, Fifth Series, Vol. VI.

March, 12. [1718/19] Dr. Cotton Mather prays again [in Council]. Preaches the Lecture from Prov. 29: 18. no Vision. [*Where there is no vision, the people perish: but he that keepeth the law, happy is he.*] The Govr., Lt. Govr., Mr. Dudley, Mr. Belcher press'd hard that there might be an order of the Govr. and Council to print it. Col. Tailor, Clark, Davenport, Sewall and others opposed it. For my part, the Dr. spake so much of his visions of Convulsion and Mutiny, mentioning our being a dependent Government, and the Danger of Parliamentary Resentments: that I was afraid the printing of it might be an Invitation to the Parliament to take away our Charter. Govr. would have it put to the vote: but when he saw how hardly it went, caused the Secretary to break off in the midst.[19]

Here is a party alignment that tells its own story, and it needs no very lively imagination to fill out the meager note and reënact the little drama. The minister, eager to make overtures of peace, falls into the Tory note, talks about mob-rule and the sinfulness of popular unrest, calls upon authority to maintain law and order, and hints at the expediency of preserving due colonial subservience in view of possible resentments on the part of certain great men in England. Sewall, as a "true New-England man," squirms somewhat under the implications, but the little group of Tories are loud in praise. Such a sermon, from so eminent a servant of God, would aid wonderfully in strengthening the spirit of loyalty to the crown, and it must be printed and circulated amongst the people. But the opposition proved too spirited, and the manuscript was not dispatched to the printer, no doubt to Cotton Mather's chagrin.

It was easy for so reactionary a nature to slide over into the Tory. There was not a grain of liberalism in his make-up. His antipathy to all popular movements was deep-rooted, for he knew no other political philosophy than that of the obsolete theocracy in which he had grown up. He was a bourgeois soul who loved respectability and was jealous of his social position; no fraternizing with the poor and outcast for him, no profitless excursions into the realms of Utopian justice. Though he might play to popular prejudices to serve his political ends, he had scant regard for popular rights. The highest privilege of the New England people, he believed, was the privilege of being ruled by the godly. His real attitude towards the plain people is revealed in a note by his son, that refers to the days following the overturn of the Andros government:

[19] Vol. II, p. 214.

Upon Discoursing with him of the Affairs he has told me that he always pressed *Peace* and *Love* and *Submission* unto a legal Government, tho' he suffered from some tumultuous People, by doing so; and upon the whole, has asserted unto me his *Innocency* and Freedom from all known Iniquity in that time, but declared his Resolution, from the View he had of the fickle Humors of the Populace, that he would chuse to be concern'd with them as little as possible for the future.[20]

As he grew older and the shadow of failure fell across his life, his bitterness towards a people that had rejected his admonitions is revealed on many a page of his diary. It was a "silly people," a "foolish people," "insignificant lice"—"The cursed clamour of a people strangely and fiercely possessed of the Devil"—"My aged father laies to heart the withdrawal of a vain, proud, foolish people from him in his age"—"It is the Hour of . . . Darkness on this Despicable Town." He could not easily forgive those who had wounded his love of power and lust of adulation, and he was too aloof from the daily life of men to understand the political and social movements of the times, too self-centered to understand his fellow villagers. He possessed none of the sympathetic friend-liness that made Samuel Sewall a natural confidant to every one in trouble. He loved the people when they honored and obeyed him, but when they hearkened to other counsels he would fall to scolding like a fishwife. Doubtless he was sincere in thinking he would gladly die to save his people from their sins, but he had no mind to neighbor with them or humor their wicked love of power. He immured himself so closely within the walls of the old theo-cratic temple that he never took the trouble to examine the groundsills, and when the rotten timbers gave way and the struc-ture came tumbling about his ears, he was caught unprepared and went down in its ruins.

Happily most of the printed output of Cotton Mather has fallen into the oblivion it deserved. It is barren of ideas, and marred by pedantic mannerisms that submerge the frequent felicities of phrase—old-fashioned on the day it came from the press. "In his *Style*, indeed," wrote his friend Thomas Prince, "he was something singular, and not so agreeable to the Gust of the Age. But like his *manner of speaking*, it was very *emphatical*." Yet he possessed very considerable gifts and under happier cir-cumstances he might have had a notable literary career; but he

[20] Wendell, *Cotton Mather, etc.*, p. 82.

was the victim of a provincial environment. He was the most widely read man of his generation in America, and one of the few who followed sympathetically the current scientific movement in England. Like old Increase he dabbled in science; he was proud of his membership in the Royal Society, to which he forwarded his characteristic *Curiosa Americana*—a hodgepodge of those marvels in which his generation delighted. It was from an English source that he got the idea of inoculation for smallpox, which he urged upon Boston so insistently that a war of scurrilous pamphlets broke out. He made use of the method in his own family, incurring thereby much stupid abuse and at least one attack of violence. It was an intelligent and courageous experiment, that is not to be forgotten in casting up the accounts of Cotton Mather.

Of his major works two only call for brief consideration: the celebrated *Magnalia Christi Americana; or, The Ecclesiastical History of New England;* and the less known *Wonders of the Invisible World.* The latter is suggestive for the light it throws on the psychology of the witchcraft mania. The fantastic devil-fear, which bit so deeply into the imagination of Puritan New England, has already been commented on. In that common seventeenth-century delusion, Cotton Mather not only ran with the mob, but he came near to outdistancing the most credulous. His speech and writings dripped with devil-talk. The grotesqueries that marked the current marvel-tales crop out nakedly in his writings. "I have set myself," he wrote in the *Diary*, "to countermine the whole *Plot* of the Devil, against New-England, in every branch of it, as far as one of my *darkness* can comprehend such a *Work* of Darkness." His conviction of the malignant activities of Satan was so vivid, that in delivering a carefully prepared sermon on the *Wiles of the Divil*, he was fain, he tells us, to pause and lift up his eyes and cry "unto the Lord Jesus Christ, that he would rate off Satan," who "all the Time of my Prayer before the Lecture" had "horribly buffeted me"—by inflicting on the fasting priest certain qualms of the stomach. How tremendous he conceived to be the battle over a human soul, he describes thus:

The *Wilderness* through which we are passing to the Promised Land is all over fill'd with Fiery flying serpents. But, blessed be God, none of them have hitherto so fastned upon us as to confound us utterly! All our way to Heaven lies by *Dens of Lions* and the *Mounts of Leopards;* there are incredible Droves of Devils in our way. . . . We are poor travellers in a world which is as well the Devil's Field, as the Devil's *Gaol;* a world in which every Nook whereof, the Devil is encamped with *Bands of Robbers* to pester all that have their Faces looking Zionward.[21]

In the light of Mather's logic, "That there is a *Devil*, is a thing Doubted by none but such as are under the influence of the Devil," and "God indeed has the *Devil* in a *Chain*, but has horribly lengthened out the Chain," his private comment on the work— "that reviled book"—becomes comprehensible.

The *Magnalia* is a far more important work, the repository of a vast miscellany of information concerning early New England that his pious zeal saved from oblivion. It is the *magnum opus* of the Massachusetts theocracy, the best and sincerest work that Cotton Mather did. The theme with which it deals, and about which he accumulates marvels and special providences together with historical facts, was the thing which next to his own fame lay nearest his heart—the glory of that theocracy which men whom he accounted foolish and wicked were seeking to destroy. The purpose of the book has nowhere been better stated than by Professor Wendell:

> Its true motive was to excite so enthusiastic a sympathy with the ideals of the Puritan fathers that, whatever fate might befall the civil government, their ancestral seminary of learning should remain true to its colours. . . . The time was come, Cotton Mather thought, when the history of these three generations might be critically examined; if this examination should result in showing that there had lived in New England an unprecedented proportion of men and women and children whose earthly existence had given signs that they were among the elect, then his book might go far to prove that the pristine policy of New England had been especially favoured of the Lord. For surely the Lord would choose His elect most eagerly in places where life was conducted most according to His will.[22]

When old Increase was near the end of his many years, a friend wrote to ask if he were still in the land of the living. "No, Tell him I am going to it," he said to his son; "this Poor World is the land of the Dying." The bitter words were sober truth. The New England of the dreams of Increase and Cotton Mather was sick to death from morbid introspection and ascetic inhibitions; no lancet or purge known to the Puritan pharmacopeia could save it.

[21] *Wonders of the Invisible World*, p. 63.
[22] *Literary History of America*, pp. 48–49.

Though father and son walked the streets of Boston at noonday, they were only twilight figures, communing with ghosts, building with shadows. They were not unlike a certain mad woman that Sewall tells of, who went crying about the town, "My child is dead within me." The child of Cotton Mather's hopes had long been dead within him, only he could not bring himself to acknowledge it. The fruit of the vine planted by the fathers was still sweet to him, and when other men complained of its bitterness, and fell to gathering from other vines, he could only rail at their perversity. He would not believe that the grapes were indeed bitter and the vine blighted; that the old vineyard must be re-plowed and planted to fresh stock. All his life he had set marvels above realities and in the end his wonder-working providence failed him. Prayers could not bring back a dead past; passionate conjurations could not strike the living waters from the cold granite of Puritan formalism. A New England flagellant, a Puritan Brother of the Cross, he sought comfort in fasts and vigils and spiritual castigations, and—it is pleasant to learn—in ways far more natural and wholesome. Incredible as it may seem, the following record is authentic, and it falls like a shaft of warm sunshine across the path of the morbid priest: "Augt, 15. [1716]. . . . Now about Dr. C. Mather Fishing in Spy-pond, falls into the Water, the boat being ticklish, but receives no hurt."[23] The restless minister who had fished overmuch in troubled waters, sometimes, it would appear, ventured for perch in Spy Pond.

[23] Sewall, *Diary*, Vol. III, p. 98.

CHAPTER III

STIRRINGS OF LIBERALISM

I

JOHN WISE

Village Democrat

In the days when Sir Edmund Andros was seeking to fasten upon Massachusetts Bay the principles and practice of Stuart prerogative, an event occurred that greatly stirred New England. Taxes having been arbitrarily assessed in Council, the several towns were bidden appoint commissioners to collect them. When the order reached Ipswich, John Wise, minister of the second church, gathered the chief members of his flock together, and it was agreed by them to choose no such commissioner at the town meeting—"We have a good God, and a good king, and shall do well to stand for our privileges," the minister is reported to have argued. Soon thereafter John Wise was summoned before a star-chamber court on the charge of sedition. Upon his plea of colonial privilege, the president of the court, Dudley, is said to have retorted, "You shall have no more privileges left you than not to be sold for slaves." "Do you believe," demanded Andros, "Joe and Tom may tell the King what money he may have?" "Do not think," put in another judge, "the laws of England follow you to the ends of the earth." Thereupon with five others, John Wise was thrown into Boston jail, where he lay one and twenty days, and whence he was released only after payment of fifty pounds, giving bond in a thousand pounds for good behavior, and suffering suspension from the ministry. "The evidence in the case," he remarked afterward, "as to the substance of it, was that we too boldly endeavored to persuade ourselves we were Englishmen, and under privileges.[1] The year following, Andros having been driven out, John Wise brought suit against Dudley for having denied him a writ of *habeas corpus*.[2]

[1] A similar plea had failed Dr. Church when he offended the oligarchy twenty years before, who quite as arbitrarily had fined him six hundred pounds.

[2] See the account in Palfrey, *History of Massachusetts*, Vol. II, Book XII, p. 327;

Two years later Wise served as chaplain in the ill-managed Quebec expedition under Sir William Phipps. He bore himself well both in council and on the field; went ashore with the storming party; and if he had succeeded in his efforts to instil some of his own force into the leaders, the grand exploit might not have dwindled to such an unhappy ending. In a long account which he sent to Increase Mather, then in London, he did not mince matters, or attempt to throw on the Lord's shoulders blame that belonged elsewhere, but charged the fiasco to the cowardice of Major Walley, in command of the assaulting troops.[3] Clearly the Ipswich minister was a fighting as well as a praying parson, whom Cromwell would have delighted in.

Posterity has been too negligent of John Wise hitherto. Although possessed of the keenest mind and most trenchant pen of his generation of New Englanders, he was uninfected by the itch of publicity that attacked so many of his fellow ministers, and so failed to challenge the attention of later times. Called to serve in an outlying portion of the Master's vineyard he discovered little opportunity there and less inclination to magnify his own importance. He was too honest to persuade himself that God's fame was bound up with his own, and he was never forward to push his claims to priority in righteousness. Nevertheless what little we know of him is to his credit. An independent man, powerful of body, vigorous of intellect, direct and outspoken in debate, he seems to have understood the plain people whom he served, and he sympathized heartily with the democratic ideals then taking form in the New England villages. Such liberalism as emerged from the simplicity of village life found intelligent response in his sympathies, and he dedicated his keen mind and wide reading to the business of providing it with a philosophical justification. Some explanation of his democratic leanings may be discovered in his antecedents. His father was a self-made man who had come over to Roxbury as an indented servant—most menial of stations in that aristocratic old Boston world. He must have been of sound

and in Wise, *Vindication of the Government of the New England Churches, Introduction.* The current Tory interpretation of the common law of sedition was severe. "In 1679, at the trial of Henry Carr [Care], indicted for some passages in a weekly paper, the Lord Chief Justice Scroggs declared it criminal at Common Law to 'write on the subject of government, whether in terms of praise or censure, it is not material; for no man has a right to say anything of government'" (*State Trials,* VII, 929; quoted in Schuyler, *The Liberty of the Press in the American Colonies, etc.*)

[3] See *Massachusetts Historical Society Proceedings,* Second Series, Vol. XV, pp. 283–296.

and rugged stock, for in addition to a magnificent physique he endowed his son with manly independence and democratic self-respect, which stood the latter in good stead when, after having made his way through Harvard College, he came to speak for the people against the tax program of Andros, the reactionary ambitions of the Presbyterians, and the schemes of the hard-money men. In John Wise, Cotton Mather was to encounter an antagonist who was more than a match for him.

With the final overthrow of the theocracy and the lessening of the political power of the clergy, a critical period in the development of the church was reached, and with it a renewal of the old conflict between the Presbyterian and Congregational principles. In the year 1705, under the leadership of the Mathers, the Presbyterian party, which numbered among its adherents most of the ministers of the larger churches, put forth a series of "Proposals," looking to a closer union of the churches, and greater control of the separate congregations by the ministerial association. This was a challenge to the Congregationalists which John Wise could not overlook. The question touched the fundamentals of church organization, and when by way of preparation he turned to examine critically the work of the fathers, he found in it quite another meaning than Cotton Mather found. It was as a liberal that he went back to the past, seeking to recover the original Congregational principle, which, since the conservative triumph in the Cambridge Platform of 1648, had been obscured. When he was quite ready, he published in 1710, his *Churches Quarrel Espoused*, reissued five years later; and in 1717, his *Vindication of the Government of the New England Churches*, reissued together with the earlier work in 1772, and again in 1860. The two works were a democratic counterblast to the Presbyterian propaganda, and they stirred the mind of New England profoundly. What Edwards did later for the doctrinal side of Congregationalism, John Wise did for the institutional. His exposition of the Congregational principle was so luminous and convincing that it soon came to be regarded as authoritative, and more than a hundred years after the *Vindication* appeared the Chief Justice of Massachusetts cited it in support of a judicial decision.

The significance of John Wise in the history of democratic America lies in the fact that he followed "an unbeaten path," justifying the principle of Congregationalism by analogy from civil polity. Seemingly alone amongst the New England clergy of his day, he had grounded himself in political theory; and the doctrine upon which he erected his argument was the theory of natural rights, derived from a study of Pufendorf's *De Jure Naturae et Gentium*, published in 1672. Locke and the other writers of the English natural-rights school he seems not to have been acquainted with; but Pufendorf he had read closely, and he discharged the new theory against his opponents with telling effect. This was the first effective reply in America to the old theocratic sneer that if the democratic form of government were indeed divinely sanctioned, was it not strange that God had overlooked it in providing a government for his chosen people? Wise was the first New England minister to break with the literal Hebraism of the old school; like Roger Williams he was willing to make use of profane philosophies, basing his argument upon an appeal to history, a method which baffled the narrow Hebraists, putting them in a quandary.

After examining the three regular forms of civil government, and showing how each is related to "the many ennobling immunities" of the subject, Wise turned to the real business in hand, which was to inquire "whether any of the aforesaid species of regular, unmixed governments, can with any good show of reason be predicable of the church of Christ on earth"; whether the monarchical form as exhibited in papacy and episcopacy, the aristocratic form as exhibited in Presbyterianism, or the democratic form as exhibited in Congregationalism, is nearest the divine model as revealed in Scripture and the law of nature?

The gross inadequacy of the monarchical principle appears to him so certain that he concludes his argument with the comment "that God and wise nature were never propitious to the birth of this monster." The inadequacy of the aristocratic principle seems to him equally clear. The principle of stewardship, ideal though it may appear in theory, did not seem to work in practice, and he put his finger shrewdly upon the weakness of oligarchical rule in Massachusetts. Government by a "select company of choice persons" might be justified, if—

we could be assured they would make the Scripture, and not their private will the rule of their personal and ministerial actions; . . . but considering how great an interest is embarked, and how frail a bottom we trust, though we should rely upon the best of men, especially if we remember what is in the hearts of good men (namely, much ignorance, abundance of small ends, many times cloaked with a high pretense in religion; pride skulking and often breeding revenge upon a small affront, and blown up by a pretended zeal, yet really and truly by nothing more divine than interest or ill nature), and also considering how very uncertain we are of the real goodness of those we esteem good men . . . and . . . how Christianity, by the aforesaid principle, had been peeled, robbed and spoiled already, it cannot consist with the light of nature to venture again upon such perils, especially if we can find a safer way home. . . . In a word an aristocracy is a dangerous constitution in the church of Christ.[4]

This "safer way home," as he then proceeded to point out, lay in following the broad path of democracy:

But to abbreviate, it seems most agreeable with the light of nature, that if there be any of the regular forms of government settled in the church of God, it must needs be . . . a democracy. This is the form of government which the light of nature does highly value, and often directs to as most agreeable to the just and natural prerogatives of human beings. . . . It is certainly a great truth, namely, that man's original liberty after it is resigned . . . ought to be cherished in all wise governments; or otherwise a man in making himself a subject, he alters himself from a freeman into a slave, which to do is repugnant to the law of nature. Also the natural equality of men amongst men must be duly favoured; in that government was never established by God or nature, to give one man a prerogative to insult over another. . . . Honor all men. The end of all good government is to cultivate humanity, and promote the happiness of all, and the good of every man in his rights, his life, liberty, estate, honor, etc., without injury or abuse to any.[5]

From which he concludes that—

. . . a democracy in church or state, is a very honorable and regular government according to the dictates of right reason, And, therefore . . . That these churches of New England, in their ancient constitution of church order, it being a democracy, are manifestly justified and defended by the law and light of nature.[6]

A vigorous thinker was John Wise, with a shrewd knowledge of men and their selfishness. He would rule himself, well or ill, and would have others do likewise. Stewards in church and state, he would have none of. "Brethren," he exclaimed, "ye have been called unto liberty, therefore Hold your hold brethren! . . . pull up well upon the oars, you have a rich cargo, and I hope we shall escape shipwreck . . . daylight and good piloting will secure all."[7] "There is strong and sharp reasoning" in his pages, more

[4] *Vindication*, edition of 1860, pp. 50–53.   [5] *Ibid.*, pp. 54–55.
[6] *Ibid.*, p. 60.
[7] *The Churches Quarrel Espoused*, p. 116.

solid meat in his two volumes than in all Cotton Mather's muddled
effusions. Like a good Englishman and a good Yankee he hated
arbitrary power as he hated the devil. "The very name of an
arbitrary government is ready to put an Englishman's blood into
a fermentation; but when it comes and shakes its whip over their
ears, and tells them it is their master, it makes them stark mad." [8]

Naturally so vigorous an advocate of democracy in the church
was disliked by the gentlemen whose ambitions he thwarted.
Such plebeian views were incomprehensible to Cotton Mather.
When *The Churches Quarrel Espoused* was reprinted in 1713,
prefaced with a commendatory letter signed by two well-known
clergymen, the latter wrote to a friend:

. . . A furious Man, called John Wise,[9] of whom, I could wish he had,
Cor bonum, while we are all sensible, he wants, *Caput bene regulatum*, has
lately published a foolish Libel, against some of us, for presbyterianizing
too much in our Care to repair some Deficiencies in our Churches. And
some of our People, who are not only tenacious of their Liberties, but also
more suspicious than they have cause to be of a Design in their pastors to
make abridgments of them; they are too much led into Temptation, by
such Invectives. But the Impression is not so great as our grand Adver-
sary doubtless hoped for.[10]

Two years later, when the *Vindication* was published, the sulky
theocrat noted in his diary:

25 [May. 1717] G[ood] D[evice]. Should not I take into Consideration
what may be done for the Service of the Ministry and Religion and the
Churches, throughout the Land, that the Poison of Wise's cursed Libel
may have an Antidote? [11]

Cotton Mather was unable to discover an antidote, and the
poison of Wise's democratic philosophy was to prove of surprising
vitality. As late as 1772, when his two works were reprinted on
subscription, no fewer than 1133 copies were taken. That the
argument of Wise was not without influence in the struggle then
developing seems reasonable; but that it greatly influenced the
thinking of the revolutionary leaders, as Professor Tyler supposes,
is scarcely probable. The argument from natural rights was well
known in 1772, and it was to Locke and not to Wise that men like
Samuel Adams turned for help. Nevertheless, in denying to him

[8] *Ibid.*, p. 209.
[9] A gratuitous insult, as Wise was well known.
[10] "Letter to Robert Wodrow, September 17, 1715:" *Diary*, in *Massachusetts
Historical Collections*, Seventh Series, Vol. VIII, p. 327.
[11] *Ibid.*, p. 450.

wide influence in the later period we are neither detracting from
the honor that is rightly his as the first colonial to justify village
democracy by an appeal to political philosophy, nor lessening the
repute in which he should be held by Americans as the early defender of local self-rule.

The instinctive sympathy of John Wise with the plain people
among whom he lived led him to stand with them in another matter
that touched the interests of the farming class. The currency question had thrust its provocative demands into political councils, and
sharply divided the electorate. City men like Samuel Sewall
were jealous to maintain the English metallic currency, partly
through custom and partly because its scarcity augmented its
value; whereas the plain people of Ipswich, like so many country
people, no doubt were impressed with the desirability of a land-
script currency. Into this mighty controversy entered John Wise,
who in the year 1721, under the pen name of *Amicus Patriae*, is
reputed to have been the author of a book entitled, *A Word of
Comfort to a Melancholy Country. Or the Bank of Credit . . . fairly
defended by a Discovery of the Great Benefit, accruing by it to the whole
Province, etc. Humbly dedicated to the Merchants in Boston.* It
was "a well-managed and witty plea for paper money and 'inflation.'" With the economics of the problem that he was delving
into, we are not concerned; many heads have wrestled with it
since; we are concerned rather to point out that the democratic
John Wise was on the same side with the democratic Franklin, in
espousing paper currency.

After all, the significant thing that emerges from the life and
work of John Wise, is the unerring directness with which he seized
upon the core of primitive Congregationalism, and the breadth
and vigor with which he defended it. After a spirited contest
lasting three-quarters of a century, theocratic Puritanism yielded
to ecclesiastical democracy. For two generations it had remained
doubtful which way the church would incline. Dominated by
gentlemen, it was warped towards Presbyterianism; but interpreted by commoners, it leaned towards Congregationalism. The
son of a plebeian, Wise inclined to sympathize with the spirit of
radical Separatism, bred of the democratic aspirations of Jacobean
underlings; and this radical Separatism he found justified by the
new political philosophy, as well as by facts of the New England
village world. The struggle for ecclesiastical democracy was a

forerunner of the struggle for political democracy which was to be the business of the next century; and in founding his ecclesiasticism upon the doctrine of natural rights, John Wise was an early witness to the new order of thought.

II
SOCIAL DRIFTS

Great changes, whether liberal or otherwise as the future might determine, were to come to Massachusetts from the new order with its Charter provision establishing a property qualification for suffrage. The venture in idealism was over and economic determinism reasserted its sway. New England was to swing back into the broad current of English political development. Following the Revolution of 1688 a new theory of the political state was rising in England—the theory that the state originated in private property and exists primarily for the protection of property; and this conception, thrust upon New England, was to cut sharply across the cleavages of the old order and create new ones. It substituted the dominance of wealth for the stewardship of righteousness; the stake-in-society principle for the Mosaic code. It set a premium upon acquisitiveness and subordinated the Puritan to the Yankee. It prepared the way for class alignments which must grow sharper with the increase of wealth, and would eventually produce a Tory group with natural longings for titles and a colonial aristocracy. How powerful this mercantile-Tory element was to become would depend upon the counter strength of the rising democratic group, with its freehold tenure of land, its town meeting, its Congregational church, and its distrust of aristocratic orders.

For the present, the world of John Wise was the real New England, thrifty, parsimonious, intensely local, driving straight towards a homespun democracy. The older fashioned New Englander, whatever his social position, did not take kindly to Toryism; and when it made its appearance in the train of the royal officials, swaggering somewhat and a bit insolent, it seemed to the colonial both alien and wicked. English Tory and Puritan Yankee frankly disliked each other; their ideals were incompatible, their manners unlike. A cloud of suspicion surrounded the English official as he walked the streets of Boston: suspicion of the hated church which he promptly set up, though not much given to worship;

suspicion of his political motives and the overseas authority which he represented.   In a vague way the New Englanders were convinced that he constituted a menace to their most cherished rights and privileges; that he was secretly bent on undermining the traditional liberties.   And the English gentleman, with his casual old-world arrogance, unwittingly aggravated the common suspicion.

How great was the chasm that separated the two worlds is sharply revealed by an episode in the career of Joseph Dudley, son of the emigrant, who was made royal governor in 1702. Dudley had lived much in England, had sat in Parliament, and had imbibed prerogative notions of government. He little relished the homely ways of New England and he bore himself somewhat haughtily. One December day in 1705, as he was driving along a country road with high snowdrifts on each side, he met with two loads of wood. The chariot coming to a stop, Dudley thrust his head out of the window and bade the carters turn aside and make way for him; but they were inclined to argue the matter in view of the drifts. Words were multiplied, and one of the carters cried—to quote Sewall—"I am as good flesh and blood as you . . . you may goe out of the way."   In a rage the governor drew his sword and struck at the fellow, who snatched the sword away and broke it. "You lie, you dog; you lie, you devill!" cried Dudley, beside himself. "Such words don't become a Christian," retorted the carter. "A Christian, you dog!" cried Dudley; "a Christian, you devill! I was a Christian before you were born!" and he snatched the carter's whip and lashed him roundly. "Being in a great passion: threatn'd to send those that affronted him to England." He arrested both carters and threw them into jail, whence they were released by the help of Sewall, who took their side though connected with Dudley through marriage. They were of good yeoman families, yet the matter hung on for nearly a year before they were discharged from their bonds.[12]

Village New England was becoming surprisingly independent in spirit when plain countrymen stood upon their rights against the Governor—"nor did they once in the Govrs . . . sight pull of their hatts," as Dudley took pains to inform the Queen's justices. Three generations in America were having their effect in the creation of a homespun democracy. "Mr. Dudley's principles,

[12] The account with affidavits is given in Sewall, *Diary*, Vol. II, pp. 144–147.

in government, were too high for the Massachusetts people," commented a later Tory, whose own principles were high:

He found it difficult to maintain what appeared to him to be the just prerogative of the crown, and at the same time to recover and preserve the esteem of the country. The government had been so popular [i. e. democratic] under the old charter, that the exercise of the powers reserved to the crown by the new charter was submitted to with reluctance.[13]

If "the prejudices against him were great," some explanation is found in a letter written by his son, Attorney-General Paul Dudley, to an English friend, which came to the hands of Cotton Mather and was published by him:

I refer you to Mr. — for an Account of everything, especially about the Government, and the Colledge; both which, are Discoursed of here, in Chimney Corners, and Private Meetings, as confidently as can be. . . . This Country will never be worth Living in, for Lawyers and Gentlemen, till the *Charter* is *Taken Away*. My Father and I sometimes Talk of the Queen's Establishing a *Court of Chancery* in this Country; I have Writ about it, to Mr. Blathwayt: If the Matter should Succeed, you might get some Place worth your Return; of which I should be very Glad.[14]

If New England had grown restive under the theocratic oligarchy, it had no intention of being toryized by English placemen.

It was during these troubled years that a new force made its appearance in Massachusetts which Sewall noted: "Sept. 25 [1690]. A printed sheet entituled publick Occurrences comes out, which gives much distaste because not Licensed. . . ." A week later he added: "Print of the Governour and Council comes out shewing their disallowance of the Public Occurrences"; and the next day, "Mr. Mather writes a very sharp letter about it." This was Increase Mather, who would tolerate no such lawlessness of the press, which must be kept as a private preserve for the orthodox party. Against the Mather conservatism it was impossible to make headway, and the little sheet did not come to a second issue. Not till fourteen years later did Sewall set down a similar note: "April 24 [1704]. I went to Cambridge. . . . I gave Mr. Willard the first News-Letter that ever was carried over the River. He shew'd it to the Fellows." So began in America, at first unlawfully, and then with due propriety, the work of making and publishing newspapers. For seventy-two years thereafter, the

---

[13] Hutchinson, *History of Massachusetts Bay Colony*, Vol. II, p. 148.
[14] Sewall, *Diary*, Vol. II, Introduction, p. 109.

News-Letter was published continuously, justifying in all its utterances the confidence of Boston conservatism, espousing naturally
the Tory side in the pre-Revolutionary quarrels, and coming to a
sudden end on the evacuation of Boston by General Gage.

On December 14, 1719, the *Boston Gazette* entered the field as a
competitor for conservative readers, and two years later, August
17, 1721, the *New England Courant* appeared, the first organ of the
opposition. It was edited by James Franklin, who possessed
much of the Franklin independence, untempered by the prudence
of Benjamin; and he set himself incautiously to the business of
assailing the strait-laced authorities of Boston. He got together a
group of brisk young men, known as the Hell-fire Club, who flung
their vivacious satires at the Mathers with such effect as to
lead Cotton Mather to undertake the following "Good Device":

> Warnings are to be given unto the wicked Printer, and his Accomplices,
> who every week publish a vile Paper to lessen and blacken the Ministers
> of the Town, and render their Ministry ineffectual. A Wickedness never
> parall'd any where upon the Face of the Earth.[15]

Although his prayers could not convert the wicked journalists,
his warnings availed with the magistrates, who took means to put
a stop to such disrespect. Twice Franklin was arraigned for
contempt, and once he spent four weeks in the common jail. By
way of counterblast to so disreputable a sheet, the *New England
Weekly Journal* appeared on March 20, 1727, an eminently respectable sheet, edited by Mather Byles and with such notable con-
tributors as the Reverend Thomas Prince. But with the coming
of the *Journal* with its staff of writers who modeled their style
upon the Augustan wits, we are in the mid-current of the eighteenth
century, that was to enlarge the influence of the public press far
beyond what could have been foreseen from its small beginnings.
It was to penetrate the inland villages and slowly wear away their
insularity of temper and outlook, bringing fresh ideas to minds
that had long stagnated. On the whole it was not a liberal press,
but its final effect was profoundly liberalizing.

[15] *Diary*, Vol. II, p. 663.

BOOK TWO: THE COLONIAL MIND

THE COLONIAL MIND

THE undistinguished years of the early and middle eighteenth century, rude and drab in their insularity, were the creative spring-time of democratic America—plebeian years that sowed what after times were to reap. The forgotten men and women of those silent decades wrote little, debated little, very likely thought little; they were plain workmen with whom ideas counted for less than the day's work. The stir of achievement filled the land, daily penetrating farther into the backwoods and bringing new farmlands under the plow. The stern demands of necessity held men in their grip, narrowing the horizon of their minds, and obscuring the vision of their larger accomplishment. Along the Appalachian watershed a vast drama, magnificent in the breadth and sweep of its movement, was being enacted by players un-conscious of their parts. Not until long after they had gone to their graves were the broad lines of that drama revealed. Today it is plain that those unremembered years were engaged in clearing away encumbrances more significant than the great oaks and maples of the virgin wilderness: they were uprooting ancient habits of thought, destroying social customs that had grown old and dignified in class-ridden Europe. A new psychology was being created by the wide spaces that was to be enormously signifi-cant when it came to self-consciousness. If this middle eighteenth century wrote little literature, it created and spread among a vigorous people something of far greater importance to America, the psychology of democratic individualism.

From this determining influence—too little recognized by later generations—the creative outlines of our history have taken shape. American ideals and institutions emerged in large part from the silent revolution which during the middle eighteenth century differentiated the American from the transplanted colonial; a change that resulted from an amalgam of the older English stock with other races, and the subjection of this new product on a great scale to the influence of diffused landholding. From these two major facts of a new race and a free environment came the social and political philosophy of older America, to which we have traditionally applied the term democratic, and which unconsciously wove itself into our daily intercourse and ways of thinking.

PART ONE: THE MIND IN THE MAKING
1720–1763

CHAPTER I

COLONIAL BACKGROUNDS

I

NEW STOCK

IMMIGRATION in the eighteenth century was almost wholly economic in motive. The reports of free land and free opportunity in America penetrated to remote hamlets of Great Britain, and more slowly to the continent, and drew hither a rude influx of the dispossessed and disinherited of Europe. From the hopeless poverty of great masses of old-world laborers, increasing numbers sought escape through emigration, accepting the hardships and uncertainties of the migration in the hope of bettering themselves ultimately. A host of English nondescripts—broken men, bond servants, "gaol birds," the lees and settlings of the old world— came overseas, voluntarily or under duress, in numbers running into the hundred thousands, and shared with German peasants from the Palatine, or Scotch-Irish from Ulster, the back-breaking labor of subduing the wilderness. About these unfortunate men and women no romance has gathered; tradition and history have not remembered their names or glorified their deeds; yet their blood runs in the veins of most Americans today of the older stock, and their contribution to our common heritage was great and lasting.

Of the different racial strains that mingled their blood with the earlier English—Irish, Huguenot-French, German, Scotch-Irish—the last was by far the most important. Not since 1630, when the *Lady Arbella* and her companion vessels brought the Puritans to Massachusetts Bay, had there been an event so momentous to America as the arrival in 1718 of some four thousand Scotch-Irish from Ulster, the vanguard of an army which by the time of the Revolution had risen to approximately two hundred thousand, or more than twelve times the number of English who settled

133

Massachusetts. They were desperately poor; the available lands near the coast were already preëmpted; so armed with axes, their seed potatoes, and the newly invented rifle, they plunged into the backwoods to become our great pioneering race. Scattered thinly through a long frontier, they constituted the outposts and buffer settlements of civilization. A vigorous breed, hardy, assertive, individualistic, thrifty, trained in the democracy of the Scottish kirk, they were the material out of which later Jacksonian democracy was to be fashioned, the creators of that "western type which in politics and industry became ultimately the American type." [1]

Next to the Scotch-Irish, who for the most part were free peasants, the most important addition to eighteenth-century America were the indented servants. Mostly from England, Scotland, Ireland, and Germany, they represented all trades and some of the professions. The white slavers of the times were well organized and plied a brisk trade with satisfactory profits; and in consequence, a steady stream of indented servants poured into America to turn the wheels of colonial industry. In his history of the German redemptioners, Diffenderfer has printed a number of newspaper advertisements which throw a curious light upon the traffic: here are two:

From the *American Weekly Mercury*, February 18, 1729:
Lately arrived from London, a parcel of very likely English servants, men and women, several of the men Tradesmen; to be sold reasonable and Time allowed for payment. By Charles Read of Philadelphia, or Capt. John Ball, on board his ship, at *Anthony Millkinson's Wharf*.

From the same for May 22, 1729, announcements of two ships:
There is just arrived from Scotland, a parcel of choice *Scotch Servants;* Taylors, Weavers, Shoemakers and ploughmen, some for five and others for seven years; Imported by James Coults, etc.
Just arrived from London in the ship *Providence*, Capt. Jonathan Clarke, a parcel of very likely *servants*, most Tradesmen, to be sold on reasonable Terms.

The several nationalities were appraised and rated by careful merchants and the fittest import seasons considered. [2] The "best

[1] See Commons, *Races and Immigrants in America*, p. 37.
[2] Sometimes the profits were unexpectedly great, as is illustrated by the case of a certain George Martin, who contracted with a shipmaster to transport himself, his wife, and five children to America for fifty-four pounds. He paid down $16, but died on the passage. On the arrival of the vessel in port, the captain foreclosed on the contract, sold the widow for twenty-two pounds, the three eldest sons at thirty

time for Servants is about the month of May," one merchant wrote to his agent in Ireland; and another warned, "Irish servants will be very dull, such numbers have already arrived from Different parts & many more expected, that I believe it will be overdone, especially as several Dutch vessels are expected here, which will always command the Market." [3]

In the middle colonies, particularly Pennsylvania, the greater number of servants came from the Rhine country. Deceived by swindling agents, thousands of German peasants, eager to get away from their war-harried and plundered homes, sold themselves into servitude to pay their passage to America. For the better part of a century these German redemptioners thronged the ports of Philadelphia and Baltimore, as the following news items testify:

From *Der Hoch Deutsche Pennsylvanische Bericht*, August 16, 1750:
Six ships with Irish servants have arrived at Philadelphia, and two ships with German Newcomers. Some say 18 more on their way here; others say 24 and still others 10,000 persons.

From the same, December 16, 1750:
Capt. Hasselwood has arrived from Holland with the latest ship that brought Germans. It is the fourteenth that has come laden with Germans this year. 4,317 have registered in the Court House. . . . Besides these, 1,000 servants and passengers arrived from Ireland and England. [4]

Of the human side of this widespread traffic some little idea may be got from the diary of a certain John Harrower, a man of modest education who became an articled schoolmaster to a Virginia family in the year 1774. Following are some entries:

Wednesday, 26th. [January, 1774.] This day I being reduced to the last shilling was obliged to engage to go to Virginia for four years, as a schoolmaster for Bedd, Board, washing and five pounds during the whole time. I have also wrote my wife this day a particular Acct of everything that has happened to me since I left her until this date. . . .
Munday 31st . . . It is surprising to see the No. of good tradesmen of all kinds, th't come on b'd every day . . . while the Clerk was filling up the Indentures the doctor search'd every serv't to see that they were sound . . . seventy-five were Intend [indented] to Capt Bowres for four Years. . . .

pounds each, and the two youngest, who were under five years of age, he sold for ten pounds, realizing one hundred and twenty-two pounds on a debt under fifty-one pounds. (Diffenderfer, *The German Immigrants into Pennsylvania*, p. 268).
[3] *Ibid.*, p. 229.
[4] *Ibid.*, Part II, "The Redemptioners," p. 209.

Munday 7th . . . at 4 pm put a servant ashore extreamly bade in a fever, and then got under saile for Virginia with seventy Servants on board all indented to serve four yeares there at their different Occupations. . . .

Munday, May 2nd. . . . At 2 pm the Capt carried five servts ashore to Hampton in order to sell their Indentures, But returned again at Midnight with[out] selling any more but one Boat Builder. . . .

Freiday, 6th . . . at Hobshole there was five Glasgow ships and an English Brigantine lying, at 2 pm we passed by Leedstown on our Star board hand where there was a ship from London lying with convicts. . . .

Wednesday, 11th. . . . At 10 A M Both Coopers and the Barber from our Mace [mess] went ashore upon tryall. At night one Daniel Turner a servt returned onb'd from Liberty so Drunk that he abused the Capt and Chief Mate and Boatswan to a verry high degree, which made him to be horse whipt, put in Irons and thumb screwed. on houre afterward he was unthumbscrewed, taken out of the Irons, but then he was hand cuffed, and gagged all night. . . .

Munday, 16th. This day severalls came on b'd to purchase servts Indentures and among them there was two soul drivers. they are Men who made it their business to go on b'd all ships who have in either Servants or Convicts and buy sometimes the whole and sometimes a parcell of them as they can agree, and then they drive them through the Country like a parcell of Sheep until they can sell them to advantage, but all went away without buying any. . . .

Munday, 23rd [May] . . . at same time all the rest of the servants were ordered ashore to a tent at Fredericksbg and several of their indentures were then sold. about 4 pm I was brought to Colonel Daingerfield, when we immediately agreed and my Indenture for four years was then delivered him and he was to send for me the next day.[5]

In some such fashion, year after year, thousands of immigrants were transported to America, there to mingle their blood with that of the earlier comers. They came as social derelicts, were greeted by the awaiting "soul-drivers," found masters, worked and got on, or lost heart and slipped away into the tempting back-country whither so many broken men went in search of refuge. They were a plebeian lot, and they endured the common fate of the underling. Very likely they transmitted to their children a bitter hostility to the ways of an aristocratic society, the residuum of old grievances, and this slowly accumulating animus was eventually to count heavily with lower-class colonials in favor of a more democratic order in the new world.

[5] For the entire diary, see *American Historical Review*, Vol. VI, pp. 65-107.

II
THE FRONTIER
Lubberland

The frontier, which exercised so creative an influence in shaping American character and institutions, was regarded in very different lights by the gentleman and the commoner. To the former it was no other than lubberland, the abode of rude leveling, the temptation to gross social laxity. It drew away servants who were needed, and kept the price of real estate low; and such very different persons as Cotton Mather and John Dickinson agreed in desiring to stop the constant drain into the backcountry, and keep settlers in the older portions. Descriptions of the frontier indited by aristocratic pens convey an idea very different from later democratic conceptions, and paint the ancestors of later Jacksonians in unlovely colors.

Among the earliest of these records is *The Private Journal kept by Madam Knight on a Journey from Boston to New York in the Year 1704*. Madam Knight was a sprightly and intelligent woman, keeper of a dame's school in Boston, who set down in the journal some of the odd things that came under her sharp eyes on her venturesome trip on horseback. As she drew away from the older settlements, signs of relaxing social convention multiplied with the worsening of the road. Connecticut, which had always been too democratic to suit the Boston taste, she found "a little too much Independant in their principalls." It was not careful to uphold proper social distinctions, but inclined to a free and easy leveling altogether offensive:

. . . They Generally lived very well and comfortable in their famelies. But too Indulgent (especially ye farmers) to their slaves: suffering too great familiarity from them, permitting ym to sit at Table and eat with them (as they say to save time), and into the dish goes the black hoof as freely as the white hand. They told me that there was a farmer lived nere the Town where I lodged who had some difference with his slave, concerning something the master had promised him and did not punctually perform; wch caused some hard words between them; But at length they put the matter to Arbitration and Bound themselves to stand to the award of such as they named—wch done, the Arbitrators Having heard the Allegations of both parties, Order the master to pay 40s to black face, and acknowledge his fault. And so the matter ended; the poor master very honestly standing to the award.[6]

[6] *The Private Journal, etc.*, p. 40.

In the unsettled country strange figures with rude decivilized ways made their appearance. Here is a description of one such product of the wilderness:

I had scarce done thinking, when an Indian-like Animal come to the door, on a creature very much like himselfe, in mien and feature, as well as Ragged cloathing; and having 'litt, makes an Awkerd Scratch with his Indian shoo, and a Nodd, sitts on ye block, fumbles out his black Junk [salt meat?], dipps it in ye ashes, and presents it piping hott to his muschee-to's (?), and fell to sucking like a calf, without speaking, for near a quarter of an hower. At length the old man said how do's Sarah do? who I under-stood was the wretches wife, and Daughter to ye old man.[7]

She thus describes a squatter's hut in the backwoods:

This little Hutt was one of the wretchedest I ever saw a habitation for human creatures. It was suported with shores enclosed with Clapboards, laid on Lengthways, and so much asunder, that the Light come throu' everywhere; the doore tyed on with a cord in ye place of hinges; The floor the bear earth; no windows but such as the thin covering afforded, nor any furniture but a Bedd with a glass Bottle hanging at ye head on't; an earthan cupp, a small pewter bason, A Bord with sticks to stand on, instead of a table, and a block or two in ye corner instead of chairs. The family were the old man, his wife and two children; all and every part being the picture of poverty. Notwithstanding both the Hutt and its Inhabitance were very clean and tydee.[8]

As Madam Knight meditated upon the causes of such poverty, she came to a characteristic Boston conclusion:

We may Observe here the great necessity and benefit both of Educa-tion and Conversation: for these people have as Large a portion of mother witt, and sometimes Larger, than those who have bin brought up in Citties; but for want of emprovements, Render themselves almost Ridic-ulos, as above.[9]

It is in the chatty narrative of Colonel William Byrd of Virginia,[10] that we find the earliest detailed description of the fringe of squat-ter settlements. Colonel Byrd was the first gentleman of Virginia, a man of old-world education and some literary taste,[11] polished manners, and a vast number of acres of choice land which he had ac-quired and held largely tax-free, by means well understood among Vir-

---

[7] *Ibid.*, pp. 29–30.   [8] *Ibid.*, p. 28.   [9] *Ibid.*, p. 45.
[10] "The History of the Dividing Line," in *The Writings of Colonel William Byrd of Westover in Virginia, Esquire*, New York, 1901.
[11] At his death his library contained some four thousand volumes, "the largest private library in the English-speaking colonies," according to his biographer.

ginia gentlemen.[12] Among the several capacities in which he served the commonwealth in return for his many acres, was to act as a member of a joint commission which in the year 1728 ran a boundary line between Virginia and North Carolina. As he sat his horse in the capacity of overseer, he observed many amusing things which he jotted down in his journal.

The backcountry, it would seem, had already developed the free and easy ways of a squatter world, shiftless, lubberly, independent, but animated by hostility towards the aristocratic Old Dominion, from which many of the settlers had come. North Carolina had long been a place of refuge for debtors, criminals, and runaway servants, who used their legs to even the score with a caste system; and Colonel Byrd regarded the lazy crew with amused contempt:

Surely there is no place in the World where the Inhabitants live with less Labour than in N Carolina. It approaches nearer to the Description of Lubberland than any other, by the great felicity of the Climate, the easiness of raising Provisions, and the Slothfulness of the People. Indian corn is of so great increase, that a little Pains will Subsist a very large Family with Bread, and then they may have meat without any Pains at all, by the Help of the Low Grounds, and the great Variety of Mast that grows on the High-land. The Men, for their parts, just like the Indians, impose all the Work upon the poor Women. They make their Wives rise out of their Beds early in the Morning, at the same time that they lye and Snore, till the Sun has run one third of his course, and disperst all the unwholesome Damps. Then, after Stretching and Yawning for half an Hour, they light their Pipes, and, under the Protection of a cloud of Smoak, venture out into the open Air; tho' if it happens to be never so little cold, they quickly return Shivering into the Chimney corner. When the weather is mild, they stand leaning with both their arms upon the corn-field fence, and gravely consider whether they had best go and take a Small Heat at the Hough; but generally find reasons to put off till another time. Thus they loiter away their Lives, like Solomon's Sluggard, with their Arms across, and at the Winding up of the Year Scarcely have Bread to Eat. To speak the Truth, tis a thorough Aversion to Labor that makes People file off to N Carolina, where Plenty and a Warm Sun confirm them in their Disposition to Laziness for their whole Lives.[13]

One thing Colonel Byrd noted everywhere: the lazy lubbers wanted chiefly to be let alone; they dreaded the possibility of falling within the Virginia line; they were content in their Eden,

---

[12] His father died possessed of 26,231 acres. He himself owned at his death "no less than 179,440 acres of the best land in Virginia."

[13] *Op. cit.*, pp. 75–76.

and had no wish to exchange their freedom for the stricter rule of the Old Dominion:

> Wherever we passed we constantly found the Borderers laid it to Heart if their Land was taken into Virginia; they chose rather belong to Carolina, where they pay no Tribute, either to God or to Caesar. . . . Another reason was, that the Government there is so Loose, and the Laws so feebly executed, that, like those in the Neighbourhood of Sydon formerly, every one does just what seems good in his own Eyes. . . . Besides, there might have been some Danger, perhaps, in venturing to be so rigorous, for fear of undergoing the Fate of an honest Justice in Corotuck Precinct. This bold Magistrate, it seems, taking upon to order a fellow to the Stocks, for being disorderly in his Drink, was, for his intemperate zeal, carry'd thither himself, and narrowly escap'd being whipp't by the Rabble into the Bargain.[14]

> They are rarely guilty of Flattering or making any Court to their governours, but treat them with all the Excesses of Freedom and Familiarity. They are of Opinion their rulers woul'd be apt to grow insolent, if they grew Rich, and for that reason they take care to keep them poorer, and more dependent, if possible, than the Saints of New England used to do their Governours.[15]

To the student of colonial politics such glimpses are suggestive. They reveal how early was the popular distrust of magistrates and government; and they serve to explain the most striking characteristic of Revolutionary political practice—the movement to minimize the power of the judiciary and the executive, and magnify the power of the legislature; to keep authority within the control of the local democracies. "Every one does just what seems good in his own Eyes"—in this attitude of social *laissez faire* that throve on a diet of corn pone and salt pork was the origin of the coonskin democracy of Old Hickory that was to bring eventual disaster to the plans of gentlemen.

III

THE FRONTIER

Land of Promise

Quite another picture of the frontier was likely to be painted by the eighteenth-century democrat. In the well-known *Letters* of Crèvecœur, and in the recently published *More Letters from an American Farmer*,[16] is an analysis of frontier life and its creative

[14] *Ibid.*, p. 87.   [15] *Ibid.*, p. 81.
[16] Published under the title of *Sketches of Eighteenth Century America* by the Yale University Press, 1925.

influence upon the emerging American character, far more sympathetic and thoughtful than the casual narratives of Madam Knight and Colonel Byrd. The author was a cultivated Norman-French gentleman, who about the year 1759 or 1760 entered the English colonies from Canada, was a surveyor for a time near Albany, a resident of Pennsylvania and of Ulster County in the province of New York, eventually acquired a farm of 120 acres in Orange County which he named "Pine Hill," married Mehetable Tippet of Yonkers, and became a competent tiller of the soil as well as a lover of country life. In disposition he was active and energetic, curious concerning the ways of nature and society. In Canada he had joined the army as lieutenant under Montcalm and was sent on a map-making expedition to the wilderness beyond the Great Lakes, and traveled from Detroit as far south as the Ohio River. After quitting Canada following the fall of Quebec, he traveled from Nova Scotia through the English colonies to the extreme south, and perhaps visited Bermuda and Jamaica, noting keenly the country and the manners of the people. Perhaps no other man before the Revolution was so intimately acquainted with the French and English colonies as a whole, with their near background of frontier and the great wilderness beyond, as this French American; and it was from long and intimate contact with the realities of colonial life that he wrote those comments that have preserved his name to the present.

The Revolution broke in upon his peaceful life with disastrous consequences. He took no part in the preliminary disputes, and was under grave suspicion by his neighbors in Orange County and by the British. He was thrown into prison in New York by his Majesty's officers, where his health was undermined and he was reduced to extreme straits. Finally permitted to sail for Europe without his family, he was shipwrecked off the coast of Ireland, but reached London where he disposed of his manuscripts, and eventually got over to France in August, 1781. After the peace he returned to America to find his wife dead, his children scattered, and his farmhouse burnt. For a time he was French consul at New York, where he interested himself in establishing a packet service between France and America, and in the improvement of agricultural methods, amongst other ways by the establishment of botanical gardens. He was a scientific farmer, introducing the system of cover crops into America and endeavoring to intro-

duce potato culture into France. He was a corresponding member
of the Académie des Sciences and the Royal Agricultural Society of
Paris, and a member of the Société d'Agriculture, Sciences, et Arts
de Meaux, and of the Société d'Agriculture de Caen. In 1790 he
returned to France where he died in 1813.

Underneath the discursive chat of his letters is the firm fabric of
economic fact. In the background of his thinking Crèvecœur was
quite definitely Physiocratic, in his warm humanitarianism as well
as in his agrarian bias. As the kindly Frenchman studied the ways
of colonial society and contemplated the future, he asked himself
the question, what was the American as he was perceptibly differentiating from his European ancestors? That a new race was
emerging in this new country, he was convinced; and that it was
not in consequence chiefly of a new mixture of blood—although
that was not without its influence—he likewise believed. A more
potent influence was at work and that influence was environment.
Crèvecœur was something of an economic determinist who sought
to explain laws, customs, institutions—the pattern of the social
web—by an inquiry into economic factors. *Mann ist was er isst.*
"Men are like plants; the goodness and flavor of the fruit proceeds
from the peculiar soil and exposition in which they grow. We are
nothing but what we derive from the air we breathe, the climate
we inhabit, the government we obey, the system of religion we
profess, and the mode of our employment." [17] Transplanted from
the meager opportunities of the old world to the rich soil and ample
spaces of America, the European undergoes a subtle transformation.

The rich stay in Europe, it is only the middling and the poor that
emigrate. In this great American asylum, the poor of Europe have by
some means met together, and in consequence of various causes; to what
purpose should they ask one another, what countrymen they are? Alas,
two thirds of them had no country. Can a wretch who wanders about,
who works and starves . . . can that man call England or any other
kingdom his country? A country that had no bread for him, whose fields
procured him no harvest, who met nothing but the frowns of the rich, the
severity of the laws, with jails and punishments; who owned not a single
foot of the extensive surface of this planet? No! urged by a variety of
motives, here they came. Every thing tended to regenerate them; new
laws, a new mode of living, a new social system; here they are become men:
in Europe they were as so many useless plants, wanting vegetable mould,

[17] *Letters* . . ., in edition of 1904, p. 56.

and refreshing showers; they withered and were mowed down by want, hunger, and war: but now by the power of transplantation, like all other plants, they have taken root and flourished! Formerly they were not numbered in any civil list of their country, except in those of the poor; here they rank as citizens. By what invisible power has this surprizing metamorphosis been performed? By that of the laws of their industry . . . his country is now that which gives him land, bread, protection, and consequence: *Ubi panis ibi patria*, is a motto of all emigrants. . . . Here the rewards of his industry follow with equal steps in the progress of his labor; his labor is founded on the basis of nature, *self-interest;* can it want a stronger allurement? [18]

From economic individualism in presence of unexploited natural resources, he deduces the natural emergence of a new American psychology that differentiates the colonial from the European peasant. If "from involuntary idleness, servile dependence, penury, and useless labor," the emigrant "has passed to toils of a very different nature, rewarded by ample subsistence"; if he has left off being a peasant and become a free-holder and citizen; will not this man "entertain new ideas, and form new opinions"? He possesses a stake in society; his horizons broaden, his ambitions quicken; this is his country.

An European, when he first arrives, seems limited in his intentions, as well as in his views; but he very suddenly alters his scale . . . he no sooner breathes our air than he forms new schemes, and embarks in designs he never would have thought of in his own country. There the plenitude of society confines many useful ideas, and often extinguishes the most laudable schemes which here ripen into maturity.[19]

He begins to feel the effects of a sort of resurrection; hitherto he had not lived, but simply vegetated; he now feels himself a man, because he is treated as such; the laws of his own country had overlooked him in his insignificancy; the laws of this cover him with their mantle. Judge what an alteration there must arise in the mind and thoughts of this man; he begins to forget his former servitude and dependence, his heart involuntarily swells and glows; this first swell inspires him with those new thoughts which constitute an American. . . . From nothing to start into being, to become a free man, invested with lands, to which every municipal blessing is annexed! What a change indeed! It is in consequence of that change that he becomes an American.[20]

He is an American, who leaving behind him all his ancient prejudices and manners, receives new ones from the mode of life he has embraced, the new government he obeys, and the new rank he holds. He becomes an American by being received in the broad lap of our great *Alma Mater.*

[18] *Ibid.*, pp. 52–55.   [19] *Ibid.*, p. 76.   [20] *Ibid.*, pp. 77, 79.

Here individuals of all nations are melted into a new race of men, whose labors and posterity will one day cause great changes in the world.[21]

Having convinced himself that economic relaxation was the creative force in determining American institutions and psychology, he was led to examine the working of that force in diverse portions of America.   It is neither in the older seacoast world, nor along the extreme frontier that he discovers his representative America; but in the broad stretches of clearings, the vigorous backcountry or "middle-settlements," where agriculture was followed soberly and effectively.   "Some few towns excepted, we are all tillers of the soil," he pointed out; and it is the farmer of the middle region of New York and Pennsylvania, with his broad acres in prosperous cultivation, his economic independence, and his manly vigor, that he most delights to dwell upon:

Europe has no such class of men; the early knowledge they acquire, the early bargains they make, give them a great degree of sagacity.   As freemen, they will be litigious; pride and obstinacy are often the cause of lawsuits; the nature of our laws and governments may be another.   As citizens it is easy to imagine, that they will carefully read the newspapers, enter into every political disquisition, freely blame or censure governors and others.   As farmers, they will be careful and anxious to get as much as they can, because what they get is theirs. . . . As Christians, religion curbs them not in their opinions; the laws inspect our actions; our thoughts are left to God.   Industry, good living, selfishness, litigiousness, country politics, the pride of freemen, religious indifference, are their characteristics.[22]

The thinly settled backwoods with their restless squatter population, Crèvecœur regards as the rough vanguard of the westward-moving settlements.   It is here, he points out, that the forces of leveling are strongest, that the last remnants of old-world distinctions and privileges are stript away, that the idea of individual freedom carries furthest, sometimes to social disaster.   "He who would wish to see America in its proper light," he says, "and have a true idea of its feeble beginnings and barbarous rudiments, must visit our extended line of frontiers where the last settlers dwell."

Now we arrive near the great woods, near the last inhabited districts; there men seem to be placed . . . beyond the reach of government, which in some measure leaves them to themselves . . . as they were driven there by misfortune, necessity of beginnings, desire of acquiring large tracts of land, idleness, frequent want of economy, ancient debts; the re-

[21] *Ibid.*, pp. 54–55.   [22] *Ibid.*, pp. 57–58.

union of such people does not afford a very pleasing spectacle. . . . The few magistrates they have, are in general little better than the rest; they are often in a perfect state of war; that of man against man, sometimes decided by blows, sometimes by means of law . . . men are wholly left dependent upon their native tempers, and on the spur of uncertain industry, which often fails when not sanctified by the efficacy of a few moral rules. There, remote from the power of example, and check of shame, many families exhibit the most hideous parts of our society. They are a kind of forlorn hope, preceding by ten or twelve years the more respectable army of veterans which come after them. In that space, prosperity will polish some, vice and law will drive off the rest, who uniting with others like themselves will recede still farther; making room for more industrious people, who will finish their improvements, convert the loghouse into a convenient habitation, and rejoicing that the first heavy labors are finished, will change in a few years that hitherto barbarous country into a fine, fertile, well regulated district. Such is our progress, such is the march of the Europeans toward the interior parts of this continent. In all society there are off-casts; this impure part serves as our precursors or pioneers.[23]

Crèvecœur's chattiness and bucolic love of nature may easily obscure for the casual reader, the solid economic core of the *Letters*. The story of Andrew, the Hebridean, with its note of idyllic simplicity, reads like a tale out of the French romantics; yet in its broad outline it is the story of many an immigrant who penetrated to the hospitable backcountry, took land, and prospered. The strong coloring of the description is only partly French; in part it is a reflection of the spontaneous optimism that was working like leaven in colonial society. It is the old-fashioned phrasing rather than the matter that makes the *Letters* seem obsolete to modern readers. Change the wording, soften the bucolic enthusiasm, and the sober American of earlier generations, as he observed the arrival of the strong-armed peasant from the north of Europe, would have discovered nothing strange in such a sentiment as this:

After a foreigner from any part of Europe is arrived, and become a citizen; let him devoutly listen to the voice of our great parent, which says to him, "Welcome to my shores, distressed European; bless the hour in which thou didst see my verdant fields, my fair navigable rivers, and my green mountains!—If thou wilt work, I have bread for thee; if thou wilt be honest, sober, and industrious, I have greater rewards to bestow on thee—ease and independence. I will give thee fields to feed and clothe thee; a comfortable fire-side to sit by. . . . I shall endow thee besides with the immunities of a freeman. . . . Go thou, and work and till; thou shalt prosper, provided thou be just, grateful, and industrious.[24]

[23] *Ibid.*, pp. 58–60. [24] *Ibid.*, pp. 90–91.

Andrew the Hebridean is a portrait painted by a Physiocratic humanitarian, but the idealism that would build peace and content on honest foundations, and would deny them to none, not even the poorest if they proved worthy, found frequent justification in the prosaic experience of colonial America. If many an immigrant found "soul-drivers" awaiting them, many others like Andrew found a more hospitable reception.

Across the peaceful scenes depicted in the *Letters* soon fell the dark shadow of civil war, and Crèvecœur's content was rudely broken in upon. As a French humanitarian he loathed war and all its works, and every instinct and argument counseled him to stand apart from the strife that seemed to him so meaningless. He liked peace and orderly ways and he could not work himself into a passion over the supposed wrongs of a people who seemed to him blessed above all others on this troubled earth. As a philosophical farmer he held the politician in contempt and refused to take seriously abstract theories of statecraft. The citizen who stuck to his plow was happier, he believed, than the citizen who talked noisily of his wrongs, and was eager to overset things. The rough leveling of the frontier he had found distasteful, and as he watched the development of the Revolutionary disputes, he seems to have discovered in the Whig program an irruption of the tumultuous frontier leveling that threatened to sweep away the common peace and well-being. The source of the unrest he traced to New England, the feculent wellspring of all the hypocrisies; it was inspired, he was convinced, by a selfish demagoguery and led by unprincipled mobsters. In so far as he held partisan sympathies, they inclined to the Loyalist side. His education in England and his breeding as a gentleman, drew him towards the Loyalist gentry with whom he associated in Orange County, and repelled him from the noisy ardor of the plebèian patriots. Yet in spirit he stood resolutely aloof, although his sympathies were cruelly hurt by the sufferings that fell under his observation. In certain letters only recently published (*Sketches of Eighteenth Century America*), he narrates the misfortunes that befell innocent men and women from the bitterness of civil strife,[25] and draws a picture of the lawlessness and greed of patriot committeemen, and the intolerance of the mob spirit, that is not pleasant to contem-

[25] See, e. g., "The Man of Sorrows," "The Wyoming Massacre," "The History of Mrs. B.," "The Frontier Woman."

plate.[26] Bitterness rarely exudes from his pen, but when he considers the ways of Whig politicians he now and then indulges in a passage that reveals his loathing of the mercenary spirit that he discovers in the new patriotism. In the conclusion of "The American Belisarius" he gives vent to his anger against those who outrage common morality; if it were not for the fact that this is a moral universe, he says ironically:

> I'd worship the demon of the times, trample on every law, break every duty, neglect every bond, overlook every obligation to which no punishment was annexed. I'd set myself calumniating my rich neighbors. I'd call all passive, inoffensive men by the name of inimical. I'd plunder or detain the entrusted deposits. I'd trade on public moneys, though contrary to my oath. Oath! Chaff for good Whigs, and only fit to bind a few conscientious Royalists! I'd build my new fortune on the depreciation of the money. I'd inform against every man who would make any difference betwixt it and silver, whilst I, secure from any discovery or suspicion by my good name, would privately exchange ten for one. I'd pocket the fines of poor militiamen extracted from their heart's blood. I'd become obdurate, merciless, and unjust. I'd grow rich, "fas vel nefas." I'd send others a-fighting, whilst I stayed at home to trade and to rule. I'd become a clamorous American, a modern Whig, and offer every night incense to the god Arimanes.[27]

A lover of peace and good will, a humanitarian concerned only with justice and the common well-being, seeking new ways to enlarge the returns of agriculture, devoid of petty ambition and local prejudice, a friend of man, Hector St. John de Crèvecœur was an embodiment of the generous spirit of French revolutionary thought, a man whom Jefferson would have liked for a neighbor. His sketchy and discursive writings may not be notable literature, but we could ill spare them from the library of eighteenth-century America.

[26] See, e. g., "The American Belisarius" and "Landscapes."
[27] *Sketches of Eighteenth Century America*, p. 249.

CHAPTER II

THE ANACHRONISM OF JONATHAN EDWARDS

I

BEFORE an adequate democratic philosophy could arise in this world of pragmatic individualism, the traditional system of New England theology must be put away, and a new conception of man and of his duty and destiny in the world must take its place. For the moment Calvinism was strengthened by the coming of the Scotch-Irish who spread the familiar dogmas along the frontier, remote from attack by old-world rationalism; nevertheless those dogmas carried within them the seeds of slow decay. The world that had created them lay in a forgotten past. The five points of Calvinism, postulated on a God of wrath, were no longer living principles answering to common experience; they were become no other than ghosts that walked on the Sabbath to terrify the timid. An intellectual *Aufklärung* was a necessary preliminary to the creation of a fruitful social philosophy. Theology must be made to square with actuality, or yield control of men's minds to more stimulating things.

But unfortunately there was no vigorous attack but only a tedious decay. The old was too deeply entrenched to be routed, and stricken with palsy it lingered out a morose old age. For years New England stewed in its petty provincialism, untouched by the brisk debates that stirred the old world. No vigorous disputant challenged its orthodoxy. In the year 1726 Cotton Mather wrote, "I cannot learn, That among all the Pastors of Two Hundred Churches, there is one Arminian; much less an Arian, or a Gentilist." [1] Nevertheless rationalism was in the air, and although it might be excluded from the minister's study, it spread its subtle infection through the mass of the people. The backwash of English deism reached the shores of New England, and by the decade of the forties a movement of liberalism seems to have got under way. The word Arminian sprinkles more freely

[1] Quoted in Walker, *History of the Congregational Churches in the United States,* p. 216.

148

the pages of controversial literature, indicating the nature of the attack being directed against Calvinism. Dogma was face to face with rationalism.

A critical movement had long been developing in England, undermining there the foundations of Calvinism; and in this work members of the Anglican clergy had aided. Hooker had been a rationalist and the influence of the *Ecclesiastical Polity* was thrown in favor of an appeal to reason and to history. He rejected a literal Hebraism for a more philosophical interpretation of the Scripture. "The Light of naturall understanding, wit and reason, is from God," he argued; "he it is which thereby doth illuminate every man entring into the World. He is the Author of all that we think or do by vertue of that light which himselfe hath given." [2] Because of this rationalizing tendency the Anglican clergy, before the middle of the seventeenth century, had passed from the Calvinistic to the Arminian position. The fundamental dogma of Arminianism was the doctrine of the freedom of the will—that the elect of God are not pre-chosen, but a righteous life and good works will bring men into the way of salvation. Destructive of the whole Calvinistic system as such doctrine was—striking at the taproot of determinism—Arminianism carried a social significance greater than its theological import: it was an expression of the ideal of individual responsibility that emerged from the decay of the feudal system. The first reformers had asserted the right to individual interpretation of the Scriptures; the Arminians threw upon the individual the whole responsibility, bidding him assert his will and achieve his own salvation.

English rationalism was carried further by a notable group of thinkers, including Milton and Locke, who rapidly passed from Arminianism to Arianism, and thence to Deism. By the beginning of the eighteenth century English Presbyterianism, which had clung to Calvinism long after the defection of the Anglicans, was undermined by the growing rationalism and finally passed over into Unitarianism. Calvinism had lost the battle in the old world and ceased to play an important part in the intellectual life of England. In the face of this steady drift away from the conception of a divine Will that dwarfed the human will and held it fixed in the mesh of the divine purpose, towards the conception of the responsibility of the individual and the significance of the moral

[2] *Ecclesiasticall Politie*, sixth edition, Book III, p. 10.

code in the work of salvation, the New England Calvinists found
their work cut out for them. A critical spirit was stirring, an incipient rationalism was beginning to ask questions; orthodoxy
for the first time was on the defensive, and ill equipped for the
pending battle.

But Calvinism had fallen into the clutch of forces greater and
more revolutionary than either minister or congregation realized.
To preach with convincing force one must appeal to the common
experience; dogma must seem to square with the evident facts of
life; it must appear to be the inevitable and sufficient explanation
of the mysteries and perplexities that beset men in the world of
reality. When it ceases to be a reasonable working hypothesis
in the light of common experience, it is no longer a controlling
influence in men's lives. And this was the unhappy predicament
in which Calvinism now found itself. Take, for example, the
doctrine of total depravity. In the corrupt worlds of Augustine
and John Calvin such a doctrine must have seemed a reasonable
explanation of the common brutality; an evil society must spring
from the evil heart of man. But in the village world of New England the doctrine had lost its social sanction. When in moments
of calm sense these provincial Calvinists asked themselves if the
human heart were in truth utterly depraved, if they themselves
and their neighbors were such vipers and worms as they professed
to be, the conviction must have grown upon them that such professions were untrue. The everyday life of the New England
village was animated by rugged virtues—by kindliness toward
neighbors and faithfulness to a strict ethical code, rather than by
hatred to God and man, or brutal wallowing in sin. In short,
these villagers knew that they were very far from a bad lot; and
when they pondered on this fact they must have discovered increasing difficulty in reconciling Sunday dogma and week-day
experience. Although they repeated the familiar creed, the
sanction for that creed was gone; it was the voice of dogma that
spoke, and not the voice of reason and experience.[3]

Such is the explanation, as well, of the decay of another of the
cardinal points of Calvinism—the dogma of special election. In
an aristocratic society it is natural to believe that God has set
men apart in classes; but as the leveling process tended to strip
away social distinctions, the new individualism undermined the

[3] See Wendell, *Literary History of America*, p. 89.

older class psychology. When the common man has freed himself from political absolutism, he will become dissatisfied with theological absolutism. The right to achieve salvation is a natural corollary to the right to win social distinction; that one's future status lay wholly beyond the reach of one's will, that it rested in the hands of an arbitrary God who gave or withheld salvation at pleasure, was a conception that ill accorded with the nascent ideal of democracy. When that ideal should be sufficiently clarified, the dogma of the elect of God, like the aristocratic conception of the king's favorite, would be quietly put away in the potter's field.

As the century advanced, the growing dissatisfaction with Calvinism received fresh impetus from the new social philosophy of France. The teaching of Rousseau that in a state of nature men were good, that they are still sound at heart, and that the evils of civilization have resulted from a perversion of the social contract, would appeal to men whose experience was daily teaching them the falseness of the traditional dogmas; and the ideal of equality would come home with special meaning to men bred up in villages and on the frontier. Such doctrines were fundamentally hostile to the spirit of Calvinism: not only did Rousseau set the doctrine of human perfectibility over against the dogma of total depravity, but he quickened the passion of revolt against every form of arbitrary authority, theological as well as political and social. Although the provincial colonial might not come in immediate contact with such speculative philosophy, in the long run he could not escape being influenced by it, and that influence would count against a decadent theology that held men's minds in its tenacious *rigor mortis*.

The crux of the question, it came finally to be seen by the apologists of the old order, lay in the fundamental problem of determinism. Was the will of man effectively free, or was it held in strict subjection to the stable will of God? According as the decision went touching this question, would stand or fall the entire metaphysical structure of Calvinism. To this problem, therefore, the best minds among the ministers directed their thought; and the historical position of Jonathan Edwards, greatest of the defenders of Calvinism, is revealed in its true perspective when his labors are studied in the light of this vital question.

II

Never had the traditional theology been so sorely in need of a champion as at the beginning of the second quarter of the eighteenth century; and such a champion God raised up—many devout Calvinists believed—in the person of Jonathan Edwards. Armed at all points—a theologian equipped with the keenest dialectics, a metaphysician endowed with a brilliantly speculative mind, a psychologist competent to deal with the subtlest phenomena of the sick soul—here was a man who might be counted on to justify the ancient dogmas to the troubled churches of New England.

The offspring of four generations of religious enthusiasts, by every right of heredity and training the child of Puritanism, Jonathan Edwards was the last and greatest of the royal line of Puritan mystics. As a young man he felt himself to be living in the very presence of God; he was conscious of the divine life flowing through and around him, making him one with the Godhood; and he was filled with yearning for personal union with the divine love in Christ. His intellectual and spiritual life was molded by a God-consciousness as passionate as that of Spinoza; and it is this fact of a lifelong devotion to the God-idea that furnishes the clue to an understanding of his later development. Not content that God had marked him for His own, he must build a philosophical universe about the Godhood, justifying his mysticism by a metaphysical idealism. He must examine critically the foundations of his creed and establish his theology upon philosophy. No obscurity must remain unprobed, no link in the chain of reasoning escape challenge: he must base the five points of Calvinism upon a metaphysics that should relate them to a universal system of thought, giving them a cosmic as well as a Biblical sanction. It was a great ambition, likely to prove too difficult even for the remarkable powers of Edwards; and if in pursuit of new arguments for old doctrines, he found himself inclosed in a mesh of subtleties, if his theology and metaphysics were never quite reconciled, blame must be laid upon the difficulty of the undertaking rather than on the incapacity of the thinker. To one cardinal principle Edwards was faithful—the conception of the majesty and sufficiency of God; and this polar idea provides the clue to both his philosophical and theological systems.

Yet with this as a guide there is much that remains perplexing. There are inconsistencies in his thought as there were in his pastoral life; and we shall understand his position only when we recognize the contrary tendencies which confused him, as the inevitable consequences of a system of thought that was at once reactionary and progressive, the outcome of certain latent inconsistencies too antagonistic for any thinker to reconcile. As the defender of the traditional theology, setting his face against the developing experience of his generation, and as a rigid disciplinarian, reverting to the older Separatist conception of a church of the elect, and rejecting the "whole way covenant" of his grandfather Stoddard, he may perhaps appear in the light of a reactionary. But as the expounder of philosophic idealism he was looking forward to Emerson; and as the advocate of the new revivalistic methods, exalting the experience of conversion as the central fact of the Christian life, and assisting the forces that were drawing church and state apart, he was a pronounced revolutionist, the schismatic leader of the New Lights and the father of later Congregationalism. That Edwards was aware of certain inconsistencies is fairly evident; that he was puzzled, hesitated, and stopped halfway in his labors, is evident too, unless we believe, with Mrs. Stowe, that certain of his speculations were too daring to put into print. The chains that bound him were too strong to be broken; the contradictions that lay at the root of the Calvinistic system could be eradicated only by grubbing up the whole, and for that the time had not yet come.

In his early years, before his conversion turned him aside from his true path, setting the apologetics of the theologian above the speculations of the philosopher, Edwards gave promise of becoming a strikingly creative thinker. Following the native bent of his genius, he plunged into the study of metaphysics with such fruitful results that it seemed likely that New England Puritanism was at last to come to flower; that the mystical perception of the divine love, which had steeped the early Puritan thought in emotion and quickened it to poetry, was now to create a system of philosophy which, like transcendentalism in the next century, should adequately express the aspirations of the New England mind. There is no more interesting phase in the early history of Edwards than the transition from religious mysticism to philosophical idealism. The yearning for the knitting of the soul to Christ, as expressed in the imagery of the Song of Songs, burgeoned into a larger ideal-ism that translated the Rose of Sharon and the Lily of the Valley into an all-pervasive spirit of divine life. In certain moods it is the mystic who cries, "My soul breaketh for the longing it hath; my soul waiteth for the Lord, more than they who watch for the morning."

> He was reading one day the words of Scripture [says Allen, paraphrasing Edwards' diary], "Now unto the King eternal, immortal, invisible, the only wise God, be honor and glory forever, Amen," when there came to him for the first time a sort of inward, sweet delight in God and divine things. A sense of the divine glory was, as it were, diffused through him. He thought how happy he should be if he might be rapt up to God in Heaven, swallowed up in him forever. He began to have an inward, sweet sense of Christ and the work of redemption. The Book of Canticles attracted him as a fit expression for his mood. It seemed to him as if he were in a kind of vision, alone in the mountains or some solitary wilderness, conversing sweetly with Christ and wrapt and swallowed up in God. . . . God's Excellency, his wisdom, his purity and love, seemed to appear in everything—in the sun, moon, and stars; in clouds and blue sky; in the grass, flowers, trees; in the water and all nature, which used greatly to fix my mind.[4]

In other moods the intellect gains ascendency over the emotions, and it is the idealistic metaphysician who speaks. With a searching curiosity that impelled him to ask what lies behind the outward semblance of things, binding them into a coherent whole and imparting to the world of experience a compelling unity, he came early to an interpretation distinctly Berkeleyan. From what source he derived it has been much debated and remains un-answered; nevertheless it is clear that it is closely related to his religious mysticism. When he inquired what lies back of the out-ward semblance, what is the thing in itself behind attributes and qualities, the existence of which is implicit in our perception of time and space, but which cannot be resolved into the things perceived, it was natural that he should have interpreted this *Ding an sich* in terms of God. "Men are wont to content them-selves by saying merely that it is something; but that something is *He* in whom all things consist."[5] The world of sensation thus translates itself into a world of ideas; and this world of ideas, the expression of the divine mind, is the only reality. The more important of his early generalizations are given by Allen in some

[4] *Jonathan Edwards*, p. 25.   [5] *Ibid.*, p. 13.

extracts from his notes on the "Mind": "Bodies have no existence of their own." "All existence is mental; the existence of all things is ideal." "The brain exists only mentally, or in idea." "Instead of matter being the only proper substance, and more substantial than anything else because it is hard and solid, yet it is truly nothing at all, strictly and in itself considered." "The universe exists nowhere but in the divine mind." "Space is necessary, eternal, infinite, and omnipresent. But I had as good speak plain. I have already said as much as that space is God." "And indeed the secret lies here,—that which truly is the substance of all bodies is the infinitely exact and precise and perfectly stable Idea in God's mind, together with His stable will that the same shall gradually be communicated to us, and to other minds, according to certain fixed and exact established methods and laws; or, in somewhat different language, the infinitely exact, precise, Divine Idea, together with the answerable, perfectly exact, precise, and stable will, with respect to correspondent communications to created minds and effects on their minds."[6]

Edwards had come to such conclusions before the normal unfolding of his mind was interrupted by his conversion. From the first a strong bias toward theology had tended to warp his interest in the purely metaphysical, and with the quickening of an active religious experience, he turned to examine the dogmas which expressed his faith. The call of the churches in distress came to him, and he made ready his logic to do battle with the enemy. Against the twin tendencies that were undermining the foundations of Calvinism—Arminianism with its humanistic emphasis and deism with its mechanistic—the deepest instincts of Edwards protested. The profound God-consciousness that filled him was stirred by what seemed an infidel attack upon the divine glory and sufficiency; the mystic and idealist was aroused to protest against a theology that conceived of religion as consisting of benevolence toward men rather than in union with God; and against a philosophy that in constructing a mechanical system was de-personalizing God into a vague First Cause, and bowing him politely out of the universe. In so great a crisis his duty seemed clear—to vindicate, not the ways of God, but God himself to men; to assert the glory

[6] For an examination of the philosophy of Edwards, see Adam Leroy Jones, "Early American Philosophers," in *Columbia University Contributions to Philosophy, Psychology and Education*, Vol. II, No. 4, Chapter 4.

and sufficiency of God even to the extent of minifying the capacities and potentialities of man.

The basis of his defense was already provided in his metaphysics, the conception of the divine idea existent in God's mind and expressed in His stable will. The needs of his polemics, however, thrust into relief the secondary rather than the primary element in his philosophy, exalting the doctrine of the divine will to the obscuring of the divine idea. How this came about is sufficiently clear in the light of the fact that in explaining the existence of evil, Calvinism fell back on determinism: the dogma of election could be fitted to the conception of a precise and stable will of God. The long feud between Arminianism and Calvinism resulted from emphasis laid upon different attributes of the Godhood. Shall God be interpreted in terms of will or love? If He is the sovereign ruler of the universe, He is also the common father; and that which broadly divides later theological systems from earlier is the shift from the former interpretation to the latter. The strategic weakness of Edwards's position lay in his assumption of the divine sovereignty as a cardinal postulate.

But in adhering to the doctrine of predetermined election by the sovereign will of God, Edwards did unconscious violence to the instincts of the mystic, that throughout his earlier speculations —and in much of his later, as well—impelled him to glorify the love of God the Father, and the sweetness of spiritual communion with Him. The practical necessities of the preacher, called upon to uphold the dogma of election in face of growing disbelief, seem to have forced him to such a position; but once having entered upon the train of speculation opened by the question of divine polity involved in "His having mercy on whom He will have mercy, while whom He will, He hardeneth," he came somewhat reluctantly to accept the doctrine of God's sovereignty as the cardinal principle of his theology, the creative source of his thinking. Thereafter he followed a path that led back to an absolutist past, rather than forward to a more liberal future. He had broken wholly with the social tendencies of his age and world.[7]

[7] For a statement of the doctrine, see Sermon XXXIV, "God's Sovereignty," in *Works*, New York, 1847, Vol. IV, p. 548.

Edwards unconsciously admits that the doctrine of sovereignty was reactionary. "From my childhood up, my mind had been full of objections against the doctrine of God's sovereignty, in choosing whom He would to eternal life, and rejecting whom He pleased, leaving them eternally to perish and be everlastingly tormented in hell." Later he came to regard such repugnance as the sinful expression of the

The philosophical conception of divine sovereignty was too abstract to concern the New England laity; it was rather against the dependent dogmas of election and total depravity that the revolt was rising. And in defense of these threatened dogmas Edwards put forth his best strength. The crux of the matter, obviously, lay in the difficult question of the power of will. The entire structure of Calvinistic theology had been erected upon the assumption of determinism; and it must stand or fall according as the argument should justify or fail to justify that hypothesis. If the human will is effectively free to choose between good and evil, the dogma of the elect must go down with the dogma of predestination; and the teachings of the Arminians—tending, as they seemed to the Calvinist, to abase the creator in exalting the creature, and minifying the sovereignty of God in magnifying the excellence of man—would be in a way to prevail. Around this crucial point the battle had long raged, and it was with full realization of the critical nature of the problem that Edwards resolved to penetrate to the root of the matter, and by subjecting the question of determinism to exact analysis, rout the enemies of Calvinism from the inmost keep of their stronghold. His celebrated work *On the Freedom of the Will*, written in 1754, not only was his most important contribution to theology, but it was the last great defense of the conservatism that was stifling the intellectual life of New England.

The argument of this knotty book rests on a psychological rather than a metaphysical basis. Compressed into the briefest terms it runs thus: will is subject to desire, and desire follows what seems to us good; hence the determining impulse is to be sought in the impulse to seek the apparent good. The ethical import of such an argument will turn, of course, upon the character of the good which the natural man may be expected to desire. To Rousseau with his benevolent interpretation of human nature nothing is to be feared from the subjection of will to desire. Nor to the younger Edwards, feeling his way along the path of tran-

natural man. As he saw further, his mind "apprehended the justice and reasonableness of . . . God's absolute sovereignty and justice with respect to salvation . . . as much as of anything that I see with my eyes; at least it is so at times. But I have often, since that first conviction, had quite another sense of God's sovereignty than I had then. I have often had not only a conviction, but a delightful conviction. The doctrine has very often appeared exceedingly pleasant, bright, and sweet. . . . But my first conviction was not so." Quoted in Allen, *Jonathan Edwards*, pp. 37–38.

scendentalism, rediscovering the doctrine of the inner light, was
such subjection to be feared. In a remarkable sermon published
in 1734, he had expounded the thesis, "That there is such a thing
as a Spiritual and Divine Light, immediately imparted to the
Soul by God, of a different nature from any that is obtained by
natural means." [8] The divine splendor which the idealist had
seen diffused through the material world the theologian was now
merging with the regenerative life of the Holy Spirit which "acts
in the mind of a saint as an in-dwelling vital principle." It is
"a kind of emanation of God's beauty, and is related to God as
the light is to the sun"; it is a new vision by means of which one
may "see the beauty and loveliness of spiritual things." In such
a reinterpretation of the Quaker doctrine—so harshly condemned
by the earlier Puritans—Edwards entered upon a train of thought
that threatened to disrupt the entire Calvinistic system. He was
at the dividing of the ways; he must abandon transcendentalism
or the dogma of total depravity.

Instead he sought refuge in compromise, endeavoring to reconcile what was incompatible. Herein lay the tragedy of Edwards's
intellectual life; the theologian triumphed over the philosopher,
circumscribing his powers to ignoble ends. The field of efficiency
allotted by the later theologian to this "in-dwelling vital principle,"
was no longer coextensive with the universe, but was narrowed
to the little world of the elect. In the primal state of man, Edwards
argued, before the sin of Adam had destroyed the harmony between
creature and creator, the light which flowed from God as from a
sun shone freely upon His universe, filling its remotest parts with
the divine plenitude; but with the fall the harmony was destroyed,
the sun was hidden, and only stray beams broke through the
rifts to shine upon those whom God willed them to shine upon; all
else in creation was given over to eternal darkness. And if the
natural man, thus cast into sudden darkness "as light ceases in a
room when the candle is withdrawn," is a being whose will is
impotent to his salvation, it follows that he will now be impelled
as inevitably towards evil as before he was impelled towards good.
Every instinct of a nature corrupt and compact of sin, and with
no wish to exchange darkness for light—having no eyes for the
divine glory—drives him to a blind and consuming hatred of God.
He is become as a loathsome "viper, hissing and spitting poison

[8] Sermon XXVII, in *Works*, Vol. IV, p. 438.

at God," the outcast and pariah of the universe. There is no drawing back from the conclusion involved in the argument; the Edwardean logic moves forward by regular steps. The punishment meted out to sin is to be measured by the excellence of which the sin is a denial. God is of infinite excellence, and denial of His excellence is therefore infinitely sinful and merits infinite punishment. As a perfectly just judge God could not decree otherwise; because of the infinite heinousness of his sin, the natural man must receive the doom of eternal damnation.[9]

Under the rod of such logic—grotesque, abortive, unseasoned by any saving knowledge of human nature—Edwards preached that remarkable series of imprecatory sermons that sank deep into the memory of New England, and for which it has never forgiven him.[10] Unfortunate as those sermons were in darkening the fame of an acute thinker, disastrous as they were in providing a sanction for other men to terrify the imaginations of ill-balanced persons, we cannot regret that Edwards devoted his logic to an assiduous stoking of the fires of hell. The theology of Calvin lay like a heavy weight upon the soul of New England, and there could be no surer way to bring it into disrepute, than to thrust into naked relief the brutal grotesqueries of those dogmas that professed thus to explain the dark mysteries which lie upon the horizons of life. For a long while yet they were to harass the imagination of New England, but the end already could be foreseen. Once the horrors that lay in the background of Calvinism were disclosed to common view, the system was doomed. It might still wear the semblance of life; it might still remain as an evil genius to darken the conscience of men and women; but its authoritative appeal was gone. In this necessary work of freeing the spirit of New England, no

[9] See Sermon IX, in *Works*, Vol. IV, p. 226. The argument is unfolded in the following propositions: "Every crime or fault deserves a greater or less punishment, according as the crime is greater or less." "A crime is more or less heinous, according as we are under greater or less obligations to the contrary." "Our obligations to love, honor, and obey any being, is in proportion to its loveliness, honorableness, and authority." "But God is a being infinitely lovely, because he hath infinite excellence and beauty." "So that sin against God, being a violation of infinite obligations, must be a crime infinitely heinous, and so deserving of infinite punishment."

[10] See in particular Sermon XI, "The Eternity of Hell Torments"; Sermon XII, "When the Wicked shall have filled up the measure of their Sin, wrath will come upon them to the uttermost"; Sermon XIII, "The End of the Wicked contemplated by the Righteous; or, The Torments of the Wicked in Hell, no occasion of grief to the Saints in Heaven"; Sermon XV, "Sinners in the Hands of an Angry God," in *Works*, Vol. IV.

other thinker played so large or so unconscious a part as Jonathan Edwards; and it was the notorious minatory sermons—the translation into vivid images of the generalized dogmas—that awakened the popular mind to an understanding of the conclusions involved in the premises.

While Edwards was thus hastening the decay of Calvinism with his lurid painting of "the landscape of hell," in another phase of his work he was engaged in awakening an interest in religion among the slothful churches. He had long been interested in the phenomena of conversion, and as the great revival of the forties, led by Whitefield, spread from England to the colonies, he joined eagerly in the work. In consequence of an earlier revival in his parish of Northampton, his attention had been drawn to the little understood psychology of the awakening soul, and with the detachment of the scientist he set himself to study the problem. The terrors aroused by his minatory sermons provided his clinical laboratory with numerous cases of abnormal emotionalism. Day after day he probed and analyzed and compared, until as a result of his close studies in vivisection, he became a specialist in the theory of conversion, commanding the eager attention of a generation that had come to look upon this as the central fact of Christian experience. It is not easy today to be sympathetic with this phase of Edwards's work; it belongs equally with his dogmas to a world of thought that is no longer ours. The repulsive records as they are set down in his *Narrative of the Surprizing Works of God*, marked by evidence of pathological states of mind not far removed from insanity, no longer seem a testimony to God's beneficent presence; the spiritual writhings which this gentle-natured student watched with such fascination, appear rather to be cases for the alienist to prescribe for. But to Edwards the terrors of a five-year-old girl were not pathological; they were the soul-labors of the spiritual rebirth, the visible signs of the supreme miracle of the universe, filling him with wonder and awe at God's infinite mercy; and like a modern psychologist he was at enormous pains to chart the successive steps in the miraculous transformation.[11]

[11] According to Edwards there were four regular stages: (1) the first stirrings, when the sinner is brought under conviction that he is lost; (2) the realization of God's justice, that he merits damnation; (3) the breaking in of the light, the first "gracious discoveries" of God's mercies; (4) peace after the storm, the joy of assurance of salvation. For a fuller statement, see Allen, *Jonathan Edwards*, pp. 133–160.

Other and greater consequences were to flow from the new revivalism. The Great Awakening was the single movement that stirred the colonial heart deeply during three generations. It reveals, among other things, that America was still living in the world of the seventeenth century: that the upper class was not yet rationalized, nor the middle class commercialized. Theology was still of greater popular interest than politics. In its chief phenomena the Great Awakening was a return to an earlier age— to those unbalanced enthusiasms of the Puritan upheaval. It was essentially a mass movement. Its use of hypnotic suggestion, its lurid terrorism, its outcries and hysterical possessions, reveal like the Ranters of a hundred years before the phenomena of mob psychology, and it made appeal to the ill-educated, the isolated, the neurotic, to the many natural victims of hypnotic excitation bred by the monotony and austerity of village life. Its after effects were revolutionary, for the quickening of religious emotionalism marked the beginning of the end of Puritan formalism.

The bitter quarrel among the churches which followed as an aftermath was more than a theological dispute; it was a sign of the breaking up of the traditional parish system. The hierarchy had long before lost its authority, but in their several parishes the ministers still enjoyed patriarchal power. The tragic dismissal of Edwards from his parish was an unprecedented revolt against that authority. But greater changes were to follow. After the Great Awakening itinerant preachers made their appearance, who presumed to enter any parish without the consent of the minister, and preach such doctrines as they would. They were non-conforming free lances, hostile to the established church, whose stock-in-trade was the new emotionalism. Under their leadership, Separatist congregations were gathered that were not only an offense to the regular establishment but a challenge to its authority. Hundreds left the old congregations and flocked to the Baptists and Methodists, and naturally they would make trouble over paying taxes to support a church they had repudiated. In short, a little revolution was under way that was to end in the complete disintegration of the parish system.

By a curious irony of fate, Jonathan Edwards, reactionary Calvinist and philosophical recluse, became the intellectual leader of the revolutionaries. His insistence upon conversion as the sole ground of admission to communion was the final blow that de-

stroyed the old theocratic system which the Mathers had labored
to uphold.   Church and state were effectively cut asunder by such
a test.   There is no evidence that Edwards was concerned about
the political or social consequences that must result from the
abandonment of the traditional "Half-way Covenant."   It was a
question of doctrine with him, involving only matters of church
discipline.   Although he was accused of being a Separatist, and of
seeking to disintegrate the parish system, he had no thought of
attacking a parochial order that he held in high esteem.   He was
unconcerned that his teachings led straight to the old Separatist
conclusion that it is the church mystical which Christ established,
and not the church visible.   Nevertheless he became the creator
of the new Congregationalism, which in accepting the democratic
principles elaborated by John Wise and establishing the local
church as an autonomous unit, effectively nullified the Presbyterian
tendencies of the old order.

As one follows the laborious career of this great thinker, a sense
of the tragic failure of his life deepens.   The burdens that he
assumed were beyond the strength of any man.   Beginning as a
mystic, brooding on the all-pervasive spirit of sweetness and light
diffused through the universe, with its promise of spiritual emancipation; then turning to an archaic theology and giving over his
middle years to the work of minifying the excellence of man in
order to exalt the sovereignty of God; and finally settling back
upon the mystical doctrine of conversion—such a life leaves one
with a feeling of futility, a sense of great powers baffled and wasted,
a spiritual tragedy enacted within the narrow walls of a minister's
study.   There was both pathos and irony in the fate of Jonathan
Edwards, removed from the familiar places where for twenty years
he had labored, the tie with his congregation broken, and sent to
the frontier mission at Stockbridge to preach to a band of Indians
and to speculate on the unfreedom of the human will.   The greatest
mind of New England had become an anachronism in a world that
bred Benjamin Franklin.   If he had been an Anglican like Bishop
Berkeley, if he had mingled with the leaders of thought in London
instead of remaining isolated in Massachusetts, he must have made
a name for himself not unworthy to be matched with that of the
great bishop whom he so much resembled.   The intellectual powers
were his, but the inspiration was lacking; like Cotton Mather
before him, he was the unconscious victim of a decadent ideal and

a petty environment.   Cut off from fruitful intercourse with other thinkers, drawn away from the stimulating field of philosophy into the arid realm of theology, it was his fate to devote his noble gifts to the thankless task of re-imprisoning the mind of New England within a system from which his nature and his powers summoned him to unshackle it.   He was called to be a transcendental emancipator, but he remained a Calvinist.

CHAPTER III

BENJAMIN FRANKLIN

Our First Ambassador

THERE was a singularly dramatic fitness in the life and career of Benjamin Franklin. America has never been more worthily represented at old-world capitals than by this unpretentious commoner, drawn from the stock of the plain people. A plebeian in an aristocratic age, he was nevertheless, by common consent, first among colonial Americans in qualities of mind and heart. A wit and philosopher, rich in learning, charming in manners, ripe in the wisdom of this world, resourceful in dealing with men and events, he was one of the most delightful as he was one of the greatest men produced by the English race in the eighteenth century.

"Figure to yourself," he wrote in his seventy-second year, "an old man, with gray hair appearing under a marten fur cap, among the powdered heads of Paris. It is this odd figure that salutes you, with handfuls of blessings." An odd figure indeed in such a setting, but a figure that captured the imagination of Paris, as it has since captured the imagination of America; so novel as to seem romantic—a charming rustic philosopher who might have stepped out of the pages of Rousseau. And so the French aristocracy patronized *le bon homme*, and laughed with him at the affectations of this preposterous world, and made much of him for the zest that it discovered in a novel sensation. It was the same odd figure that had stood at the bar of the House of Commons and matched his intelligence against that of celebrated English lawyers; the same figure that had been called in council by the great Pitt—who thought himself too great to learn anything even from Franklin; that had been lashed by the scurrilous tongue of Wedderburn; that had seen a thousand bribes dangled before him by Lord Howe and other gentlemen—a figure that seems strangely out of place in that old-fashioned Tory world, with its narrow sympathies and narrower intelligence. And yet considered in the light of social revolutions, what other figure in eighteenth-century

164

Europe or America is so dramatically significant? The figure of
the self-made democrat, with some three millions of his fellows
at his back, and countless other millions to come, who was entering
on a world-wide struggle for political mastery, the end of which no
one can yet foresee? His presence in the councils of gentlemen was
a tacit denial of their hitherto unquestioned right of supremacy.
It was a rare personal triumph; but it was far more significant than
that, it was the triumph of a rising class and a new social ideal.

Although Franklin's origins, whether Boston or Philadelphia,
were narrowly provincial, his mind from early youth to extreme
old age was curiously open and free, and to such a mind the intellectual wealth of the world lies open and free. From that
wealth he helped himself generously, to such good effect that he
early became an intellectual cosmopolitan, at ease with the best
intellects and at home among the diverse speculative interests of
the eighteenth century: the sane and witty embodiment of its
rationalism, its emancipation from authority, its growing concern
for social justice, its hopeful pursuit of new political and economic
philosophies, its tempered optimism that trusted intelligence to
set the world right. No other man in America and few in Europe
had so completely freed themselves from the prejudice of custom.
The Calvinism in which he was bred left not the slightest trace
upon him; and the middle-class world from which he emerged did
not narrow his mind to its petty horizons. He was a free man who
went his own way with imperturbable good will and unbiased
intelligence; our first social philosopher, the first ambassador of
American democracy to the courts of Europe.

Fortune was kind to Franklin in many ways: kind in that it
did not visit upon him the fate that befell his elder brother Ebenezer, of whom Sewall noted, "Ebenezer Franklin of the South
Church, a male-Infant of 16 months old, was drowned in a Tub
of Suds, Febr. 5, 1702/3"; kind also in that it set him in a land
where opportunity waited upon enterprise, and where thousands
of kindred spirits were erecting a society that honored such qualities as he possessed. In England he must have remained middle-
class, shut in by a wall of prejudice; but in colonial America he
found a congenial environment. Like Samuel Sewall, he swam
easily in the main current of colonial life, won increasing honors,
until—as he naïvely remarked—he came more than once to stand
before kings. How fortunate he was is revealed by contrast with

the career of his great English counterpart and fellow spirit, Daniel Defoe, whose *Essay on Projects*—a classic document of the rising middle class—might well have been Franklin's first textbook.

The earliest literary representative of the English middle class, Defoe preached the same gospel of social betterment. With his head full of projects for the advancement of trade and the material well-being of his fellows, he preached the new gospel of practical efficiency to a generation of wits, going so far as to assert that the ideal statesman should be sought, not among gentlemen but among merchants, whose training in business affairs had made them shrewd judges of men and capable in dealing with practical matters. But the London of Queen Anne was not a place in which to rise by preaching efficiency. Defoe's day had not yet come in England, and in spite of great abilities and arduous labors he remained a Grub Street hack, the servant and not the counselor of aristocratic politicians. Instead of coming to stand before kings—like the more fortunate Franklin—he stood often before constables; instead of cracking his joke and his bottle at Will's Coffee House, he was forced to study the ways of the unprosperous at Bridewell. But if he failed in his ambition to get on, he found a certain solace in the vicarious realization of his ideal. Robinson Crusoe, the practically efficient man making himself master of his environment, was the dream of Daniel Defoe; Franklin was the visible, new-world embodiment of that dream.

It was Franklin's supreme capacity for doing well the things which his fellow Americans held in esteem, that enabled him to rise out of obscurity to a position of leadership. Before he should be intrusted with the confidence of his fellow citizens, he must prove himself worthy of such confidence, and even in colonial America the task was far from easy. In the wealthier communities society was exclusive and select—nowhere more so than in Philadelphia— and it could not be expected to view with approval the advancement of a printer-tradesman, especially if he were a member of the plebeian anti-Proprietary party. It was an evidence of Franklin's discretion that he removed from Boston, where neither his father's chandlery shop, nor his brother's baiting of the ruling gentry, would serve his purpose. In Philadelphia, free from family entanglements, he bent himself to the task of securing a competence, understanding how easily the wheel turns on a well-greased axle;

and by the time he had come to his early forties he had kept his shop so well that henceforth it would keep him. He was ready to do his real work in the world; and in the choice of that work he revealed the curious *flair* for the timely that was so characteristic. His extraordinary successes in the field of civic betterments gained him the good will of the commonalty, and his experiments in natural philosophy won the approbation of the gentry. Interest in scientific inquiry, particularly in physics, had spread widely in England since the founding of the Royal Society, and to be an authority on magnetism was as evident a mark of breeding in Georgian England as discriminating judgment in the matter of manuscripts and mistresses had been a sign of culture among Florentine cinquecentists. In establishing a reputation as a natural philosopher, therefore, Franklin not only was acquiring dignity at home, but he was providing himself with a sure passport to European favor. And it was the seal of European approval that finally won for Franklin the grudging recognition of the first families of Philadelphia. A few held out against him and to the day of his death regarded him with disapproval; but in the end his personal charm prevailed with all but a handful of elderly Tory ladies. So delightful a wit and so useful a citizen could not be dismissed as a pushing tradesman.

Franklin first entered politics as a member of the popular party, then engaged in a bitter struggle with the Proprietors over tax matters, defense of the frontier, and other questions of acute popular concern. There was the usual colonial alignment between the backcountry yeomanry and the town gentry; between the agrarian and mercantile interests; and the dispute had reached a point where the yeomanry determined to appeal to the King to convert the commonwealth into a Crown Colony. As one of the leaders of the popular party, Franklin was singled out for attack. A bitter election went against him, and he lost his seat in the Assembly, only to be chosen Colonial Agent to England, there to begin his long diplomatic career. Probably no other attack which Franklin suffered was so coarse or vindictive as this assault by the Proprietary party, led by the first gentlemen of Philadelphia, John Dickinson among them. Unpleasant as the experience was, it proved of service to Franklin, for it taught him how quickly the hornets would be about the ears of anyone who disturbed the nest of official perquisites; and this was worth knowing to a colonial diplomat on his first mission to a court and parliament where yellow jackets were uncommonly abundant.[1]

He was nearly threescore when he set out on his diplomatic mission, which beginning modestly as temporary agent of the anti-Proprietary party of Pennsylvania, was to broaden immensely as the American difficulties increased, until he became in the eyes of all the world the spokesman of the colonial cause; first at London to King, Parliament, and people, and later at Paris to all Europe. It was a mission of discussion and argument, curiously illuminating to a colonial bred in a simple, decentralized world. Before he went abroad Franklin had been a democrat by temperament and environment; when he returned he was a democrat by conviction, confirmed in his preference for government immediately responsible to the majority will. Centralized Tory governments had taught him the excellence of town-meeting ways. At London he discovered widespread political corruption. It was a world flyblown with the vices of irresponsible power. The letters of Franklin are full of the scandal of bribe-taking and pension-mongering, of gross parliamentary jobbery. The elections of 1768 were a debauch, the brisk bidding of Indian nabobs sending the market price of parliamentary seats up to four thousand pounds. "It is thought," he wrote on March 13, "that near two millions will be spent on this election; but those, who understand figures and act by computation, say the crown has *two millions in places and pensions* to dispose of, and it is well worth while to engage in such a seven years lottery, though all that have tickets should not get prizes." [2] To expect such a government to be swayed by appeals to justice or abstract rights was plain folly, Franklin very quickly learned.

[1] "You know," wrote Franklin to his wife on the eve of his departure, "that I have many enemies . . . and very bitter ones; and you must expect their enmity will extend in some degree to you." He was forced to slip away and get secretly on board the vessel. His activities were reproved thus by a certain Tory lady:

Oh! had he been wise to pursue
The track for his talents designed,
What a tribute of praise had been due
To the teacher and friend of mankind.

But to covet political fame
Was in him a degrading ambition,
The spark that from Lucifer came,
And kindled the blaze of sedition.

(In *Works*, Vol. VII, p. 267.)

In Sargent's *Loyal Verses of Joseph Stansbury and Doctor Jonathan Odell*, these verses are attributed to a less likely source.
[2] *Works*, Vol. VII, p. 398.

The colonial goose was there to be plucked, and gentlemen who gained their livelihood by skillful plucking would not easily be denied. "To get a larger field on which to fatten a herd of worthless parasites, is all that is regarded," wrote the celebrated London physician, Dr. Fothergill, to Franklin.[3] Even war with the colonies might not seem undesirable to some, for "an auditor of the exchequer has sixpence in the pound, or a fortieth part, of all the public money expended by the nation, so that, when a war costs forty millions, one million is paid to him."[4]

It was a bitter experience for one who had grown up in respect for England and veneration for English traditions. Franklin was not a man of divided loyalties, and his love of the old home was deep and sincere. He had many warm friends there, and the idea of American separation from the empire was profoundly repugnant to him. It was not till he was convinced beyond hope that America could expect from the English government nothing but ignoble dependence that he accepted the idea of independence. Again and again he complained bitterly of "the extreme corruption prevalent among all orders of men in this rotten old state."[5] "I wish all the friends of liberty and of man would quit that sink of corruption, and leave it to its fate." "I do not expect that your new Parliament will be either wiser or honester than the last. All projects to procure an honest one, by place bills, etc., appear to me vain and impracticable. The true cure, I imagine, is to be found in rendering all places unprofitable, and the King too poor to give bribes and pensions. Till this is done, which can only be by a revolution (and I think you have not virtue enough left to procure one), your nation will always be plundered, and obliged to pay by taxes the plunderers for plundering and ruining. Liberty

---

[3] *Ibid.*, Vol. V, p. 81.

[4] *Ibid.*, Vol. II, p. 428. A good deal of light is thrown upon the ways of the ministry in Franklin's account, *Negotiations in London.* See in particular pp. 37, 68, 76 of Vol. V, where Lord Hyde and Lord Howe exhibit special solicitude for his advancement. His letters tell of successive attempts to approach him, and among his works is a little skit in which he speaks of himself thus: "Your correspondent *Brittannicus* inveighs violently against Dr. Franklin, for his ingratitude to the ministry of this nation, who have conferred upon him so many favors. They gave him the post-office of America; they made his son a governor; and they offered him a post of five hundred a year in the salt-office, if he would relinquish the interests of his country; but he has had the wickedness to continue true to it, and is as much an American as ever. As it is a settled point in government here, that every man has his price, it is plain they are bunglers in their business, and have not given him enough." (*Works*, Vol. IV, pp. 534–535.)

[5] *Ibid.*, Vol. VIII, p. 146.

and virtue therefore join in the call, COME OUT OF HER, MY PEO-
PLE!"[6] "The people of England . . , are just and generous,"
wrote his friend David Hartley, member of Parliament, "and,
if it were put to the sense of the people of England, you would
not be left in any doubt whether it was *want of will*, or *want of power*,
to do you justice. You know the blot of our constitution, by
which, to our disgrace, and to your misfortune, a corrupt ministry,
sheltered by Parliamentary influence, are out of our immediate
control. A day of account may come, when the justice of the
nation may prevail; and if it comes not too late, it may prove a
day of reconciliation and cordial reunion between us and America."[7]
He is blind indeed who cannot see in such experience the explanation of Franklin's later efforts in Pennsylvania and in the constitutional convention to keep government in America responsive to
the will of the people.

During the long years of his ambassadorship, so rich in intellectual opportunity, Franklin was intimately concerned with economics
and politics, and he found in them subjects congenial to his talents.
By temperament he was what we should call today a sociologist.
He cared little for abstract reasoning, but much for social betterment; and this led him to examine critically current economic
theory in the light of present fact. All his life economics was a
major interest with him, and his several contributions entitle him
to be regarded as our first important economist, the only one
indeed before the nineteenth century. His chief guides in this
little explored field seem to have been Sir William Petty, the
statistician of the Restoration period, in his younger days, and the
French Physiocrats in later years. He was the first American to
abandon the traditional mercantile school—a generation before
other American thinkers had repudiated it; and he was the first to
ally himself with the rising school of *laissez faire*.

In the year 1729, when he was just turned twenty-three, Franklin
entered the field of economics with a pamphlet entitled *A Modest
Inquiry into the Nature and Necessity of a Paper Currency*. It is
a curiously suggestive work, not only for the light which it sheds
on his economic views, but on his social and political sympathies.
It marks his early alignment with the agrarian party, to which he
adhered to the end of his life. From the days when Samuel Sewall
first confronted the question of land-banks in the Massachusetts

<hr />

[6] *Ibid.*, Vol. VIII, pp. 215, 505.   [7] *Ibid.*, Vol. VIII, p. 177.

legislature till the British government forbade all issues of bills
of credit, the currency question was bitterly debated in the several
colonies. It was primarily a class issue, in which the town merchants and money lenders found themselves outvoted by the
agrarian debtors and small men. Little light had come from those
debates on the nature of money and its social functions; but much
heat had been engendered over the supposed question of honest
versus dishonest money. With this cheap fallacy Franklin was
not concerned; but he was greatly concerned in this and in later
papers in expounding the quantitative theory of money, the
nature of credit, and the important fact, overlooked by the hard-
money men, that gold and silver are themselves commodities,
fluctuating in value with supply and demand. This first pamphlet,
Franklin afterward remarked, "was well received by the common
people in general; but the rich men disliked it, for it increased and
strengthened the clamor for more money; and, they happening
to have no writers among them that were able to answer it, their
opposition slackened, and the point was carried by a majority in
the House." [8]

By much the most interesting idea in the pamphlet, however,
is the elaboration of the labor theory of value. Commenting on
this, McMaster says in his *Life of Franklin:*

> Bad as were his notions of political economy, his pamphlet contained
> one great truth,—the truth that labor is the measure of value. Whether
> he discovered, or, as is not unlikely, borrowed it, he was the first openly
> to assert it; and his it remained till, forty-seven years later, Adam Smith
> adopted it and reaffirmed it in "The Wealth of Nations." [9]

Unfortunately the biographer's knowledge of the history of economic thought was as faulty as, in his judgment, were Franklin's
economic principles. In his *Treatise of Taxes*, written in 1662,
Sir William Petty—whom Franklin in many ways greatly resembled—clearly elaborated the principle of labor-value; [10] it
was restated by Vauban in 1707, in his *Projet d'une disme Royale*,
by Hume in 1752, and later by the Physiocrats; and when Adam
Smith wrote it was pretty widely known. There can be little
doubt where Franklin got it. The similarity between his work
and that of Sir William Petty is too evident to escape comment.
But that does not lessen the significance of the fact that a self-

---

[8] *Works*, Vol. II, p. 254.   [9] P. 64.
[10] See *Economic Writings of Sir W. Petty*, Cambridge Press, Vol. I, pp. 43–51.

trained provincial of three and twenty should have read Petty's work, seized upon the salient idea and turned it to effective use, years before economic students generally were acquainted with it. All his life Franklin took up ideas like a sponge, and what he took he incorporated with the solid results of his own observations.

During his stay in England Franklin came in close contact with the body of Physiocratic writings, which seem to have greatly stimulated his interest in economic thought. The school was at the height of its influence between the years 1763 and 1772, and had pretty well undermined the position of the mercantilists. They were the founders of modern social science and their teachings contained in germ the liberal doctrine of economics in its entirety. In their emphasis upon free trade and *laissez-faire* competition, on the police theory of the state, on property, security, liberty, on the natural laws of association and self-interest, and especially in their emphasis on land as the sole source of wealth, they presented a system of economics that fitted American conditions as Franklin understood those conditions. In one important point— their acceptance of an absolute prince—Franklin broke with them wholly; but their preference for agriculture over manufacturing and commerce accorded with his deepest convictions. America was notably happy and contented in comparison with Europe, and America would remain happy and contented, he believed, so long as land was abundant and her farmers remained freeholders. The new middle-class gospel of industrialism he profoundly distrusted. He shared Goldsmith's concern over the destruction of the English peasantry and the creation of a degraded proletariat. Manufacture and trade developed only where free land was inadequate or the peasants were dispossessed; industrialism sprang from the national poverty and was nourished by it. Writing in 1760 he said:

Unprejudiced men well know, that all the penal and prohibitory laws that were ever thought on will not be sufficient to prevent manufactures in a country, whose inhabitants surpass the number that can subsist by the husbandry of it. . . . Manufactures are founded in poverty. It is the number of poor without land in a country, and who must work for others at low wages or starve, that enables undertakers to carry on a manufacture, and afford it cheap enough to prevent the importation of the same kind from abroad, and to bear the expense of its own exportation. But no man, who can have a piece of land of his own, sufficient by his labor to subsist his family in plenty, is poor enough to be a manufacturer, and work for a master. Hence while there is land enough in America for our people, there can never be manufactures to any amount or value.[11]

Nine years later, in his *Positions to be Examined, concerning National Wealth*, he stated the Physiocratic theory thus:

There seem to be but three ways for a nation to acquire wealth. The first is by *war*, as the Romans did, in plundering their conquered neighbors. This is *robbery*. The second by *commerce*, which is generally *cheating*. The third by *agriculture*, the only *honest way*, wherein man receives a real increase of the seed thrown into the ground, in a kind of continual miracle, wrought by the hand of God in his favor.[12]

Franklin's prejudice against trade somewhat lessened in after years, as he considered the economic need of free exchange of commodities. In 1774, two years before the publication of *The Wealth of Nations*, he collaborated with George Whately in writing a pamphlet entitled *Principles of Trade*, that suggests Adam Smith. Franklin was acquainted with Smith, had visited him, and doubtless had discussed with him the theory of *laissez faire*, division of labor, use of machinery, and other principles of the new school, but no mention of him is made.[13] The central doctrine is thus elaborated:

Perhaps, in general, it would be better if government meddled no farther with trade, than to protect it, and let it take its course. Most of the statutes, or acts, edicts, *arrêts*, and placarts of parliaments, princes, and states, for regulating, directing, or restraining of trade, have, we think, been either political blunders, or jobs obtained by artful men for private advantage, under pretense of public good. When Colbert assembled some wise old merchants of France, and desired their advice and opinion, how he could best serve and promote commerce, their answer, after consultation, was, in three words only, *Laissez-nous faire:* "Let us alone." It is said by a very solid writer of the same nation, that he is well advanced in the science of politics, who knows the full force of that maxim, *Pas trop gouverner:* "Not to govern too much." Which, perhaps, would be of more use when applied to trade, than in any other public concern. It were therefore to be wished, that commerce was as free between all the nations of the world, as it is between the several counties of England; so would all, by mutual communication, obtain more enjoyments. Those counties do not ruin one another by trade; neither would the nations. No nation was ever ruined by trade, even seemingly the most disadvantageous.[14]

As a colonial, long familiar with the injustice of Navigation Laws, Boards of Trade, and other restrictions in favor of British tradesmen, Franklin agreed with Adam Smith on the principle

[11] *Works*, Vol. IV, p. 19.   [12] *Ibid.*, Vol. II, p. 376.
[13] *Ibid.*, Vol. II, p. 438.   [14] *Ibid.*, Vol. II, p. 401.

of free trade; but with later developments of the *laissez-faire*
school—its fetish of the economic man and its iron law of wages—
he would not have agreed. Plugson of Undershot was no hero
of his, and the social system which Plugson was creating would
have seemed to him as vicious as the old system with its "bad,
wasteful, plundering governments, and their mad destructive
wars." In his later speculations he was rather the social philosopher than the economist, puzzled at the irrationality of society
that chooses to make a pigsty of the world, instead of the garden
that it might be if men would but use the sense that God has given
them. "The happiness of individuals is evidently the ultimate
end of political society,"[15] he believed, and a starvation wage-
system was the surest way of destroying that happiness.[16] In
one of the most delightful letters that he ever wrote, Franklin
commented on the ways of men thus:

It is wonderful how preposterously the affairs of this world are managed.
Naturally one would imagine, that the interests of a few individuals should
give way to general interest; but individuals manage their affairs with so
much more application, industry, and address, than the public do theirs,
that general interest most commonly gives way to particular. We assemble parliaments and councils, to have the benefit of their collected wisdom;
but we necessarily have, at the same time, the inconvenience of their
collected passions, prejudices, and private interests. By the help of these,
artful men overpower their wisdom and dupe its possessors; and if we may
judge by the acts, *arrêts*, and edicts, all the world over, for regulating commerce, an assembly of great men is the greatest fool upon earth?. . . .
What occasions then so much want and misery? It is the employment
of men and women in works, that produce neither the necessaries nor
conveniences of life, who, with those who do nothing, consume necessaries
raised by the laborious. . . . Look round the world, and see the millions
employed in doing nothing, or in something that amounts to nothing, when
the necessaries and conveniences of life are in question. What is the bulk
of commerce, for which we fight and destroy each other, but the toil of
millions for superfluities, to the great hazard and loss of many lives? . . .
It has been computed by some political arithmetician, that, if every man
and woman would work for four hours each day on something useful, that
labor would produce sufficient to procure all the necessaries and comforts of
life, want and misery would be banished out of the world, and the rest of
the twenty-four hours might be leisure and happiness.[17]

But the immediate problem of Franklin as representative of the
colonies at St. James's, was political—how to reconcile the antag-

[15] *Ibid.*, Vol. II, p. 323.
[16] See "Reflections on the Augmentation of Wages, etc.," in *Ibid.*, Vol. II, p. 436.
[17] "On Luxury, Idleness, and Industry," in *Ibid.*, Vol. II, pp. 448–451.

onistic ambitions of the sundered bodies of Englishmen; and the solution which he set forth with admirable clearness, bears the impress of a mind intent upon the reality behind parchment pretense. While lawyers were befogging the issue with legal quibble, and politicians were proving the unconstitutionality of the forces stirring in eighteenth-century America, Franklin was more concerned with adjusting imperial policy to existing fact. On one side were the colonies, in which the practice of local self-government had taken deep root; whether the practice was sanctioned by their charters or the British constitution was beside the question. On the other side was the British parliament, serving as a legislative body for its proper constituency, the people of the British Isles. Over both colonies and parliament, providing an effective but ungalling tie to bind the parts together, was the King, to whom both paid willing allegiance. So long as England was content to maintain the *status quo*, the colonies, Franklin believed, would remain loyal to the empire; but if the ministry persisted in its program of extending parliamentary sovereignty over the colonies, the outcome must be one of two things, federation or separation.

To the principle of federation Franklin was an early and faithful friend. The conception of a federal union of the several colonies was slowly spreading in America, and no other colonial had done so much to further it; in his well-known Plan of Union he had sketched the outlines of a federal constitution; what was more natural, therefore, than for him to think in terms of a Federated British Empire, as a statesmanlike solution of the present perplexities. The plan involved two problems: first, an inquiry into the nature and constitution of an imperial parliament, and second, provision for an equitable representation of the several divisions of the empire. The present difficulties had arisen out of the ambition of the British parliament to assume sovereignty over the colonial legislatures, thereby reducing them to a dependent status; those difficulties would be settled only by constitutional recognition of local rights and local sovereignties. "The British state," he argued, "is only the Island of Great Britain," and if by reason of familiarity with local needs, "the British legislature" is "the only proper judge of what concerns the welfare of that state," why does the principle not hold for the several colonial legislatures?

Here appears the excellency of the invention of colony government, by separate, independent legislatures. By this means, the remotest parts of a great empire may be as well governed as the centre; misrule, oppressions of proconsuls, and discontents and rebellions thence arising, prevented. By this means, the power of a king may be extended without inconvenience over territories of any dimensions, how great soever. America was thus happily governed in all its different and remote settlements, by the crown and their own Assemblies, till the new politics took place, of governing it by one Parliament, which have not succeeded and never will.[18]

In this dream of a British Empire Franklin was far in advance of his time. On both sides of the ocean selfish and unimaginative men stood ready to thwart all such proposals; little Englanders and little colonials in vast numbers were concerned with more immediate and personal interests than those of the English race. Nevertheless Franklin was convinced that the gods, if not the Tories, were on the side of the colonies. The enormous increase in material strength that the years were swiftly bringing to America was an augury of good hope; the legitimate demands of America would be granted when America had grown too strong to be denied, which must be shortly. In the meantime it was the duty of Englishmen, British and colonial alike, to endeavor "with unfeigned and unwearying zeal to preserve from breaking that fine and noble China vase, the British empire." It was the traditional policy of "protract and grow strong"—a wise and sane policy—and Franklin clung to it until he was convinced of its utter futility. One other choice remained—separation; and he made that choice sadly, understanding better than most what it involved.

The years which followed were filled to the brim for Franklin as well as for America. Ideals changed and principles clarified swiftly; but his social philosophy was founded on too wide and sobering an experience with men and governments, to sway with every gusty passion of the times. He had been a democrat from his youth up and in those critical first days of independence, when the forces of agrarianism were taking possession of state governments, he threw in his lot with them, and joined heartily in the stimulating work of providing a democratic constitution for Pennsylvania. During the later years of reaction following the peace, when so many Revolutionary leaders endeavored to stay the agrarian movement and undo its work, he saw no cause to lose faith in government immediately responsive to the majority will. He was a forerunner of Jefferson, like him firm in the con-

[18] *Works*, Vol. IV, p. 282. For Franklin's views on American representation in Parliament, see Vol. VII, pp. 315, 329.

viction that government was good in the measure that it remained close to the people. He sat in the Constitutional Convention as one of the few democrats, and although he was unable to make headway against the aristocratic majority, he was quite unconvinced by their rhetoric. For years he had been an advocate of unrestricted manhood suffrage, annual parliaments,[19] and a single-chamber legislature; and when he heard eloquent young lawyers argue that a single-chamber legislature, responsive to a democratic electorate, must lead to mob legislation, and that good government required a carefully calculated system of checks and balances, he remarked:

It appears to me . . . like putting one horse before a cart and the other behind it, and whipping them both. If the horses are of equal strength, the wheels of the cart, like the wheels of government, will stand still; and if the horses are strong enough the cart will be torn to pieces.[20]

When in 1790 it was proposed to substitute a bicameral system for the single-chamber in Pennsylvania, Franklin came to the defense of the simpler, more democratic form, with a vivacity little staled by years:

Has not the famous political fable of the snake, with two heads and one body, some useful instruction contained in it? She was going to a brook to drink, and in her way was to pass through a hedge, a twig of which opposed her direct course; one head chose to go on the right side of the twig, the other on the left; so that time was spent in the contest, and before the decision was completed, the poor snake died with thirst.[21]

Both his economic principles and his views on government have been condemned by Federalistic critics as tainted with populism. They both sprang from the same root of agrarian democracy. Whether Franklin or his critics more adequately represented the larger interests of eighteenth-century America is beside the present question; it is enough to note that all such criticism is leveled primarily at Franklin's democratic philosophy as a thing in itself undesirable, if not dangerous.

Franklin may often have been wrong, but he was never arrogant, never dogmatic. He was too wise and too generous for that. In the midst of prosperity he never forgot the unprosperous. All his

[19] See the pamphlet indorsed *Some Good Whig Principles*, of the probable date of 1768–69, in *Works*, Vol. II.
[20] *Works of Thomas Paine*, edited by Moncure D. Conway, Vol. IV, p. 465.
[21] In "Queries and Remarks Respecting Alterations in the Constitution of Pennsylvania," in *Works*, Vol. V, p. 167.

life his sympathy went out to whoever suffered in person or fortune from the injustice of society: to the debtor who found himself pinched by the shrinking supply of currency; to the black slave who suffered the most elementary of wrongs; to impressed seamen; to the weak and wretched of earth. He was a part of that emerging humanitarian movement which, during the last half of the eighteenth century, was creating a new sense of social responsibility. True to his Physiocratic convictions, Franklin was social-minded. He was concerned not with property or class interests, but with the common welfare; and in his quick sympathy for all sorts and conditions of men, in his conviction that he must use his talents to make this world better and not exploit it, he reveals the breadth and generosity of his nature. Reason and work, in his pragmatic philosophy, are the faithful handmaids of progress, of which war, whether public or private, is the utter negation. After long years of thought he rendered a judgment which later experience has not reversed,—"there is no good war and no bad peace."

It is to little purpose that certain shortcomings of Franklin are dwelt upon. "There is a flower of religion, a flower of honor, a flower of chivalry, that you must not require of Franklin," said Sainte-Beuve; a judgment that is quite true and quite obvious. A man who is less concerned with the golden pavements of the City of God than that the cobblestones on Chestnut Street in Philadelphia should be well and evenly laid, who troubles less to save his soul from burning hereafter than to protect his neighbors' houses by organizing an efficient fire-company, who is less regardful of the light that never was on sea or land than of a new-model street lamp to light the steps of the belated wayfarer—such a man, obviously, does not reveal the full measure of human aspiration. Franklin ended as he began, the child of a century marked by sharp spiritual limitations. What was best in that century he made his own. In his modesty, his willingness to compromise, his openmindedness, his clear and luminous understanding, his charity—above all, in his desire to subdue the ugly facts of society to some more rational scheme of things—he proved himself a great and useful man, one of the greatest and most useful whom America has produced.

PART TWO: THE AWAKENING OF THE AMERICAN MIND
1763–1783

CHAPTER I

IMPERIAL SOVEREIGNTY AND HOME RULE

I

BACKGROUND FACTS

THE American Revolution remains after a hundred and fifty years somewhat of a puzzle to historians. Much careful investigation has been done in the last two decades, but we still know too little to speak confidently or with a sense of finality. The appeal to arms would seem to have been brought about by a minority of the American people, directed by a small group of skillful leaders, who like Indian scouts, covered their tracks so cleverly that only the keenest trailers can now follow their course and understand their strategy. On the other hand, the philosophy of revolution is familiar to us. Revolutions are born of an abnormal state of mind, sensitized by an accumulated body of experience. They are psychological explosions, resulting from irritations commonly economic in origin, and they are conditioned in their programs by the stock of knowledge and aspiration peculiar to their time and place. Two determining facts, then, would seem to lie at the root of the American Revolution: the American psychology which shaped the colonial outlook, and the peculiar situation of the British Empire at the close of the French and Indian war.[1]

In old age John Adams "hazarded an opinion, that the true history of the American revolution could not be recovered," for "the revolution was effected before the war commenced. The revolution was in the minds and hearts of the people."[2] Accepting Adams's thesis of a change in American psychology, we may hazard a further opinion that the revolution resulted from the emergence

[1] An excellent short statement of the causes of the American Revolution is given by A. M. Schlesinger in *New Viewpoints in American History*, Chapter VII. Compare C. H. Van Tyne, *The Causes of the War of Independence*.

[2] Letter to Mr. Niles, January 14, 1818.

in the two countries of divergent interpretations of the theory and practice of sovereignty, which may be sufficiently distinguished by the terms local home rule and imperial centralization. In the beginning it was a clash of jurisdiction between colonial self-government and absentee paternalism; but later it developed into an open challenge of the monarchical principle. A popular will to self-rule had long been developing in America, and when the outbreak of hostilities clarified its latent objective, it speedily asserted a conscious republican purpose. To many of the early supporters of the colonial protest, this republican outcome was unforeseen and deeply regretted; but it was implicit in the whole history of colonial development, and must ultimately stand sharply revealed, once its aspirations were balked.

If the crisis was precipitated almost casually by the program of parliamentary regulation, the long drift towards alienation was far from casual. An American mind had been created by the silent pressure of environment. A large measure of economic freedom had developed an American liberalism, frankly and vigorously individualistic. It was not consciously democratic, or even republican. There were few avowed democrats in the stolid mass of colonial provincialism; a busy and commonplace routine offered little opportunity for revolutionary appeal to a people grown lethargic from economic abundance. Of social unrest, the common fuel of revolutionary fires, there was practically none; and but for a blundering ministerial imperialism that challenged this nascent liberalism, throwing over it the mantle of patriotism, the colonies would have written a very different history. Once the crisis was precipitated, however, and it became clear that imperial centralization was encroaching upon local rights, the liberal impulses in the background of the American mind assumed a militant form and purpose.

The existence of this native liberalism had been stupidly overlooked and ignored by responsible statesmen. With the exception of Franklin, colonial spokesmen were commonly members of the aristocratic group, among whom the Tory philosophy was spreading fast. Gentlemen in Boston, New York, Philadelphia, and Charleston fashioned their manners upon the polite world of St. James's and caught the Tory ways in politics as naturally as the London style in wigs. They associated with the royal officials, traveled in England, corresponded with members of Parliament, advised in all matters of colonial policy, and proved themselves the most shortsighted of counselors. Upon their heads rest in part the blunders of the ministry. In failing to understand the native liberalism of America, they not only shared responsibility for an unwise policy, but they hastened their own destruction. Samuel Adams could not have played so effectively upon the popular prejudices if the Hutchinsons and Olivers had not brought the Tory ways into wide disrepute by their arrogance.

Colonial liberalism, on the other hand, was not so simple and homogeneous as we long believed. It was rather a somewhat vague composite of the aspirations of three diverse geographical areas, with different economic interests, social ways, and political ideals. The middle and northern coast region, with its mercantile cities, was a distinct area; the tidewater region from Maryland to Georgia, with its plantation economy, constituted another; and the indefinite backcountry beyond the older settlements, stretching from Maine southward along the Alleghany watershed, constituted a third. The first was dominated by a merchant group—wholesale importers and exporters—wealthy and conservative, but with a great majority of the population—small tradesmen, mechanics and yeomen—far more democratic than the leaders. The second was controlled by the aristocratic planters, whose leadership during the crises of the dispute with England was rejected by an economically strong but socially inferior body of factors or alien middlemen. The third was composed of thousands of small freeholders, largely Scotch-Irish and German, who acknowledged no leadership, were unconsciously democratic in their ways, suspicious of the seacoast aristocracy, wedded to an agrarian philosophy. The merchant group was liberal only to the extent that liberalism meant profit: their commercial relations with England constituted them the closest tie between the two countries, and their timid love of established ways made them naturally conservative rather than revolutionary. The planter group possessed the traditional independence of English gentlemen: they would tolerate no outside dictation in matters concerning their own parishes, and their burdensome debts to English merchants cooled the ardor of their loyalty to Great Britain. The frontier agrarians, on the other hand, were pronounced liberals by environment and training to whom English ties were at the strongest only sentimental. They were republican in temper, and

becoming class conscious during the ten years of debate, they grew
rapidly in power and finally turned America against England. A
recent historian has thus characterized the change of temper which
brought these agrarians to the front as the fighting strength of
the republicans:

A new class, formed within a decade, growing rapidly in numbers, was
rising to power. In Pennsylvania, as in a number of other colonies, it con-
sisted of small farmers in the back country, Scotch-Irish and German
immigrants, reënforced by the voteless laborers and artisans of Philadelphia or other seaboard cities. . . . For over a decade this rising democracy
had struggled for power against the little seaboard aristocracy of wealth
and accepted social leadership. . . . The colonial masses could no longer
be controlled by reverence for the high-born. The Quaker merchants of
Philadelphia, the holders of manors on the Hudson, the tobacco and rice
planters of Virginia and South Carolina, and even the great merchants,
clergy, and professional men of New England, could no longer rule without
question their social inferiors. . . . Thus, in 1774, came the climax in the
struggle between rich and poor, East and West, those with a vote and
those who were voteless, between privilege and the welfare of the common
man. The two classes might work in harmony or might clash on the
question of resistance to Great Britain, but they were pretty sure to be in
opposition on the issue of individual rights. A merchant . . . might
welcome the support of the mechanics and small shopkeepers against a
grievous tax by the British Government, but the price, a right to vote and
to hold office, he was sure to resent, and he grew more and more alarmed as
the pressure became more insistent.[3]

From the imperial point of view there were the soundest reasons
why, following the Treaty of Paris in 1763, Parliament should
have desired to set about reorganizing the far-spread British
Empire. Within a few years vast territories had been added to
the crown, and if the scattered parts were to be gathered into a
cohesive and powerful whole there was need of a definite policy
of coördination and integration. The American colonies were
only a small part of the total empire, and it was generally agreed
among English statesmen that the old policy of "salutary neglect"
could no longer serve imperial interests. If the Whig imperialists
under the leadership of Pitt had been put in charge of imperial
reconstruction, the outcome very likely would have been peaceful.
But unfortunately for the empire the colonial problem became
embroiled with English domestic politics. The purpose of the
King was to set up a personal autocracy with Tory help, over-

[3] Van Tyne, *Causes of the War of Independence*, pp. 424–426.

throw the rule of the Whig families, eliminate from the ministry the more intelligent Old Whig leaders—Pitt, Camden, Barré, Burke, Shelburne—and bring in a narrow-minded group who held to the obsolete mercantilist theory of colonial dependency. The immediate outcome was the inauguration of a policy that ran counter to the economic interests of the three major colonial regions and aroused the hostility of important colonial groups. Every successive enactment was a greater blunder, until the crowning stupidity of the tea monopoly—which used colonial interests as a pawn in a game of the East India Company—threw the colonial fat into the fire.

The grievances of the merchants resulting from the regulatory trade acts were real and serious. However the ministry might justify those acts before Parliament, their effects were disastrous to substantial colonial interests, and to American eyes seemed designed to bring colonial trade into further subjection to English merchants. The attempt to suppress the widespread practice of smuggling was ill advised even though logical, for it aroused the consuming public as well as the middlemen, and gave popular backing to the protests of the merchants. The total political result was to align against Parliament the most influential groups in the trading towns—the wealthy importers and the professional classes—and provided opportunity to the radicals to spread their propaganda under cover of respectable leadership. The movement of resistance thus set on foot by the class-conscious merchants eventually slipped from their control and passed into the hands of the Sons of Liberty, who drove faster and farther than conservative business men would willingly follow; yet these latter soon found themselves coerced by tumultuous forces which they had unwittingly loosed. In consequence there came a time of divided counsels, and when independence was finally declared large numbers of the wealthiest and most dignified merchants turned Loyalist and threw in their lot with the King. More than two hundred quitted Boston on its evacuation by General Gage. Others stood apart as neutrals till the war was over, and then drew together in a compact organization to stem the tide of post-war agrarianism and assist in setting up a federal government after their liking.[4]

[4] For an admirable study, see A. M. Schlesinger, *The Colonial Merchants and the American Revolution: 1763-1776.*

The grievances of the plantation group were less obvious but none the less real. Probably more critical than taxation or the debts owed to English merchants, was the question of the western lands. The Quebec Act stirred the South as the tea monopoly stirred Boston and New York and Philadelphia. Involved in that act were certain long accepted colonial rights of domain, on the strength of which vast speculation in backcountry lands had been engaged in by English and colonial land companies and individuals.[5] The question was extraordinarily complicated, involving the rights of the Indians, the ambition of the Hudson Bay Company to retain the western wilderness as a vast fur preserve, the rights of Catholics in the French settlements, the rights of the imperial treasury to income from the sale of the lands, the rights of soldiers of the French wars to lands granted by colonial legislatures, the rights of frontiersmen to free settlement and exploitation, as well as specific grants to several colonies, in particular Massachusetts, Connecticut and Virginia. From this mass of conflicting interests, all eager to exploit an incalculably rich domain, little hope of satisfactory solution offered, and a wiser ministry would have kept hands off. But an ill-considered Parliamentary enactment cut the knot in a way to arouse the quick and keen resentment of America. Whatever may be said for the solution, one thing is clear; it set aside by arbitrary statute cherished rights which Virginian gentlemen, with their eyes on rich plantations to the West, deeply resented. It was a matter of vital concern to colonies like Virginia that they should control their wilderness frontier. The Quebec Act not only alienated thousands of western colonials, but it provided them with influential leaders like Washington and Robert Morris. It was more fuel to the radical bonfire. •

In the end the fortunes of the revolutionary movement rested with the yeomanry, and this yeomanry with its agrarian outlook and republican sympathies, was in a mood to respond to radical appeal. That the farmer was induced to take down his squirrel rifle and fight King George was made possible by a number of irritations—his deep-rooted prejudice against aristocracy, his instinctive dislike of crown officials, his inveterate localism that

[5] This important subject has been examined by C. W. Alvord, *The Mississippi Valley in British Policies;* C. A. Beard, *An Economic Interpretation of the Constitution;* C. H. Van Tyne, *The Causes of the War of Independence.*

resented alien interference—as well as by substantial class interests. In every colony the party of incipient populism had been checked and thwarted by royal officials; and it was this mass of populistic discontent, seeing itself in danger of being totally crushed, and its interests ignored, that provided the rank and file of armed opposition to the King. Already Parliament had brought acute financial distress to the colonies by forbidding the emission of bills of credit; and other attacks on popular policies followed. The strength of the popular opposition to royal programs had lain heretofore in the legislative control of the purse; by threatening to withhold salaries, the democratic legislatures had been able to coerce the royal governor and the judges, and keep them somewhat responsive to the popular will. To the Tories such coercion was proof that the democratic claws needed cutting, and one of the purposes of the Stamp Act was the providing of a fund to pay the royal officials out of the royal chest. It was a skillful plan, but it overreached itself. Party alignment had become too sharp, agrarian suspicions had grown too sensitive, for the plan to succeed. The immediate, fatal result was the accession of a numerous body of fighting men to the other malcontents.

The American Revolution was one of the first fruits of a short-sighted imperialism. A generous policy of imperial federation would have returned incredible revenues to Great Britain; but the Tory ministry was not intelligent enough to let sleeping dogs lie. A sentimental attachment had kept America loyal. So long as his customary and traditional rights remained undisturbed, the colonial would throw up his cap for King George; but if he were driven to choose between loyalty and self-interest, between sentiment and profit, the choice was certain. If the heavy debts which the foolish wars of Pitt had bequeathed to the Empire had not seemed to offer a justification, the Tory blunderers would not have forced the issue; but once it was joined, vast numbers of Americans came to believe that the development of their country had reached a point where it would be hampered by further overseas regulation; that America must be free to exploit her resources to her exclusive advantage; and that such economic freedom would be possible only with political independence. It was the ill luck of the ministry to present the question so concretely that the colonial radicals were given an opportunity to awaken the latent forces of American liberalism and turn them against English sovereignty.

A militant nationalistic psychology resulted from a widespread propaganda, and the last ties with England were broken.

II

ARGUMENT AND PROPAGANDA

We understand the ways of propaganda today better than our fathers understood them, and the official pronouncements of diplomats and statesmen we have grown somewhat skeptical of. Historians of the American Revolution have paid rather too exclusive attention to formal speeches and state papers, forgetting that those speeches and papers too often served the purpose of obscuring and evading the real issues. The ten years of dreary debate preceding the clash of arms, during which theory and precedent were examined by partisan lawyers, did little more than serve party purposes on both sides of the Atlantic, investing immediate interests with nationalistic or imperialistic idealism. Honest men talked themselves into a passion, but they took good care that their cause should appear dressed to advantage.

On the American side the argument fell into two broad divisions: an attempt to justify the colonial position by appeal to the British constitution, and when that failed by an appeal to the extra-legal doctrine of natural right. To understand the obscure constitutional wrangle, it must be recalled that important changes in English constitutional practice had taken place since the colonies were founded. Parliamentary sovereignty had superseded royal sovereignty, or in other words, the sovereignty of property had superseded divine right autocracy; and this in turn was undergoing change in the second half of the eighteenth century—the sovereignty of landed property was challenged by the rising capitalism. The Revolution of 1688 had established the general principle that the state can take no property in the form of taxes or levies without the consent of the owner, given by himself or by his representative sitting in Parliament. But in current practice the system of representation had become so misshapen that a new theory had arisen to give constitutional sanction to existing methods. Refusal to reapportion representation had resulted in the notorious rotten-borough system, control of which boroughs was too valuable an asset to the ruling oligarchy to be surrendered. To justify the scandal a new theory of virtual representation was developed—a theory upon which turned much of the early revolutionary debate. In brief the theory asserted that as Parliament speaks for the total body of Englishmen, it makes no practical difference who elects them, where they live, who they are, or what interests they represent. Within the halls of Parliament they can be trusted to think and legislate for the nation as a whole. The essential constitutional principle requires only that there shall be a respectable body chosen from among the commons of England, in whose hands shall rest the custody of the purse, and who shall serve as a check upon the royal prerogative. Such was the parliamentary situation in 1763, and when appeal was made by the colonials to the principle of no taxation without representation, it was answered by appeal to the theory of virtual representation.

American constitutional practice, on the other hand, had developed in a contrary direction. Quite as consciously as Parliament, the several colonial legislatures rested on the principle of property rights, but a different system of representation had developed. By easy logic a geographical theory had emerged, by the terms of which a legislator must be a freeman of the district rather than of the realm, that he should hold power for a short period and frequently submit his conduct to the scrutiny of the electors, and that a district should bear a just per capita relation to the total population. The doctrine of virtual representation was alien to colonial theory, although in fact it might be applied to the large body of disfranchised non-property-holders. The broad difference, then, in the legislative practice of the two countries lay in the important distinction between local, numerical representation, and a grotesque system of borough jobbing. Both systems rested on a narrow suffrage, although the colonial basis was very much broader. The difference was without significance so long as the traditional relations between America and England continued; but when Parliament proposed to extend the theory of virtual representation to the colonies, and treat Massachusetts and Virginia as on a constitutional footing with Birmingham and Manchester, the difference became acute. No American colony was willing to become the pawn of parliamentary placemen, at the mercy of parliamentary jobbery.

The debate over this vital question was involved in obscurities by reason of the vagueness of the British constitution. If an

unwritten constitution be no other than established practice—
and it is true of the English constitution in spite of the body of
principles existing in such pronouncements as Magna Charta, the
settlement of 1689, and the Common Law—then the current
practice of Parliament must be accepted as constitutional. This
was the fatal weakness of the colonial argument, as it was the
weakness of Pitt and other defenders of America in Parliament.
When Pitt exclaimed with characteristic grandiloquence, "I come
not here armed at all points with law cases and acts of Parliament,
with the statute-book doubled down in dog-ears, to defend the
cause of liberty," he abandoned the legal ground to appeal to the
sense of justice and right of Englishmen. But the question could
not so easily be transferred from the domain of constitutional law.
For upwards of a hundred years Parliament had been sovereign,
and for the colonials now to deny its sovereignty meant one of
two things: either to go back to the obsolete principle of divine
right, or to postulate an extra-parliamentary body of constitutional law, unknown to English practice. A sovereignty inhering
neither in King nor Parliament, but in a super-constitution, was a
conception that had been played with by Coke in an endeavor to
exalt the Common Law, and hinted at by later Whig statesmen,
but which had never established itself in practice. The colonials
recognized the dilemma and made half-hearted attempts to evade
it. John Adams and Franklin endeavored to argue that as the
colonial charters were from the crown, and antedated the rise of
Parliament, Americans owed allegiance to the King and not to
Parliament, and hence parliamentary pretentions to sovereignty
over America were only a new form of unconstitutional prerogative. But the argument was taken seriously by neither side, and
was soon put away.[6]

It finally became clear to American leaders that if their cause
were to make headway, appeal must be made to broader principles.
Their case must rest on philosophical rather than on legal grounds.
This suffices to explain the shift from constitutionalism to abstract
rights, which marked the middle period of the debate. By 1773
it had become evident to thoughtful observers that the cause of
American liberalism must fail, or become revolutionary in purpose and intent, and to become such it must seek justification in

[6] For an excellent discussion of the constitutional questions involved, see C. H.
Van Tyne, *The Causes of the War of Independence*, Chapters VIII and IX.

extra-constitutional principles. And this justification it discovered
in the writings of English liberals of the seventeenth century—in
Sidney and Milton, and above all in Locke. The influence of
Locke had long been paramount in English political speculation.
He had been the apologist and defender of the settlement of 1689;
the principles which he expounded lay at the base of the dynastic
rights of the reigning house, and were nominally accepted by all
the parliamentary leaders. The relations between natural rights
and parliamentary sovereignty had not wholly clarified, and in
the background of English constitutional thought still lingered
a vague notion of certain natural rights above the constitution,
and limiting parliamentary statutes. Thinkers as different as
Blackstone and Camden subscribed to such doctrine, but it daily
became more tenuous in the face of a growing acceptance of unlimited parliamentary sovereignty.[7]

In turning to Locke, therefore, the colonial debaters went back
a century and picked up the argument of liberalism as it existed
before it had been nullified by later English practice. They
occupied a position similar to that defended by him a hundred
years before; they were combating the same arbitrary rule that
had brought on the Revolution of 1688. He had laid down the
basic principle of revolution in the doctrine of certain natural rights
of the subject which no state may subvert without peril to the
original compact; he had asserted that taxation without representation constituted such subversive tyranny; and he gave high sanction
to the right and duty of resistance to an encroaching sovereignty.
The noble words, "Chains are but an ill wearing how much soever
we gild or polish them," uttered a note of defiance to arbitrary
power which struck a responsive chord in the breast of the colonial
liberal. In short, Locke's two *Treatises on Civil Government*,
aimed at Sir Robert Filmer's absurd *Patriarcha*, were turned against
Parliament and became the textbook of the American Revolution.

The ground had been well prepared. The argument of Locke
went home with such convincing force to the colonial liberal because it embodied conclusions towards which America had long
been moving. It was an eloquent confirmation of native experience, a sober justification of the psychology of individualism.
The self-governing state had so long been an established fact in
colonial life as to have assumed the complexion of a natural

[7] For this see Van Tyne, *ibid.*, pp. 234–238.

right. The political compact had taken form in American political thought, a generation before Locke gave currency to the theory, and Jefferson was expressing native conclusions drawn from American experience when he argued that "governments derive their just powers from the consent of the governed," and that "all men are created equal, that they are endowed by their Creator with certain unalienable Rights, that amongst these are Life, Liberty and the pursuit of Happiness." It is not true to assert that Jefferson was only reciting Locke, with modifications derived from the French humanitarians. It is nearer the truth to say that he made use of old-world philosophy to express and justify certain native tendencies then seeking adequate statement.

To such an experience, armed with such a philosophy, there must come eventually the conviction that both monarchy and aristocracy were irrational; that the ambitions of a coercive alien sovereignty were fraught with danger to the rights of the American citizen. The resurgent absolutism of Stuart times, with its doctrine of the omnicompetent state, which the King was reviving through the instrumentality of Parliament, was broken by the stubborn colonial resistance. Absolutism under whatever form was doomed in America, however slowly it might linger out its life. Jonathan Boucher might seek to revive Sir Robert Filmer, and preach to Americans the dogma of divine right through royal primogeniture from Adam, and other colonial Tories might applaud; but they were fast becoming anachronisms. The Revolution was to overthrow for Americans the principle of the absolutist state, and substitute a modified sovereignty, circumscribed by the utilitarian test of its relation to the common well-being of its citizens. For the first time in modern history it was discovered that "the true meaning of sovereignty," as a recent student has put it, is to be sought "not in the coercive power possessed by its instrument [the state,] but in the fused good-will for which it stands." [8]

III

CERTAIN SOCIAL CONSEQUENCES

The swift crystallization of colonial sentiment in favor of republicanism, as the crisis developed, produced the American revolution of which John Adams wrote. The long leveling process

[8] H. J. Laski, *The Problem of Sovereignty*, p. 12; see also Appendices A and B.

of a hundred and forty years, with its psychology of decentralization, fruited naturally in a new political philosophy fitted to new-
world conditions. Monarchy, with its social appanage of aristocracy, was a caste institution wholly unsuited to an unregimented
America. The war brought this revolutionary fact home to the
consciousness of thousands of colonials; and the liberalism that
before had been vaguely instinctive quickly became eager and
militant. The old order was passing; the day of the Tory in
America was over for the present; the republican was henceforth
to be master of the new world. Out of this primary revolution were
to come other revolutions, social and economic, made possible by
the new republican freedom.

The swift rise of a political philosophy traditionally regarded as
mean and traitorous was inexplicable to Tory gentlemen, and
aroused a fierce retaliatory opposition. A social war of the classes,
bitter, vindictive, followed upon hostilities against England. The
arrogance of the gentry during those brisk days when the new
spirit was rising is scarcely comprehensible to later Americans
unused to such frankness. The republicans were scorned by the
superior classes as unprincipled sedition-mongers, plotting treason
against the King and society. If commoners flocked to town-
meetings and outvoted the gentlemen, the latter were outraged
at the presumption of the "mobsters" in flouting their betters.
For the plain people to take things into their own hands was no
other than anarchy. The familiar records of the day are filled
with such aristocratic jests as this:

> Down at night a bricklayer or carpenter lies,
> Next sun a Lycurgus, a Solon doth rise.[9]

"The dirty mob was all about me as I drove into town," said
Mistress Peggy Hutchinson, as she looked out on turbulent Boston
from her father's chariot; and her feminine contempt for the
common people was an echo of the universal Tory contempt for
republican mechanics and farmers. It was the duty of the vulgar,
as loyal subjects, to pay taxes and not lay them; to obey the law
and not make it. By far the most important consequence of the
Revolution was the striking down of this mounting aristocratic
spirit that was making rapid headway with the increase of wealth.
It sifted the American people as the migrations of the seventeenth

[9] Moore, *Diary of the Revolution*, Vol. II, p. 22.

century had sifted the English people, keeping the republicans at home and sending forth the Tories, weakening the influence of the conservatives and increasing the influence of the liberals. Few experiences in our history have proved so momentous in results as this shift of power and change in personnel that resulted from the great schism. A middle-class America was to rise on the ruins of the colonial aristocracy.

The unfortunate Loyalists were victims of their own blindness. They did not rightly estimate the driving power of the liberal forces released by the struggle, and failing to understand, they staked everything on the issue, and lost, and were driven rudely out of the land by the plebeian republicans whom they despised. The disruption of colonial society resulting from the expulsion of the Loyalists was far graver than we commonly assume. Ship-loads of excellent gentlemen, and among them the most cultivated minds in America, were driven from their firesides and sent forth to seek new homes, whether in "Hell, Hull or Halifax" mattered little to the victors. Upward of forty thousand sought refuge in Canada; thousands more went to the Bahamas; and still other thousands returned to the old home. "There will scarcely be a village in England without some American dust in it, I believe, by the time we are all at rest," wrote the Loyalist Dutchman, Peter Van Schaak. Much suffering was endured and much bitterness engendered, and if for years the dominant temper in Canada was fiercely hostile to the United States, the mood is traceable to the expatriated gentlemen who transmitted to their children a grudge against the victorious republicans. It was an unhappy business, but it was scarcely avoidable once appeal was made to the sword. There was no longer place in America for the foolish dream of a colonial aristocracy.

The change of temper that came over American society with the loss of the Loyalists, was immense and far-reaching. For the first time the middle class was free to create a civilization after its own ideals. In rising to leadership it brought another spirit into every phase of life. Dignity and culture henceforth were to count for less and assertiveness for more. Ways became less lei-surely, the social temper less urbane. The charm of the older aristocracy disappeared along with its indisputable evils. Al-though a few of the older wits like Mather Byles lingered on bitterly, and others like Gouverneur Morris accepted the situation philosophically, they belonged to the past. A franker evaluation of success in terms of money began to obscure the older personal and family distinction. New men brought new ways and a vulgar clamor of politics went hand in hand with business expansion. The demagogue and the speculator discovered a fruitful field for their activities. The new capitalism lay on the horizon of republican America, and the middle class was eager to hasten its development. But a new economic order required a new political state, and as a necessary preliminary, the spirit of nationalism began that slow encroachment upon local frontiers which was to modify profoundly the common psychology. Americanism superseded colonialism, and with the new loyalty there developed a conception of federal sovereignty, overriding all local authorities, checking the movement of particularism, binding the separate commonwealths in a consolidating union. This marked the turning point in American development; the checking of the long movement of decentralization and the beginning of a counter movement of centralization—the most revolutionary change in three hundred years of American experience. The history of the rise of the coercive state in America, with the ultimate arrest of all centrifugal tendencies, was implicit in that momentous counter movement.

CHAPTER II

THE MIND OF THE AMERICAN TORY

So nearly forgotten by later generations is the American Tory of Revolutionary times that it will be well to examine the genus with some care; for only by understanding the great authority inhering in his traditional leadership can we measure his power to thwart the ambitions of the republicans. In numbers the Tories were a very small minority; unendowed with wealth and position they would have been negligible; but as members of the local gentry they enjoyed great prestige which was highly serviceable to the royal cause. Although native born they aped the English aristocracy, and reproduced on a less magnificent scale the manners of the English landed families. Less arrogant than their old-world models, certainly much less corrupt in their politics, they exuded the same aristocratic prejudices and the same narrow sympathies. Their most cherished dream was the institution of an American nobility, with the seal of royal favor set upon their social pretensions. They were the embodiment of the aristocratic eighteenth century, in a world instinctively hostile to all aristocracies. Out of a numerous company of distinguished Tories, three will serve for consideration—Thomas Hutchinson, Royal Governor, Daniel Leonard, lawyer, and Jonathan Boucher, minister.

I

THOMAS HUTCHINSON

Royal Governor

The career of the last royal governor of Massachusetts affords a suggestive study in the relation of material prosperity to political principles. Descended in the fourth generation from the Antinomian enthusiast, Mistress Anne Hutchinson, whom all the authorities of Boston could neither terrify nor silence, but who suffered contumely and exile rather than submit her will to official censors, Thomas Hutchinson reveals in his stiff conservatism the common change that follows upon economic well-being. The House

194

of Hutchinson had long since abandoned all unprofitable radicalisms and had taken to the safer business of acquiring property
and respectability; in which work it had by God's blessing greatly
prospered, until it came to be reckoned the first house in the
province. With growing wealth political honors multiplied. The
grandfather of the governor had been the first Chief Justice of the
Common Pleas, Commander of the Forces, Assistant, and Councilor; and at his death in 1717 he was as eminent a citizen as Chief
Justice Sewall, the diarist. The governor's father, Thomas Hutchinson, Sr., devoted more attention to his calling of merchant
than to politics, nevertheless he sat in the Council for twenty-five
years, and was a colonel in the provincial militia. With the advent
of Thomas Hutchinson upon the scene, the respectability of the
house was assured, abundant wealth had been accumulated, and
the path of political preferment was open. The little colony was
eager to confer honors on so promising a son. He was ambitious
and thrifty, and he coveted the distinction and the material
rewards which officeholding brought. No Boston gentleman of
his day had a sharper eye for the main chance. He added office
to office, and at one and the same time he was Member of the
Council, Judge of Probate, Chief Justice, and Lieutenant Governor; and such other offices as he could not himself possess he
maneuvered to get into the hands of his sons, and brothers-in-law,
and dependents. One of those brothers-in-law, Samuel Mather,
son of Cotton Mather, who refused to follow his kinsman into the
Tory camp, called him "an avaritious man"; and avaricious of
power, even more than of money, he certainly was.

   With his abundant offices and honors, there was every temptation to conservatism. Unless there was hidden in him some lingering idealism, some seed of the ancestral radicalism to sprout and
grow into discontent, Thomas Hutchinson was marked for a
reactionary. And unhappily in his conventional soul there was
not the faintest spark of idealism. The enthusiasm of Mistress
Anne was washed clean out of the Hutchinson blood, leaving only
the native stubbornness; which stubbornness, dominating a
character cold, formal, arrogant, dogmatic, unimaginative, self-
righteous, was finally to play havoc with Thomas Hutchinson's
good fortune. The son of a merchant, he was a careful, methodical
soul, who studied how to save and invest; in a later generation he
would have been a great banker, but in his own he preferred to

invest in politics. How suggestive of Yankee thrift is such an entry as this:

All the time he was at College he carried on a little trade by sending ventures in his father's vessels, & kept a little paper Journal & leger, & enterd in it every dinner, supper, breakfast, & every article of expense, even of a shilling; which practice soon became pleasant; & he found it of great use all his life. . . . Before he came of age, he had, by adventuring to sea from two or three quintalls [hundredweight] of fish, given him by his father, when about 12 years old, acquired four or five hundred pounds sterling.[1]

After a number of years in his father's countinghouse, learning the ways of eighteenth-century trade, he abandoned the mercantile career and entered politics at the age of six-and-twenty. From May 31, 1737, when he first took his place in the House of Deputies as one of the "Boston Seat," to June 1, 1774, when he quitted his country home at Milton to take ship for London and exile, he was a power in the political life of Massachusetts, reaching eventually the highest station. During that long period of thirty-seven years he was a spokesman of the New England gentry, always on the side of government, never in the opposition. That he ever critically examined the foundations of his political creed, there is nothing in the printed record to indicate. He had some of the tastes of the book-lover and scholar. He was deeply interested in the Puritan past, and his *History of Massachusetts Bay* was based on a wide knowledge of manuscript sources which he had been at great pains to collect. But in spite of a praiseworthy care for accuracy and impartiality, he lacked the creative imagination to reconstruct the past. He had pretty much freed his mind from religious bigotry, but he could not rid himself of a narrow partisanship, and his treatment of the agrarian movement was grossly unfair. His shortcomings as a political thinker were more striking. His knowledge of the political classics was of the slightest. When Samuel Adams made use of the natural-rights theory, Hutchinson's comment would indicate that he had no acquaintance with the theory and had not even read Locke.[2] He was little given to intellectual interests, and ill at ease in dealing with general principles. He possessed the mental qualities of a lawyer rather than a speculative thinker, and his long immersion in office contracted a mind naturally sterile to the routine habits of an administrator.

[1] *Diary and Letters*, Vol. I, pp. 46–48.
[2] See Hosmer, *Life of Samuel Adams*, p. 259.

He hardened early, and thereafter he was incapable of changing his views or liberalizing his sympathies. Consistency he erected into a fetish and once he had taken a position he would not budge from it. He did not understand the liberal America that was rising about him—neither the economic forces that were creating it nor the spokesmen who represented it; and he saw no reason for change. The House of Hutchinson had prospered under existing conditions, and other houses would prosper likewise, he believed, if they were equally honest and diligent. So he went his tactless, unintelligent way, barking his shins on every liberal tendency of the times, and hating the men who gave him trouble.

Hutchinson, in short, was a complete Tory, and if we would understand him and his class, we must first take into account the current Tory philosophy. Compressed into a sentence it was the expression of the will-to-power of the wealthy. Its motive was economic class interest, and its object the exploitation of society through the instrumentality of the state. Stated thus, the philosophy does not appear to advantage; it lays itself open to unpleasant criticism by those who are not its beneficiaries. In consequence, much ingenuity in tailoring was necessary to provide it with garments to cover its nakedness. Embroidered with patriotism, loyalty, law and order, it made a very respectable appearance; and when it put on the stately robe of the British Constitution, it was enormously impressive. The Tory theory of the British Constitution may well be regarded as a masterpiece of the gentle art of tailoring. Government by king, lords, and commons it asserted, approximated the ideal of a "mixt government," embracing the total wisdom of the realm, ruling in the interests of all, avoiding the evils of class domination, and chastising the refractory only for the common good. Gentlemen might well praise the "glorious British Constitution." It was their little jest at the expense of the English people, who were content to be exploited by them.

In this game of political pretense Hutchinson willingly shared. He knew that Parliament did not represent the English people; that it was controlled by a group of landed gentlemen with mercenaries in their pay; and yet in reply to repeated charges he revealed no hint of the truth, but reiterated the familiar Tory interpretation in the face of shrewd enemies who knew that he was insincere. In private among other gentlemen, Hutchinson

was frank enough.   He knew what was at stake in America—
whether political control should remain in the hands of "gentlemen
of principle and property," with the assistance of English Tories,
or whether it should pass into the hands of the majority.   And
so while declaiming against mobs, and preaching loyalty to the best
of kings, he secretly busied himself with influential persons in
devising methods to frustrate the Whig ambitions.   Moreover
in dealing with his enemies he was a thorough realist.   In his
comment on American Whigs and their political methods, he set
down many a shrewd and just estimate of their actions and motives.
But in defense of the English ministry he refused to face reality.
He quibbled and misrepresented and denied, stooping to dirty
politics to hold his party together and strengthen it.

At the moment when Hutchinson assumed the duties of governor the situation was tense.   Bernard had muddled things sadly,
and "the rage against him became, at length, so violent, that
it was judged necessary to recall him," [3] and he slipped off to
England to receive a baronetcy and a pension.   But he had brought
the commonwealth to the parting of the ways, and Hutchinson
found himself in a difficult position.   The roots of the trouble are
laid bare in the following affidavit of Bernard:

In the Province of Massachusetts Bay, when civil authority was reduced
so low as to have nothing left but the form of a government, and scarce
even that, an enquiry into the causes of so great a weakness in the governing power was unavoidable; and there was no entering upon such an
enquiry, without observing upon the ill effects of that part of the constitution of that government, whereby the appointment of the Council is left
to the people, to be made by annual election; and yet the Royal Governor,
in all Acts of prerogative, is subject to the controul of the Democraticall
Council.   This solecism in policy has been as hurtful in practice as it is
absurd in theory, and it is the true cause of the extreme imbecility of the
power of the crown in this government, at times when the exertion of it is
most wanted.   This is not an observation of a new date; it is of many years
standing; . . . ever since he has felt the effects which the popular constitution of the Council has had upon the Royalty of the government,
which is above three years ago; within which time, he has seen the King
deprived of the service of every man at the Council Board, who has
resolution enough to disapprove the opposition to the authority of the
King and the Parliament, and their supremacy over the *American* Colonies.
This, and this only, is the foundation of the charge of their endeavouring to
overthrow the charter; whereas his real desire has been, that the charter
should have a more durable stability, by means of a necessary alteration,

[3] Hutchinson, *History of Massachusetts Bay*, Vol. III, p. 255.

without which, he is persuaded it cannot have a much longer duration; as the abuse of the appointment of the Council now prevailing, must oblige the Parliament to interfere sooner or later.[4]

The more thoughtfully one considers this frank statement the more clearly it appears what grounds for party dissension lay in the "solecism" of a constitution whereby the "Royal Governor, in all Acts of prerogative," was "subject to the controul of the Democraticall Council." It would not be easy to patch up a working compromise between an absentee prerogative and the local democratic will; one or the other must be sovereign; and because the terms of the charter enabled the democracy to nullify the prerogative, Bernard concluded that the charter must be revised and the abuse corrected. In this Hutchinson agreed, and from the imperial point of view not without reason. "By an unfortunate mistake," he wrote in apology to Gage, "soon after the charter, a law passed which made every town in the Province a corporation perfectly democratic." With every passing year the mistake was becoming more unfortunate, and the vital problem before government, in the opinion of Hutchinson, was how to correct this unfortunate mistake, together with other like mistakes, with such happy skill as to check the democratic branch without arousing popular resentment. On this reef Hutchinson foundered.

As early as 1764 the meddlesome Bernard had proposed to the home government a complete remodeling of colonial governments on the English Tory plan; and by way of suggestion he forwarded some proposals looking to the eventual consolidation of the several colonies under a single royal government, the erection of a house of lords as a balance to the popular party and a comprehensive tax policy. It was one of numerous suggestions then being made for incorporating America into the British Empire, and extending the imperial power over the continent. Bernard's bias is sufficiently revealed in the following:

86. There is no government in America at present, whose powers are properly balanced; there not being in any of them, a real and distinct third legislative power mediating between the king and the people, which is the peculiar excellence of the British constitution.

87. The want of such a third legislative power, adds weight to the popular, and lightens the royal scale; so as to destroy the balance between the royal and popular powers.

[4] "Answer of Bernard to the Petition of the House of Representatives to the King," in *Works of Samuel Adams*, Vol. I, pp. 365-367.

88. Although America is not now . . . ripe enough for an hereditary nobility; yet it is now capable of a nobility for life.

89. A nobility appointed by the king for life, and made independent, would probably give strength and stability to the American governments, as effectually as an hereditary nobility does to that of Great Britain.[5]

It is not known to what extent Hutchinson indorsed so ambitious and comprehensive a plan. For years he had been Bernard's understudy, and supported him in all his policies; but being cautious by nature and attached to local custom, he probably would have rejected the plan of continental consolidation unless his personal ambition had been enlisted. Hosmer's attempt to clear his skirts [6] is not convincing. Recalling that Hutchinson yielded invariably to royal or ministerial suggestions, no matter how contrary to local custom, there is no reason to believe that he would have objected to any coercive program, which provided adequately for the colonial Tories.

In another matter that touched the political life of Massachusetts to the quick, Hutchinson was deeply engaged. The source of the power of the popular party lay in the democratic town meeting. In earlier days the Tories had made no objection to it, for it was amenable to control by the "better sort of people." But under the skillful politics of Samuel Adams and his fellows, it had become the chief instrument of opposition, and Hutchinson was determined to cut its claws. On so delicate a matter, however, it was only to the ministry that he could speak frankly; he must not appear to be laying a plot against an institution so long established as a part of the political machinery of the commonwealth. Under date of March 26, 1770, he wrote to the secretary of Lord Hillsboro:

There is a Town Meeting, no sort of regard being had to any qualification of voters, but all the inferior people meet together; and at a late meeting the inhabitants of other towns who happened to be in town, mixed with them. . . . It is in other words being under the government of the mob. This has given the lower part of the people such a sense of their importance that a gentleman does not meet with what used to be common civility, and we are sinking into perfect barbarism. . . . If this town could be separated from the rest of the Province, the infection has not taken such strong hold of the parts remote from it. The spirit of anarchy which prevails in Boston is more than I am able to cope with.[7]

[5] Quoted in John Adams, *Novanglus*, Second Letter.
[6] See his *Life of Thomas Hutchinson*.
[7] Quoted in *ibid.*, p. 189.

Writing to Hillsboro on April 19, 1771, he complained:

In these votes and in most of the public proceedings of the town of
Boston, persons of the best character and estate have little or no concern.
They decline attending Town Meetings where they are sure to be out-
voted by men of the lowest order.[8]

A month later, writing to his old crony, ex-Governor Bernard, he
suggested a remedy which in one form or another he was constantly
holding before the ministry, as an inducement to act:

The town of Boston is the source from whence all the other parts of the
Province derive more or less troubled water. When you consider what is
called its constitution, your good sense will determine immediately that
it never can be otherwise for a long time together, whilst the majority
which conducts all affairs, if met together upon another occasion, would
be properly called a mob, and are persons of such rank and circumstance
as in all communities constitute a mob, there being no sort of regulation of
voters in practice; and as these will always be most in number, men of
weight and value, although they wish to suppress them, cannot be induced to attempt to do it for fear not only of being outvoted, but affronted
and insulted. Call such an assembly what you will, it is really no sort of
government, not even a democracy, at best a corruption of it. There is no
hope of a cure by any legislative but among ourselves [*i.e.*, ministerial
supporters] to compel the town to be a corporation.[9] The people will not
seek it, because every one is sensible his importance will be lessened. If
ever a remedy is found, it must be by compelling them to swallow it, and
that by an exterior power,—the Parliament.[10]

In such advice—the destruction of the democratic machinery
by an "exterior power" in order that control of government
should lie beyond the reach of the popular will—we may discover
ample grounds for democratic dissatisfaction with the governor.
Hutchinson believed that when matters of state were settled by
gentlemen over their wine, good government resulted; but when
discussed by common people over their cider, the door was thrown
wide open to anarchy. His particular *bête noire* was the mob, by
which name he designated any gathering that had not received his
gracious permission to assemble. It was his shortsighted willingness to arm himself with external authority against his fellow
countrymen, that filled the years of his administration with so
much bitterness. The more he lost ground, the more anxiously he

---

[8] *Ibid.*, p. 206.
[9] Hutchinson assumes the act of incorporation will lay restrictions upon the
right of suffrage and the powers of the town meeting.
[10] *Ibid.*, pp. 206–207.

pleaded for help from the ministry. When certain of his private letters came to the hands of Franklin and were sent home, Hutchinson was put in a rage. He had long been fearful of such a diplomatic leak and urged secrecy, for if his private correspondence should become public, he explained, "I have no security against the rage of the people." [11] Much ink was used by his friends in declaiming against the infamy of making public a gentleman's private letters, and Hutchinson characterized it as an "affrontery" such as "was never known before." That such private correspondence was in effect official correspondence, in that it aimed at shaping parliamentary policy towards Massachusetts, was ignored by these outraged gentlemen. Diplomats who plan privately rarely like to be read publicly, especially when the public reads how it is being bought and sold.

Very likely the Assembly overstated the case in declaring that "there has been, for many years past, measures contemplated, and a plan formed, by a set of men, born and educated among us, to raise their own fortunes, and advance themselves to posts of honor and profit, not only to the destruction of the charter and constitution of this province, but at the expense of the rights and liberties of the American colonies." [12] Hutchinson was too cautious and too conservative to seek any revolutionary end; at the same time he was too yielding to make a stand against any encroachment that had legal sanction. From his narrow mind no help could be expected touching the great matter of imperial federation. In seeking a way out of the difficulties in which the British Empire was daily becoming entangled, the royal governor could discover no wiser plan than the abridgment of fundamental privileges which a hundred and fifty years of slow growth had made the peculiar possession of the colonies. The unhappy conclusion towards which the American Tories were drifting he set forth in words which were to become the most notorious he ever penned.

I never think of the measures necessary for the peace and good order of the colonies without pain. There must be an abridgment of what are called English liberties. I relieve myself by considering that in a remove from a state of nature to the most perfect state of government, there must be a great restraint of natural liberty. I doubt whether it is possible to project a system of government in which a colony 3000 miles distant from the parent state shall enjoy all the liberty of the parent state. I am cer-

[11] *Ibid.*, p. 199.
[12] *Resolves of the House of Representatives of Massachusetts Bay*, June 16, 1773.

tain I have never yet seen the projection. I wish the good of the colony when I wish to see some further restraint of liberty rather than the connexion with the parent state should be broken; for I am sure such a breach must prove the ruin of the colony.[13]

Later writers, forgetful of Hutchinson's self-seeking record and of his Tory philosophy, have inclined to leniency in judging him for his stand on this crucial point. But in spite of his wig and scarlet broadcloth robes he was only an unintelligent politician, who served the hand that fed him. No better commentary could be asked than is found in the caustic remark of the keenest Englishman of his day on the ministerial policy. In a letter of April, 1777, Horace Walpole asked, "What politicians are those who have preferred the empty name of *sovereignty* to that of *alliance*, and forced subsidies to the golden ocean of commerce?" Hutchinson was stubborn rather than wise. He would make no compromise in the matter of sovereignty; there could be no lawful will but the will of Parliament. "I know of no line that can be drawn between the supreme authority of Parliament and the total independence of the colonies," he replied to the Assembly, when it was struggling with the idea of federation.[14] When the Council and House were outlining a plan of imperial union, and seeking to demonstrate that the "subordinate authorities" of the colonies were sovereign within their fields, and "that, in fact, two such powers do subsist together, and are not incompatible"; the governor with patient finality explained to them the true "nature of supreme power,"

. . . and urged, as an undeniable principle, that such a power is essential in all governments, and that another power, with the name of subordinate, and with a right to withstand or control the supreme in particulars, is an absurdity—for it so far ceases to be subordinate, and becomes itself supreme; that no sensible writer upon government ever denied what he asserted; and whilst the council continued to hold, that two supreme powers were compatible, it would be to no purpose to reason upon the other parts of their message to him, or to deny what they adduced from a principle so contrary to reason.[15]

Hutchinson's position as the King's representative soon became so difficult that a wiser man would have resigned. He was constrained to be the executive of a policy of government by ministerial

[13] *Ibid.*, p. 436. Compare the view of Van Tyne, *The Causes of the War of Independence*, p. 85.
[14] Speech of January 6, 1773.
[15] *History of Massachusetts Bay*, Vol. III, pp. 381–382.

instructions. Again and again he vetoed a measure, or dissolved the legislature, or took action contrary to the spirit of the charter; and the sole justification which he pleaded was a secret letter of instructions, the terms of which he refused to make public, and the object of which must be judged by his acts. "So long as he continued commander-in-chief," he replied to the House in one of their perennial wranglings, "he should think himself bound to conform to every signification of his majesty's pleasure." To the denunciations of the popular party he remained outwardly indifferent, strong in the supposed integrity of his official purpose. In time, he believed, the evil spoken of him by ambitious men would be forgotten, and his course would find vindication. The words of Bernard might well have been his:

He denies, that the opinion of the whole people of that Province can now be taken and ascertained, labouring as it does at present, under the baneful influence of a desperate faction, who by raising groundless fears and jealousies, by deluding one part of the people, and by intimidating the other part, has destroyed all real freedom, not only of action, but even of sentiment and opinion. But the Respondent doubts not but that his Administration has been approved by the generalty of the best and most respectable men of the Province.[16]

In spite of Hutchinson's endeavors to build up a prerogative party the drift of public opinion went steadily against him until he was convinced that he stood almost alone. "He was not sure of support from any one person in authority," he commented stoically, in telling of the tea troubles. The Council, the Assembly, the very constables were against him. Yet he went his way obstinately; he would fulfill to the last word the instructions of his superiors. The ministry might be unwise, but better the legal folly of Parliament than the madness of the democracy. To encroach upon the royal prerogative, Hutchinson believed was to endanger the nice balance of the constitution. He was convinced that "the present easy, happy model of government" was as near perfect as the ingenuity of Englishmen could devise; that the welfare of America was dependent upon a proper subordination of the colonies to the mother country; and that the popular party was plotting treason against their country and their king. The third volume of his history is a long argument to demonstrate the

[16] *Answer of Bernard to the Petition of the House of Representatives.*

wisdom of his own and Bernard's administrations. The liberal
governor, Thomas Pownall, Hutchinson disliked, partly because
of his easy familiar ways, but chiefly because he was not a prerogative man.[17] But if Pownall had been in Hutchinson's place,
the history of the relations of Massachusetts and England would
have run very differently.

It was his ingrained snobbery which, more than anything else,
brought about his undoing. The aristocratic governor never
differed with a lord, and rarely agreed with a commoner. It was
intolerable to him that common fellows should dispute his reasoning or sit in judgment upon his official acts. It was their duty as
loyal subjects to obey without question the mandates of the King's
appointed spokesmen; and when town-meeting resolutions, put
through by mechanics and petty tradesmen, criticised his conduct,
or refused to accept the decision of the supreme court that the
"Boston massacre" was not legally a "massacre," he saw in such
acts only the madness of the mobocracy. That the people should
suspect the probity of his majesty's judges was painful to him.
As partisan bitterness increased, he became acutely suspicious
of all who disagreed with him, and shut his mind against every
argument. The debates and resolves in House and Council
"abounded with duplicity and inconclusive reasonings." "The
disingenuity and low craft, which appeared in so many of the
messages, resolves, and other publick instruments," he commented,
descended "to the level and vulgarity of a common newspaper
essay." [18] To the leaders of the popular party, the group of keen
debaters and parliamentarians who kept him constantly on the
defense, he attributed an artful malignancy. The fathers of the
Revolution do not appear to advantage in the pages of his history.
The Otises had gone over to the opposition because the father
had been disappointed on the occasion of Hutchinson's elevation
to the coveted chief-justiceship. John Hancock's "ruling passion
was a fondness for popular applause. . . . His natural powers
were moderate, and had been very little improved by study."
John Adams was a man whose "ambition was without bounds. . . .
He could not look with complacency upon any man who was in
possession of more wealth, more honours, or more knowledge than
himself," and he went over to the opposition because of a slight

[17] For Hutchinson's statement of the Tory case, see Vol. III, pp. 352–355.
[18] *History of Massachusetts Bay*, Vol. III, p. 399.

upon him by refusal of a place on the bench. For Samuel Adams, his most relentless enemy, Hutchinson's hatred was boundless. He had defaulted as collector of taxes and for equivalent of his arrears of public money he had set up as defender of the public liberties, and he "made more converts by calumniating governors, and other servants of the crown, than by strength of reasoning." His main business in life was "robbing men of their characters."

It is unlikely that time will bring any vindication of the later career of Thomas Hutchinson. He was a stiff-necked official of scrupulous principle, whose principles were grossly reactionary. He was sincerely attached to the great ideal of imperial unity, but he conceived of that unity as embodied in the coercive sovereignty of the crown and parliament, with Tory gentlemen as exclusive administrators. Samuel Adams was not unjust in declaring, "It has been his principle from a boy that mankind are to be governed by the discerning few; and it has ever since been his ambition to be the hero of the few." Courteous and conscientious, with very considerable administrative ability, it was his misfortune to defend a social philosophy alien to the rough individualism of his fellow countrymen. He would think only in terms of imperial centralization, and they would think only in terms of local home rule. He conceived of the political state as a private preserve for gentlemen to hunt over, and they conceived of it as a free hunting-ground for all. He never understood the assertive, capitalistic America that was rising about him, and in joining issue with it he destroyed himself. "If we were not mad," he lamented, "I have no doubt we might enjoy all that liberty which can subsist with a state of government." It was the complaint of the Tory upon a democracy that preferred self-rule to the blessings of a trusteeship, which, like a lawyers' squabble, consumed the estate in fees. Quite evidently the "mobility," in the days of Thomas Hutchinson, was running into madness, for it demanded greater liberty than was compatible with a "state of government" sanctioned by crown officials—a fact which the royal governor grieved over but was helpless to restrain.

II
DANIEL LEONARD
Tory Lawyer

Probably the most finished prose writer, certainly one of the most cultivated minds, among the notable group of American Loyalists, was a young man of excellent family, who if events had turned out otherwise would have made a much greater name for himself. Daniel Leonard was a Harvard graduate and a member of the Boston bar, an effective speaker, of some weight in commonwealth politics, and aligned with Hutchinson, Sewall, and the crown party. In temperament and taste he seems to have been conspicuously aristocratic. He delighted in fine clothes and set up his coach and pair to drive from his countryseat to Boston— a gesture of opulence that excited the laughter of sober people, and led Mercy Warren to introduce him into her comedy, *The Group*, under the name of Beau Trumps. According to John Adams, who was a decided gossip, it was this cavalier love of display that led to his political undoing, overcoming his native sympathy with the party of revolution.

He wore a broad gold lace round the rim of his hat, he made his cloak glitter with laces still broader, he had set up his chariot and pair and constantly traveled in it from Taunton to Boston. This made the world stare— it was a novelty. Not another lawyer in the province, attorney or barrister, of whatever age, reputation, rank, or station, presumed to ride in a coach or chariot. The discerning ones soon perceived that wealth and power must have charms to a heart that delighted in so much finery, and indulged in such unusual expense. Such marks could not escape the vigilant eyes of the two arch-tempters, Hutchinson and Sewall, who had more art, insinuation, and address, than all the rest of their party.[19]

Under the pen name of "Massachusettensis," Leonard published a series of weekly letters addressed to "the Inhabitants of the Province of Massachusetts Bay," running from December 12, 1774, to April 3, 1775, a fortnight before the affair at Lexington. They were begun soon after the adjournment of the Continental Congress, and may be taken as the final statement of the Tory argument. They were exceedingly skillful partisan pamphlets, adapted with great adroitness to current prejudices and old loyalties. Their main appeal was to the psychology of the colonial,

[19] *Works*, Vol. X, pp. 194–195; quoted in Tyler, *Literary History of the American Revolution*, Vol. I, Chapter XVI.

and if the springs of that psychology had not been sapped by the
rising liberalism, the appeal would have been extraordinarily
persuasive. Probably the King's cause was never presented more
convincingly, and the American Tories were delighted with the
letters. "On my return from Congress," said John Adams, "I
found the Massachusetts Gazette teeming with political speculations, and Massachusettensis shining like the moon among the
lesser stars." [20] He at once replied to them under the pen name
"Novanglus," beginning with a slashing attack in which the
seventeenth-century republicans are called in to refute Leonard,
and then reciting some plain facts about the British government
and its American spokesman, which somewhat tarnished the
latter's eulogies. But he soon strayed off into abstract disquisition, and the controversy was brought to an abrupt end with the
news from Lexington.

As in most Loyalist pamphlets, Leonard's appeal was primarily
to the law and the constitution, and it is tagged with references
to statutes like a proper lawyer's brief. But underlying the
argument is a political philosophy which fairly represents the
current Tory theory. The immediate purpose of the Letters was
to make the rebellious spirit of the colonial Whigs toward their
lawful sovereign appear both wicked and groundless, dangerous
to the peace and well-being of society and inspired by the personal
ambitions of demagogues. This major purpose involved him in
two main arguments: first, on the heinousness of rebellion in
general; and second, on the special heinousness of the Whig leaders.
Leonard's political philosophy is implied rather than elaborated.
With other American Loyalists he evaded broad principles; nevertheless his total argument rests on a philosophical foundation too
well known to be glossed over. He derived immediately from
Hobbes, and he follows the *Leviathan* in his exaltation of the
sovereign state. Men in a state of nature, he argued, live in a
condition of anarchy, with the hand of all against all. Amid such
chaos civilization is impossible, and the common need of security
for person and property impelled men to erect the coercive state
as an instrument of social protection. It first arose and has since
been maintained from the necessity of holding in check the spirit
of anarchy which continually threatens from the ambitions of
designing men. This is the great danger that lies always in

[20] Preface to *Novanglus and Massachusettensis*, 1819.

wait, ready to destroy society. Government is a guarantee of
the protection of the weak against the strong, and every friend
of law and order must enlist his loyalty on the side of the lawful
prince against all who would foment rebellion; for rebellion is the
mischief-maker that unlooses all the evils of Pandora's box.

This was no more than the familiar stock-in-trade of the Tory,
nevertheless Leonard becomes quite terrifying in describing the
evils of sedition:

Rebellion is the most atrocious offence, that can be perpetrated by man,
save those which are committed more immediately against the supreme
Governor of the Universe, who is the avenger of his own cause. It dis-
solves the social band, annihilates the security resulting from law and
government; introduces fraud, violence, rapine, murder, sacrilege, and the
long train of evils, that riot, uncontrouled, in a state of nature. Allegiance
and protection are reciprocal. The subject is bound by the compact to
yield obedience to government, and in return, is entitled to protection
from it; thus the poor are protected against the rich; the weak against
the strong; the individual against the many; and this protection is guar-
anteed to each member, by the whole community. But when government
is laid prostrate, a state of war, of all against all, commences; might over-
comes right; innocence itself has no security, unless the individual seques-
ters himself from his fellowmen, inhabits his own cave, and seeks his own
prey. This is what is called a state of nature.[21]

The "seeds of sedition" having been sown, they spring up and
bring forth fruits of death; the "people are led to sacrifice real
liberty to licentiousness, which gradually ripens into rebellion and
civil war."

And what is still more to be lamented, the generality of the people, who
are thus made the dupes of artifice, and the mere stilts of ambition, are
sure to be losers in the end. The best they can expect, is to be thrown
neglected by, when they are no longer wanted; but they are seldom so
happy; if they are subdued, confiscation of estate and ignominious death
are their portion; if they conquer, their own army is often turned upon
them, to subjugate them to a more tyrannical government than that they
rebelled against.[22]

Leonard then proceeds to supplement the Hobbesian argument
by an elaborate appeal to the history of English law, and discovers
ample sanction in a recital of a long list of statutory enactments
and court decisions against the evil of sedition. As treason is the
gravest social crime, so it has always been visited with the severest
punishments. He states the history of legislation against treason,

[21] Letter of February 6, 1775, in *Novanglus and Massachusettensis*, pp. 187–188.
[22] *Ibid.*, pp. 152–153.

and points out how the statutes have been construed to reach so far as to embrace the gathering of private men in a warlike manner, with a design to redress public grievances or to better their economic condition. He makes a parade of the brutal laws of feudal times, and the decisions of Tudor and Stuart judges, justifying those pronouncements as a necessary defense of society against sedition-mongers and their subversive ambitions. By a natural transition he brings the argument home to his American readers. The aims and methods of the Whigs, he contends, constitute a clear violation of the law of treason. They are playing with the gallows, with their Committees of Correspondence—"the foulest, subtlest, and most venomous serpent that ever issued from the eggs of sedition," and the imperative need of the hour was to put a stop to all treasonable thought and action.

I saw the small seed of sedition, when it was implanted; it was, as a grain of mustard. I have watched the plant until it has become a great tree; the vilest reptiles that crawl upon the earth, are concealed at the root; the foulest birds of the air rest upon its branches. I now would induce you to go to work immediately with axes and hatchets, and cut it down, for a twofold reason; because it is a pest to society, and lest it be felled suddenly by a stronger arm and crush thousands in the fall.[23]

From the first major proposition, that all sedition is heinous, Leonard passed to his second, that the sedition of the American Whigs was peculiarly wicked, for it was grounded in no injustice on the part of England. If loyalty is the highest social virtue, that loyalty might justly be claimed by Great Britain as her due. "Has she not been a nursing mother to us, from the days of our infancy to this time? Has she not been indulgent almost to a fault?" The Whigs, he asserted broadly, have been patching together their supposed grievances out of cloth that never came from an English loom. It is the shoddiest of homespun, mean, and shameful.

We had always considered ourselves, as a part of the British empire, and the parliament, as the supreme legislature of the whole. Acts of parliament for regulating our internal policy were familiar. We had paid postage, agreeable to act of parliament, . . . duties imposed for regulating trade, and even for raising a revenue to the crown without questioning the right, though we closely adverted to the rate or quantum. We knew that in all those acts of government, the good of the whole had been consulted, and whenever through want of information any thing grievous had been ordained, we were sure of obtaining redress by a proper representation of

[23] Letter of January 2, in *ibid.*, p. 159.

it. We were happy in our subordination; but in an evil hour, under the influence of a malignant planet, the design was formed of opposing the stamp-act, by a denial of the right of parliament to make it.[24]

Our patriots exclaim, "that humble and reasonable petitions from the representatives of the people have been frequently treated with contempt." This is as virulent a libel upon his majesty's government, as falsehood and ingenuity combined could fabricate. Our humble and reasonable petitions have not only been ever graciously received, when the established mode of exhibiting them has been observed, but generally granted. Applications of a different kind, have been treated with neglect, though not always with the contempt they deserved. These either originated in illegal assemblies, and could not be received without implicitly countenancing such enormities, or contained such matter, and were conceived in such terms, as to be at once an insult to his majesty, and a libel on his government. Instead of being decent remonstrances against real grievances, or prayers for their removal, they were insidious attempts to wrest from the crown, or the supreme legislature, their inherent, unalienable prerogatives or rights.[25]

The prerogative might not be argued, according to Leonard, nor the sovereignty of parliament discussed, for any such comment was "an insult to his majesty, and a libel on his government." The illegal Continental Congress had done both and thereby proved itself seditious.

The prince, or sovereign, as some writers call the supreme authority of a state, is sufficiently ample and extensive to provide a remedy for every wrong, in all possible emergencies and contingencies; and consequently a power, that is not derived from such authority, springing up in a state, must encroach upon it, and in proportion as the usurpation enlarges itself, the rightful prince must be diminished; indeed, they cannot long subsist together, but must continually militate, till one or the other be destroyed.[26]

The true animus of the Whig attack upon the nice balance of the British constitution Leonard professed to discover in a dangerous republican ambition. From the beginning there had been an excess of the democratic element in the charters and practice of many of the colonies; and this overbalance must in the end be rectified.

Our council boards are as destitute of the constitutional authority of the house of lords, as their several members are of the noble independence, and splendid appendages of peerage. The house of peers is the bulwark of the

[24] Letter of December 19, in *ibid.*, p. 147.
[25] Letter of March 27, in *ibid.*, pp. 217–218.
[26] *Ibid.*, p. 219.

British constitution, and through successive ages, has withstood the shocks of monarchy, and the sappings of democracy, and the constitution gained strength by the conflict.[27]

Lacking a peerage, which Leonard regrets, but which will come with time, American political practice is less stable than the English, more exposed to "the sappings of democracy"; but necessary steps have already been taken to stabilize it. The hands of the royal governor and judges have been strengthened against the democratic House, and "town meetings are restrained to prevent their passing traitorous resolves." The ideal towards which America must travel as fast as circumstance and the colonial temper will permit, is the wise balance of the English government, with local powers vested in colonial lords and commons, supervised by the King and the Imperial Parliament. In the midst of these present agitations, wickedly fomented by Whig smugglers—"a smuggler and a whig are cousin germans, the offspring of two sisters, avarice and ambition"—it should be remembered that "the terms whig and tory have been adopted according to the arbitrary use of them in this province, but they rather ought to be reversed; an American tory is a supporter of our excellent constitution, and an American whig a subverter of it." To bring these American subverters of the glorious British constitution to a sense of their obligations, Leonard refers them to the words of James Otis written ten years before:

It is a maxim, that the king can do no wrong; and every good subject is bound to believe his king is not inclined to do any. We are blessed with a prince who has given abundant demonstrations, that in all his actions, he studies the good of his people, and the true glory of his crown, which are inseparable. It would therefore be the highest degree of impudence and disloyalty, to imagine that the king, at the head of his parliament, could have any but the most pure and perfect intentions of justice, goodness and truth, that human nature is capable of. All this I say and believe of the king and parliament, in all their acts; even in that which so nearly affects the interests of the colonists; and that a most perfect and ready obedience is to be yielded to it while it remains in force. The power of parliament is uncontroulable but by themselves, and we must obey. They can only repeal their own acts. There would be an end of all government, if one or a number of subjects, or subordinate provinces should take upon them so far to judge of the justice of an act of parliament, as to refuse obedience to it. If there was nothing else to restrain such a step, prudence ought to do it, for forcibly resisting the parliament and the king's laws is high

[27] Letter of January 9, in *ibid.*, p. 171.

treason. Therefore let the parliament lay what burdens they please on us, we must, it is our duty to submit and patiently bear them, till they will be pleased to relieve us.[28]

The argument comes back finally to a threat; sovereignty rests not on good will but on coercion. The insincerity and unreality of the Tory appeal are only too patent. Those old pleaders were true to their breeding and their interests, for they regarded fact as little as a modern diplomat. They ignored or denied open and plain evidence. Nowhere, perhaps, does the weakness of Leonard's argument become more evident than in his refusal to admit the theoretical right of revolution. He professed allegiance to a king whose claim to the crown rested on revolution, and was justified by the apostle of Whiggery, Locke. But nowhere does he refer to Locke, and not until he was prodded by John Adams, who insisted that the Whig principles were "the principles of Aristotle and Plato, of Livy and Cicero, and Sydney, Harrington and Locke," did he concede that any other interpretation of revolution than the Hobbesian, was justifiable. In his last paper, of April 3, 1775, he replied to Adams thus:

I hold the rights of the people as sacred, and revere the principles, that have established the succession to the imperial crown of Great Britain, in the line of the illustrious house of Brunswick; but that the difficulty lies in applying them to the cause of the whigs . . . for admitting that the collective body of the people, that are subject to the British empire, have an inherent right to change their form of government, or race of kings, it does not follow, that the inhabitants of a single province, or of a number of provinces, or any given part under a majority of the whole empire, have such a right. By admitting that the less may rule or sequester themselves from the greater, we unhinge all government.[29]

By such logic does he whittle away the doctrine of the right of revolution. As a lawyer Daniel Leonard discovered a distinction between the Continental Congress of 1774 and the Revolutionary Convention of 1689, which rendered the former treasonable and the latter glorious. But the rising liberalism of America could see no such nice distinction, and a year later the brilliant young lawyer was forced to withdraw to Halifax. He was rewarded by a grateful King with the post of chief justice of Bermuda, lived to be nearly ninety, and died in London in 1829, one of the last of the exiled Loyalists.

[28] Letter of January 23, in *ibid.*, p. 181.   [29] *Ibid.*, p. 225.

III

JONATHAN BOUCHER

Tory Priest

The extremest expression of American Toryism came not un-fittingly from an Anglican priest. The English church has always been the mother of loyalty, and Jonathan Boucher of Virginia and Maryland was the spiritual son of a notable line of bishops and priests who upheld the royal prerogative through evil times and good, throwing the august sanction of religion about the monar-chical state. A fearless, capable, outspoken man was this English-born southerner, taking counsel of his own thought, not over-tolerant of those who differed with him, holding himself *in loco parentis* to his parishioners, and exacting obedience from them. He was another Increase Mather, with the same love of domination, the same directness of purpose and strength of will. A man of conspicuous parts and equally conspicuous position: not only a clergyman, but a gentleman of affairs, owner of a large plantation and many slaves, concerned with public business and a volunteer statesman: a sort of unofficial adviser and secretary to draft pro-vincial laws. Above all of independent mind. He would truckle to no man, and he subjected the opinions of his neighbors to the same scrutiny that he gave his own. For the popular orator and the demagogue he had frank contempt, and mass prejudices and mob power held no terrors for him.

There was both courage and futility in his free, outspoken career. He refused to be intimidated or turned aside by popular disfavor. "For more than six months I preached, when I did preach, with a pair of loaded pistols lying on the cushions; having given notice that if any one attempted, what had long been threatened, to drag me out of the pulpit, I should think myself justified in repelling violence by violence." One day he promptly knocked down a burly blacksmith who had been set on him, but there came a time when his church was filled with armed men, and his friends, fearing for his life, held him back forcibly from mounting the pulpit. That episode marked the end of his career in America. He had plainly become obsolete, and he was driven home to his native England. There as an old man, he published in 1797 thirteen sermons, preached in America between 1763 and 1775, with an historical preface, under the title, *A View of the Causes and Consequences of the American Revolution*, and dedicated to his old neighbor and friend, General Washington.

The political philosophy of Jonathan Boucher, as elaborated in these discourses, is frank and unequivocal. It is the voice of seventeenth-century Cavalier England, speaking to an alien people, bred up in another philosophy of government. Church and state, the Bible and the British constitution, the divine authority of God and the divine authority of the *status quo*, have got themselves curiously fused—and confused—in the mind of this disciple of Laud. It was the result not of ignorance but of conviction. When the revolutionary movement began to make a stir about him, the parish priest took the situation seriously and set about preparing himself to cope with it. Before then he had been no student of political theory, but now he turned to his books. "With sincerity in my heart, and my Bible in my hand," he said, "I sat down to explore the truth . . . to read and study what had been collected and laid down on the subject of government by writers . . . who got their materials . . . from the only pure sources of information, the law of God, and the law of the land." [30] The restriction in his choice of writers is suggestive of his bias; it eliminated at one stroke the main body of political speculation, not only the English thinkers of the preceding century, but the continental followers of the natural-rights school. Actually, however, Boucher did not limit himself so narrowly, for he refers frequently to Locke, and he was fairly familiar with the main doctrines of the revolutionary philosophy. But his most cherished discovery was Sir Robert Filmer's *Patriarcha*, and having digested Filmer's quaint theory, thenceforth he remained a confirmed patriarchist. The absurd jumble of Hebraic precedent and Tory prejudice which Filmer had laboriously put together and which Locke had knocked to pieces, was wholly convincing to this belated advocate of divine right, who proceeded to wipe the dust off the precious volume and expound its doctrines to an amazed congregation.

The single and sacred duty of the subject, Jonathan Boucher was convinced, is faithful obedience to the powers that are set over him. Those powers derive from God and are instituted for the subject's good. It follows, therefore, that the unpardonable sin is rebellion against lawfully constituted authority. "The doctrine

[30] *A View of the Causes, etc.*, p. 591.

of *obedience for conscience sake*," he asserted, "is . . . the great *cornerstone* of all good government." [31] With Daniel Leonard he makes much of it, but he appeals rather to the sanctions of religion than to the law.

> Obedience to Government is every man's duty, because it is every man's interest; but it is particularly incumbent on Christians, because . . . it is enjoined by the positive commands of God. . . . If the form of government under which the good providence of God has been pleased to place us be mild and free, it is our duty to enjoy it with gratitude and with thankfulness. . . . If it be less indulgent and less liberal than in reason it ought to be, still it is our duty not to disturb the peace of the community, by becoming refractory and rebellious subjects, and *resisting the ordinances of God*.[32]

> Those great and good men, who, *like wise master-builders*, have from time to time so *fitly framed together* our glorious Constitution, well knew that *other sure foundation no man could lay* than . . . obedience, not only *for wrath*, but *for conscience sake*.[33]

Because this spirit of obedience was openly flouted in America, where every influence made for rough individual liberty, Jonathan Boucher feared for the future. Loose principles were abroad, notions of popular sovereignty under the majority will, that must give "rise to a low and unworthy opinion of government," unless the people were recalled to their duty. Particularly dangerous, he thought, was "that loose notion respecting government, which has long been disseminated among the people at large with incredible industry, namely, that all government is the mere creature of the people, and may therefore be tampered with, altered, newmodelled, set up or pulled down, just as tumultuous crowds of the most disorderly persons in the community (who on such occasions are always so forward to call themselves *the people*) may happen in some giddy moments of overheated ardour to determine." [34]

The unhappy results of such evil principles Boucher saw spread through America. With the insidious undermining of respect for law and government, the vicious conception of republicanism made its appearance. "Everything in America had a republican aspect," he commented in after years; and he agreed with Bernard that "the splitting America into many small governments weakened the governing power, and strengthened that of the people." [35] If Parliament had been wise enough to consolidate government in

[31] *Ibid.*, p. 309.   [32] *Ibid.*, pp. 507–508.   [33] *Ibid.*, p. 306.
[34] *Ibid.*, p. 313.   [35] *Ibid.*, p. xliv.

America, drawing it to a single head, and investing it with dignity and authority, the country would not have become, like revolutionary France, "a mean and odious republic." As a minister and a loyal British subject, Jonathan Boucher would not seduce the American people "by any flowery panegyrics on liberty. Such panegyrics are the productions of ancient heathens and modern patriots: nothing of the kind is to be met with in the Bible, nor in the Statute Book. The word *liberty*, as meaning civil liberty, does not, I believe, occur in all the Scriptures." [36]

> To respect the laws, is to respect liberty in the only rational sense in which the term can be used; for liberty consists in subserviency to law. "Where there is no law," says Mr. Locke, "there is no freedom." . . . True liberty, then, is a liberty to do everything that is right, and the being restrained from doing anything that is wrong.[37]

The evils which flow from disrespect for authority carry much further than the unsettling of the political *status quo;* they end by overturning the entire social order. If any group or class rejects the divine plan according to which God has set each in its due place, society as a whole is involved in strife that may lapse into anarchy. It was an unhappy scene, prophesying an unhappier future, that the minister beheld in contemporary America.

> There never was a time when a whole people were so little governed by settled good principles. . . . Both employers and the employed, much to their mutual shame and inconvenience, no longer live together with anything like attachment and cordiality on either side; and the laboring classes, instead of regarding the rich as their guardians, patrons, and benefactors, now look on them as so many overgrown colossuses whom it is no demerit in them to wrong. A still more general . . . topic of complaint is, that the lower classes, instead of being industrious, frugal, and orderly (virtues so peculiarly becoming their station in life) are become idle, improvident, and dissolute.[38]

With social morality thus dangerously undermined, the Americans were a natural prey to demagogues, who filled the land with their clamor of patriotism and liberty. The situation in Virginia was peculiarly dangerous by reason of long-standing debts to English merchants which the planters were unable to pay; they found themselves in consequence, impaled on the horns of an unhappy dilemma, "to be loyal and be ruined, or to rebel and be damned." [39]

Instructed by the colonial troubles, Jonathan Boucher elaborated

[36] *Ibid.*, p. 504.
[38] *Ibid.*, p. 309.
[37] *Ibid.*, pp. 509 and 511.
[39] *Ibid.*, Preface, p. xlii.

a theory of the true origin and purpose of government, a theory taken straight out of Filmer, which he expands thus:

> As soon as there were some to be governed, there were also some to govern. . . . The first father was the first king: and . . . it was thus that all government originated, and monarchy is the most ancient form.[40]

> The glory of God is much concerned, that there should be good government in the world: it is, therefore, the uniform doctrine of the Scriptures, that it is under the deputation and authority of God alone that *kings reign and princes decree justice.* Kings and princes (which are only other words for supreme magistrats) were doubtless created and appointed, not so much for their own sakes, as for the sake of the people committed to their charge: yet they are not, therefore, the creatures of the people. So far from deriving their authority from any supposed consent or suffrage of men, they receive their commission from Heaven; they receive it from God, the source and original of all power.[41]

Instituted by God and functioning under divine sanction, government becomes, therefore, a divine instrument, for the security of which He is greatly concerned: "Everything our blessed Lord either said or did, pointedly tended to discourage the disturbing a settled government." "Unless we are good subjects, we cannot be good Christians." Jesus "thought it would be better, both for Judea in particular, and for the world in general, that . . . the people should not be distracted by a revolution, and . . . that there should be no precedent to which revolutionists might appeal." "The only very intolerable grievance in government is, when men allow themselves to disturb and destroy the peace of the world, by vain attempts to render that perfect, which the laws of our nature have ordained to be imperfect." "To suffer nobly indicates more greatness of mind than can be shown by acting valiantly."[42]

Jonathan Boucher was the high Tory of the Tory cause in America. He refused to strike his flag to the pirate craft of republicanism; he would not truckle to newfangled notions; but stood up stoutly to be counted for God and the King. In laying bare the heart of Toryism, he unwittingly gave aid and comfort to the detested cause of liberalism. It is reasonable to assume that such militant loyalty to the outworn doctrine of passive submission was a real disservice to the ministry, for it revealed the prerogative in a light peculiarly offensive to American prejudices. What a godsend to the liberals was such doctrine on the lips of so eminent a divine!

[40] *Ibid.*, p. 525.   [41] *Ibid.*, p. 534.   [42] *Ibid.*, pp. 535, 538, 542, 543.

CHAPTER III

JOHN DICKINSON

The Mind of the American Whig

FOR many colonials it was a hard and bitter choice that was thrust upon them by the political situation. They had no wish to choose between loyalty to the British Empire and love for their native land. So long as the quarrel remained a legal dispute over parliamentary encroachments, colonial sentiment was fairly united in opposition to the ministerial policy; differences of opinion arose over methods of defense, rather than the need of it. The threatened loss of home rule drew together radical and conservative. Although Governor Hutchinson asserted that the feeling against England was the work of a small populistic element—"in Massachusetts Bay the exception to the constitutional authority of Parliament was first taken, and principally supported, by men who were before discontented"[1]—it is clear that the active Tory party numbered at first few more than the royal officials and their beneficiaries. But when it came to the point of severing colonial relations with the mother country, comparatively few among the upper classes in the northern and middle colonies went with the party of independence. The moderate men, the conciliationists, were crushed between the two extremes, and the Tory party was greatly increased in numbers and influence.

Of this moderate party of conciliationists, the outstanding figure during the years of tedious debate was John Dickinson, of Philadelphia. His *Letters from a Pennsylvania Farmer*, published between December 2, 1767, and February 15, 1768, created considerable stir both in America and England, and if Hutchinson may be trusted, they "formed a temporary political creed for the colonies." Later he was chief draftsman of a notable series of state papers: the Declaration of Rights of the Stamp Act Congress; the two Petitions to the King and the Address to the Inhabitants of Quebec of the first Continental Congress; and finally the Articles

[1] *History of Massachusetts Bay*, Vol. III, p. 257.

of Confederation. Professor Tyler has fastened upon him the title of "penman of the Revolution"; but a juster title, and more in accord with the facts, would be "spokesman of the Colonial Whigs." From his first entrance into public life to the adoption of the Constitution, Dickinson was a consistent advocate of the political philosophy of which John Pym was the early representative, Locke the philosophical defender, and Pitt the parliamentary advocate—a philosophy which he accepted as the final embodiment of the long struggle for English freedom.

English Whiggery has been fortunate in its advocates. It has been expounded with great fervor and glossed with much eloquence. Its ends have been so persistently proclaimed as at one with the cause of human liberty, that in the mind of English-speaking people it early became synonymous with English liberalism. In so far as it represented a protest against divine right, such an interpretation was historically just. It was the expression of a rising class, and every rising class in its ostensible program professes to be liberal. But in the outcome Whiggery proved to be very different from generic liberalism. Examined critically the program of Whiggery is seen to have been compounded of substantial economic interests. Although the Whig party created the modern House of Commons and ministerial government, and wrote into the British constitution the principle of no taxation without representation, back of such revolutionary changes was a middle-class, property theory of society. It laid down as the first principle of political science the dogma that government is instituted for the protection of property; and it advanced by inevitable stages to the position that government should use its powers to extend the field of profitable operations and safeguard exploitation, the natural outcome of which was a policy of imperialism. On the pretense of furthering human liberty it carried the British flag and British goods to the ends of the earth. The great Pitt, grandson of the unscrupulous exploiter of India, completed the work begun by John Pym more than a century before; the American Revolution was the natural sequence of an imperialistic policy begun by Cromwell's Navigation Act, which, aimed immediately at the Dutch carriers, put the power of the government behind British shipping to the disadvantage of American competitors.

The philosophy of Whiggery had spread widely in America before the Revolution and numbered among its advocates probably

the great majority of thoughtful Americans. Of these John
Dickinson became the best known, although he was certainly not
the ablest—less able, indeed, than his fellow Marylander, Daniel
Dulany. Of Quaker extraction, Dickinson was a country gentleman who inherited broad acres, an honorable name, and high
social position. His dignified standing was further assured by his
marriage with the only surviving child of Isaac Norris, long Speaker
of the Pennsylvania Assembly, and the most influential amongst
a little group of wealthy merchants who had long ruled the commonwealth in patriarchal fashion. By his wife he came into
possession of Fairhill, a country place of several hundred acres on
the outskirts of Philadelphia, one of the show places of the city,
of which the mansion with its stately façade, its waxed floors and
red-cedar wainscoting, its books and paintings and statuary,
its setting of gardens and fishponds and conservatories, was vastly
impressive to a world that loved dignified display.

With such advantages of wealth and position he could hardly
fail to get on in his profession, and within a short time after his
return from the Inns of Court at London, where he had his training
in the law, he became one of the leaders of the Philadelphia bar and
was soon deep in commonwealth politics. He was a gentleman in a
society of gentlemen and preferment came easily to him. His
natural parts were respectable, he had improved himself by considerable reading in history and politics, he possessed a cultivated
pen and some facility in debate. He understood commercial problems, could talk trade, was ready with statistics of imports and
exports, and was an advocate of the paper money which Philadelphia merchants had discovered to be a stimulus to business.
Among his intimate friends were Robert Morris, Thomas Willing,
and George Clymer, representatives of the younger generation of
Philadelphians, whose speculative enterprises were not approved
by their conservative elders. And so by consequence he became
the spokesman of the mercantile interests in their remonstrance
against the ministerial policies.

But Dickinson was more than a legal adviser to clients who
were in trade. As lawyer and statesman he was true to the best
traditions of the English law and the British constitution, faithful
to what he conceived to be the larger interests of the British Empire.
In all his public acts he was animated by a scrupulous sense of
duty, swerving no whit from the line of conduct marked out by

his principles in spite of the clamor of opposition. From first to last he seems to have been guided by a fine sense of responsible stewardship that came to him from his English heritage. Certainly the dignity of John Dickinson and the integrity of his political career suffer little by contrast with certain popular representatives who governed their conduct by expediency rather than principle. The great ideal of imperial unity possessed him completely, and he would do nothing to bring it into jeopardy. He sacrificed his great influence with the radicals by his refusal to go with the majority for independence; he would not assist in disrupting the British Empire even though he could not preserve it. The refusal was difficult and it destroyed his popularity in a moment. He withdrew from active participation in political affairs, and for years afterwards, to the eyes of former associates, his conduct seemed to have been pusillanimous.

By temperament and breeding Dickinson was a conservative, and this native bias was emphasized by his English training in the law. The lawyers of the middle and southern colonies were far better trained than those of New England. Many were from the Inns of Court, where they had steeped themselves in the Common Law and had imbibed profound respect for the orderly processes of English legal procedure. They found intellectual satisfaction in tracing the evolution of constitutional practice, and their methods of thought were too strictly legal to suffer them to stray into the domain of extra-legal political speculation. Their appeal was to the law and the constitution; never to abstract principles. If, on the other hand, the revolutionary leaders of New England—and Virginians like Jefferson and Patrick Henry—were poorer lawyers they were better political scientists, for their legal training had been too casual and too scanty to contract their minds to statutes and precedents. Jefferson and John Adams were alike in this respect; their interests were speculative rather than legal; and they wrote more convincingly when defending the principles of Locke than in expounding Coke.

But John Dickinson remained always the lawyer. The English political thinkers of the seventeenth century scarcely touched the fringe of his mind. In consequence his writings are a long constitutional argument. He rarely refers to political authorities. The philosophy of Locke—whom he had read—is largely ignored, and Hume—"this great man whose political speculations are so much admired"—is quoted only in support of a constitutional interpretation. "The constitutional modes of relief are those I wish to see pursued on the present occasion," he insisted in reply to the natural-rights advocates, and the attitude is eloquent of the man. This scrupulous legalism he carried to such lengths that when the new constitution for Pennsylvania was adopted he refused to take office under it because he doubted the legality of the convention that framed it.

With such temperament and training Dickinson would seem to have had the making of an excellent Tory in him. What cause had he to quarrel with Great Britain, and why should he have risked his lot with the party of protest? It was not because he denied the ministerial theory of parliamentary sovereignty in America, for he acknowledged both the fact and the necessity for such sovereignty:

He, who considers these provinces as states distinct from the *British Empire*, has very slender notions of *justice*, or of their *interests*. We are but parts of a *whole* and therefore there must exist a power somewhere to preside, and preserve the connection in due order. This power is lodged in the parliament; and we are as much dependent on *Great-Britain* as a perfectly free people can be on another.[2]

Nor was it because of old trade grievances—shipping restrictions, the spying of customs officers, prohibitions laid on manufactures, and the like. He accepted without challenge the English mercantile view of the economic relations of colonies to the mother country, and he professed to see in existing trade regulations only the incidental and necessary burdens of a system both salutary and just; he had no protest to urge against the principle of the Navigation Acts.

Colonies have been settled by the nations of *Europe* for the purposes of trade. These purposes were to be attained, by the colonies raising for their mother country those things which she did not produce herself; and by supplying themselves from her with things they wanted. These were the *national objects*, in the commencement of our colonies, and have been uniformly so in their promotion. . . . The parent country, with undeviating prudence and virtue, attentive to the first principles of colonization, drew to herself the benefits she might reasonably expect, and preserved to her children the blessings, on which those benefits were founded. She made laws, obliging her colonies to carry to her all those products which she wanted for her own use; and all those raw materials

2 "Farmer's Letters," in *Works*, Vol. I, p. 312.

which she chose herself to work up. Besides this restriction, she forbad them to procure *manufactures* from any other part of the globe, or even the *products* of *European* countries, which alone could rival her, without first being brought to her. In short, by a variety of laws, she regulated their trade in such a manner as she thought most conducive to their mutual advantage, and her own welfare.[3]

Not only did Dickinson concede to the mother country the right to regulate the entire system of colonial trade and industry to the primary advantage of British merchants, even going so far as to justify it by a false historical explanation of the rise of the colonies; not only did he profess to believe that such regulation had been exercised in a spirit of unselfish concern for the well-being of the empire; but he professed a faith in the King and the English people that suggests Hutchinson and Bernard. Consider such naïve adulation as the following:

We have an excellent prince, in whose good dispositions towards us we may confide. We have a generous, sensible and humane nation, to whom we may apply. They may be deceived. They may, by artful men, be provoked to anger against us. I cannot believe they will be cruel or unjust; or that their anger will be implacable. Let us behave like dutiful children, who have received unmerited blows from a beloved parent. Let us complain to our parent; but let our complaints speak at the same time the language of affliction and veneration.[4]

With so much conceded, what ground of serious quarrel remained? What was there to justify an American protest against the parliamentary program? Nothing less than the vital principle of taxation. In this matter the ministerial policy overrode the fundamental tenet of Whiggery. The situation was critical, for if the Tories denied the validity of the Whiggish principle in dealing with the colonies, they might deny it at home and the old battle of 1688 must be fought over. The right of control of the public purse by a chamber in which the property owners were represented, and which they would dominate, was a principle too vital to be yielded, and the English Whigs in Parliament, led by Pitt and Camden, took vigorous issue with the ministerial tax proposals. To American Whigs the proposed innovation was a calamity. To suffer control of the American purse to pass out of their hands into those of a group beyond their reach meant a return to a system of Tory spoliation; it meant that property and the rule of property

[3] *Ibid.*, p. 337.   [4] *Ibid.*, p. 327.

in America were threatened. To the colonial Whig the constitutional representative chamber could be no other than the assembly of the commonwealth of which he was a taxpayer. The English Parliament was alien if not hostile to his interests; and if the right of imposing taxes upon the colonies were held to lie in this overseas body, the colonials would find themselves in the identical position of their ancestors of the days of King Charles. No longer masters of their property, they would not be a free people.

All this John Dickinson understood perfectly, and as a large property owner he hastened to the defense of the principle of self-taxation. He proposed to show that the policy of the ministry, in advancing the new tax program, was a usurpation of power and a violation of the constitutional rights of American property owners; and that as such it should be resisted on constitutional grounds. This is the burden of the celebrated *Letters from a Pennsylvania Farmer*. In arguing their case the American debaters were embarrassed by a long series of precedents which seemed to prove that Parliament possessed sovereignty over the colonies; that such sovereignty had in fact been repeatedly acknowledged; and that a hundred years of fiscal legislation, unchallenged heretofore, had clearly established the parliamentary right of taxation. To this difficult point Dickinson directed his argument. The real point at issue, he contended, lay in the fundamental distinction between a tax and an imposition; Parliament possessed the constitutional right to impose the latter, but not the former. An imposition, he pointed out, is a fiscal arrangement made by the proper representatives, primarily "for the regulation of trade," and with a view to the general interests of the whole; whereas a tax is a "gift of the people to the crown, to be employed for public uses." The one is regulatory in intent, imposed in a paternal spirit; and though the result may lessen or increase the opportunity of the individual or the community to acquire property, it does not take away what has already been got; whereas a tax reaches into the pocket of the individual and takes from him what belongs to him alone. Unless the subject "give and grant of his own free will," such a tax had long been held unconstitutional. Of necessity, every tax must be internal, and since by their charter governments the colonies were granted the right to impose "internal taxes," Parliament has no right to impose them.

A "TAX" means an imposition to raise money. Such persons therefore as speak of *internal* and external "TAXES," I pray may pardon me, if I object to that expression, as applied to the privileges and interests of these colonies. There may be *internal* and *external* IMPOSITIONS, founded on *different principles*, and having *different tendencies*, every "tax" being an imposition, tho' every imposition is not a "tax." But *all taxes* are founded on the same *principles*; and have the *same tendency*. External impositions, for the regulation of our trade, do not "grant to his Majesty *the property of the colonies*." They only *prevent the colonies acquiring property*, in things not necessary, in a manner judged to be injurious to the welfare of the whole empire. But the last statute respecting us, "grants to his Majesty *the property of the colonies*," by laying duties on the manufactures of *Great-Britain* which they MUST take, and which she settled on them, on purpose that they SHOULD take. What *tax* can be more internal than this? Here is money drawn, *without their consent*, from a society, who have constantly enjoyed a constitutional mode of raising all money among themselves.[5]

This line of argument was not original with Dickinson. It had earlier been elaborated by Daniel Dulany of Maryland, in an able pamphlet,[6] which had provided argument to Pitt for his speech on the repeal of the Stamp Act.[7] Dickinson in turn quoted from Pitt's speech in support of his position.[8] How intimate was the connection between English and American Whigs, and how like was their reasoning, is made clear from a passage of a later speech by Pitt which Dickinson quoted in the preface to a collected edition of his works issued in 1801:

This universal opposition to your arbitrary system of taxation, might have been foreseen; it was obvious from the nature of things, and from the nature of man, and *above all* . . . from the spirit of WHIGGISM flourishing in *America*. The spirit which *now* pervades *America*, is *the same* which formerly opposed loans, benevolences, and ship-money in this country; is *the same spirit* which roused all *England* to action at the revolution, and which established at a remote era, your liberties, on the basis of that grand fundamental maxim of the constitution, that no subject of *England* shall be taxed, but by his own consent. To maintain this principle, is the *common cause* of the WHIGS, on the other side of the *Atlantic*, and on this. *It is liberty to liberty engaged*. In this great cause they are immoveably allied. It is the alliance of *God* and *nature*, immutable, eternal, fixed as the firmament of heaven. As an *Englishman*, I recognize to the *Americans*, their supreme unalterable right of property. As an *American*, I would

[5] *Ibid.*, pp. 332–333.
[6] *Considerations on the Propriety of Imposing Taxes in the British Colonies, for the Purpose of Raising a Revenue by Act of Parliament.*
[7] See Tyler, *Literary History of the American Revolution*, Vol. I, p. 111.
[8] *Works*, Vol. I, p. 320.

equally recognize to *England*, her supreme right of regulating commerce and navigation. This distinction is involved in the abstract nature of things; property is private, individual, absolute: the touch of another annihilates it. Trade is an extended and complicated consideration; it reaches as far as ships can sail, or winds can blow; it is a vast and various machine. To regulate the numberless movements of its several parts, and combine them into one harmonious effect, for the good of the whole, requires the superintending wisdom and energy of the supreme power of the empire. On this grand practical distinction, then, let us rest: taxation is theirs, commercial regulation is ours. As to metaphysical refinements, attempting to shew, that the *Americans* are equally free from legislative controul, and commercial restraint, as from taxation, for the purpose of revenue, I pronounce them futile, frivolous, and groundless.[9]

How characteristic of Pitt is the shrewd purpose, covered over with pretentious rhetoric, to seize the imperialistic substance of trade control for the London merchants, and graciously yield in the name of liberty, the shadow of taxation!

Discussion of abstract rights interested Dickinson no more than it did Pitt; but he cared greatly for English liberty, by which he meant the rights of propertied gentlemen recognized by the British constitution, for which his ancestors had struggled. He had no wish to enlarge those rights, for he believed they were adequate to the well-being of Englishmen. No thought of a republican form of government crossed his mind. He had no sympathy with democracy; he believed in a "mixed government" as exemplified in the British system; and while he was not an outspoken advocate of an American peerage, he would have approved of its institution. Like so many upper-class Americans, he was English as well as colonial; he could not conceive that the heritage of England to her sons was circumscribed by geographical lines, and he habitually thought and spoke in terms of the British Empire, and never in local terms. What he most feared was a misunderstanding that would widen into rupture. There is more than a hint of the doctrine of passive resistance in his counsel of moderation:

The cause of *liberty* is a cause of too much dignity to be sullied by turbulence and tumult. It ought to be maintained in a manner suitable to her nature. Those who engage in it, should breathe a sedate, yet fervent spirit, animating them to actions of prudence, justice, modesty, bravery, humanity, and magnanimity. . . . I hope, my dear countrymen, that you will, in every colony, be on your guard against those, who may at any time endeavour to stir you up, under pretense of patriotism, to any measures

[9] *Ibid.*, pp. xv-xvii.

disrespectful to our Sovereign and our mother country. Hot, rash, disorderly proceedings, injure the reputation of a people, as to wisdom, valour,
and virtue, without procuring them the least benefit. I pray GOD, that he
may be pleased to inspire you and your posterity, to the latest ages, with a
spirit of which I have an idea, that I find a difficulty to express. To express it in the best manner I can, I mean a spirit, that shall so guide you,
that it will be impossible to determine whether an *American's* character is
most distinguishable, for its loyalty to his Sovereign, his duty to his mother
country, his love of freedom, or his affection for his native soil.[10]

In these earlier years of the controversy Dickinson seems to
have remained placidly unaware of the sordid realities of parliamentary huckstering, the details of which Franklin was daily
noting in his letters. He seems honestly to have believed in the
justice and good intentions of the King and his ministers, and he
felt little sympathy for the New England malcontents. But as
the debate dragged on, and the English politicians in whose recti-
tude he had professed confidence, clearly were playing into the
hands of British trading interests, going so far as to seek to bolster
up the falling fortunes of the East India Company at the expense
of colonial merchants, he was impelled to speak with plebeian
warmth. His *Two Letters on the Tea Tax*, written in November,
1773, are as vigorous in denunciation as Samuel Adams could
have penned.

Five Ships, loaded with TEA, on their Way to *America*, and this with a
View not only to *enforce* the *Revenue Act*, but to *establish* a *Monopoly* for the
East-India Company, who have espoused the Cause of the Ministry; and
hope to repair their broken Fortunes by the Ruin of *American* freedom and
Liberty! No Wonder the Minds of the People are exasperated . . . to a
degree of Madness. . . . Pray have you heard, whether *they* and the
Ministers have not *made a Property* of US, and whether WE, our WIVES and
CHILDREN, together, with the HARD EARNED FRUITS OF OUR LABOUR, are
not *made over* to this almost *bankrupt Company*, to augment their Stock,
and to *repair* their *ruined Fortunes?* Justice seems to have forsaken the
old World. . . . The Rights of free States and Cities are swallowed up in
Power. Subjects are considered as Property. . . . Are we . . . to be
given up to the Disposal of the *East-India Company?* . . . . Their conduct in Asia, for some Years past, has given ample Proof, how little they
regard the Laws of Nations, the Rights, Liberties, or Lives of Men. They
have levied War, excited Rebellions, dethroned lawful Princes, and
sacrificed Millions for the Sake of Gain . . . hackneyed as they are in
Murders, Rapine, and Cruelty, [they] would sacrifice the Lives of Thousands to preserve their Trash, and enforce their measures.[11]

[10] "Farmer's Letters," in *Works*, Vol. I, pp. 324–325.
[11] *Works*, Vol. I, pp. 459–461.

The ideal of a beneficent British Empire, extending English freedom through the world, appealed to the imagination of Dickinson; but the reality of British imperialism, "hackneyed in murders, rapine and cruelty," seeking to extend its exploitation to America, striking at the trade interests of Philadelphia and his merchant friends, was enough to disturb his legal calm. What fate awaited American rights and liberties if the London imperialists were permitted to prey upon them, he began to comprehend. The bones would be picked clean, and America would become another India. It was the deepening fear of such a possibility that sapped Dickinson's loyalty, and reconciled him to independence after the thing was done.

The later years of Dickinson were happier than those of the middle period. The conservative reaction that set in with the conclusion of peace carried the emerging party of nationalism back to the position of Whiggery, which Dickinson had tenaciously occupied. The leaders of that party were coming to agree on the necessity for a closer alignment in defense of property rule, and they gladly accepted Dickinson as an ally and co-worker. He was chosen a member of the Constitutional Convention, and there found a congenial audience for the exposition of his political principles. In the debates he spoke as a high Federalist who would like to go further toward the model of the British system than the state of the public mind rendered expedient. A strong and stable government, he believed, depended upon a just balance of king, lords, and commons.

A limited monarchy he considered as *one* of the best governments in the world. He was not certain that the same blessings were derivable from any other form. It was certain that equal blessings had never yet been derived from any of the republican forms. A limited monarchy, however, was out of the question. The spirit of the times, the state of our affairs, forbade the experiment, if it were desirable. Was it possible, moreover, in the nature of things, to introduce it, even if these objects were less insuperable? A house of nobles was essential to such a government. Could these be created by a breath, or by a stroke of the pen? No. They were the growth of ages, and could only arise under a complication of circumstances none of which existed in this country. But, though a form the most perfect, *perhaps*, in itself, be unattainable, we must not despair.[12]

Granted the necessity of a republican form of government, the question so vital to Whiggery remained, how could property secure

12 *Elliot's Debates*, Vol. V, p. 148.

and maintain a commanding position in the government? The reply was obvious; it must be through limitation of suffrage rights. If the vote could be restricted to property holders, even though small freeholders were included, the common rights of property would be secure.

Mr. Dickinson had a very different idea of the tendency of vesting the rights of suffrage in the freeholders of the Country. He considered them as the best guardians of liberty; And the restriction of the right to them as a necessary defence agst. the dangerous influence of those multitudes without property & without principle, with which our country like all others, will in time abound.[13]

A further safeguard offered in the proper constitution of the Senate. As a representative of a small state, Dickinson was concerned that the several states should enjoy a parity of power in the upper house, as he was concerned that the Senate should provide a safeguard for property interests. It must be rendered secure from factional unrest and democratic aggression. He was very likely at one with his friend George Clymer, in holding that "a representative of the people is appointed to think *for* and not *with* his constituents"; and to the end that the right persons should be chosen to do the national thinking, he laid down the principle that, "In the formation of the Senate, we ought to carry it through such a refining process as will assimilate it as nearly as may be to the House of Lords in England."[14] Such expressions throw sufficient light upon Dickinson's opinions of democratic government, but they do not prepare us for a curious inconsistency that marked his last years, namely, his friendship for Jefferson and his sympathy with the Jeffersonian program. The reasons for this strange shift are not clear, but it is generally attributed to his fear of consolidation that might end in subordinating the small states to the greater ones. It certainly was not due to any sympathy with agrarianism.

Dickinson was in no sense a serious political thinker. He was a cultivated lawyer who defended with skill and grace a ready-made philosophy, unconcerned about the social significance of that philosophy. Scarcely anywhere else in his writings does he show to such poor advantage as in the nine *Letters of Fabius* written in defense of the Constitution during the great debate. There is in them not a single illuminating comment. His most anxious concern is shown in his reply to George Mason's direct charge, that the "government will commence in a moderate aristocracy; it is at present impossible to foresee whether it will, in its operation, produce a monarchy, or a corrupt oppressive aristocracy." [15] After searching the records of the past he concludes that "the uniform tenor of history . . . holds up the *licentiousness* of the people, and *turbulent temper* of some of the states, as *the only causes* to be dreaded, not the conspiracies of federal officers." [16] The argument had been somewhat staled by Federalistic repetition, but Dickinson soberly accepted it as sound historical interpretation. His cleverest defense he found in an appeal to the analogy of the British constitution, which has only one democratic branch, and that "diseased" by inadequate representation, to withstand the power and influence of king and lords; if English liberty has been thus safeguarded, what danger can threaten America with "a constitution and government, every branch of which is so extremely popular"?[17]

However greatly the writings of Dickinson, from the Farmer's Letters to the *Letters of Fabius*, may have appealed to Whiggish lawyers, it is inconceivable that they should have appealed to the rank and file of Americans. As an eighteenth-century gentleman he little understood the spirit of liberalism that was stirring in many minds; he did not sympathize with the turbulent forces that were driving towards a different social order; and in consequence his technical arguments seem today curiously old-fashioned. Franklin's common sense kept him a realist; but Dickinson's loyalty made him an idealist, incapable of understanding current economic forces either in England or America. The colonial was so ingrained in his habits of thought that it was hard for him to become an American. So long as it was politic to profess loyalty to England while remonstrating against ministerial policies, John Dickinson was the man for the business. But when it became necessary to throw aside the mask of loyal professions, to stand up and fight, he was thrust aside to make room for more vigorous spokesmen. No doubt there were desirable things which the radicals overlooked; no doubt the ideal of imperial unity, of a world-wide federation of the several bodies of Englishmen, possessed a

[15] Quoted in Ford, *Pamphlets on the Constitution*, p. 332.
[16] *Ibid.*, p. 200.   [17] *Ibid.*, p. 212.

grandeur which ardent patriots held too cheap. But that ideal did not prevail, despite Dickinson's earnest endeavors; and in the new order which arose he probably never felt quite at home, or was free from a lingering regret. He belonged still in that older world in which he was bred.

CHAPTER IV

SAMUEL ADAMS

The Mind of the American Democrat

In the history of the rise of political democracy in America Samuel Adams occupies a distinguished place. He was by no means the first American to espouse the democratic cause, but he was the first to conceive the party machinery to establish it in practice. The single purpose of his life was the organization of the rank and file to take over control of the political state. He was the instrument of a changing world that was to transfer sovereignty from the aristocratic minority to the democratic majority. Political sovereignty inheres potentially in the mass will of the people; but if that will is restrained from exercising its strength by an undemocratic psychology, it remains powerless in presence of an organized minority. The America in which Samuel Adams labored was ripe to throw off the inhibitions of the popular will; and it was his perception of that fact, and the tenacity and skill with which he cajoled the mass to "make a push for perfect political liberty," that made him an outstanding figure in our history. In his hands the majority will became in reality the sovereign will. But before he could wield it he must create it; and before he could create it he must understand the mass mind. He must turn popular prejudice to his own purpose; he must guide the popular resentment at grievances into the way of revolution; he must urge the slow moving mass forward until it stood on the threshold of independence, beyond which lay the ultimate goal of his ambitions, the democratic state. And so, in pursuit of his life purpose, Samuel Adams became a master political strategist, the first of our great popular leaders.

The modern term, professional agitator, most adequately characterizes him. He was an intriguing rebel against every ambition of the regnant order. He hated every sort of aristocratic privilege, whether in the form of overseas prerogative or in the later guise of native Federalism; it must be swept away and a new, democratic order take its place. In the pursuit of this great end he daily counseled treason and made rebellion his business. Loyalty to the government *de facto* was no virtue in his political ethics; he was not frightened into conformity by the stigma attaching to the term rebel. America was founded in rebellion, he well knew, and it should continue in rebellion till every false loyalty was cast off and concern for the common well-being accepted as the single loyalty worthy of respect. "What has commonly been called rebellion in the people," he commented wisely, "has often been nothing else but a manly and glorious struggle in opposition to the lawless power of rebellious Kings and Princes." [1] He was the outstanding example in his day of the militant idealist to whom the dissemination of unrest was a matter of principle. No cause goes forward without its leaders, and democratic America owes Samuel Adams a debt which it has too grudgingly acknowledged.

He was born and grew up in an atmosphere of politics. His father was a prosperous, well-read gentleman who found politics a pleasant avocation; he established the Caucus Club for political discussion, and became one of the leaders of the popular party that opposed the Tory group, gathered about the royal officials. Its personnel can only be guessed at, but it was probably composed of small merchants, with a following of mechanics and other unimportant folk. It seems to have been greatly interested in currency reform, and the elder Adams was one of the principal organizers and stockholders of the Land Bank, a project for increasing the money of the commonwealth. The institution was roughly liquidated by government decree at the instigation of commercial rivals interested in "tight money"; the father lost heavily and the son was pretty much ruined by later attempts at arbitrary collection on his stock. It seems to have been a petty and altogether sordid move on the part of government, in which Hutchinson played an important part. With the loss of his money Samuel Adams, Jr., settled down to a meager, somewhat precarious existence, preferring politics to profits, and began that long, arduous career which resulted so momentously for America.

He had taken his two degrees at Harvard in the expectation of becoming a minister; but while an undergraduate he was more interested in the political classics than in theology, and he rejected the ministry for the law. But a brief experience with Coke sufficed, and he turned to more congenial fields. With a group of like-

[1] *Works*, Vol. II, p. 269.

minded young men he founded in 1748 *The Public Advertiser*,
a weekly magazine of politics. In the essays which as a young
man of twenty-six he wrote for that paper, he expounded a political
creed frankly liberal. He began as he ended, anti-Tory and pro-
democratic. From then till the beginning of the tax troubles he
was a tireless contributor to the newspapers, and except during
the administration of the liberal Pownall, always in the opposition.
Hutchinson stated the exact truth when he said, "He was for
near twenty years a writer against government in the public
newspapers." The need was urgent, for during those years the
government of Massachusetts was being subtly changed. With
increasing prosperity, ways of thinking, like styles of dress, were
becoming more like those of St. James's. Ambitious young men
were drawn into the circle of the ruling group and caught with
the bait of preferment. An aristocracy was emerging that wanted
only titles to make ready to set up a House of Lords. Quite
plainly it was time for the liberals to arouse the rank and file of
the people to the danger, and this became the daily business of
Samuel Adams.

The evidence available is insufficient to explain the motives
which impelled him to take up and carry forward so difficult and
thankless a work. The cost in personal ease and the good opinion
of respectable people was great, the peril certain, and the reward
dubious. Not lightly will a serious man compromise with treason;
to talk republicanism was not profitable in Tory New England;
and Samuel Adams, no more than another, was anxious to come to
close acquaintance with the hangman. What secret motives
inspired the heart of this ascetic Puritan—"he eats little, drinks
little, sleeps little, thinks much," said the Loyalist Galloway, half
sneeringly, half out of respect—we can only guess at. Very likely
there was an old grudge at a government that had ruined him;
very likely love of power stimulated his hatred of the ruling clique;
very likely his close association with tradesmen colored his resentment at overseas regulation, for better than most, he knew that
the American goose was reserved for English plucking. Nevertheless the more intimately one comes to know Samuel Adams
the more inadequate seem all cynical and sordid interpretations
of his strange career. He was no self-seeking politician, but a
man of vision. He believed ardently in the principle of local
home rule. Love of the New England town-meeting democracy

was bred in his bones. More clearly than others he saw the danger of erecting a governing class irresponsive to the popular will. He was, in short, the embodiment of the rising spirit of the eighteenth century that found expression in individualism, that exalted liberty and hated tyranny—a spirit that had for its ultimate purpose the reduction of the powers of the political state.

His critical study of the methods of Tory politicians early stripped from government the last vestige of glamor so appealing to the ignorant. Adams understood too perfectly the secret springs and backstairs intrigues that determined governmental policies, to be taken in by appeal to his loyalty. English politics was a sordid business, conducted by professional traders, to whom loyalty and patriotism were no more than gestures to gull the simple. Quite as well as Franklin, Adams understood its ways. He had watched the steady unfolding of the ministerial program: how it was proposed to free the royal governor and judges from popular restraint by the payment of salaries from the royal chest; to change the charter in the interest of prerogative by vesting the nomination of the councilors in the governor; to disarm the democracy by destroying the town meeting as a political instrument; in short to substitute government by ministerial instructions for government by the people. As he watched the calculated encroachments upon the historical rights of the commonwealth— rights that were sanctioned by a hundred and forty years of exercise, and were now in danger from carelessness—he would have been faithless to his duty if he had not sought to arouse the people of Massachusetts to the danger. There was no idle rhetoric in the words, "No time can better be employed than in the preservation of the rights derived from the British constitution . . . . No treasure can be better expended, than in securing that true old English liberty, which gives a relish to every other enjoyment."[2]

In the fulfillment of this purpose to defend the democratic rights of Massachusetts, Adams became no mean master of political theory. In the works of no other writer is the total body of Revolutionary thought so adequately revealed. He was deeply read in the political classics, and all the great names—Hooker and Grotius, Pufendorf and Vattel, Coke and Blackstone, Locke and Milton and Sidney and Hume and Montesquieu—are spread largely through his pages to buttress his argument. In spite of the elusive

[2] *Works*, Vol. I, p. 348.

"meanders and windings" of his thought, veering and tacking as the winds blew, three broad lines of defense are clearly discernible. He rested his case on an appeal to the natural rights of man, to the particular rights and privileges of the British subject under the constitution, and to the express terms of the compact between the crown and its emigrant subjects laid down in the several colonial charters. Inasmuch as the American cause was to be argued before an old-world court, it was common prudence to seek to justify the seeming innovations of American institutional development, by old-world precedent and authority. If he could base the American grievance on the Whig doctrine of representation, he might rally the English Whigs to the American cause. This was sound constitutionalism, and Adams was too shrewd not to profess the highest respect for the glorious British constitution. "You know there is a charm in the word 'constitutional,'" he slyly suggested to a fellow colonial; and such respect, not to say veneration, he trumpeted to the world, until it may well have seemed that he did protest too much.

In his first line of defense Adams was on familiar ground, and he was supported by the authority of Locke, whose opinions were sacred in the eyes of English Whigs. What use he made of him is evident; "the immortal Locke," he calls him at one time, and at another, "one of the greatest men that ever wrote." He had been a disciple of Locke since his first interest in political theory, and he thought and spoke habitually in terms of the natural-rights school. It is sometimes asserted that the appeal to natural rights was made only after the breakdown of the colonial argument drawn from constitutional practice.[3] But as early as 1765 Adams based his argument on Locke in assuming the economic origin of government, and the inevitable connection between property and parliamentary representation.[4] How heavily he leaned on the natural-rights school appears again and again; particularly in a brilliant series of articles, signed "Candidus," written in 1771, where he paraphrases the *Second Treatise on Government:*

[3] Hutchinson seems to justify such a view from a passage written in 1770: "The leaders here seem to acknowledge that their cause is not to be defended on constitutional principles, and Adams now gives out that there is no need of it; they are upon better ground; all men have a natural right to change a bad constitution for a better, whenever they have it in their power." (Hosmer, *Life of Samuel Adams,* p. 259.)

[4] *Works.* Vol. I, p. 135.

Mr. Locke has often been quoted in the present dispute . . . and very much to our purpose. His reasoning is so forcible, that no one has ever attempted to confute it. He holds that "the preservation of property is the end of government, and that for which men enter into society. It therefore necessarily supposes and requires that the people should have property, without which they must be suppos'd to lose that by entering into society, which was the *end* for which they enter'd into it; too gross an absurdity for any man to own. Men therefore *in society having property*, they have such right to the goods, which by the law of the community are theirs, that no body hath the right to take *any part* of their subsistence from them without their consent: Without this, they could have no property at all. For I truly can have no property in that which another can by right take from me when he pleases, against my consent. Hence, says he, it is a mistake to think that the supreme power of any commonwealth can dispose of the estates of the subject arbitrarily, or *take any part* of them at pleasure. The prince or senate can never have a power to take to themselves the whole or any part of the subjects' property without *their own* consent; for this would be in effect to have no property at all."—This is the reasoning of that great and good man. And is not our own case exactly described by him? [5]

This was excellent doctrine in the eyes of the English Whigs, and it explains in part the support which Pitt and Camden lent to the colonial cause. But in his second line of defense, namely, that the English constitution was a fundamental charter of the natural rights of the subject, and that a statute which disregarded those natural rights was null and void, Adams was on less tenable ground. Every attempt to establish such a principle, whether that fundamental law be conceived of as the "law of God and nature," special compacts like the Magna Charta, or the Common Law, has met with failure in English constitutional practice. Nevertheless Adams made use of the argument, derived, very likely, from Coke.

Magna Charta itself is in substance but a constrained Declaration or proclamation, and promulgation in the name of King, Lords, and Commons, of the sense the latter had of their original, inherent, indefeazible natural Rights, as also those of free Citizens equally perdurable with the other. That great author, that great jurist, and even that Court writer Mr. Justice Blackstone holds that this recognition was justly obtained of King John sword in hand: and peradventure it must be one day sword in hand again rescued and preserved from total destruction. [6]

[Magna Charta] is affirm'd by Lord Coke to be declaratory of the principal grounds of the fundamental laws and liberties of England. "It is

[5] *Works*, Vol. II, p. 299.
[6] "The Rights of the Colonists," in *Works*, Vol. II, pp. 355–356.

called *Charta Libertatum Regni, the Charter of the Liberties of the kingdom,* upon great reason . . . because *liberos facit, it makes and preserves the people free."* . . . If then according to Lord Coke, *Magna Charta* is declaratory of the principal grounds of the *fundamental* laws and liberties of the people, and Vatel is right in his opinion, that the supreme legislature cannot change the constitution, I think it follows, whether Lord Coke has expressly asserted it or not, that an act of parliament made against Magna Charta in violation of its essential parts, is void.[7]

Adams was probably fully aware of the weakness of the argument. The well known attempt of Coke to establish a body of super-parliamentary law that sanctioned the annulling of a statute had been a total failure. Parliament had refused to yield sovereignty to the lawyers. The Tories were on stronger ground in asserting Hume's doctrine that "the only rule of government is the established practice of the age, upon maxims universally assented to"; and the established practice was sufficient reply to the argument that "it is the glory of the British constitution that it hath its foundations in the law of God and nature." Moreover the doctrine of virtual representation was at hand to cover any discrepancy between natural rights and existing practice; the argument from Locke was met by a legal refinement which held that as the charter of Massachusetts was as of the manor of East Greenwich, the freemen of Boston were personally represented by the parliamentary member from that borough.

When Adams fell back upon his third line of defense, the appeal to the colonial charter, he broke with the English Whigs completely. The royal charters, by authority of which the colonies had been founded and governed hitherto, were exalted by him into a secondary fundamental law, subordinate to the English constitution, but with authority beyond an act of parliament. This organic law of the charter was "the only medium of their political connection with the Mother State," he argued, and as sacred to Americans "as Magna Charta is to the People of Britain, as it contains a Declaration of all their Rights founded in natural Justice."[8]

Thus we see that Whatever Governmt in general may be founded in, Ours was manifestly founded in Compact. . . . By this Charter, we have an exclusive Right to make Laws for our own internal Government & Taxation: And indeed if the Inhabitants here are British Subjects . . . it seems necessary that they should exercise this Power themselves; for

[7] "Candidus," in *Works*, Vol. II, pp. 325–326.   [8] *Works*, Vol. I, p. 28.

they are not represented in the British Parliamt & their great Distance
renders it impracticable: It is very probable that all the subordinate
legislative Powers in America, were constituted upon the Apprehension
of this Impracticability.[9]

After all, the futility of argument as a colonial defense against
Grenville or Townshend was evident to so shrewd a student of
political realism as Samuel Adams. If the colonies were to preserve
their traditional liberties, more effective means must be found than
appeal to justice or colonial use and wont.   Force must be used,
and that force—short of armed rebellion—could be only an aroused
public opinion.   It was like to prove a difficult business, this
arousing of an effective public opinion, and not wanting in danger;
but neither difficulty nor danger would deter a calculating enthusiast like Adams from undertaking it.   He was ready to devote his
life to the work of creating and guiding a popular interest in political measures.

The means which he made use of were as novel as they were
repugnant to the Tory statecraft.   He was the first American to
understand the power of publicity, and not the least of his services
to democracy was his attack upon the principle of secret government.   Affairs of state had always been guarded jealously from
public knowledge, on the theory long before stated by Sir Robert
Filmer that the subject must "have nothing to do to meddle with
mysteries of state, such *arcana imperii*, or cabinet councils, the
vulgar may not pry into."   Adams now proposed to lay them open
to common inspection.   He insisted that questions of governmental
policy be taken out of the exclusive jurisdiction of secret councils,
and transferred to Faneuil Hall where the freemen of Boston might
examine them, and where the "Cause of Liberty" might "be
warmly espoused and ably vindicated."   Here was a revolutionary
proposal indeed, with its demand for public discussion and a
popular referendum; and naturally it gave offense to the crown
officials.   It meant the vulgarization of government.   It was a
disturbing thought to such men that government might come to
be regarded as the common concern of the tax-paying public;
that the town meeting might fall under the control of the plebeian
mass and crowd in with its demands upon the aristocratic Council.
How could gentlemen deliberate freely and determine wisely, with
demagogues sitting in judgment on every word and vote?   So

[9] *Ibid.*, Vol. I, p. 29.

disturbing to gentlemen was any criticism that one of Hutchinson's followers went so far as to charge Adams with "Indecency in 'undertaking to answer a Governor's Message,'" to which he replied:

I know very well that it has been handed as a political Creed of late, that the Reasoning of the People without Doors is not to be regarded— But every ' transient Person" has a Right publickly to animadvert upon whatever is publickly advanc'd by any Man, and I am resolv'd to exercise that Right, when I please, without asking any Man's Leave.[10]

Effective organization of the rank and file of the people was the business at hand. It was a new problem and there was need of new methods. The Caucus Club, founded by his father, served as a training school for the leaders; there the policies were determined upon for the town meeting and the assembly, and there the plans for a continental union were laid in Non-Importation Agreements, organization of Committees of Correspondence, and the like. The program there agreed upon Adams made it his business to put through the town meeting, as the first step. When he faced his fellow Bostonians in Faneuil Hall he relied upon the influence which long years of familiar intercourse with all sorts and conditions of men had won for him, and many a Boston freeman went to the meeting ready to vote for "whatever the old man wanted." Behind the imposing figure of John Hancock, or the eloquence of John Adams, was certain to be the directing mind of the "master of the puppets," as Hutchinson sneeringly called Samuel Adams.

His hours of triumph in Boston town meeting or in the assembly were preceded by an incredible amount of labor with the pen as well as with the tongue, for this master politician was the journalist as well as the organizer of the New England revolution. The public opinion on which he depended was daily being made in chimney corners and tavern talk, and he proposed to mold it through the agency of a party press. No other pen in Boston was so busy as his. "There is Sam Adams writing against the Tories," his fellow townsmen are said to have remarked when they saw his familiar candle burning long into the night. When he was away in attendance on the Continental Congress he reproached his friends at home for neglecting the work of publicity. "Your presses have been too long silent. What were your Committees of Corre-

[10] "A Chatterer," in *Works*, Vol. II, pp. 45-46.

spondence about? I hear nothing of circular Letters—of joynt
Committees &c. Such Methods have in times past raised the
Spirits of the people—drawn off their Attention from picking up
Pins, & directed their Views to great objects." [11]

With such neglect Samuel Adams could not be charged. As clerk
of the inevitable Committee of Grievances appointed by the Boston
town meeting in accordance with his prearranged plan, he wrote
those plain-spoken papers that stirred the wrath of Tory gentlemen; as clerk of the assembly he was the chief author of successive
state papers, which under guise of replying to the prerogative
principles of Bernard and Hutchinson, set forth in masterly fashion
the whole theory of colonial rights; and as Chairman of the Committee of Correspondence he appealed to his fellow Americans of
every colony. Yet his official writings constitute only a minor
part of his total work. His letters were innumerable and his
newspaper articles crowded the desk of every friendly editor. The
labors undergone and the energy consumed were enormous. It
was no holiday task to create and guide a public opinion that was
so constantly falling into apathy.

Running through the third volume of Hutchinson's *History of
Massachusetts Bay* is a note of indignant protest at "the machina-
tions of selfish and designing men" who at the precise time when
the feeling between the two countries was friendliest, and an
amicable settlement of differences seemed likeliest, were assiduous
to breed fresh discord and frustrate the hopes of peace. That he
had Adams chiefly in mind there can be little doubt. During the
"calm interval" of the summer of '71, when, according to Hutchinson, "the province was more free from real evils" than for years,
and when "to keep up a spirit of discontent, recourse was had,
either to evils merely imaginary, or to such as were at a distance,
and feared rather than felt," [12] Adams wrote the ablest of his
many able newspaper articles.[13] In no other phase of his work is
the craft of the man so evident as in these anonymous newspaper
discussions. There was cunning as well as caution in his method.
Changing his style with every fresh quill and every new pen name,
putting forth an idea for the sake of denying it, then examining
its merits cautiously, and finally advocating it boldly, he created

[11] *Works*, Vol. III, p. 289.
[12] *History of Massachusetts Bay*, Vol. III, p. 349.
[13] See in particular the "Candidus" articles in *Works*, Vol. II, in which he elabo
rated his views on government by ministerial instructions.

like Falstaff a host of patriots out of a single Bostonian in brown homespun, making it appear that many were troubled over evils that were visible only to him. On occasion his style possesses the light touch, the leisurely detail, the easy pleasantry of a Spectator essay; [14] again, there is a note of biting irony and studied insult; [15] and again, there is dignified discussion in which Adams argues dispassionately with his countrymen, or pleads with them to stand together in defense of the common welfare. But in whatever vein or under whatever disguise he wrote, the conclusion of every argument was the implied suggestion, how much better it would be if the American people were to take into their own hands the management of their affairs.

But before the colonial could be induced to strike for governmental control, the old psychology of subserviency to the ruling class must be uprooted; and an effective means to that end was to lay bare the selfish motives of the aristocracy. To stimulate what we call today class consciousness was a necessary preliminary to a democratic psychology; and to this task Adams devoted every energy. The ways of the iconoclast are rarely lovely, and the breaking of idols is certain to wound sensitive souls. There was abundant justification for the charge of Hutchinson that "robbing men of their characters" was the "patriotic business" of Samuel Adams; but he missed the point in attributing to him the motive, *Gubernatorum vituperatio populo placet*. The respect that attached to Bernard and Hutchinson by virtue of their official positions was a powerful ally of ministerial authority; their words carried weight beyond the sanction of their logic; for the good of America their power must be destroyed. Doubtless Adams was ungenerous in attack; certainly he was vindictive in his hates; but the cold record as we read it today justifies one in the belief that the men whom he attacked were tools of the ministry, and must be struck down if the rights of Massachusetts were to be preserved. And it was due to the bitter denunciations of Adams that Thomas Hutchinson was driven from his native land and forced to take refuge in England, the best hated man in all the colonies.

But it was not enough to pull down the courtly Hutchinson, for behind the governor was a group of lawyers and judges, equally

[14] See "Puritan" articles, in *Works*, Vol. I, p. 201 *et seq.*
[15] See "Candidus," in Vol. II, p. 246; "Chatterer," in Vol. II, pp. 35, 39, 43; "Layman," in Vol. I, p. 322.

subservient to prerogative, adepts in the art of interpreting away rights by due process of law. It became part of the day's work, therefore, to lay open the sacred precincts of the courts to common inspection; to create a public opinion to review judicial decisions when those decisions were political rather than legal. It was a startling innovation for a private citizen to assert in the public press that "*state-lawyers*, attorneys and sollicitors general, & persons advanced to the highest stations in the courts of law, *prostitute* the honor of the profession, become *tools of ministers*, and employ their talents for *explaining away*, if possible, the Rights of a kingdom." Never before had the integrity of the colonial courts been openly attacked and the motives of the judiciary impugned. But it was far more startling for Adams to lay down the thesis, that in matters which concern the general welfare, the letter of the law is not to be considered final, and "the opinions . . . and determinations of the greatest Sages and Judges of the law in the Exchequer Chamber, ought not to be considered as decisive or binding . . . any further, than they are consonant to natural reason." [16] If Franklin was concerned to create a new economics in harmony with democratic needs, Samuel Adams was concerned to democratize the New England law. He was dissatisfied with a legal system created by a Tory past, and that had lately received a fresh Tory impress at the hands of Blackstone. Such a body of law could not answer the needs of a free people; it must be reshaped to conform to new needs. And the conclusion towards which his thinking pointed was the principle of a referendum of judicial decisions, for how otherwise could it be determined whether a given decision were "consonant to natural reason"?

Samuel Adams was little given to striking at the air, and he set himself to the work of cutting the claws of the more obnoxious judges with the same cool skill that marked his baiting of the governor. Certain of them who held plural offices he maneuvered out of the Council, on the ground that they ought not to exercise both legislative and judicial functions; and when Bernard protested that they had been members of the Council for years and by reason of "their knowledge of the public business, were almost necessary to the body," he replied that they were to be released "from the cares and perplexities of politics . . . to make further advances in the knowledge of the law"—which thrust, in view of

[16] *Works*, Vol. II, p. 436.

the notorious fact that few of them had been trained in the law, but had risen to the bench through political influence, must be reckoned a palpable hit.[17]   Others beyond his immediate reach found their characters assailed and their motives aspersed, until popular respect for them was destroyed; and the unlucky judges who accepted payment from the royal chest found such a hue and cry raised against them that they were driven to make choice between the royal guineas or answering to the mob—a rude but effective way of stimulating their loyalty to the commonwealth. In short, this "master of the puppets," measuring the power of the judges and fearing their prerogative bias, did not scruple over ways and means of rendering them more responsive to the popular will, which in the eyes of the best people of Boston was no less than incendiary.

The work of Samuel Adams was largely done before the word democrat was given vogue by the French Revolution, and he cautiously refrained from using it; nevertheless he was probably the most thoroughgoing democrat of his generation of Americans. He was wholly persuaded that the sovereign people have a right to change their fundamental law, together with the interpretation and administration of it, whenever they desire; and that pending such change it was well to nullify an act of prerogative subversive of their interests.   "We contend, that the People & their Representatives have a Right to withstand the abusive Exercise of a legal & constitutional Prerogative of the Crown," he argued in reply to Hutchinson; "whenever instructions cannot be complied with, without injuring the people, they cease to be binding." [18] From the necessary corollary, that the people are competent to judge of their own good and manage their own affairs, Adams did not shrink.   Stated thus in general terms, the theory possessed no novelty.   The sovereignty of the people had long been a staple of Whiggish theory; but Adams gave to the doctrine democratic significance.   The people, in his philosophy, were something more than the wealthy and cultured minority to whom the Whigs appealed; they were the mass of men—the yeoman, the tradesman, the mechanic—all that multitude of homespun folk who had hitherto been mere pawns in the political game.   Such a passage as this, written four years before Lexington, reads like Tom Paine and his doctrine of the *res publica:*

[17] *Works*, Vol. I, p 80.   [18] *Works*, Vol. II, pp. 22, 26.

The *multitude* I am speaking of, is the *body of the people*—no contempti-
ble multitude—for whose sake government is instituted; or rather, who
have themselves erected it, solely for their own good—to whom even
kings and all in subordination to them, are strictly speaking, servants and
not masters. . . . Philanthrop [Jonathan Sewall] I think, speaks somewhat unintelligently, when he tells us that the well being and happiness
of the whole depends upon *subordination*; as if mankind submitted to
government for the sake of being subordinate. . . . Mankind have entered into political societies, rather for the sake of restoring *equality*. . . .
I am not of levelling principles: But I am apt to think, that constitution
of civil government which admits equality in the most extensive degree,
consistent with the true design of government, is the best.[19]

Accepting the sovereignty of the people, Adams was led to a
pure democracy, based on the town meeting. He rejected every
form of "mixt government," whether in the form of king, lords
and commons, or in the form of constitutional checks and balances. That sober men should profess to prefer the dominion of
the few to the rule of all, he could not understand. "I find everywhere some Men, who are afraid of a free Government," he said
in 1776, "lest it be perverted, and made Use of as a Cloke for
Licenciousness. The fear of the Peoples abusing their Liberty is
made an Argument against their having the Enjoyment of it; as
if anything were so much to be dreaded by Mankind as Slavery."[20]
Democracy he believed was inevitable, for "in these times of
Light and Liberty, every man chuses to see and judge for himself."[21]
He was quite untroubled by any fear of the tyranny of the mass;
he was a good enough historian to know that it is always the
minority and not the mass that creates tyranny. Though Toryism
might infect the government circles, and aristocracy appeal to
the wealthy and ambitious, the great body of Massachusetts
people were democratic, and he looked forward hopefully to a new
political order, created by the popular mind. It came more quickly
than he had expected, once the old inhibitions were removed.
"New Govts are now erecting in the several American states
under the Authority of the People," he wrote soon after Independence. "Monarchy seems to be generally exploded. And it
is not a little surprising to me that the Aristocratick Spirit, which
appeard to have taken deep Root in some of them, now gives
place to that of Democracy." [22]

During the difficult after-years of reconstruction Adams re-

[19] *Works*, Vol. II, p. 150.   [20] *Works*, Vol. III, p. 244.
[21] *Ibid.*, Vol. II, p. 39.   [22] *Ibid.*, Vol. III, p. 305.

mained true to his democratic principles. As he had earlier resisted the encroachments of monarchical centralization, he later fought against Federalistic consolidation. He distrusted the Constitution as an undemocratic instrument, fearing a centralized authority removed from immediate control; and he joined heartily in the work of securing a Bill of Rights. He welcomed the French Revolution and followed closely the developing democratic philosophy which that great upheaval did so much to clarify and disseminate. He remained an unrepentant Jacobin during those acrimonious years when the Federalists were filling the air with their anti-Jacobin fustian. He had heard gentlemen rant before and was probably amused when, as Governor, he attended Harvard Commencement and listened to young Robert Treat Paine fulminate against the red atheism of France and its American spawn. Although a kinsman of John Adams and warm friend, he welcomed the election of Jefferson as a return to democratic principles after an unhappy period of "prejudice and passion," although he warned him, "you must depend upon being hated . . . because they hate your principles." The last letter in the collected edition of his works, addressed to his old friend Tom Paine, November 30, 1802, is an appeal for democratic unity; and the words with which it concludes—*felix qui cautus*—embody the principle of his amazing political strategy. In playing for great stakes it is well to be wary.

His anti-Federalism, aggravated by his frank advocacy of Jacobin principles, cost him heavily in after days, and like Philip Freneau his just fame was long obscured by partisan spleen. Although he retained his hold on the affections of the Massachusetts electorate, and was annually chosen Governor until the infirmities of age determined his withdrawal from public affairs, he was silently dropped from the roll of American patriots whose deeds were celebrated in current panegyrics. His manuscripts were scattered after his death, and he was in the way of being forgotten till Bancroft, in the next century, gave fresh currency to his earlier reputation. Since then the figure of Samuel Adams has grown steadily larger, although he still awaits a biographer who will set him in his due place in the history of American liberalism.

CHAPTER V

LITERARY ECHOES

THE Revolutionary upheaval produced no polite literature in any respects comparable to its utilitarian prose. The expiring wit literature of England was an exotic that refused to be naturalized, and the times were unpropitious for the creation of a native poetry. An occasional dilettante like Mather Byles aspired to be a wit, but the reputation of the clever Bostonian owed more to his tongue than to his pen, and he is dimly remembered for the letter that he received from the great Mr. Pope, rather than for notable verse. Nevertheless in the early seventies pure literature was beginning to make a perceptible stir in New England. Clever young men in the colleges were turning moderns and making ready to wage a new battle of the books. They preferred the refinements of verse to the didacticism of sermons; they were discovering the charm of playful satire; and they found in the currently fashionable tetrameter a brisk vehicle for their attacks on academic dullness. They admired Churchill, then at the height of his brief fame, but they were restrained by a decent modesty and dared not go his length in brutal frankness. It was from these young men, amateurs in verse writing and amateurs likewise in politics, that the American cause mainly recruited its literary defenders. They might be flaming Whigs but they were also well-bred young gentlemen who studied the amenities and sought to unite patriotism with good form.

I

THE WHIG SATIRISTS

1. JOHN TRUMBULL

There was the best of Yankee blood in the veins of John Trumbull. Among his kinsmen were the Reverend Benjamin Trumbull, historian of Connecticut, Governor Jonathan Trumbull—Washington's "Brother Jonathan"—and John Trumbull the painter. On his mother's side he was descended from the vigorous Solomon

248

Stoddard, grandfather of Jonathan Edwards. His father was a scholarly minister, long a trustee of Yale College, at which school the son spent seven years as undergraduate and tutor. He was a precocious youth with a strong love of polite letters, and a praiseworthy desire to achieve literary distinction. Greek and Latin had been the toys of his childhood and when he was seven years of age he passed the entrance examination to college. During the period of his tutorship he joined with Timothy Dwight and Joseph Howe in the work of overhauling the stale curriculum, supplementing Lilly's Grammar and Calvin's Institutes with Pope and Churchill. Like other aspiring youths of the day he dabbled in Spectator papers, practiced his couplets, and eventually produced *The Progress of Dulness*, the cleverest bit of academic verse till then produced in America. At heart Trumbull was thoroughly academic, and nothing would have suited his temperament better than the life of a Yale professor; but the prospects proving unfavorable, he began to mingle Blackstone with the poets in preparation for his future profession.

He was thus engaged during the middle years of the long dispute with England, the bitter wranglings of which seem to have disturbed him little in his quiet retreat. But in 1773 he resigned his tutorship to prepare himself further in the law. Removing to Boston he entered the office of John Adams, then rising to prominence as a spokesman of the popular party; and he took lodgings in the house of Caleb Cushing, Speaker of the Massachusetts Assembly. Placed thus at the storm center of provincial politics, he was soon infected with the Whig dissatisfactions and joined himself to the patriotic party. When Adams went to Philadelphia to sit in the Continental Congress, Trumbull withdrew to Hartford, where he established himself. Before quitting Boston he had published an *Elegy on the Times*, a political tract that seemed to Adams so useful to the cause that he marked the young poet for future service, and the year following he encouraged the writing of *M'Fingal*, the first part of which appeared in 1775. So great was the prestige it met with that Trumbull tinkered with it for seven years, publishing it finally in its completed form in 1782. The law seems to have been a jealous mistress then as now, and his dreams of further literary work were inadequately realized. He is believed to have had a hand in *The Anarchiad*, and he wrote some minor poems; but he soon drifted into politics, went on the bench,

finally removed to Detroit in 1825, and died there in 1831, at
the age of eighty-one. He had outlived his Revolutionary generation, long outlived his literary ambitions, and was pretty much
forgotten before he died. His collected works, published in 1820,
proved a losing venture for the printer. America in 1820 was
turning romantic, and few, it seems, cared to invest in two volumes
of echoes.

Trumbull's reputation rests exclusively on *M'Fingal*. It was so
popular in its time that more than thirty pirated editions were
issued. It was broadcasted by "news-papers, hawkers, pedlars,
and petty chapmen," and it served its partisan purpose. The
author was complimented by the Marquis de Chastellux on
fulfilling all the conditions of burlesque poetry as approved since
the days of Homer; but in spite of the indisputable cleverness of
some of the lines, it is not a great work. In its final form it is
spun out to extreme length, and pretty much swamped by the
elaborate machinery on which the poet visibly prided himself.
Even in the thick of attack Trumbull did not forget his academic
reading, but he explains his allusions with meticulous care. He
seems, indeed, rather more concerned about the laws of the mock
epic than the threatened rights of America. The Scotch Tory
hero is a figure so unlike the real Tory—the Olivers and Leonards
and Hutchinsons, with their love of power and dignified display—
that the caricature loses much in historical veracity. Trumbull's
patriotism was well bred and unmarked by fierce partisanship.
His refined tastes were an ill equipment for the turmoil of revolution. The ways of the radical were not lovely in his eyes; the Sons
of Liberty with their tar-pots and feather-beds were too often
rough fellows, and although they provided him with comic material
to set off the blunderings of the Squire, they probably seemed to
him little better than tools of demagogues. Very often this tousle-
headed democracy behaved like a mob, and Trumbull in his tie-
wig did not approve of mobs.

The more thoughtfully one reads *M'Fingal*, throwing upon it
the light of the total career of its author, the more clearly one
perceives that John Trumbull was not a rebellious soul. In the
year 1773, while projecting some fresh ventures in the Spectator
vein, "he congratulated himself on the fact 'that the ferment of
politics' was, as he supposed, 'pretty much subsided,' and that at
last the country was to enjoy a 'mild interval from the struggles

of patriotism and self-interest, from noise and confusion, Wilkes and liberty.'" He had then no wish for embroilment in civil war, no dreams of political independence. All his life he seems to have suffered from ill health, which probably sapped his militancy and lessened his pugnacity. From this temperamental calmness came a certain detachment that allowed his partisanship to remain cooler than the hot passions of the times commonly suffered. He could permit himself the luxury of a laugh at the current absurdities; and it is this light-heartedness that made *M'Fingal* so immediately effective. The rollicking burlesque of the Tory argument, the telling *reductio ad absurdum* of the Tory logic, must have tickled the ears of every Whig and provoked many a laugh in obscure chimney-seats. Laughter is a keen weapon, and Trumbull's gayety laid open weak spots in the Tory armor that were proof against Freneau's invective. It was a rare note in those acrimonious times, and one likes Trumbull the better for minding his manners and engaging in the duel like a gentleman. After all, this son of Yale had certain characteristics of the intellectual, and if his environment had been favorable and the law had not claimed him, very likely he would have given a better account of the talents that were certainly his. He wrote with ease if not with finish, and he possessed the requisite qualities of a man of letters. A lovable man he seems to have been, but somewhat easy-going, too lightly turned away from his purpose; and in consequence his later life failed to realize the expectations of his early years.

That he was not a Loyalist was probably due in large measure to environment and his family connections. Considering his temperament, it is not easy to discover any logical reason why he should have turned Whig. He had never suffered in his own fortune from existing arrangements; he was not a political idealist to throw the glamor of republicanism about the struggle; he had not subjected the colonial question to critical analysis. He was an academic dilettante, unconcerned with political principles, little more than an echo of the Connecticut gentry in such matters; and if he espoused the Whig cause it is a pretty good indication that Yale College was indoctrinated in Whig principles. An echo he remained throughout his life. When later he became a Federalist and enjoyed some of the emoluments of party victory, and when later still democracy lifted up its head in Connecticut, wearing the

French cockade, and bringing down upon it the wrath of all respectable people, he reflected faithfully the views of his class. John Trumbull was a moderate liberal, but no leveler, no democrat, no friend to Jeffersonian heresies. Democracy he detested heartily, and he joined with the other Hartford Wits to draw its portrait in unflattering terms. As a Connecticut gentleman he was insistent on the supremacy of the tie-wig in government as well as in society; he would scarcely have been a Connecticut gentleman had he thought otherwise.

2. FRANCIS HOPKINSON, ESQ.

If the career of Trumbull indicates that Whiggery existed among the young collegians of Connecticut, the career of Francis Hopkinson suggests that the culture of Philadelphia, the great center of fashion and wit, was Whiggish also. That it should have been so is the more noteworthy, for the Quaker spirit of Philadelphia was far less militant than the Puritan spirit of Boston; more peaceful, if not more conservative. The city had long been dominated by a group of sober merchants who detested the leveling tendencies of New England. But the domination of these older men was passing; a younger generation, more aggressive in trade and speculation, was rising to power; and that Philadelphia finally went with the Whigs was due to the influence of these younger merchants. When it became clear that the commercial interests of men like Robert Morris and George Clymer were disadvantaged by the connection with England, the ardor of patriotism grew stronger, and talk of independence became common. No sooner had business come out for independence than culture swung over; the wit which would gladly have remained loyal applauded the comments of the countinghouse, and the newspaper essay reflected the new patriotic sentiments.

Chief among the Philadelphia wits was Francis Hopkinson, Esq., a charmingly versatile dilettante, who to the vocation of the law and the bench of admiralty, joined the polite avocations of painting, music, natural philosophy, and literature. He was indisputably clever, full of innumerable sprightly enthusiasms, and master of cultivated speech and manners. Of his skill in painting and music we cannot judge, but of his literary accomplishments the record has been preserved. Life seems to have been an agreeable experience to him, and if his dainty enthusiasms were a marvel to John Adams,[1] it would indicate that society in Philadelphia in 1775 was far more refined than in provincial Boston.

Hopkinson possessed ample means to gratify his polite tastes, and had long moved in the most exclusive circles. The son of an eminent lawyer, he had received the best education available in the colonies, after which he went abroad to acquire old-world polish. Some fourteen months were spent in England, where, as a near kinsman of the Bishop of Worcester, he frequented the best English society, made the acquaintance of eminent men, and even enjoyed the distinction of dining with my Lord North. On his return he prudently fell in love with an heiress of the Bordens, of Bordentown, and turned Jerseyman the better to administer his wife's estates. He entered the law, and doubtless at the solicitation of his kinsman the Bishop, he became a beneficiary of ministerial patronage: receiving appointment in 1772 to a sinecure post as collector of customs at Newcastle, and two years later being made mandamus councilor for New Jersey—a somewhat hazardous post, considering the nature of the office and the temper of the people. Already in Massachusetts certain gentlemen had learned that the compliment of royal recognition might cost too dear a price. That Hopkinson should have been tendered such an appointment as late as 1774, shows that he was regarded by the ministry as good Tory material.

During the anxious months of 1774, when intelligent Americans were trying to forecast the outcome of the growing radicalism of the colonial temper, Hopkinson must have done some serious thinking; with the result that when in September the Continental Congress assembled in Philadelphia, he offered to the members as his contribution to the discussion a clever little allegory wherein the whole question at issue between England and the colonies was sketched with a light touch that is an agreeable relief from the arguments of the official debaters. In *A Pretty Story* Hopkinson is frankly pro-colonial, and offers his wit to the service of his country. It is not a great work, but it shows that he had definitely put aside the ministerial temptation—probably to the disgust of the good Bishop—and had gone over to the Whigs. Two years later he took a seat in the Congress, and within a week voted for the Declaration of Independence, aligning himself against the conservative group led by his fellow townsman, John Dickinson.

[1] See *Familiar Letters of John and Abigail Adams*, p. 217.

What impelled Hopkinson to so momentous a shift in political opinion can be explained by no records that have been preserved, and must remain a matter of conjecture. Even less than Trumbull was he revolutionary in temper. His Whiggery was probably commercial in origin, a reflection of the economic interests of the merchant class with which he mingled. That he went so far as to attack the aristocratic spirit of the English government—its debauching of public servants and its sordid motives—may have been due quite as much to a refined integrity as to partisan advantage; but for an aristocrat to attack the aristocratic principle of government was unusual as it was dangerous for his class. But though he turned Whig he was no agrarian to substitute the majority will for the royal prerogative; and when the war was over and political re-alignment was under way, Hopkinson went with his group, became a stout Federalist, defended the Constitution, and enjoyed his share of the party emoluments. His wit was unembittered by the acrimonious disputes of Jacobin days, and his partisanship retained its note of casual sprightliness through the dogdays of the nineties.

His chief contributions to the debate over the Constitution were *The New Roof* and *Objections to the Proposed Plan of a Federal Government for the United States, on Genuine Principles.* They are delightfully clever, but the cleverness cannot conceal a good-natured contempt for the democratic underling and all his ways. The attitude of aristocratic superiority is the more striking for its easy bearing. The first is an implied eulogy of James Wilson, Scotch lawyer of Philadelphia, who as master-architect finds his plans for erecting a splendid roof over a "certain Mansion-house" violently opposed by Margery, a slattern midwife, for no better reason than that "in the construction of the new roof, her apartments would be considerably lessened." Margery, of course, is agrarian democracy, and to further her interests she incites three worthless servants to testify that the old leaky roof is better than the one proposed. Naturally their flimsy arguments are laughed out of court, and the wisdom of the architect is apparent to all except a "half-crazy fellow" [2] who filled the air with his "fustian," making himself a general nuisance to the disgust of all respectable people.

In the second of the two works, Hopkinson gives freer rein to

[2] "Philadelphiensis," one of the anti-Federalist pamphleteers.

his polite fancy, figuring the opposition to the Constitution under the form of a Wheelbarrow Society at the city gaol. Within those walled precincts, he suggests, the most advanced advocates of natural liberty may be found, and there the monstrous crime of the Constitution is most eloquently exposed. How foolish is this America that persists in believing what able lawyers and reputable gentlemen say of the merits of the document, and refuses to intrust the making of a fundamental law to such true liegemen of democracy as these knights of the chain-gang! It is all very witty, and provokes its laugh, and serves its purpose of heaping on the head of the opposition the class prejudice that was indignant at the insolence of plebeians in holding contrary views on a subject quite beyond their comprehension. But times change, and the sprightliest wit may lose its savor. Those old Federalist skits are as dead today as the marvelous pageant got up by Hopkinson to celebrate the adoption of the Constitution, an affair which greatly pleased the amiable little gentleman, a detailed account of which he prepared for the definitive edition of his works, where it may be read by the curious.

If Francis Hopkinson is no very important figure in our literary history, he is not without significance as a representative of our colonial culture that deliberately chose to be Whig rather than Tory. He risked much and he was amply rewarded. For years he sat on the bench of the Court of Admiralty, sparkled at dinners, and was a respected and influential member of a genteel society. If the recompense for his services during the perilous days was greater than fell to the lot of a democrat like Philip Freneau, who will wonder? Like rewards like, and the days of democratic rewards were not yet come in America.

II

THE TORY SATIRISTS

1. JONATHAN ODELL

Amongst the occasional writers who dedicated extemporized couplets to the defense of Toryism in America, there can be no doubt to whom belongs the primacy. Jonathan Odell was easily first as a purveyor of virulent Loyalist rhyme. Of the sternest Puritan ancestry, Odell was educated in medicine, and saw service in the West Indies as surgeon to his Majesty's forces. Turning

Anglican he was ordained priest in London, and came home to his native colonies as a missionary, to further the cause of episcopacy. Busily engaged with parochial duties, he chose to remain aloof from all political disputes, and during the early months of the war he refrained from taking sides. Unfortunately, however, he made acquaintances among some captive British officers, for whom he wrote a song in honor of the King's birthday, which was sung with much drinking of wine on June 4, 1776, the news of which getting abroad stirred the Whig partisans to anger. Soon thereafter matters grew too warm for Odell to remain longer neutral; he suffered certain humiliating personal experiences and was driven to seek refuge within the British lines. Thenceforth none was more ardent in the royal cause. He busied himself with innumerable intrigues to undermine the Whig strength, amongst others serving as a go-between in the unlucky André-Arnold affair. He remained implacable to the end, and not until the last Redcoat was withdrawn from the independent states, did he leave off urging reprisals. When it was all over he withdrew sullenly to Nova Scotia, was amply rewarded by his King, and sat down to nourish to the end of a long life the most virulent hatred of all Whigs and republicans. "Toryissimus," Professor Tyler calls him, borrowing Sir Walter's word; and the term hits to a nicety the bitter arrogant nature which so closely resembled in its essentials the "proud prelate Laud," from whom his ancestors had fled a hundred and fifty years before.

A vigorous man was Jonathan Odell, strong, capable, uncompromising, possessing a clear intellect and a heart little touched by Christian charity—a stern Hebraist who would sweep away with the besom of wrath all the enemies of his God and his King. He felt no hesitation in making out the list of the proscribed: the enemies of the King were *ipso facto* the enemies of God—rebels who were daily signing their own death warrants in overt acts of treason. Watching the seditious crew of "Congress men" seducing the colonials into unnatural rebellion against the best of kings and fathers, he took it to be his Christian duty to lay the rod of correction upon their shoulders. If they would not be warned they must be hanged. Not content with active intrigue, he pressed his pen into service, and during the year 1779 he wrote four pieces which for bitterness of satire outdid Freneau at his frankest. Freneau was bitter and brutal in all conscience, but he was never nasty; there were infamies of personal insult that he would not stoop to, vulgarities of innuendo that he was not guilty of. If he studied the art of Churchill, he stopped short of Churchill's grossness. But Odell the priest was unhampered by scruple; the meanest gossip found a place in his "acrid rhyme." No Christian charity spread its mantle over the shortcomings of his enemies, no Christian forgiveness found lodgment in his unforgiving heart. He was a son of the Old Testament and he girded up his righteousness with prayer.

> Ask I too much? then grant me for a time
> Some deleterious pow'rs of acrid rhyme:
> Some ars'nic verse, to poison with the pen
> These rats, who nestle in the Lion's den! [3]

The four satires which embody his holy wrath and which were little calculated to spread sweetness and light in a world sorely in need of them, are *The Word of Congress*, *The Congratulation*, *The Feu de Joie*, and *The American Times*—all written, probably, in the last months of the year 1779. Of these the first and the last are the most suggestive in their denunciation. The spirit which prompted him to turn to satire is given in the preface to the 1780 edition of *The American Times*.

The masters of Reason have decided, that when doctrines and practices have been fairly examined, and proved to be contrary to Truth, and injurious to Society, then and not before may Ridicule be lawfully employed in the Service of Virtue. This is exactly the case of the grand American Rebellion; it has been weighed in the balance, and found wanting: able writers have exposed its principles, its conduct, and its final aim. Reason has done her part, and therefore this is the legitimate moment for Satire. Accordingly the following Piece is offered to the Public. What it is found to want of Genius, the Author cannot supply; what it may want of Correction, he hopes the candor of the Public will excuse on account of the fugitive nature of the subject: next year the publication would be too late; for in all probability there will then be no Congress existing.

When we examine the work of Odell to discover the deeper springs of his thought, we come upon naked class prejudice, undiluted Toryism. His social philosophy is erected upon that unstable foundation; the actions of men are judged solely by that light. Of any valid or reasoned philosophy, social or political, he was as wanting as a child. Of any real understanding of his

[3] *Loyalist Poetry*, p. 55.

fellow Americans who had espoused the Whig cause, he was as
lacking as General Clinton, whose "warfare," Odell asserted, "was
the war of God." The colonial grievances which other Tories
acknowledged to have some foundation, Odell casually ignored.
There was no cause in heaven or earth for colonial disloyalty, he
was convinced, except Whiggish perversity, and for such perversity
there must be due punishment—the rope. In his mind's eye he
sees the "impious crew," one after another silenced by the halter.
There must be no ill-judged mercy; the best of the rebels must
swing with the worst, for they are all sedition-mongers, all attainted
traitors. From his vast ignorance Odell derived an equally vast
confidence in the ultimate triumph of truth. There is a note of
finality in his judgments that amazes, an infallibility that amuses.
The Reverend Jonathan frankly acknowledges himself to be the
boon companion of Reason, the favored suitor of Truth—from
them only has he taken instruction and in their name he professes
to speak. Whereas the Whigs are poor fellows who have held
commerce with neither.

Odell is careful of his workmanship and organizes his materials
with an eye to climax. *The American Times* is formally divided
into three parts. The poem opens with a summoning of the in-
fernal crew of sedition and the abuse of them severally, rising to a
rhetorical conclusion in an address to Washington; then the leering
portrait of the mother of all mischiefs, Democracy, is painted;
finally comes a pure and lofty strain which summons Reason to
decide in the great cause. Taxation, Independence, are haled
before her august throne and there condemned, and the whole
concludes with a vision of Britannia's guardian angel bearing a two-
edged sword and proclaiming:

> At length the day of Vengeance is at hand:
> The exterminating Angel takes his stand:
> Hear the last summons, rebels, and relent:
> Yet but a moment is there to repent.
> Lo! the great Searcher ready at the door,
> Who means decisively to purge the floor:
> Yes, the wise Sifter now prepares the fan
> To separate the meal from useless bran.
> Down to the centre from his burning ire
> Ye foes of goodness and of truth, retire:
> And ye, who now lie humbled in the dust,
> Shall raise your heads, ye loyal and ye just;

Th' approving sentence of your Sov'reign gain.
And shine refulgent as the starry train.
Then, when eternal justice is appeas'd;
When with due vengeance heav'n and earth are pleas'd;
America, from dire pollution clear'd,
Shall flourish yet again, belov'd, rever'd:
In duty's lap her growing sons be nurs'd,
And her last days be happier than her first.[4]

Into this framework Odell has fitted a surprising number of personal attacks. His ink blots out the good name of every Whig on whom it drips. To the present generation it furnishes food for wonder to see what a paltry appearance the fathers make in the verse of this plain-speaking Tory. Jefferson, Paine, Morris, Adams, Washington, and a host of others, are shallow creatures, in the judgment of Odell, bereft of reason, void of honor, the very scum of the revolutionary pot; whereas Clinton and Gage, Hutchinson and Galloway, are holy instruments in the hand of God to cleanse the land of pollution. The attack is rankly and grossly partisan, with no saving grace of humor or humanity. The alpha and omega of Odell's political faith was loyalty to the crown, and the bankruptcy of such a creed in revolutionary America is nowhere thrust into harsher relief than in the bitter verses of this bitter heart. Empty Jonathan Odell of prejudice, class interest, passion for the prerogative, with their corollary of praise for an unmanly truckling to the King, and nothing remains, the empty sack collapses. It was a hardship that he should have been driven out of his native country upon the failure of the King's cause, but what could be done with a fellow who insisted that his empty sack was stuffed with all the virtues? He was harshly intolerant in his Toryism, and he encountered a victorious republican harshness.

2. SAMUEL PETERS

It is amusing to turn from the implacable Odell to the mendacious Peters, only to meet with another tale of abortive missionary zeal. The Anglican clergy played a conspicuous part during the Revolutionary troubles—a part that in many cases inspired small regard for the establishment in the minds of a dissenting laity. Not in vain did the church teach loyalty to authority, for while the British Empire was breaking asunder, the Anglican ministers were visible pillars of prerogative and with pen and voice lent

[4] *Loyalist Poetry*, p. 36.

effective aid to the royal cause. Sometimes their ardor outran
their intelligence, their devotion betrayed their discretion; nevertheless their zeal contributed notably to the number and quality
of the Loyalist writings.

For some inconceivable reason Samuel Peters was seized with a
desire to plant the Anglican church in Congregational Connecticut—surely the strangest of desires and the strangest of men to
undertake such a work. To uplift the banner of episcopacy in a
commonwealth that for over a hundred years had been militantly
Separatist, that did not want bishops and would not have them—
here was missionary zeal that a plain man understands with difficulty. To have made headway at all there was need of apostolic
fervor and an ingratiating tact; and Samuel Peters possessed
neither. He was a gentleman who preened himself on his quality,
exuding in speech and action a pride of caste that led him to speak
of the American farmers as peasants—the only native Loyalist
who thus aped the English. His abilities were far from mean,
but his better qualities were corroded by overweening conceit.
Possessed of all the arrogance of a lord and all the ostentation of a
brewer, he was scarcely the man to serve the Connecticut laity
with due Christian humility. He pointed out the truth authoritatively and then took it as a personal affront if his hearers failed to
agree with him. And so, after explaining to the Congregationalists
of Connecticut the infallible truth of the Anglican way, and being
ready to minister to them according to that way, he fell into a pet
when they refused to turn churchmen. The more he argued the
more he got himself disliked, and when his tactless loyalism brought
down the Sons of Liberty upon him and he was driven to Boston—
whence he sailed for England where he survived for thirty-one
years—he took a spirited revenge by writing his *History of Connecticut*, a work that solaced the early years of expatriation, and
provided material for many an after argument.

It is an amazingly provocative book, over which the sons of
Connecticut have disputed acrimoniously for a hundred years
without coming to agreement. Fortunately those disputes are of
far less concern today than the political philosophy tucked away
in the pages of the *History;* the scandal is far less interesting than
the shrewd comment on the causes of the American Revolution.
Samuel Peters was a high Tory with the virtue of frankness, which
defeat had made the more open. From his secure refuge in England

he looked back upon the revolutionary upheaval, and his analysis of causes is the more suggestive from the fact that he had nothing to gain from truckling to popular opinion. His judgments are interesting even when he exaggerates. The colonial Tory is no longer serving immediate partisan ends, but after the battle has been fought and lost he takes a grim pleasure in pointing out to the English government its costly blunders. Affairs went ill in America, not because of too much Toryism on the part of government, but because of too little and too late applied. The explanation of the origin and spread of unrest in America, Peters regarded as very simple. The tap-root of the disaffection was republicanism, which through the criminal negligence of government was not severed in the days when the plant was small, but which was suffered to grow till the tree could not be pulled up or destroyed.

It appears to me, that the British government, in the last century, did not expect New-England to remain under their authority; nor did the New-Englanders consider themselves as subjects, but allies, of Great Britain. It seems that England's intent was to afford an asylum to the republicans who had been a scourge to the British constitution; and so, to encourage that restless party to emigrate, republican charters were granted, and privileges and promises given them far beyond what an Englishman in England is entitled to. The emigrants were empowered to make laws, in church and state, agreeable to their own will and pleasure, without the King's approbation.[5]

From the first they have uniformly declared, in church and state, that America is a new world, subject to the people residing in it; and that none but enemies to the country would appeal from their courts to the King in Council. They never have prayed for any earthly king by name. They always called themselves republicans and enemies to kingly government. . . . They hate the idea of a parliament. . . . They never have admitted one law of England to be in force among them, till passed by their assemblies. . . . They hold Jesus to be their only King, whom if they love and obey, they will not submit, because they have not submitted to the laws of the King of England.[6]

The natural fruits of this pernicious root of republicanism were the colonial hostility to the monarchical and aristocratic elements of the British constitution, together with all the domestic turbulence and lawlessness which have marked the history of New England from the first. If gentlemen wished an object lesson in republicanism, none better than Connecticut could be had; there

[5] *A General History of Connecticut*, Appendix, p. 374. [6] *Ibid.*, p. 290.

from the earliest days, "republicanism, schisms, and persecutions," have gone hand in hand; and it was to make this clear to the world that Samuel Peters took the trouble to write his *History*.

> In the course of this work, my readers must necessarily have observed, in some degree, the ill effects of the democratical constitution of Connecticut. I would wish them to imagine, for I feel myself unable adequately to describe, the confusion, turbulence, and convulsion, arising in a province, where not only every civil officer, from the Governor to the constable, but also every minister, is appointed as well as paid by the people, and faction and superstition are established. The clergy, lawyers, and merchants or traders, are the three efficient parties which guide the helm of government. . . . *En rabies vulgi*—I must beg leave to refer my readers to their own reflections upon such a system of government as I have here sketched out.[7]

That such a people would respect the King's laws at a late day, when those laws lessened their profits, was foolish to expect. There had been much complaint from ministerial gentlemen in respect to colonial smuggling; but how idle was it to complain of the natural consequences of ministerial laxness chronic for a hundred years!

> Smuggling is rivetted in the constitutions and practice of the inhabitants of Connecticut . . . and their province is a storehouse for the smugglers of the neighboring colonies. They conscientiously study to cheat the King of those duties, which, they say, God and nature never intended should be paid. From the governor down to the tithing-man, who are sworn to support the laws, they will aid smugglers, resist collectors, and mob informers.[8]

In contemplating these open and notorious facts, which every member of government must have known, Samuel Peters came very near anger at the gross stupidity of the ministerial policy. The way to have met these difficulties was plain—the itch of democracy should have been cured with the salve of aristocracy. The natural leaders in the several colonies should have been taken care of by a judicious distribution of titles of nobility.

> The people of New-England are rightly stiled republicans: but a distinction should be made between the learned and unlearned, the rich and poor. The latter form a great majority; the minority, therefore, are obliged to wear the livery of the majority, in order to secure their election into office. Those very republican gentlemen are ambitious, fond of the power of governing, and grudge no money nor pains to obtain an annual office. What would they not give for a dignity depending not on the fickle will of a multitude, but on the steady reason and generosity of a King?[9]

[7] *Ibid.*, pp. 282–285.   [8] *Ibid.*, p. 320.   [9] *Ibid.*, p. 377.

There was shrewd, unclerical wisdom in the comment of Samuel Peters. If the gentlemen of England had founded their colonial policy on the principle of sharing the emoluments of rank and power with ambitious gentlemen in America, there might well have been quite another story to tell. But because they begrudged the small rewards, because they would have the shadow as well as the substance, they lost everything. An outcome so untoward and so stupid hurt Samuel Peters to the quick; but it was not his fault, and he doubtless found a crumb of malicious satisfaction in pointing out the ministerial stupidity after the mischief was done.

BOOK THREE: LIBERALISM AND THE CONSTITUTION
1783–1800

PART ONE: THE AGRARIAN DEFEAT
1783–1787

CHAPTER I
AGRARIANISM AND CAPITALISM

I

THE BACKGROUND OF IDEAS
English and French Contributions

WITH the close of the war the question of the times was the urgent problem of the form and control of the new political state to be erected: whether it should be the coercive sovereign of the whole, or should share its sovereignty with the several states. Although the problem was political, the forces that were driving to a solution were economic, and were commonly recognized as such. Agrarian and mercantile interests opposed each other openly and shaped their political programs in accordance with their special needs. Not until French romanticism popularized the doctrine of social equalitarianism was there any serious questioning of the principle of the economic basis of politics. The fact of property rule was challenged in America no more than in England, and the laws of suffrage in the several states were founded on that principle. The new state, therefore, took its shape from men who were political realists, deeply read in the republican literature of the seventeenth century, and inspired by the ideals of the rising English middle class. The opponents of the new state, on the other hand, were economic liberals who rejected English middle-class ideals, and inclined increasingly to the humanitarian theory of the French thinkers, though with an eye always upon American conditions. The struggle between these two schools of thought determined the final outcome of a long and acrimonious contest.

The English middle class had received its creative bent from seventeenth-century Puritanism. That vast movement survived political defeat and effected a silent revolution in English character that projected its ideals far into the future. It permeated the rising tradesman class, stimulated its ambition, and gave it an ethics precisely fitted to its needs. In inculcating the doctrine of a sacred calling to work, it substituted the modern attitude towards production for the medieval. It rejected the older conception of work for the sake of a livelihood, of production for consumption, and substituted the ideal of work for its own sake, of production for the sake of profit. It implicitly condemned the leisurely, play-loving and pleasure-taking activities of medieval England, and substituted a drab ideal of laborious gain, that measured life in terms of material prosperity and exalted the business of acquisition as the rational end of life. In the sanction of such an ethics, wealth became the first object of social desire; and this ideal, that answered the ambitions of the rising middle class, was preached under the authority of religion. To labor diligently in the vocation to which one is called of God, it was believed, was to labor under the great Taskmaster's eye, and in the confident hope of eternal reward.

No conceivable discipline was better calculated to breed a utilitarian race and create a nation of tradesmen. The immediate result was the emergence of a middle-class, unimaginative, laborious, prudential, who devoutly believed that the right to rise in the world, to pursue economic well-being in a competitive society, was the most sacred of human rights; that those who were faithful in little things, God would make rulers over great things. To scant one's service, whether to God or one's master, was the cardinal sin; work, thrift, self-denial, were the cardinal virtues. This amazing revolution in the ethics of work laid the basis upon which modern England was to rise; it carried in its loins the industrial revolution. The rise of the new ethics coincided historically with the final disintegration of the craft guilds, and the emergence of the great trading companies. It provided a desirable sanction for the modern principle of exploitation, and the development of the middleman system of distribution; and these conceptions the Puritanized English commercial class seized upon eagerly, and in capable fashion set about the work of creating the system of modern capitalism.

Every rising group is jealous of its interests and active in asserting them. It joins forces with whatever movements of current liberalism promise to further its purpose, but it will see to it that the wider movement shall serve its narrower ends. The commercial class gathered strength swiftly during the early seventeenth century, and with the gentry formed the backbone of discontent with the strong rule of Strafford. London was growing fast, "the abode of smoke, disease and democracy," as a contemporary gentleman phrased it; and the London burgesses supported Parliament heartily. The new money-economy wanted to be free from governmental restrictions and exactions, and the simplest way seemed to lie in asserting parliamentary sovereignty. That hope was frustrated after 1660 when control of Parliament passed into the hands of the landed gentry. The aristocracy was too strong for the middle class, and the latter was forced to buy its privileges in the open parliamentary market. Not until the intellectual liberalism of the later eighteenth century clarified its conception of the minimized state, did the money economy rise to fresh political consciousness, and then it joined heartily with the new liberalism in an attack upon the centralized powers of the political state.

The philosophy of this new liberalism was derived largely from two notable thinkers of the preceding century, Harrington and Locke, supplemented later by Adam Smith. The influence of the *Oceana* upon later thinkers was profound. In grasping and applying the principle of the economic interpretation of history Harrington laid the foundation of modern political theory. The true source of political power, he asserted, is economic power—"empire follows the balance of property." The form of government in a given country, whether monarchical, aristocratic, or democratic, according to the doctrine of economic determinism, depends upon the ownership of land, whether vested largely in one, in a minority, or in many. This primary economic power is modified, however, by the presence in every society of a natural aristocracy; the authority of character and ability imposes a natural leadership on those less capable, and disturbs the simple economics of the situation. Because of the resulting clash of interests, political stability can be secured only by a judiciously calculated system of checks; and the system which Harrington elaborated provided for a bicameral legislature—the aristocratic branch proposing and debating, and the democratic branch resolving—rotation in office, and the ballot, to the end that there should be a government of laws and not of men. His ideal was rulership by the best and wisest under well-considered laws, circumscribed by a written constitution.

Locke followed Harrington in founding his political theory upon economics, but he gave to it a characteristically middle-class interpretation. Harrington had been primarily concerned with a land economy; Locke was to become unconsciously a spokesman of a money economy. The persistent problem of that economy was the security of private property against sequestration, and the ultimate effect of Locke's teachings was to secure and strengthen the rights of property in the state. In basing his doctrine of property ownership upon labor, he prepared the way for a conception of economic power dissociated from land. In the universal communism which marks the state of nature, he argued, private property rights result from labor bestowed, and are ethically and socially valid. But in such a state of nature, the possession and enjoyment of property thus detached from the communal whole are at constant hazards. "The great and chief end, therefore, of men uniting into commonwealths and putting themselves under government, is the preservation of their property." [1] If such was the original purpose for which government was instituted among men, it follows that government must regard property rights with particular tenderness; for if the state prove untrustworthy, the original compact upon which it was erected is dissolved, and society returns to a state of nature. Locke therefore went far in asserting the inviolable rights of property, laying it down as a guiding principle that the sovereign in time of war may lawfully enforce conscription upon the bodies and lives of his subjects, but not upon their property. "The supreme power cannot take from any man any part of his property without his own consent," for "to invade the fundamental law of property" is to subvert "the end of government." [2] In thus asserting the sacredness of property, Locke laid the foundation of the new philosophy of capitalism.

As English capitalism grew stronger it began to envisage more critically the fundamental problem of the powers and functions of the political state. A state controlled by the landed interests, given to imposing vexatious restrictions upon trade, could not answer its needs; freedom rather than regulation was requisite to healthy development. From the Physiocratic teachings had come the new conception that economic well-being cannot be imposed from above by governmental paternalism, but results from un-

[1] *Second Treatise on Civil Government*, Chapter IX.   [2] *Ibid.*, Chapter XI.

trammeled individual enterprise. The great concern of government should be to assist and not hamper industry and trade; political policies should follow and serve commercial interests. Thus was provided the background from which emerged *The Wealth of Nations*, the declaration of independence of modern capitalism. Adam Smith completed the work of Locke, and gave definite form to the middle-class liberalism of eighteenth-century England, a liberalism that in the pursuit of commercial freedom found it desirable to limit the powers of the state. The Tory state had been centralized and paternal, the capitalistic state was to be reduced to the position of umpire between competitors. The net results, thus, of two hundred years of English middle-class struggle to free its economic ambitions from governmental restrictions was the conception of the social, political, and economic sufficiency of *laissez faire*. "Let alone" had been erected into a fetish.

In France, on the other hand, the economic interpretation of history dominated political thinking far less than in England, and the liberal movement owed more to a group of intellectuals than to the middle class. The French leaders were a remarkable group, far removed in temper from Harrington and Locke and Adam Smith. The Physiocrats were agrarians and the romantics were humanitarians. They followed the path of logic to broad principles. As leadership passed from Montesquieu to Rousseau, French liberalism abandoned the cautious historical appeal, and turned to generalization that carried far beyond liberalism. The Rousseau school became advanced radicals, aiming at the regeneration of society as a whole, seeking political justice by a universal appeal to reason. This explains the breadth and suggestiveness of their thinking, as well as the smallness of their immediate achievement. In seeking much they overreached accomplishment, for they had behind them no disciplined, class-conscious group, pursuing definite ends. But in outrunning their own time, they became leaders of later times; and the unfulfilled program of Rousseau carried over to become the inspiration of later humanitarianism.

The creative impulse of French romantic philosophy was a passionate social idealism. A disciple of Locke, Rousseau went further than his master and translated politics and economics into sociology. That a juster, more wholesome social order should take the place of the existing obsolete system; that reason and not interests should determine social institutions; that the ultimate ends to be sought were universal liberty, equality, and fraternity—such in brief were the main conceptions of his philosophy. "Regard for the general good" must be accepted as the sole test of laws and institutions. He attacked the problem by way of psychology, essaying a revaluation of human nature. Incalculable harm had been done, and grave mistakes made, Rousseau believed, by the old slanderous interpretation; to assume that every man is a knave, governed solely by self-interest, was an assumption contrary to fact. It was a generalization deduced from certain acquired characteristics. If in a competitive society men prove to be selfish, ambitious of power and distinction, brutal in seeking egoistic ends, the blame attaches to a vicious social system that has debased them from their natural state. In a state of nature men are kindly, rational, sociable; but in society the great rewards fall to the self-seeking. A ruthless social order is forever perverting the natural man; whereas if social rewards were bestowed on the social-minded, the innate sense of justice would speedily modify and control the impulse to egoism. The solution of the vexing social problem, Rousseau concluded, lay in a return to a state of nature, where under the determining influence of wholesome environment the individual should develop naturally, unperverted by false standards and unjust rewards.

French radicalism, then, was driving in the same direction with English liberalism, but it went much further. Both desired a loosening of the machinery of centralized power as represented by the political state; but whereas English liberalism protested against a paternalism that diminished its profits, French radicalism struck at the principle of centralization. Political institutions it regarded as artificial agencies for the purposes of exploitation—the state was little more than a tax machine; whereas the living source and wellspring of every true civilization is social custom, voluntary association, free exchange. The root of French radicalism was anarchistic, and its ideal was an agrarian society of free-holders. It would sweep away the long accumulated mass of prescriptive rights, the dead hand of the past, and encourage free men to create a new society that should have as its sole end and justification, the common well-being. A pronounced individualism characterized both movements, French and English; but in the one case it was humanitarian, appealing to reason and seeking social justice, in the other it was self-seeking, founded on the right of exploitation, and looking toward capitalism.

During the period with which we are concerned, American thought, become militantly self-conscious but still vague and inchoate touching any ultimate program, drew inspiration from both sources; but the deeper, controlling influence came finally to be English rather than French. The common doctrine of decentralization fitted American conditions, but to many Americans decentralization, whether social or political, had proved undesirable. The common doctrine of liberty accorded with the passions released by the Revolution, but the French humanitarian conceptions of equality and fraternity found little response in a middle-class, competitive world. On the contrary, the English doctrine of economic individualism made universal appeal. In presence of vast, unpreëmpted resources, the right of every man to preëmpt and exploit what he would, was synonymous with individual liberty. Any government which should endeavor to limit such exploitation would be bitterly assailed; and if the small man were free to enjoy his petty privilege, the greater interests might preëmpt unchallenged. The total influence of old-world liberalism upon the America of post-war days was, therefore, favorable to capitalistic development and hostile to social democracy. Until the early years of the nineties the democratic spirit of French radicalism was little understood in America, and the field remained free to the English middle-class philosophy, which appealed equally to the agrarian and the capitalistic groups.

II

THE POLITICAL SITUATION

Against this background of ideas, the political tactics of the year 1787 are sufficiently comprehensible. Two major problems had been settled by the war, namely, that henceforth the exploitation of America was to remain the prerogative of Americans, and that in the new country there was no place for a king or a titled aristocracy. But with these preliminaries settled, the problem remained to determine the form and powers of a national government. Should that government be entrusted with coercive sovereignty, or should it remain the titular head of confederated sovereign commonwealths? The latter solution had been accepted during the period of war, and in proposing abolition of the Articles of Confederation and the substitution of a new instrument, the burden of proof fell upon the advocates of the new. How the problem was met and the solution achieved by a skillful minority in face of a hostile majority is a suggestive lesson in political strategy. It is a classic example of the relation of economics to politics; of the struggle between greater property and smaller property for control of the state.

The strategic position of the large property interests in the year 1787 was favorable to a bold stroke. In the northern and middle states the controlling influence was wielded by a powerful money group that had been slowly rising during pre-Revolutionary days, and had greatly increased its resources and augmented its prestige as a result of war financing and speculation in currency and lands. They at once assumed the leadership which before had belonged to the gentry. Like all eighteenth-century realists they exhibited a frank property-consciousness that determined all their moves. With them affiliated such members of the older gentry as remained, the professional classes, ambitious Revolutionary officers who had set up the militant Order of the Cincinnati, together with a numerous body of the disappointed and the disaffected; the net result of which was a close working alliance of property and culture for the purpose of erecting a centralized state with coercive powers. They were powerfully aided by two outstanding characteristics of the eighteenth-century mind: an aristocratic psychology which was deeply ingrained in the colonial through the long unchallenged rule of the gentry; and the universal belief in the stake-in-society theory of government, evidenced by the general disfranchisement of non-property-holders. Property had always ruled in America, openly and without apology, and the money group could count on a spontaneous response to its demand that property should reorganize the feeble central government and set up one more to its liking. In the South this reorganization was unnecessary, for the planter aristocracy, in siding with the Revolution, remained masters of their society, and the money group had not risen to challenge their supremacy. It remained only for the northern interests to join forces with the planters to bring the great property interests of the country under one banner.

The status of the small property holders, on the other hand, was much less happy. They were in possession of many of the state governments, and were strongly wedded to the Articles of Confederation; but they were deep in populism and their agrarian measures offered rallying points for a powerful opposition. They lacked disciplined cohesion and were wanting in a broad program. The militant mood of Revolutionary days had given place to suspicion and disillusion, and their fighting strength was greatly weakened. They were suffering the fate of all post-war governments. The widespread depression was attributed to populist policies, and all the evils from which the country was suffering were laid at the doors of agrarian legislatures. Under such conditions the political strategy of the money group was predetermined. The issue was ready-made. Astute politicians like Hamilton seized the opportunity and crystallized the discontent by the ingenious argument that the trouble was too much agrarianism, that agrarianism resulted from too much democracy, and that the inevitable end of too much democracy was universal anarchy. The root of all the troubles, it was asserted, was the pernicious slackness of the Articles of Confederation which prevented a vigorous administration. There could be no prosperity until a competent national government was set up on a substantial basis.

The inevitable consequence was that the ideal of popular democratic rule received a sharp setback. The aristocratic prejudices of the colonial mind were given a more militant bias by skillful propaganda. Democracy was pictured as no other than mob rule, and its ultimate purpose the denial of all property rights. Populistic measures were fiercely denounced as the natural fruit of democratic control; all America was in danger of following the destructive example of New Hampshire and Rhode Island. "Look at the Legislature of Rhode Island," exclaimed a speaker in the New York Constitutional Convention, "what is it but the perfect picture of a mob!" The virus of democracy was a poison that destroyed the character of the people as well as government; was not the fate of Rhode Island a warning to the rest of the country? Here is a picture of that commonwealth, drawn by an English gentleman before agrarianism had done its worst. ·

The government of this province is entirely democratical, every officer, except the collector of the customs, being appointed . . . either immediately by the people, or by the general assembly. . . . The character of

the Rhode Islanders is by no means engaging, or amiable, a circumstance
principally owing to their form of government. Their men in power, from
the highest to the lowest, are dependent upon the people, and frequently
act without that strict regard to probity and honour, which ought invariably to influence and direct mankind. The private people are cunning,
deceitful, and selfish: they live almost entirely by unfair and illicit trading.
Their magistrates are partisan and corrupt: and it is folly to expect justice
in their courts of judicature; for he who has the greatest purse is generally
found to have the fairest cause. . . . It is needless, after this, to observe
that it is in a very declining state.[3]

"Under the Articles of Confederation," comments a recent
student, "populism had a free hand, for majorities in the state
legislatures were omnipotent. Any one who reads the economic
history of the time will see why the solid conservative interests
of the country were weary of the talk about the 'rights of the
people,' and were bent upon establishing firm guarantees for the
rights of property."[4] The money-economy had made up its mind
that such government as that of Rhode Island could not longer
be tolerated. An example must be made of such hotbeds of
anarchy; if reason would not be listened to, force must be used.
An ardent Federalist, Judge Dana of Massachusetts, offered a
possible solution:

This state [Rhode Island] will not choose delegates to the convention,
nor order on their delegates to Congress. I hope they will not, as their
neglect will give grounds to strike it out of the union, and divide its territory between their neighbors. . . . According to my best observation,
such a division of this state would meet the best approbation of the commercial part of it, though they are afraid to take any open measures in the
present state of things, to bring it about. Their interest must dictate
such a measure; they never can be secure under the present form of government, but will always labor under the greatest mischief any people can
suffer, that of being ruled by the most ignorant and unprincipled of their
fellow citizens. This state is too insignificant to have a place on an equal
footing with any of the others in the Union, unless it be Delaware. Therefore a bold politician would seize upon the occasion their abominable anti-
federal conduct presents, for annihilating them as a separate member of
the Union.[5]

"It is fortunate," wrote General Varnum to Washington, con-
firming Judge Dana's analysis of the economic divisions of Rhode

---

[3] Burnaby, *Travels through the Middle Settlements in North America in the Years
1759 and 1760.*
[4] Beard, *The Supreme Court and the Constitution.*
[5] Austin, *Life of Elbridge Gerry*, Vol. II, pp. 66–67.

Island, "that the wealth and resources of this state are chiefly in possession of the well affected, and they are entirely devoted to the public good."

It was Shays's Rebellion, that militant outbreak of populism that set all western Massachusetts in uproar, and spread to the very outskirts of Boston, which crystallized the anti-democratic sentiment, and aroused the commercial group to decisive action. With its armed attack upon lawyers and courts, its intimidation of legislators, its appeal for the repudiation of debts, it provided the object lesson in democratic anarchy which the "friends of law and order" greatly needed. The revolt was put down, but the fear of democracy remained and called aloud for stronger government. "We see the situation we are in," exclaimed a Boston member in the Massachusetts Constitutional Convention. "We are verging toward destruction, and every one must be sensible of it." Shays had failed, but with political power in the hands of agrarian legislatures, friendly to debtors, what dangers must not the future hold in store? Was it not the patriotic duty of the sober conservators of society to set up betimes a strong constitutional defense, before the rights of property were swept away by the fierce tide of democracy? Writing to Washington under date of October 23, 1786, General Knox argued:

On the very first impression of faction and licentiousness, the fine theoretic government of Massachusetts has given way, and its laws are trampled under foot. . . . Their creed is, that the property of the United States has been protected from the confiscation of Britain by the joint exertions of all, and therefore ought to be the common property of all. . . . This dreadful situation, for which our government have made no adequate provision, has alarmed every man of principle and property in New England. They start as from a dream, and ask what can have been the cause of this delusion? What is to give us security against the violence of lawless men? Our government must be braced, changed, or altered to secure our lives and property. We imagined that the mildness of our government and the wishes of the people were so correspondent that we were not as other nations, requiring brutal force to support the laws. But we find we are men—actual men, possessing all the turbulent passions belonging to that animal, and that we must have a government proper and adequate for him. The people of Massachusetts . . . are far advanced in this doctrine, and the men of property and the men of station and principle there, are determined to establish and protect them in their lawful pursuits. . . . Something is wanting and something must be done.[6]

[6] Brooks, *Henry Knox*, pp. 194–195.

During these years of unrest the problem of a new fundamental law was carefully studied by the anti-agrarian leaders and solutions suggested. A remarkable change had come over their thinking. They discarded the revolutionary doctrines that had served their need in the debate with England. They were done with natural rights and romantic interpretations of politics and were turned realists. They parted company with English liberalism in its desire for a diminished state. Their economic interests were suffering from the lack of a strong centralized government, and they were in a mood to agree with earlier realists who held that men are animals with turbulent passions, and require a government "proper and adequate" for animals; and in view of local agrarian majorities, a proper and adequate government could not be had without a strong centralized state. The solution, they were convinced, lay in a return to some form of seventeenth-century republicanism, possibly modeled after Harrington, but with further checks upon the power of the democratic branch of the legislature, and a stronger executive. Hobbes with his leviathan monarchy had gone too far, but he had, at least, understood the need of a strong state; and a strong state, subservient to their interests, the business and landed groups were determined to set up as a barrier against a threatening agrarianism.

The great obstacle to such a program was the political power of the farmers, bred up in the traditional practice of home rule, jealous of local rights, and content with the Articles of Confederation. These home rulers would not take kindly to any suggestion of a centralized state, even though it should be republican in form. The thing must be done skillfully, if it were to succeed. To nullify where they could not override the political power of the agrarians, therefore, became the practical problem of the money-economy. The fear aroused by Shays's Rebellion provided the strategic opportunity, and the best brains of the country suggested the method. The struggle had begun which was to provide a new fundamental law for the United States.

CHAPTER II

THE GREAT DEBATE

WHEN one considers the bulk of commentary that has grown up about the Constitution, it is surprising how little abstract political speculation accompanied its making and adoption. It was the first response to the current liberal demand for written constitutions as a safeguard against tyranny, but it was aimed at the encroachments of agrarian majorities rather than at Tory minorities. It was the work of able lawyers and men of affairs confronting a definite situation, rather than of political philosophers; and it was accompanied by none of that searching examination of fundamental rights and principles which made the earlier Puritan and later French debate over constitutional principles so rich in creative speculation. Not a single political thinker comparable to the great English and French philosophers emerged from the struggle. The debate drew freely upon the materials supplied by those thinkers, but it added little that was new.

The Constitution was a venture in republicanism, on a scale and under conditions without historical precedent. It was inevitable, therefore, that the debate should concern itself greatly with the nature of republicanism and its adaptability to American conditions. As the argument developed, two major questions assumed critical importance: the question of the powers of the Federal state, and the question of the sovereign rights of the majority; and in dealing with both the debaters were on ground inadequately surveyed. Of definite republican theory little was available except the writings of a small group of seventeenth-century republicans. Of democratic theory, on the other hand, even less was available. American democratic aspiration had far outrun old-world liberalism, and had produced no independent speculation of its own. French democratic theory still awaited the rise of Jacobinism to clarify its principles. The party of Commonwealth Levelers, to be sure, with their doctrines of a "paramount law," manhood suffrage, and annual parliaments, offered much that might have proved suggestive; but the literature of the Levelers was buried too deep under Tory obloquy to be resurrected, and nowhere else was to be found any considerable body of democratic theory. It was inevitable, therefore, that the debaters should go back to the English liberals of the preceding century.

Consider for a moment the authorities bandied to and fro in the great debate. With such exceptions as Machiavelli, Vattel, Pufendorf, Montesquieu, they were the well-known English theorists, Hobbes, Harrington, Milton, Sidney, Halifax, Hume, and Blackstone. Unhappily for the democrats every one of these great names counted against their aspirations. Hobbes was a state absolutist whose *Leviathan* provided sharp weapons for those who wished to tone the government high; Hume was a Tory who accepted the traditional interpretation of human nature in the light of which democracy was the open door to anarchy; Blackstone was a Tory lawyer, who interpreted the British constitution by a narrow legalism that was obsolete before the *Commentaries* came from the press. Harrington, Milton, and perhaps Sidney, were republicans of strong aristocratic bias, and Halifax and Locke—the latter by much the most influential of all—were constitutional monarchists.[1] Every one of these great authorities either distrusted or violently condemned democracy, yet they provided the major body of theory made use of by the Federalists.

On the other hand, the slowly accumulating democratic theory was unknown to the members of the convention. In 1761 Robert Wallace had advanced an Owenite theory of property, attacking the principle of economic individualism as responsible for the current evils of government by landed property; but his book, *Various Prospects*, made no ripple on the placid waters of English liberalism.[2] In 1768 Joseph Priestley, a thinker who later was to exercise great influence in America, who lived here for a number of years and was intimate with Jefferson, published his essay, *First Principles of Government*, a work embodying the first English interpretation of the perfectibility of man, the rule of reason, the theory of the diminished state, and the Benthamite principle of utilitarianism or expediency in statecraft, which struck at the principle of coercive sovereignty. But the ideas of Priestley were probably little known in America in 1787, and his influence was

[1] These English liberals have been often regarded as democrats. Thus Merriam says of Locke, "He was the most famous of seventeenth century democratic thinkers." *American Political Theories*, p. 90.
[2] See Laski, *Political Thought from Locke to Bentham*, p. 188.

undermined further by a theological attack which sought to fasten upon him the stigma of atheism. In short, in this war of ideas the democrats were provided with little ammunition and fought at a great disadvantage. If the debate had taken place five years later, after the French Revolution had provided new democratic theory, the disparity of intellectual equipment would have been far less marked.

One other fact must be kept in mind, namely, that the great debate was in reality two debates, one carried on in the quiet of the convention hall, the other in the open. Each interprets the other, and taken together they reveal the conflict of forces and ideas that determined the form of the Constitution. In the privacy of the convention the speakers were free to express their views frankly, and in consequence a loose rein was given to the play of ideas; fundamental principles were examined critically and economic motives and class interests openly acknowledged. But in arguing the case before the generality of voters without doors a more cautious approach was necessary; arguments must be tempered to well-known prejudices, and circumspection must take the place of frankness. In the earlier debate, among innumerable lesser problems, two main questions dominated the argument: the question of the form of the centralized state—whether it should be aristocratic or republican; and if republican—as was inevitable—the question of what should be done about the majority will—how representation should be so refined as to guarantee stability to the government and security to the minority. In the second debate the appeal was to expediency rather than to principles, and turned on three chief points: the need of adoption in view of the desperate condition of the country; the adaptation of the proposed republican form to the vast extent of territory and diversity of interests; and the necessity of providing checks upon political parties if anarchy were to be avoided.

In the convention the need of a strong state, with powers beyond local legislatures, was not so much debated as assumed. By common consent it was agreed that the present lack of a centralized, coercive sovereignty, was the source of all current evils. How many members preferred monarchy to republicanism, in principle, it is impossible to determine; but they all realized the inexpediency of attempting to set it up; even Hamilton yielded to the logic of Colonel Mason's argument: "Notwithstanding the oppression

and injustice experienced among us from democracy, the genius
of the people is in favor of it, and the genius of the people must
be consulted." Accepting then the principle of republicanism as
a compromise between the extremes of monarchy and democracy,
the practical problem remained of erecting a system that should
secure the minority against the aggressions of political faction.
If the danger lay in an uncontrolled majority will, the way of
safety lay in imposing restraints upon that will. In elaborating a
system of checks and balances the members of the convention were
influenced by the practical considerations of economic determinism
more than by the theories of Montesquieu. They were realists
who followed the teachings of the greatest political thinkers from
Aristotle to Locke in asserting that the problem of government
lay in arranging a stable balance between the economic interests
of the major classes. The revolutionary conception of equalitarianism, that asserted the rights of man apart from property and
superior to property, did not enter into their thinking as a workable
hypothesis. The very conditions of the unsettled times were an
argument against it. Property, they argued, is the stabilizing
force in society; it is conservative and cautious; having everything
to lose by social upheavals, it is a restraining force upon factional
unrest. The propertyless, on the other hand, having nothing to
lose, easily become the victims of demagogues and embroil society
with foolish experiments. The republican experiment might work
in America because property was widely distributed, but in the
course of time a propertyless majority would arise, whose fickle
and subversive will must be held in check. The problem, therefore,
was to provide in time against such an eventuality. Certain
members of the convention did not go so far in their fear of the
propertyless, but relied upon the ability of property to protect
itself by extra-legal means. "Give the votes to people who have
no property," argued Gouverneur Morris, "and they will sell them
to the rich, who will be able to buy them." [3] But the more general
view was expressed by Madison:

The landed interest, at present, is prevalent, but in process of time . . .
when the number of landholders shall be comparatively small . . . will
not the landed interests be overbalanced in future elections? and, unless
wisely provided against, what will become of our government? In England, at this day, if elections were open to all classes of people, the property

[3] *Elliot's Debates*, Vol. I, p. 386.

of landed proprietors would be insecure. An agrarian law would take place. If these observations be just, our government ought to secure the permanent interests of the country against innovation. Landholders ought to have a share in the government, to support these invaluable interests, and to balance and check the other. They ought to be so constituted as to protect the minority of the opulent against the majority.[4]

This conception of the natural sovereignty of the landed interest with its stake-in-society theory of political rights, America inherited from England; and although the new Constitution professed to rest on the sovereignty of the people, the men who framed it refused to interpret the term, sovereignty of the people, in an equalitarian sense. They did not profess to be, in the words of John Quincy Adams, "slavish adorers of our sovereign lords the people." Every principle of their social and political philosophy taught them the desirability of limiting the majority will in order that the wiser minority will might rule. Paul Leicester Ford has asserted that "the Federal compact was the first deliberate attempt and assent of a majority to tie its own hands; to give to the minority guarantees of fair and equal treatment, without which democratic government is well-nigh impossible, save when developed along the lines of socialism." [5] Such partisan misinterpretation of plain historical fact is characteristic of our Federalist historians. If the hands of the disfranchised majority were tied by the voting minority, it is a bit absurd to attribute the resulting guarantees to an altruistic sense of justice, deliberately expressed by the former. Very possibly in a world so aristocratic as was America in 1787, no other course would have succeeded; but there is not a single historical fact to justify so naïve an interpretation, and the bitter partisan warfare which followed is sufficient to disprove it.

We are too prone to forget the wide popular disfavor with which the new Constitution was received. No sooner did the second debate open than it became evident that the majority opinion held quite a different conception of the sovereignty of the people than was expressed by the convention. It had no desire to tie its own hands; it did not take kindly to the proposal to transfer power from the several states to the Federal government. The villagers and small men were afraid of the new instrument; they asserted that it had been prepared by aristocrats and moneyed

[4] *Ibid.*, Vol. I, pp. 449–450.   [5] *The Federalist*, Introduction, p. viii.

men, and they repudiated the stake-in-society principle. "The Constitution," said General Thompson in the Massachusetts Convention, "and the reasons which induced gentlemen to frame it, ought to have been sent to the several towns to be considered by them. My town considered it seven hours, and after this there was not one in favor of it." In Rhode Island, where it was thus submitted, it was rejected "by a very great majority." The state of mind of the agrarian majority was thus expressed by Amos Singletary, of Sutton, Massachusetts:

These lawyers, and men of learning, and moneyed men, that talk so finely, and gloss over matters so smoothly, to make us, poor illiterate people, swallow down the pill, expect to get into Congress themselves; they expect to be the managers of this Constitution, and get all the power and all the money into their own hands, and then they will swallow up all us little folks, like the great leviathan.[6]

Among the host of pamphlets and newspaper articles that quickly appeared, *The Federalist* written by Hamilton and Madison with some help from Jay, and *Letters from the Federal Farmer to the Republican*, by Richard Henry Lee, fairly adequately present the opposing arguments. By common consent *The Federalist* was at once accepted by its party as an unanswerable defense of the Constitution; and its fame has grown greater with the passing years. No other work on political theory in the American library has been rated so high, or been more frequently cited. From the mass of contemporary pamphlets it emerges like a colossus. It "has been seriously and reverently called the Bible of Republicanism," says a legal historian, which "for comprehensiveness of design, strength, clearness, and simplicity . . . has no parallel among the writings of men, not even excepting or overlooking those of Montesquieu and Aristotle,"[7]; and a literary historian pronounces authoritatively, "it is so wisely thoughtful that one may almost declare it the permanent basis of sound thinking concerning American constitutional law." [8]

The Federalist was the work of able lawyers, with whom was joined a notable political thinker. In very large part it is of interest only to students of early constitutional theory and practice. It was designed as a frankly partisan argument to appeal to an

[6] Quoted in Harding, *The Federal Constitution in Massachusetts.*
[7] Carson, *History of the Supreme Court*, quoted by Ford, *The Federalist*, p. xxix.
[8] Wendell, *Literary History of America*, p. 118.

influential group in New York, many members of which had
followed George Clinton and Robert Yates in opposition to the
Constitution. On the political side it develops four main theses:
the necessity for taking effective action in view of the self-confessed
failure of the Articles of Confederation; the urgent need of a
sovereign, unitary state, to avoid the horrors which must follow
from "the political monster of an *imperium in imperio*"; the necessity of providing that justice shall prevail over the majority will;
and the adaptability of the republican form to a great extent of
territory and divergent interests. Of these the second and third
lay bare the heart of Federalist political theory; and in the treatment of them there is no shrinking from the conclusions of the
earlier debate, although the tone is conciliatory.

The argument for a unitary, sovereign state, developed by
Hamilton, and the argument for justice, developed by Madison,
rest upon the same basis and are regarded as the twin problems
of government. The true sanction of government is found, not
in good will, as Bentham and later democratic thinkers have urged,
but in coercion; [9] and coercion is accepted as necessary because
of universal selfishness. "Why has government been instituted
at all? Because the passions of men will not conform to the
dictates of reason and justice, without restraint." [10]   Granted
coercive sovereignty, government must guarantee justice to all;
and justice demands that the majority shall suffer needful restraint
equally with the minority. The great and insidious danger to
good government has always been faction, the argument runs,
and a chief merit of the Constitution lay in its provisions to lessen
the disasters of factional ambition. "Complaints are everywhere
heard from our most considerate and virtuous citizens, equally
the friends of public and private faith, and of public and personal
liberty, that our governments are too unstable, that the public
good is disregarded in the conflict of rival parties, and that measures
are too often decided, not according to the rules of justice and
the rights of the minor party, but by the superior force of an
interested and overbearing majority." [11]

No theory is more representative of the time than the theory
of faction. It was a first line of defense thrown up against the
advancing democratic movement. The term had long served
conveniently to stigmatize any popular unrest, the "factious

[9] Number 15.   [10] *Ibid.*   [11] Number 10.

multitude" having been held synonymous in earlier usage with mob; but in the eighteenth century the word was applied generally to political parties. In a world moving inevitably towards manhood suffrage, a sharp alignment of parties with definite platforms was greatly feared by the minority, for the organization of the rank and file of voters must end in majority control. An honest appeal to the people was the last thing desired by the ·Federalists, and the democratic machinery of recalls and referendums and rotation in office, which had developed during the war, was stigmatized as factional devices which in the end must destroy good government. "As every appeal to the people would carry an implication of some defect in the government," argued Madison,[12] "frequent appeals would in a great measure deprive the government of that veneration which time bestows on everything, and without which the wisest and freest governments would not possess the requisite stability." "The danger of disturbing the public tranquillity by interesting too strongly the public passions is a still more serious objection against a frequent reference of constitutional questions to the decisions of the whole society."

In the remarkable tenth number, which compresses within a few pages pretty much the whole Federalist theory of political science, Madison has explained the Federalist objections to political parties and party government.

By a faction, I understand a number of citizens, whether amounting to a majority or minority of the whole, who are united and actuated by some common impulse of passion, or of interest, adverse to the rights of other citizens, or to the permanent and aggregate interests of the community. . . . If a faction consists of less than a majority, relief is supplied by the republican principle, which enables the majority to defeat its sinister views, by regular vote. . . . When a majority is included in a faction, the form of popular government, on the other hand, enables it to sacrifice to its ruling passion or interest, both the public good and the rights of other citizens. To secure the public good and private rights, against the danger of such a faction, is then the great object to which our inquiries are directed. . . . By what means is this great object attainable? Evidently by one of two only. Either the existence of the same passion or interest in a majority at the same time must be prevented; or the majority, having such coexistent passion or interest, must be rendered by their number and local situations, unable to concert and carry into effect schemes of oppression. If the impulse and the opportunity be suffered to

[12] Number 49.

coincide, we well know, that neither moral nor religious motives can be relied on as an adequate control.

In full agreement with the greater political thinkers of the past, Madison then traces political parties to economic sources. Since in every society the diversity of economic groups creates diversity of political programs, party divisions and party alignments are inevitable in the ordinary course of events. The unequal distribution of property is the realistic basis of all politics, and the "*sentiments* and *views* which arise from the possession of different degrees and kinds of property form the stuff of so-called 'political psychology.'" [13]

The diversity in the faculties of men, from which the rights of property originate, is . . . an insuperable obstacle to a uniformity of interests. The protection of these faculties is the first object of government. From the protection of different and unequal faculties of acquiring property, the possession of different degrees and kinds of property immediately results; and from the influence of these on the sentiments and views of the respective proprietors, ensues a division of the society into different interests and parties.

The latent causes of faction are thus sown in the nature of man; and we see them everywhere brought into different degrees of activity, according to the different circumstances of civil society. A zeal for different opinions . . . [has] divided mankind into parties, inflamed them with mutual animosity, and rendered them much more disposed to vex and oppress each other than to co-operate for their common good. . . . But the most common and durable source of factions has been the various and unequal distribution of property. Those who hold and those who are without property have ever formed distinct interests of society. Those who are creditors, and those who are debtors, fall under a like discrimination. A landed interest, a manufacturing interest, a mercantile interest, a moneyed interest, with many lesser interests, grow up of necessity in civilized nations, and divide them into different classes actuated by different sentiments and views. The regulation of these various and interfering interests, forms the principal task of modern legislation, and involves the spirit of party and faction in the necessary and ordinary operations of the government.

As a means of securing a necessary balance between rival interests, Madison approved a republican rather than a democratic form of government:

The two great points of difference, between a democracy and a republic, are, first, the delegation of the government, in the latter, to a small number of citizens elected by the rest; secondly, the greater number of citizens,

[13] Beard, *The Economic Basis of Politics*, pp. 29–32.

and greater sphere of country, over which the latter may be extended.
The effect of the first difference is, on the one hand, to refine or enlarge
the public views, by passing them through the medium of a chosen body of
citizens, whose wisdom may best discern the true interests of their country, and whose patriotism and love of justice, will be least likely to sacrifice it to temporary or partial considerations. Under such a regulation,
it may well happen, that the public voice, pronounced by the representatives of the people, will be more consonant to the public good, than if
pronounced by the people themselves, convened for the purpose. . . .
The other point of difference is, the greater number of citizens, and extent
of territory, which may be brought within the compass of republican, than
of democratic government; and it is this circumstance principally which
renders factious combinations less to be dreaded in the former, than in
the latter. . . . Extend the sphere, and you take in a greater variety of
parties and interests; you make it less probable that a majority of the
whole will have a common motive to invade the rights of other citizens;
or if such a common motive exists, it will be more difficult for all who
feel it to discover their strength, and act in unison with each other.[14]

In such argument Madison was adapting to his purpose the views
of Milton and other seventeenth-century republicans, to whom
in the dangerous days when the Puritan Commonwealth was
breaking up, the "noise and shouting of the rude multitude," the
drunken ribaldry of the London rabble, was prophetic of "new
injunctions to manacle the native libertie of mankinde." But
it has long since become a commonplace of political observation
that the minority and not the majority is the more dangerous to
the common well-being, for it is the minority that most frequently
uses government to its own ends.

The contrast in temper and argument between *The Federalist*
and Richard Henry Lee's *Letters from the Federal Farmer*,[15] is
striking. The calmness and fair-mindedness of the work persuade
one that it ill deserves the name partisan; it comes near to being a
frank and disinterested examination of the proposed instrument of
government. Its sharpest strictures are tempered by ready acknowledgment of excellent features. The burden of Lee's accusa-
tion is that the instrument is undemocratic; that it must result
in placing the majority under control of the minority; and that
it in no wise reflects the sober judgment of the body of the people.
He is more restrained than Elbridge Gerry, who asserted that it

[14] Number 10.

[15] The full title is: *Observations leading to a fair examination of the system of government, proposed by the late Convention; and to several essential and necessary alterations
in it. In a number of Letters from the Federal Farmer to the Republican.* Reprinted
in Ford's pamphlets.

was the outcome of a conspiracy hatched in secret, a work of "such motley mixture, that its enemies cannot trace a feature of Democratic or Republican extract." But the Farmer's restraint adds weight to the serious charges which he brings against the instrument, and the unseemly haste of its advocates in urging its speedy adoption. It was not to destroy the work of the Convention that he pleaded for delay; but that it should receive full and fair consideration, and be disposed of as its merits or defects should warrant.

His first concern is that the Constitution should not be adopted with the inconsiderate haste for which *The Federalist* was pressing. "The first principal question that occurs, is, Whether, considering our situation, we ought to precipitate the adoption of the proposed Constitution?" Hamilton had made much of the desperate state of affairs that admitted of no delay; Lee replied by denying, with Franklin and other competent observers, that the present state was desperate. Matters were improving daily, peace was restoring the ravages of war.

I know uneasy men, who with very much to precipitate, do not admit all these facts; but they are facts well known to all men who are thoroughly informed in the affairs of this country. It must, however, be admitted, that our federal system is defective, and that some of the state governments are not well administered; but . . . we impute to the defects in our governments many evils and embarrassments which are most clearly the result of the late war. . . . When we want a man to change his condition, we describe it as wretched, miserable, and despised; and we draw a pleasing picture of that which we would have him assume. . . . It is too often the case in political concerns that men state facts not as they are, but as they wish them to be. . . . Men who feel easy in their circumstances, and such as are not sanguine in their expectations relative to the consequences of the proposed change, will remain quiet under the existing governments. Many commercial and monied men, who are uneasy, not without just cause, ought to be respected; and by no means, unreasonably disappointed in their expectations and hopes. . . . It is natural for men, who wish to hasten the adoption of a measure, to tell us, now is the crisis— now is the critical moment which must be seized or all will be lost; and to shut the door against free enquiry, whenever conscious the thing presented has defects in it, which time and investigation will probably discover. . . . If it is true, what has been so often said, that the people of this country cannot change their constitution for the worse, I presume it still behoves them to endeavor deliberately to change it for the better.

Granted that experience has demonstrated the need of revising the Articles of Confederation in certain essential points, Lee maintains that the enemies of democracy have been making undue capital out of the shortcomings of an emergency government, in the hope of subverting the democratic state governments and substituting a more aristocratic form.

The confederation was formed when great confidence was placed in the voluntary exertions of individuals, and of the respective states; and the framers of it, to guard against usurpation, so limited, and checked the powers, that, in many respects, they are inadequate to the exigencies of the union. . . . During the war, the general confusion, and the introduction of paper money, infused in the minds of people vague ideas respecting government and credit. We expected too much from the return of peace, and of course we have been disappointed. Our governments have been new and unsettled; and several legislatures, by making tender, suspension, and paper money laws, have given just cause of uneasiness to creditors. By these and other causes, several orders of men in the community have been prepared by degrees, for a change of government; and this very abuse of power in the legislatures, which in some cases has been charged upon the democratic part of the community, has furnished aristocratical men with those very weapons, and those very means, with which, in great measure, they are rapidly effecting their favourite object.

The methods by which the convention was brought together at a time when the "idea of destroying ultimately, the state government, and forming one consolidated system, could not have been admitted," is traced briefly with penetrating comment, and the unfortunate decision of some excellent republicans to take no part in the work is regretted:

Here the favorable moment for changing the government was evidently discerned by a few men, who seized it with address. . . . Tho' they chose men principally connected with commerce and the judicial departments, yet they appointed many good republican characters—had they all attended we should see, I am persuaded, a better system presented. The non-attendance of eight or nine men, who were appointed members of the convention, I shall ever consider as a very unfortunate event to the United States.—Had they attended, I am pretty clear that the results . . . would not have had that strong tendency to aristocracy now discernible in every part of the plan . . . the young visionary men, and the consolidating aristocracy, would have been more restrained than they have been.

Lee frankly concedes that the instrument possesses many excellent features, but he considers it greatly vitiated by the "want of that one important factor in a free government, a representation of the people." "Because we have sometimes abused democracy, I am not among those who think a democratic branch a nuisance."

"Every man of reflection must see, that the change now proposed, is a transfer of power from the many to the few." The present agitation may be traced to its source in "two very unprincipled parties," between whom stand the great mass of honest and substantial people:

One party is composed of little insurgents, men in debt, who want no law, and who want a share of the property of others; these are called levellers, Shaysites, &c. The other party is composed of a few, but more dangerous men, with their servile dependents; these avariciously grasp at all power and property; you may discover in all the actions of these men, an evident dislike to free and equal government, and they go systematically to work to change, essentially, the forms of government in this country; these are called aristocrats, m—ites, &c. Between these two parties is the weight of the community: the men of middling property, men not in debt on the one hand, and men, on the other, content with republican governments, and not aiming at immense fortunes, offices and power. In 1786, the little insurgents, the levellers, came forth, invaded the rights of others, and attempted to establish governments according to their wills. Their movements evidently gave encouragement to the other party, which, in 1787, has taken the political field, and with its fashionable dependents, and the tongue and the pen, is endeavouring to establish in a great haste, a politer kind of government. These two parties . . . are really insignificant, compared with the solid, free, and independent part of the community.

Calm voices such as Lee's were few in those strident days, and the Federalists fairly overwhelmed the silent majority with clamorous argument. Polite culture and professional learning joined forces to write down the agrarians. The Hartford Wits dedicated smart couplets to the cause; Francis Hopkinson made merry over their ways; Noah Webster confuted them with his economic interpretation of politics; lawyer-scholars like James Wilson and John Dickinson exposed their heresies; solid business men like Peletiah Webster contributed after the measure of their intelligence. In their ardor the Federalists went further. "What can be the views of those gentlemen in Boston," asked Lee pertinently, "who countenanced the printers in shutting up the press against a fair and free investigation?" From the strident debate emerged not only the Constitution, but political parties, no longer to be spoken of as factions, but eventually to be accepted as necessary agencies in republican government; and to understand their rival policies we must turn to examine the political philosophies of the outstanding leaders.

CHAPTER III

POLITICAL THINKERS

The English Group

OF this great age of American political thought, two important characteristics emerge: it was overwhelmingly English in its antecedents; and it was already differentiating its program from that of contemporary English liberalism. Nearly all the outstanding men—Jefferson, Adams, Washington, Wilson, Mason, Madison, Gouverneur Morris—were of the older liberal tradition, and with some notable exceptions, of the school of Pitt. Contemporary English liberals such as Priestley, Bentham, and Godwin numbered few adherents among the leaders of American thought. Economic conditions in America already were imposing conclusions that pointed in a direction other than that which English liberalism was traveling. The doctrine of the diminished state, which was making persistent headway among English liberals, could make no appeal to men who desired an augmented state; and liberalism as a policy was in ill repute at a time when men believed thay were suffering from too much liberalism. American political thought, therefore, followed an independent path, and in spite of its English origin came to conclusions that differentiated it broadly from the old-world theory.

I

ALEXANDER HAMILTON

The Leviathan State

Of the disciplined forces that put to rout the disorganized party of agrarianism, the intellectual leader was Alexander Hamilton, the brilliant Anglo-French West Indian, then just entered upon his thirties. A man of quite remarkable ability, a lucid thinker, a great lawyer, a skillful executive, a masterly organizer, a statesman of broad comprehension and inflexible purpose, he originated and directed the main policies of the Federalist group, and brought them to successful issue. For this work he was singularly well equipped, for in addition to great qualities of mind and persuasive ways he was free to work unhampered by the narrow localisms and sectional prejudices that hampered native Americans. He was rather English than American, with a certain detachment that refused to permit his large plans to be thwarted by minor, vexatious details, or the perversity of stupid men. He was like the elder Pitt in the magnificence of his imperial outlook.

Such a man would think in terms of the nation rather than of the state. He would agree with Paine that the continental belt must be more securely buckled. The jealousies and rivalries that obstructed the creation of a centralized Federal government found no sympathy with him. He was annoyed beyond all patience with the dissensions of local home rule. In his political philosophy there was no place for "the political monster of an *imperium in imperio*"; he would destroy all lesser sovereignties and reduce the several commonwealths to a parish status. For town-meeting democracies and agrarian legislatures he had frank contempt. The American villager and farmer he never knew and never understood; his America was the America of landed gentlemen and wealthy merchants and prosperous professional men, the classes that were most bitterly anti-agrarian. And it was in association with this group of conservative representatives of business and society that he took his place as directing head in the work of reorganizing the loose confederation into a strong and cohesive union. When that work was accomplished his influence was commanding, and for a dozen years he directed the major policies of the Federalist party. His strategic position as Secretary of the Treasury enabled him to stamp his principles so deeply upon the national economy that in all the intervening years since he quitted his post they have not been permanently altered. That we still follow the broad principles of Hamilton in our financial policy is a remarkable testimony to the perspicacity of his mind and his understanding of the economic forces that control modern society. And hence, because the Hamiltonian principles lie at the core of the problem which has proved so difficult of solution by modern liberalism, the life and work of Hamilton are of particular significance in our democratic development.

Hamilton was our first great master of modern finance, of that finespun web of credit which holds together our industrial life; and because his policies opened opportunities of profit to some and entailed loss upon others, they have been debated with an acrimony such as few programs have endured. About the figure of the brilliant Federalist the myth-makers have industriously woven their tales, distorting the man into either a demigod or a monster. The individual has been merged in the system which he created, and later interpretation has been shot through with partisan feeling; political and economic prejudice has proved too strong for disinterested estimate. Any rational judgment of Hamilton is dependent upon an interpretation of the historical background that determined his career, and in particular of the state of post-Revolutionary economics; and over such vexing questions partisans have wrangled interminably. Thus Sumner, in his life of Hamilton, asserts dogmatically that Federalism was no other than the forces of law and order at war with the turbulent, anarchistic forces unloosed by the Revolution, and that the putting down of the scheme of repudiation was the necessary preliminary to the establishment of a great nation. In the light of such an interpretation, Hamilton the far-seeing, courageous and honest master of finance, was the savior of nationality, the one supreme figure rising above an envious group of lesser men. But, as has been sufficiently pointed out in preceding chapters, the historical facts are susceptible of quite other interpretation; and as our knowledge of the economic struggle then going on becomes more adequate, the falsity of such an explanation becomes patent. If, on the other hand, we concede that the crux of the political problem in 1787 was economic—the struggle waging between farmer and business groups for control of government—then the position of Hamilton becomes clear; he was the spokesman of the business economy. He thought in terms of nationality and espoused the economics of capitalism, because he discovered in them potentialities congenial to his imperialistic mind.

The career of Hamilton followed logically from the determining facts of temperament and experience. He came to New York an alien, without position or influence, ambitious to make a name and stir in the world; and in the America of his day there could be little doubt what doors opened widest to preferment. He made friends easily, and with his aristocratic tastes he preferred the rich and distinguished to plebeians. Endowed with charming manners and brilliant parts, he fascinated all whom he met; before he was of age he was intimate with all the Whig leaders, civil and

military, on Washington's staff and elsewhere, lending his brains
to the solution of knotty problems, prodding stupider minds with
illuminating suggestions, proving himself the clearest thinker in
whatever group he found himself. It was by sheer force of intellect
that he gained distinction. Singularly precocious, he matured
early; before his twenty-fifth year he seems to have developed
every main principle of his political and economic philosophy, and
thereafter he never hesitated or swerved from his path. He was
tireless in propaganda, urging on the proposed Constitutional convention, discussing with Robert Morris his favorite project of a national bank, outlining various systems of funding, advocating tariffs
as an aid to domestic manufacture, and sketching the plan of a
political and economic system under which native commercialism
could go forward. His reputation as an acute and trustworthy
financial adviser was well established with influential men north
and south, when the new government was set up, and Washington
turned to him naturally for the Treasury post, to guide financial
policies during the difficult days immediately ahead. But so able
a man could not be restricted within a single portfolio, and during
the larger part of Washington's two administrations Hamilton's
was the directing mind and chief influence. He regarded himself
as Prime Minister and rode roughshod over his colleagues. Major
policies such as that of no entangling alliances must receive his
careful scrutiny and approval before they were announced; and
in consequence more credit belongs to Hamilton for the success
of those first administrations than is commonly recognized.

But when we turn from the administrator and statesman to the
creative thinker, there is another story to tell. The quickness of
his perceptions, the largeness of his plans and efficacy of his
methods—his clear brilliancy of understanding and execution—
are enormously impressive; but they cannot conceal certain intellectual shortcomings. There was a lack of subtlety in the swift
working of his mind, of shades and *nuances* in the background of
his thought, that implied a lack of depth and richness in his intellectual accumulation. Something hard, almost brutal lurks in his
thought—a note of intellectual arrogance, of cynical contempt.
He was utterly devoid of sentiment, and without a shred of idealism, unless a certain grandiose quality in his conceptions be accounted idealism. His absorbing interest in the rising system of
credit and finance, his cool unconcern for the social consequences

of his policies, reveal his weakness. In spite of his brilliancy Hamilton was circumscribed by the limitations of the practical man.

In consequence of such limitations Hamilton was not a political philosopher in the large meaning of the term. In knowledge of history he does not compare with John Adams; and as an open-minded student of politics he is immensely inferior to Jefferson. Outside the domain of the law, his knowledge does not always keep pace with his argument. He reasons adroitly from given premises, but he rarely pauses to examine the validity of those premises. The fundamentals of political theory he seems never to have questioned, and he lays down a major principle with the easy finality of a dogmatist. Compare his views on any important political principle with those of the greater thinkers of his time, and they are likely to prove factional if not reactionary. The two tests of eighteenth-century liberalism were the doctrine of individualism, and the doctrine of the minimized state; and Hamilton rejected both: the former in its larger social bearing, and the latter wholly. He was not even abreast of seventeenth-century liberalism, for that was strongly republican, and Hamilton detested republicanism only a little less than democracy. Harrington and Locke were no masters of his; much less were Bentham or Priestley or Godwin. He called the French revolutionary writers "fanatics in political science"; to what extent he read them does not appear. The thinkers to whom he owed most seem to have been Hume, from whom he may have derived his cynical psychology, and Hobbes whose absolute state was so congenial to his temperament. But political theory he subordinated to economic theory. He was much interested in economics. With the Physiocratic school and its agrarian and sociological bias he could have no sympathy, but with the rising English school that resulted from the development of the industrial revolution, he found himself in hearty accord. Capitalism with its credit system, its banks and debt-funding and money manipulation, was wholly congenial to his masterful temperament. He read Adam Smith with eagerness and *The Wealth of Nations* was a source book for many of his state papers. To create in America an English system of finance, and an English system of industrialism, seemed to him the surest means to the great end he had in view; a centralizing capitalism would be more than a match for a decentralizing agrarianism, and the power of the state would augment with the increase of liquid wealth.

But granted that he lacked the intellectual qualities of the philosopher, it does not follow that his significance diminishes. On the contrary his very independence of contemporary European theory enlarged his serviceableness to party. He was free to employ his intelligence on the practical difficulties of a new and unprecedented situation. English liberalism did not answer the needs of Federalism, if indeed it could answer the needs of the country at large. The time had come to decide whether the long movement of decentralization should go further, and confirm the future government as a loose confederacy of powerful states, or whether an attempt should be made to check that movement and establish a counter tendency towards centralized, organized control. If the former, it meant surrendering the country to a democratic *laissez faire*, and there was nothing in the history of political *laissez faire* as it had developed in America, that justified the principle to Hamilton. It had culminated in agrarianism with legislative majorities riding down all obstacles, denying the validity of any check upon its will, constitutional, legal or ethical. The property interests of the minority had been rendered insecure. There had been altogether too much *laissez faire*; what was needed was sharp control of legislative majorities; the will of the majority must be held within due metes and bounds. Even in the economic world the principle of *laissez faire* no longer satisfied the needs of the situation. Parliamentary enactments had aided British interests in their exploitation of America before the war; it was only common sense for an American government to assist American business. The new capitalism that was rising stood in need of governmental subsidies. Business was languishing; infant industries could not compete on even terms with the powerful British manufacturing interests, long established and with ample capital. From a realistic contemplation of these facts Hamilton deduced the guiding principle that has since been followed, namely, that governmental interference with economic laws is desirable when it aids business, but intolerable and unsound when it aims at business regulation or control, or when it assists agriculture or labor.

Throughout his career Hamilton was surprisingly consistent. His mind hardened early as it matured early, and he never saw cause to challenge the principles which he first espoused. He was what a friendly critic would call a political realist, and an enemy would pronounce a cynic. With the practical man's contempt for theorists and idealists, he took his stand on current fact. He looked to the past for guidance, trusting to the wisdom of experience; those principles which have worked satisfactorily heretofore may be expected to work satisfactorily in the future. Whoever aspires to become a sane political leader must remember that his business is not to construct Utopias, but to govern men; and if he would succeed in that difficult undertaking he must be wise in the knowledge of human nature. At the basis of Hamilton's political philosophy was the traditional Tory psychology. Failure to understand human nature, he believed, was the fatal weakness of all democratic theorists; they put into men's breeches altruistic beings fitted only for a Utopian existence. But when we consider men as they are, we discover that they are little other than beasts, who if unrestrained will turn every garden into a pigsty. Everywhere men are impelled by the primitive lust of aggression, and the political philosopher must adjust his system to this unhappy fact. He must not suffer the charge of cynicism to emasculate his philosophy; "the goodness of government consists in a vigorous execution," rather than in amiable intentions; it is the business of the practical man and not of the theorist.

It needs no very extensive reading in Hamilton to discover ample justification for such an interpretation of his political philosophy; the evidence lies scattered broadly through his pages. At the precocious age of seventeen he laid down the thesis, "A vast majority of mankind is entirely biassed by motives of self-interest"; and as political systems are determined by the raw material of the mass of the people, they must be conditioned by such egoism. A year later he discovered in Hume the central principle of his philosophy:

Political writers, says a celebrated author, have established it as a maxim, that, in contriving any system of government, and fixing the several checks and controls of the constitution, *every man* ought to be supposed a *knave*; and to have no other end, in all his actions, but *private interest*. By this interest we must govern him; and, by means of it, *make him co-operate to public good*, notwithstanding his insatiable avarice and ambition. Without this, we shall in vain boast of the advantages of *any constitution*.[1]

At the age of twenty-seven he reiterated the doctrine, "The safest reliance of every government, is on men's interests. This is a principle of human nature, on which all political speculation, to

[1] *Works*, Vol. II, p. 51.

be just, must be founded." [2] Obviously this was not a pose of youthful cynicism, but a sober judgment confirmed by observation and experience.

Accepting self-interest as the mainspring of human ambition, Hamilton accepted equally the principle of class domination. From his reading of history he discovered that the strong overcome the weak, and as they grasp power they coalesce into a master group. This master group will dominate, he believed, not only to further its interests, but to prevent the spread of anarchy which threatens every society split into factions and at the mercy of rival ambitions. In early days the master group was a military order, later it became a landed aristocracy, in modern times it is commercial; but always its power rests on property. "That power which holds the purse-strings absolutely, must rule," he stated unequivocally. The economic masters of society of necessity become the political masters. It is unthinkable that government should not reflect the wishes of property, that it should be permanently hostile to the greater economic interests; such hostility must destroy it, for no man or group of men will be ruled by those whom they can buy and sell. And in destroying itself it will give place to another government, more wisely responsive to the master group; for even a democratic people soon learns that any government is better than a condition of anarchy, and a commercial people understands that a government which serves the interests of men of property, serves the interests of all, for if capital will not invest how shall labor find employment? And if the economic masters do not organize society efficiently, how shall the common people escape ruin?

Such are the fundamental principles which lie at the base of Hamilton's philosophy. He was in accord with John Adams and James Madison and Noah Webster, in asserting the economic basis of government, with its corollary of the class struggle. He not only accepted the rule of property as inevitable, but as desirable. As an aristocrat he deliberately allied himself with the wealthy. That men divide into the rich and the poor, the wise and the foolish, he regarded as a commonplace too evident to require argument. The explanation is to be sought in human nature and human capacities. For the common people, about whom Jefferson concerned himself with what seemed to Hamilton sheer

2 *Ibid.*, p. 298.

demagoguery, he felt only contempt. Their virtues and capacities he had no faith in. "I am not much attached to the *majesty of the multitude*," he said during the debate over the Constitution, "and waive all pretensions (founded on such conduct) to their countenance." His notorious comment—which the American democrat has never forgiven him, "The people!—the people is a great beast!"—was characteristically frank. Hamilton was no demagogue and nothing was plainer to his logic than the proposition that if the people possessed the capacity to rule, their weight of numbers would give them easy mastery; whereas their yielding to the domination of the gifted few proves their incapacity. A wise statesman, therefore, will consider the people no further than to determine how government may be least disturbed by their factional discontent, and kept free to pursue a logical program. Under a republican form good government is difficult to maintain, but not impossible. The people are easily deceived and turned aside from their purpose; like children they are diverted by toys; but if they become unruly they must be punished. Too much is at stake in government for them to be permitted to muddle policies.

It is sufficiently clear that in tastes and convictions Hamilton was a high Tory. The past to which he appealed was a Tory past, the psychology which he accepted was a Tory psychology, the law and order which he desired was a Tory law and order. His philosophy was not liked by republican America, and he knew that it was not liked. Practical business men accepted both his premises and conclusions, but republicans under the spell of revolutionary idealism, and agrarians suffering in their pocketbooks, would oppose them vigorously. He was at pains, therefore, as a practical statesman, to dress his views in a garb more seemly to plebeian prejudices, and like earlier Tories he paraded an ethical justification for his Toryism. The current Federalist dogma of the divine right of justice—*vox justiciae vox dei*—was at hand to serve his purpose and he made free use of it. But no ethical gilding could quite conceal a certain ruthlessness of purpose; in practice justice became synonymous with expediency, and expediency was curiously like sheer Tory will to power.

In certain of his principles Hamilton was a follower of Hobbes. His philosophy conducted logically to the leviathan state, highly centralized, coercive, efficient. But he was no idealist to exalt the state as the divine repository of authority, an enduring entity apart from the individual citizen and above him. He regarded the state as a highly useful instrument, which in the name of law and order would serve the interests of the powerful, and restrain the turbulence of the disinherited. For in every government founded on coercion rather than good will, the perennial unrest of those who are coerced is a grave menace; in the end the exploited will turn fiercely upon the exploiters. In such governments, therefore, self-interest requires that social unrest shall be covered with opprobium and put down by the police power; and the sufficient test of a strong state lies in its ability to protect the privileges of the minority against the anarchy of the majority. In his eloquent declamation against anarchy Hamilton was a conspicuous disciple of the law and order school. From the grave difficulties of post-Revolutionary times with their agrarian programs, he created a partisan argument for a leviathan state, which fell upon willing ears; and in the Constitutional convention, which, more than any other man, he was instrumental in assembling, he was the outstanding advocate of the coercive state.

In his plan of government presented to the Convention, the principle of centralized power was carried further than most would go, and his supporting speeches expressed doctrines that startled certain of his hearers. He was frankly a monarchist, and he urged the monarchical principle with Hobbesian logic. "The principle chiefly intended to be established is this—that there must be a permanent *will*." "There ought to be a principle in government capable of resisting the popular current."

Gentlemen say we need to be rescued from the democracy. But what [are] the means proposed? A democratic assembly is to be checked by a democratic senate, and both these by a democratic chief magistrate. The end will not be answered, the means will not be equal to the object. It will, therefore, be feeble and inefficient.[3]

The only effective way of keeping democratic factionalism within bounds, Hamilton was convinced, lay in the erection of a powerful chief magistrate, who "ought to be hereditary, and to have so much power, that it will not be his interest to risk much to acquire more," and who would therefore stand "above corruption." Failing to secure the acceptance of the monarchical principle, he devoted himself to the business of providing all possible checks upon the power of the democracy. He "acknowledged himself

[3] Brief of speech submitting his plan of Constitution, in *Works*, Vol. II, p. 415.

not to think favorably of republican government; but he addressed
his remarks to those who did think favorably of it, in order to
prevail on them to tone their government as high as possible." [4]
His argument was characteristic:

All communities divide themselves into the few and the many. The
first are the rich and well born, the other the mass of the people. The
voice of the people has been said to be the voice of God; and, however
generally this maxim has been quoted and believed, it is not true to fact.
The people are turbulent and changing; they seldom judge or determine
right. Give, therefore, to the first class a distinct, permanent share in the
government. They will check the unsteadiness of the second; and as they
cannot receive any advantage by a change, they therefore will ever maintain good government. Can a democratic assembly, who annually revolve
in the mass of the people, be supposed steadily to pursue the public good?
Nothing but a permanent body can check the imprudence of democracy.
Their turbulent and uncontrollable disposition requires checks. [5]

The argument scarcely needs refuting today, although curiously
enough, it was rarely questioned by eighteenth-century gentlemen.
It was the stock in trade of the Federalists, nevertheless Hamilton
was too acute a thinker not to see its fallacy. It denied the fundamental premise of his political philosophy. If men are actuated
by self-interest, how does it come about that this sovereign motive
abdicates its rule among the rich and well born? Is there a magic
in property that regenerates human nature? Do the wealthy
betray no desire for greater power? Do the strong and powerful
care more for good government than for class interests? Hamilton
was fond of appealing to the teaching of experience; but he had read
history to little purpose if he believed such notions. How mercilessly he would have exposed the fallacy in the mouth of Jefferson!
It was a class appeal, and he knew that it was a class appeal, just
as he knew that success knows no ethics. He was confronted by a
situation in practical politics, and in playing ignobly upon selfish
fears he was seeking to force the convention towards the English
model. He had no confidence in the Constitution as finally adopted,
and spoke in contemptuous terms of its weakness; whereas for
the British constitution he had only praise, going so far, according
to Jefferson, as to defend the notorious corruption of parliament
on the ground of expediency: "purge it of its corruption"—
Jefferson reports him as saying—"and give to its popular branch
equality of representation, and it would become an *impracticable*

[4] *Elliot's Debates*, Vol. V, p. 244.   [5] *Ibid.*, Vol. I, p. 422.

government; as it stands at present, with all its supposed defects, it is the most perfect government which ever existed." [6] The argument savors of cynicism, but it is in keeping with his philosophy; the British constitution owed its excellence to the fact that in the name of the people it yielded control of the state to the landed aristocracy.

It was as a statesman that the brilliant qualities of Hamilton showed to fullest advantage. In developing his policies as Secretary of the Treasury he applied his favorite principle, that government and property must join in a close working alliance. The new government would remain weak and ineffective so long as it was hostile to capital; but let it show itself friendly to capital, and capital would make haste to uphold the hands of government. Confidence was necessary to both, and it was a plant of slow growth, sensitive to cold winds. The key to the problem lay in the public finance, and the key to a strong system of finance lay in a great national bank. This, Hamilton's dearest project, was inspired by the example of the Bank of England. No other institution would so surely link the great merchants to government, he pointed out, for by being made partners in the undertaking they would share both the responsibility and the profits. It was notorious that during the Revolution men of wealth had forced down the continental currency for speculative purposes; was it not as certain that they would support an issue in which they were interested? The private resources of wealthy citizens would thus become an asset of government, for the bank would link "the interest of the State in an intimate connection with those of the rich individuals belonging to it." "The men of property in America are enlightened about their own interest, and would easily be brought to see the advantage of a good plan." Hence would arise stability and vigor of government.

Moreover, the bank would be of immense service in the pressing business of the public debt. In regard to this difficult matter Hamilton was early convinced that only one solution was possible: all outstanding obligations, state and national, must be assumed by the Federal government at face value, and funded. Anything short of that would amount to repudiation of a lawful contract, entered into in good faith by the purchaser; and such repudiation would destroy in the minds of the wealthy the confidence in the

[6] *Works of Jefferson*, Ford edition, Vol. I, p. 165.

integrity of the new government that was vital to its success. It was true that speculators would reap great and unearned profits; but the speculators for the most part were the principal men of property whose support was so essential that any terms were justifiable, and nothing would bind them so closely to the government as the knowledge that it would deal generously with them. It was true also that thousands of small men would lose by such a transaction; but under any existing social economy the small man was at a disadvantage, and the present state of affairs was not such as to justify Utopian measures. To alienate the rich and powerful in order to conciliate the poor and inconsequential seemed to him sheer folly. The argument of expediency must prevail over abstract justice; the government must make terms with those in whose hands lay the success or failure of the venture.

His report on the public credit, of January 14, 1790, is one of the significant documents in the history of American finance. It is the first elaboration by an American statesman of the new system of capitalization and credit developed in eighteenth-century England, and it laid a broad foundation for later capitalistic development. To less daring financiers of the time the public debt was no more than a heavy obligation to be met; but to Hamilton it offered an opportunity for revivifying the whole financial life of the nation. Let the debts be consolidated and capitalized by a proper system of funding, and the augmented credit would multiply capital, lower the rate of interest, increase land values, and extend its benefits through all lines of industry and commerce. It was a bold plan and it encountered bitter opposition, which was not lessened by the heavy taxation that it called for. In his tax proposals Hamilton revealed his political philosophy so nakedly as almost to prove his undoing. His doctrine of the blessing of a national debt smacked rather too strongly of English Toryism for the American stomach.

A national debt, if it be not excessive, will be to us a national blessing. It will be a powerful cement to our Union. It will also create a necessity for keeping up taxation to a degree which, without being oppressive, will be a spur to industry. . . . It were otherwise to be feared our popular maxims would incline us to too great parsimony and indulgence. We labor less now than any civilized nation of Europe; and a habit of labor in the people, is as essential to the health and vigor of their minds and bodies, as it is conducive to the welfare of the State.[7]

[7] *Works*, Vol. I, p. 257.

A further struggle was encountered over the proposals of an internal revenue and a tariff. In his advocacy of the former Hamilton encountered the vigorous opposition of the backcountry. The total lack of adequate means of transportation rendered the problem of a grain market a chronic difficulty to the frontier farmers. The most convenient solution lay in distilling, and so whisky had become the chief commodity of the farmer that was transportable and brought a cash price. In placing a tax upon distilled liquors, therefore, Hamilton struck so directly at the economic interests of thousands of backwoodsmen, as to bring a rebellion upon the new administration. He knew what he was doing, but he calculated that it was safer to incur the enmity of farmers than of financiers; nevertheless the fierceness of the opposition surprised him, and aroused all the ruthlessness that lay in the background of his nature. He called for the strong arm of the military and when the rising was put down, he was angered at Washington's leniency in refusing to hang the convicted leaders. In his advocacy of a tariff he was on safer ground, for he was proposing a solution of the difficult situation confronting the manufacturers. Something must be done to revive industry so long stagnant. The old colonial machinery had been destroyed and new machinery must be provided. Industrial independence must follow political independence; and the easiest way lay in providing a tariff barrier behind which the infant industries of America might grow and become sufficient for domestic needs.

In his notable report on manufactures, submitted on December 5, 1791, Hamilton showed his characteristic intelligence in his grasp of the principles of the industrial revolution. Certainly no other man in America saw so clearly the significance of the change that was taking place in English industrialism, and what tremendous reservoirs of wealth the new order laid open to the country that tapped them. The productive possibilities that lay in the division of labor, factory organization, the substitution of the machine for the tool, appealed to his materialistic imagination, and he threw himself heart and soul into the cause of industrial development in America. He accepted frankly the principle of exploitation. He was convinced that the interests of the manufacturers were one with the national interests, and he proposed to put the paternal power of the government behind them. With the larger social effects—the consequences to the working classes, congestion of population, the certainty of a labor problem—he concerned himself no more than did contemporary English statesmen. He was contemptuous of Jefferson's concern over such things. He had no Physiocratic leanings towards agriculture; material greatness alone appealed to him; and he contemplated with satisfaction the increase in national wealth that would accrue from levying toll upon the weak and helpless.

Besides this advantage of occasional employment to classes having different occupations, there is another, of a nature allied to it, and of a similar tendency. This is the employment of persons who would otherwise be idle, and in many cases, a burthen on the community, either from bias of temper, habit, infirmity of body, or some other cause, indisposing or disqualifying them for the toils of the country. It is worthy of particular remark, that, in general, women and children are rendered more useful, and the latter more early useful, by manufacturing establishments, than they would otherwise be. Of the number of persons employed in the cotton manufactories of Great Britain, it is computed that four-sevenths, nearly, are women and children; of whom the greatest proportion are children, and many of them of a tender age.[8]

If the material power and splendor of the state be the great end of statesmanship—as Hamilton believed—no just complaint can be lodged against such a policy; but if the well-being of the individual citizen be the chief end—as Jefferson maintained—a very different judgment must be returned.

Although the fame of Hamilton has been most closely associated with the principle of constitutional centralization, his truer significance is to be found in his relation to the early developments of our modern capitalistic order. In his understanding of credit finance and the factory economy, he grasped the meaning of the economic revolution which was to transform America from an agrarian to an industrial country; and in urging the government to further such development, he blazed the path that America has since followed. "A very great man," Woodrow Wilson has called him, "but not a great American." In the larger historical meaning of the term, in its democratic implications, that judgment is true; but in the light of our industrial history, with its corporate development and governmental subsidies, it does not seem so true. As the creative organizer of a political state answering the needs of a capitalistic order—a state destined to grow stronger as imperialistic ambitions mount—he seems the most modern and the most

[8] *Works*, Vol. III, pp. 207-208.

American of our eighteenth-century leaders, one to whom our industrialism owes a very great debt, but from whom our democratic liberalism has received nothing.

II

JOHN ADAMS

Realist

Midway between Hamilton and Jefferson stands John Adams, the most painstaking student of government and the most widely read in political history, of his generation of Americans. The noble art of government was a lifelong passion with him—the sublimest subject, in his opinion, which a free citizen could study. Solid, pragmatic, unimaginative, he was an admirable representative of the later eighteenth century with its vigorous understanding, its distrust of idealisms, its contempt for social theory. He was the political counterpart of Dr. Johnson. To a generation sniveling over the sorrows of life and seeking panaceas in Rousseau sentimentalisms, the English Tory proffered the consolation of the realist. Things are bad enough, heaven knows; poverty, injustice, disease, death, are evils which no optimism can shut its eyes to. But what can be done? The malady of human nature is a disease beyond the reach of romantic plasters. No quack remedies will cure ills that lie too deep for laws or kings—they only aggravate the trouble. Be sensible therefore. Endure like men what cannot be cured. Stop sniveling and make the best of things as they are.

The analogy between these two vigorous exponents of common sense is too obvious to miss. For years the chief business of John Adams was to bring home to Americans the lesson in realism which Samuel Johnson was urging upon his countrymen. The mischief of romantic idealisms was spreading widely in America, disseminated by propagandists like Tom Paine and theorists like Jefferson; there was high need that the people be brought back to sober reality. This duty he took upon himself. He was an uncompromising realist who refused to be duped by fine dreams or humanitarian panaceas; he was much given to throwing cold water on the hope of social regeneration through political agencies. And the reward which he gained for his voluntary labors was a personal unpopularity beyond that of any other statesman of the time. He was charged with apostacy from his earlier democratic faith, and the charge had sufficient foundation, unfortunately, to make it credible if one wished to believe it.

During the revolutionary struggle he had been a member of the left wing; during the early struggles under the Constitution he was a member of the right wing. The young man had been a stalwart defender of human rights, the old man was a stalwart defender of property rights; and this shift of position was fatal to his reputation with the rising democratic party. The French Revolution marked the critical turning point in his intellectual development. As a politician he was well-nigh ruined by it; but as a political thinker he owed it much. Before that vast upheaval came to challenge his somewhat conventional mind, he was a hard-working lawyer-politician, with a liking for legalistic constitutional theory; but as the Revolution went forward, he was forced into uncompromising reaction. While ardent young Americans were becoming pro-French, he became pro-British; while they were accepting the new leveling principles, he searched history to prove how inevitable are social distinctions and economic classes; while they looked hopefully forward to a democratic future, he gathered his materials for an interpretation of political forces that revealed aristocracy as the dominant factor in every society. Both Adams and his critics were products of the French upheaval, but facing in different directions; naturally, the antagonism between them became sharp and bitter.

The severest critic cannot deny to John Adams excellent qualities of mind and heart. A sound lawyer, a capable statesman, a vigorous thinker and courageous debater, he fought his way from obscurity to high position and many honors, and in every responsibility he acquitted himself in a fashion altogether worthy of the notable Adams posterity. A stubborn intellectual independence and a vigorous assertiveness were his distinguishing characteristics. He revealed to the full the Adams trait of going its own way and coming to its own conclusions. He was never the victim of mob psychology, and he was never careful of occasion or circumstance in speaking out his convictions. America has had too few independent minds, and much of Adams's unpopularity was the result of his refusal to hunt with the pack. Unfortunately his admirable qualities were offset by a blundering tactlessness and a colossal vanity that brought many troubles upon his head. He

loved to be in the public eye and he studied the little arts of
self-advertising. In his youthful diary he set down these characteristic words: "Reputation ought to be a perpetual subject of
my thoughts, and aim of my behavior. How shall I spread an
opinion of myself as a lawyer of distinguished genius, learning,
and virtue?" Self-confident, domineering, and jealously suspicious—always on the lookout lest some honor due him should fall
to another—he struggled through a career strewn with animosities
and heartburnings that a nicer tact and a more generous nature
would have avoided. He was his own worst enemy. He did not
spare himself in public service, but he demanded strict payment
and was inclined to haggle over the terms; in consequence his
later days were embittered and his fame was less than he deserved.

Our present concern, however, is with the political scientist
and not with the politician; with the theories of government that
occupied so much of his thought, rather than with the policies of
the statesman. He wrote voluminously, heavily, with no grace
of style or savor of wit, and the long row of his collected writings
may well appall the reader who proposes to make his acquaintance.
Ponderous treatises are supplemented by lesser works and flanked
by innumerable letters; his industry was prodigious and no one
will wonder at his exclamation, "My hand is impatient of the pen
and longs to throw it down." His important work divides broadly
into two main divisions: his contribution to the colonial debate
with England, and his elaborate system of government formu-
lated during the years of French revolutionary debate. A brief
consideration will suffice for the first, but the second requires more
careful examination.

In his contributions to the colonial debate Adams concerned
himself mainly with questions of constitutional law. He placed
little reliance on the appeal to natural rights, and showed scant
respect for "popular talk and those democratical principles which
have done so much mischief in this country." [9] The American
cause, he believed, should be based on constitutional principles,
but those principles required restatement in the light of existing
fact. They must be rescued from the narrow interpretation of
little Englanders and adapted to meet the pressing needs of imperial
federation. The English people were not all residents of the British
Isles, and a constitutional practice suited to compact groups in a

[9] "Autobiography," in *Works*, Vol. II, p. 310.

common environment, was ill adapted to the needs of widely
sundered bodies of British subjects. Into this difficult and momentous business of imperial federation, Adams plunged earnestly
in an endeavor to chart the unexplored field. That the problem
was the gravest then confronting Englishmen is abundantly
evident today; that it received grossly inadequate consideration
on both sides of the Atlantic is equally clear. In this field John
Adams was a pioneer and his work possesses still some historical
interest. This fact, too frequently overlooked, has been emphasized by a recent student, who has summarized the final results
of Adams's thinking in the following theses: that the empire was
an association of equals, each with independent legislative powers;
that the British constitution was the fundamental law of the
empire, defining the relationship of the constituent parts; and
that it was the function of the judiciary to disallow a legislative
act of any of the several legislatures which did not comport with
the fundamental law, or which attempted to impose the will of
one of the partners in violation of the fundamental understanding
and its guarantee.[10]

Such, in compressed form, was Adams's elaboration and justification of the dogma of Otis, that an act against the constitution
was void. In its relation to current English constitutional practice
it was at once revolutionary and reactionary. It implied a double
attack upon parliamentary sovereignty, first in limiting its powers
by a super-parliamentary constitution, and then in subjecting its
acts to judicial review. The final result would be the transfer of
sovereignty from the legislature to the judiciary. The idea had
been toyed with by English lawyers, but never seriously considered;
it was alien to the whole theory and history of parliamentary
development. English landed gentlemen have never been minded
to grant the veto power to the judiciary, but have persistently
retained sovereignty in the legislature. Nevertheless in such
early speculation is found the germ of our later practice, as it
finally developed through the decisions of Chief Justice Marshall.

In the works of his later period, such as *A Defence of the Constitution of Government of the United States of America* and *Discourses on Davila*, Adams emerged from the narrow field of constitutional law and elaborated a theory of government based on

[10] R. G. Adams, *Political Ideas of the American Revolution*, Trinity College Press,
1922, pp. 92-93.

wide reading and long observation. It was by way of reply to
the French thinkers, and it contributed in large measure to the
partisan passions of the time. Unfortunate circumstances attended
the publication of the works. The *Defence of the Constitution*
appeared at the moment when newspaper accounts of the absurd
dress in which he appeared at the Court of St. James's were provoking republican jests; and the *Discourses on Davila* came out
in the *Gazette of the United States*, when the country was buzzing
about his childish fondness for titles and ceremonies. It was
impolitic for Adams to publish in the *Gazette*, a virulently Federalistic sheet and anathema to all liberals. His unpopular theories
could not fail to arouse republican antagonism when set over
against such seeming commentary as this:

*Take away thrones and crowns from among men and there will soon be an
end of all dominion and justice.* There must be some adventitious prop-
erties infused into the government to give it energy and spirit, or the
selfish, turbulent passions of men can never be controlled. This has
occasioned that artificial splendor and dignity that are to be found in the
courts of many nations. The people of the United States may probably
be induced to regard and obey the laws without requiring the experiment
of courts and titled monarchs. In proportion as we become populous and
wealthy must the tone of the government be strengthened.[11]

The unfortunate effect of *Davila* upon a highly wrought public
opinion Adams himself records: "the rage and fury of the Jacobini-
cal journals against these discourses, increased as they proceeded,
intimidated the printer, John Fenno, and convinced me, that to
proceed would do more hurt than good. I therefore broke off
abruptly."[12] But the mischief to his reputation had been done;
henceforth Adams was popularly regarded as anti-republican.
Debating the nature of aristocracy in the New York Constitutional
Convention, one of the speakers said, "I would refer the gentleman
for a definition of it to the Hon. John Adams, one of our natural
aristocrats." Madison went so far as to charge that he was secretly a monarchist. The charge was absurd, as any examination
of his political theory will convince. "It is a fixed principle with
me," he wrote to Samuel Adams in 1790, "that all good government
is and must be republican." But that he advocated a system of
government hostile to agrarianism, that he was bitterly antagonistic

[11] *Gazette of the United States*, March, 1790; quoted in Forman, "The Political
Activities of Philip Freneau," in *Johns Hopkins Studies in History and Political
Science*, XX, Nos. 9-10.
[12] *Works*, Vol. VI, p. 272, note.

to French Jacobinism and all its works, is apparent to the most casual reader. He was a realist of the seventeenth-century school of English republicanism, attacking what he regarded as the delirium of democracy, appealing to experience in answer to abstract theory.

Adams erected his political system upon what he called "self-evident truths." He went to the root of the matter and directed his inquiry into the validity of the humanitarian psychology which asserted that men are good by nature, and may be trusted to deal justly with their fellows. He appealed to the whole unhappy record of past misrule to disprove the thesis. Instead of discovering in the average man a kindly, rational being—as Jefferson professed to discover—Adams found quite the contrary; and he summoned a host of historians and philosophers to witness that Machiavelli was right in his contention that "those who have written on civil government lay it down as a first principle . . . that whoever would found a state, and make proper laws for the government of it, must presume that all men are bad by nature; that they will not fail to show that natural depravity of heart whenever they have a fair opportunity."[13] In further substantiation of this fact he examined the history of governments past and present, and he found everywhere testimony to the truth that the mass of men are naturally indolent, selfish, given to luxury, shortsighted, jealous, tending to faction and all mischievous intrigue. Never does he find them given to virtue, choosing wisdom, seeking justice. They cannot endure that others should be superior in virtue, or rank, or power; but driven by ambition they strive to pull down their superiors in order themselves to rise. The men in any society who possess sufficient virtue to set justice above self-interest, are few and count for little in the scale against the selfish many.[14]

This Calvinistic doctrine that "human nature is not fit to be trusted," and that "men are never good but through necessity," being accepted—and John Adams was as clearly satisfied of its truth as "of any demonstration of Euclid"—he proceeded to translate it into political terms, and examine the bearing of it upon systems of government. At once a second fallacy of the humanitarian school emerged—men are impelled not by ideals

---

[13] *Works*, Vol. IV, p. 408.
[14] See "Defence of the Constitution, etc.," in *Works*, Vol. VI, pp. 9, 57, 97.

but by needs, not by reason, as Godwin argued, but by the desire for goods. In a social state the natural selfishness of human nature impels to economic aggression. Underneath the turbulent unrest which threatens every government is economic ambition. This is the rock on which all schemes of social justice founder—a rock which every sound political thinker will chart and recognize as a danger reef. Economics and biology provide the major social drives. "That the first want of every man is his dinner and the second want his girl were truths well known . . . long before the great philosopher Malthus arose to think he enlightened the world by his discovery."[15] The supposed liberty of a democratic state proves in practice to be no other than anarchy, running swiftly into license and ending in tyranny. All human societies are rooted in exploitation, the bitter fruit of which is domestic warfare.

The universal social state is one of ruthless class struggle, wherein the strong conquer the weak—this is the third deduction from the premises which Adams laid down. It cannot be otherwise, he argued, from the natural inequality of men. The rude mass being shiftless, ignorant, spendthrift, they are at the mercy of the strong, ambitious, and capable, who exploit them freely. Hence in every society emerges the division between patricians and plebeians, developing into caste as the social order grows complex. The self-interest of the patricians teaches them the need of class solidarity, and with intelligent solidarity the few easily seize control of the state and use it to their ends. Hence arises an aristocracy or oligarchy, which maintains its power through control of the economic resources of society. Control of property means control of men; for sovereignty inheres in economics. In presence of this historical fact it is foolish to declaim about natural rights; there are no rights except such as are won either by property or the sword.

That there should long exist a society without a property aristocracy Adams regarded as inconceivable. The French democrats with their talk of equality and fraternity were mischievous visionaries. "Every democracy . . . has an aristocracy in it as distinct as that of Rome, France, England." In older societies the aristocracy maintained supremacy through possession of the land. In America the vast extent of territory and the wide diffusion of land-

[15] Letter to John Taylor, in *Works*, Vol. VI, p. 516.

holding presented the most favorable opportunity in history for democratic development if such were possible; nevertheless the evidences of an aristocracy developing here were too patent to miss. The abundance of economic resources, Adams pointed out, was an invitation to gigantic exploitation, the logical outcome of which must be the emergence of a master group, richer and more powerful than the world has ever known. The power of economic appeal was nullified in America by no special providence.

Paper wealth has been a source of aristocracy in this country, as well as landed wealth, with a vengeance. Witness the immense fortunes made *per saltum* by aristocratical speculations, both in land and paper. . . . But, sir, land and paper are not the only source of aristocracy. There are master shipwrights, housewrights, masons, &c. &c., who have each of them from twenty to a hundred families in their employment, and can carry a posse to the polls when they will. These are not only aristocrats, but a species of feudal barons. . . .

Should a planter in Virginia sell his *clarissimum et illustrissimum et celeberricum locum* with his thousand negroes, to a merchant, would not the merchant gain the aristocratical influence which the planter lost by his transfer? Run down, sir, through all the ranks of society . . . from the first planter and the first merchant to the hog driver, the whiskey dram-seller, or the Scottish peddler, and consider, whether the alienation of lands, wharves, stores, pike stock, or even lottery tickets, does not transfer the aristocracy as well as the property.[16]

Believe—as John Adams believed regarding the funding opera-tions—that "paper wealth is the madness of the many for the profit of the few,"[17] it is nevertheless a modern illustration of the old truth that the few do profit from the madness of the many, and by reason of such profit set themselves up as masters. If then the historian cannot escape the conclusion that political systems and social classes rest upon economic foundations, this fundamental fact must preside over the speculations of the political philosopher. Democracy is out of the question, even if it were desirable. The great and sole object of political science must be the preservation of liberty—the right of every individual to life, freedom, property, in an aristocratic society—and the frustration of the universal drive of self-interest which leads on the one hand to tyranny, and on the other to anarchy. Between these two poles of tyranny and anarchy, of oligarchy and democracy, every society oscillates; to prevent such oscillation and discover some mean between the extremes must be the business of the political philosopher. The

[16] *Ibid.*, pp. 508–509.　　　　[17] *Ibid.*, p. 508.

pregnant fallacy of the French school, Adams insisted, lay in its doctrines of equality and fraternity. The meanest underling does not desire equality; men kiss the feet above them and trample on the fingers beneath. That the people love a lord is a sign of their abundant folly. Should the democrats abolish the principle of hereditary rank by law, it would still remain in fact; for the property basis on which it rests is transmitted legally from father to son, and each successive generation gains an adventitious advantage from its substantial heritage as well as from the historical splendor of the family name. On this rock every attempt at a democracy has foundered.

If these words are true, no well ordered commonwealth ever existed; for we read of none without a nobility, no, not one, that I can recollect, without a hereditary nobility; . . . It would be an improvement in the affairs of society, probably, if the hereditary legal descent could be avoided; and this experiment the Americans have tried. But in this case a nobility must and will exist, though without the name, as really as in countries where it is hereditary.[18]

The mortal weakness of democracy, Adams agreed with Madison and the Federalists generally, lay in faction, a disease which in the nature of the case he regarded as incurable. The use of party power other than justly was factional, and because the mass of men do not set justice above present interest, the unbridled rule of the majority drives straight towards mass tyranny. Despoiled by the superior ability of the aristocracy, the exploited plebeians fight back blindly; and where the constitution of government permits them to band together in a political party, they override the rights of the minority as ruthlessly as the latter before had denied the rights of the majority. Aristocratic exploitation leads to democratic leveling; and the resultant anarchy is but prelude to the rise of another aristocracy to repeat the unhappy process.

The passions and desires of the majority of the representatives being in their nature insatiable and unlimited by any thing within their own breasts, and having nothing to control them without, will crave more and more indulgence, and, as they have the power, they will have the gratification.[19]

If you give more than a share in the sovereignty to the democrats, that is, if you give them the command or preponderance in the sovereignty,

18 "Defence of the Constitution, etc.," in *Works*, Vol. VI, pp. 124-125.
19 *Ibid.*, p. 64.

that is, the legislature, they will vote all property out of the hands of you aristocrats, and if they let you escape with your lives, it will be more humanity, consideration, and generosity than any triumphant democracy ever displayed since the creation. And what will follow? The aristocracy among the democrats will take your places, and treat their fellows as severely and sternly as you have treated them.[20]

The end of every democratic experiment, Adams pointed out, has been the man on horseback. So inevitably does democracy culminate in despotism, that "in reality, the word democracy signifies nothing more nor less than a nation of people without any government at all, and before any constitution is instituted." [21] "Democracy never has been and never can be so desirable as aristocracy or monarchy, but while it lasts, is more bloody than either. Remember, democracy never lasts long. It soon wastes, exhausts, and murders itself. There never was a democracy that did not commit suicide." "The proposition that the people are the best keepers cf their own liberties is not true. They are the worst conceivable, they are no keepers at all; they can neither judge, act, think, or will, as a political body. Individuals have conquered themselves; nations and large bodies never." [22]

Having thus examined the major doctrines of the French democratic school, namely, that men are good by nature, that the social end is liberty, equality, fraternity, and that social well-being will result from an appeal to reason, Adams had cleared the problem of what he regarded as misconceptions, and was ready to lay out a system of government which should demonstrate his skill in political architecture. The determining factor in laying down the main lines was sufficiently clear. Since property lies at the root of the problem of government, the business of devising a just and stable system of government resolves itself into the question, What shall be done about property? As an orthodox Whig Adams found part of his answer ready to hand. With Locke he believed that property rights are sacred, and that it is a chief business of government to protect private property against unjust expropriation. The security of property may be taken as the measure of the stability of government. "The moment the idea is admitted into society, that property is not as sacred as the laws of God, and that there is not a force of law and public justice to protect it,

[20] "Letter to John Taylor," in *Works*, Vol. VI, p. 516.
[21] *Works*, Vol. VI, p. 211.
[22] See "Defence of the Constitution, etc.," and in particular Vol. IV of *Works*

anarchy and tyranny commence."[23] "The very name of a republic implies, that the property of the people should be represented in the legislature, and decide the rule of justice," he argued,
quoting Cicero.[24] Moreover, the futility of any other arrangement
was axiomatic in his philosophy. If property is not granted
representation, it will usurp it; if attacked, it will know how to
defend itself; and the end will be the setting up of an oligarchy on
the ruins of the republic. But if Adams agreed with Hamilton
that the state should deal tenderly with the rights and interests of
property, he refused to go with the latter in his sole concern for
the wealthy. Greater property interests must be held in due
balance with the smaller, for if unchecked the strong will drive
on to ruthless exploitation of the weak, and society will be endangered from the top as in a democracy it is endangered from
the bottom. It was this desire for a mean between oligarchy or
monarchy on the one hand, and democracy on the other, that determined his choice of a republican form of government.

The difficult problem of property-power in the state, Adams
was convinced, could be solved justly and permanently only by
a judicious system of balanced interests. Subjected, as every
government must be, to a persistent stress of rival interests, it
must be constructed with calculated nicety, or the structure would
fall of its own weight; and the sole principle, he believed, is that
of the Gothic arch—the principle of thrust and counter-thrust.
Provide in such manner that the selfishness of one group in society
shall be neutralized by the counter selfishness of other groups,
let the buttress support the arch at its weakest point, and upon
such an equilibrium of counterforces great vaults and noble towers
may be erected. It is the apotheosis of the system of checks and
balances.

It is agreed that "the end of all government is the good and ease of the
people, in a secure enjoyment of their rights, without oppression"; but it
must be remembered, that the rich are *people* as well as the poor; that they
have rights as well as others; that they have as clear and as sacred a right
to their large property as others have to theirs which is smaller; that
oppression to them is as possible and as wicked as to others. The rich,
therefore, ought to have an effectual barrier in the constitution against
being robbed, plundered, and murdered, as well as the poor; and this can
never be without an independent senate. The poor should have a bulwark

---

[23] "Defence of the Constitution, etc.," in *Works*, Vol. VI, p. 9.
[24] *Works*, Vol. IV, p. 295.

against the same dangers and oppressions; and this can never be without a house of representatives of the people. But neither the rich nor the poor can be defended by their respective guardians in the constitution, without an executive power, vested with a negative, equal to either, to hold the balance even between them, and decide when they cannot agree.[25]

Such in brief was the master principle of that system of mixed government which John Adams advocated so persistently in the teeth of the popular demand for a simpler, more responsive form. It based itself frankly upon the dogma of the class struggle; it provided each class—as he recognized them in his simple social analysis—with a legislative arm with which to defend itself; and it set as arbiter between them an executive, carefully selected, who was supposed to represent that abstract *tertium quid*, the public. The keynote is struck in a line from Pope set on the title-page of the *Defence*—"All Nature's difference keeps all Nature's peace." That Adams greatly admired his handiwork is beyond doubt; that he was intellectually honest with himself is very likely true; but that there is a note of disingenuousness, a failure to take into account his pronounced bias towards property interest, is certain. There was ample ground for the popular dislike of his theory. This is not the place to enter upon an examination of the system of checks and balances, nor to insist that any such system becomes in practice an impossibility. It is more to the point to remark upon certain fallacies in his theory which Adams himself must have seen if his mind had been quite free from bias.

Adams's intelligent analysis of social forces should have saved him from the major fallacy of the doctrine of checks and balances. In imposing the doctrine of a separation of powers upon the doctrine of property power, he effectively denied the validity of the latter. Assuming for the sake of the argument that the Senate will represent property, what reason justified the assumption that the House would represent the small men, or that the President would speak for the whole? If property is sovereign, as Adams maintained—"Harrington has shown that power always follows property. This I believe to be as infallible a maxim in politics, as that action and reaction are equal, is in mechanics" [26]—will it not rule the House equally with the Senate? above all, will it not control so important an officer as the President? The theory

[25] "A Defence of the Constitution, etc.," in *Works*, Vol. VI, p. 65.
[26] *Works*, Vol. IX, p. 376.

that the President represents an abstract public is a disingenuous political fiction; in the light of Adams's theory of economic determinism it is a gross absurdity. Moreover, Adams invalidated his entire system by refusing to provide the necessary machinery by which the House could represent the small man. In denying manhood suffrage, he eliminated the proletarian and the renter from the political equation, and left them without political power; in his definition the small man was the freeholder, the representative of the middle class. The House, therefore, equally with the Senate, was the mouthpiece of property interests; the former more likely to be representative of land, the latter of capital.

Where did Adams get the major ideas of his political philosophy?[27] An omnivorous reader, he gathered from many sources, and his memory was a well-stocked storehouse of fact and theory. As a young man he was disciple of Locke and the natural-rights school, but as he grew older he abandoned the natural-rights theory. His interpretation of human nature he took over from Machiavelli, Hobbes and Hume, discovering in their psychology of self-interest and emulation—often mean but many times admirable—a conception in harmony with the Calvinism of his early training. He owed much to Bolingbroke, whom he read five times, but to James Harrington, the Commonwealth intellectual, he turned with a zest of discovery so great that he may not unjustly be called one of Harrington's disciples. From the *Oceana* he drew so abundantly that the most casual student of political theory must remark his indebtedness. Many of the major doctrines of Adams, which by dint of iteration have become associated with his name, were taken straight out of Harrington: such as the doctrine of a natural aristocracy; the economic basis of sovereignty, discovered in the close relation of property to power; the necessity of effecting a balance between rival interests, with the ideal state rendered static by a nice balance of governmental machinery; the conception of government by laws and not by men; and finally, the historical method of approach, the cautious appeal to past experience. Since Harrington's time many of these ideas had been restated: the defense of property rights by Locke; the principle of the separation of powers and the historical method by Montesquieu; the psychology of emulation by Hume and Robert Wallace, the latter

---

[27] For a detailed examination of the sources of his philosophy, see the excellent discussion in C. M. Walsh, *The Political Science of John Adams*, Chapters XV, XVI.

of whom is another Adams in his thesis, "Lust of power sets man against his neighbor to the profit of the rich." But in spite of these later reinterpretations and his own additions, John Adams remained essentially a seventeenth-century republican, preferring with Milton the rule of the aristocracy to that of plebeians, and hating all Jacobin radicalisms as the spawn of a dangerous romanticism that disregarded the plain teachings of history and the admonitions of common sense.

Though Adams was fiercely assailed as an advocate of class government, he was far less hostile to agrarianism than was Hamilton. He was no believer in unchecked government by wealth. His honest realism taught him the sophistry of Hamilton's assumption that gentlemen of property are equally gentlemen of principle, and that wealth voluntarily abdicates selfish interest. He feared the aggressions of the rich as much as the turbulence of the poor. The bulk of his property was in land, and his sympathies were enlisted on the side of a law-abiding agrarianism, rather than on the side of a speculative capitalism.[28] He would put down vigorously all such leveling as was implied in Shays's program, and the repudiations of Rhode Island; but he would not permit the powerful to exploit the poor through the instrumentality of government. This may explain in part his hostility to Hamilton and his partial sympathy with Jefferson. He stood between the two rival economies, arguing for a system of government that should be neither agrarian nor capitalistic, but should maintain a static mean; and in consequence he pleased nobody. His four years in the presidency disrupted the Federalist party, and prepared the way for the triumph of Jefferson. Though tactless and blundering in dealing with trimming politicians, he was an honest and courageous man, and his many sterling qualities merit a larger recognition than has been accorded them by a grudging posterity. In spite of his dogmatisms and inconsistencies he remains the most notable political thinker—with the possible exception of John C. Calhoun—among American statesmen.

[28] See Beard, *The Economic Origins of Jeffersonian Democracy*, p. 317.

PART TWO: POLITICAL DEMOCRACY
GETS UNDER WAY
1787–1800

CHAPTER I

THE IMPACT OF THE FRENCH REVOLUTION

THE dramatic impact of the French Revolution upon a situation which for months had been overwrought entailed disturbing consequences. Within a week after the setting up of the new government there began that long series of events in France which carried far and gave birth to extraordinary hopes and fears; and throughout the remaining years of the century the French movement exercised a determining influence upon American parties and issues. In the words of Colonel Higginson, it "drew a red-hot ploughshare through the history of America as well as through that of France. It not merely divided parties, but molded them; gave them their demarcations, their watchwords and their bitterness. The home issues were for a time subordinate, collateral; the real party lines were established on the other side of the Atlantic." [1] The stirring of political passions afresh resulted in greatly clarifying political philosophies, and in rendering more exact, political alignments that before had been vague and inchoate.

The creative influence of the French Revolution upon the western world resulted from the enormous impetus which it gave to the movement to democratize American life and institutions. In no other country to which the sparks of revolution drifted was there such quantity of combustible material ready for the torch; and in setting afire this native material the French upheaval put a stop to the aristocratic reaction which had carried everything before it during the previous decade. It spread widely the spirit of leveling, and destroyed the last hope of the "monarchy men." But it did more—it gave a wide and popular currency to

[1] Quoted in Hazen, "Contemporary American Opinion of the French Revolution," in *Johns Hopkins University Studies in History and Political Science*, Extra Vol. XVI. The material in this excellent study has been used freely in the present chapter.

the ideal of democracy. Before the French Revolution the American mind had been curiously sensitive over the term democrat; even Samuel Adams had been driven by expediency to reject the word, and, amongst the radicals, few had the boldness to avow themselves democrats. By common consent the term had been covered with opprobrium; democracy was no other than a *bellua multorum capitum*, the hydra-headed monster of earlier Tories, licentious, irreligious, the very spawn of anarchy. But now the old conceptions were rapidly swept away, and democracy was accepted by liberals as the ultimate form of political organization, to which the American experiment was to be dedicated.

In thus imparting social idealism to political speculation, the Revolution not only elevated the democratic ideal, but it provided a body of philosophy, the lack of which had so seriously handicapped the democrats during the great debate. And this new philosophy gained extraordinarily wide currency in America under the stimulus of revolutionary enthusiasm. It made direct appeal to the vast majority who still remained among the political disinherited; it aroused them to political consciousness and intensified the class alignment that followed. The country divided sharply between left and right, and political discussion became more intense as the French movement developed. The English declaration of war upon France produced a crisis in America, and sharpened the party cleavage. The Federalists went with Great Britain and turned fiercely upon the democratic movement, assailing it with increasing venom. The democrats, on the other hand, became French partisans, and denounced all aristocrats with true republican fervor, becoming more radical as French Jacobinism developed. Never before had political passion risen to such heights in America, not even during the early days of the American Revolution; and never before had political ideas taken such hold upon the common people. Out of this increasing ferment emerged certain consequences of vast significance to the democratic movement: not only was an effective barrier erected against the further spread of aristocratic Federalism, but certain of its most characteristic doctrines disintegrated and disappeared. The current dogma of faction gave way to a more democratic interpretation of the majority will; the doctrine of the ethical absolute—the *vox justiciae, vox dei*—quietly yielded to the more practical conception of expediency; and the lately resurrected ideal of an augmented state received a temporary check, the majority preferring to intrust power to local bodies rather than to a central authority.

At the beginning the sympathy of America as a whole went heartily with the revolutionary movement in France. The adherence of Lafayette justified the cause to the most conservative. But with the advent of the Girondists to power a division in American sentiment appeared: Hamilton, John Adams, and other extreme Federalists drew back in disapproval; and with the rise of the Jacobins, party cleavage became sharp and bitter. All over America the liberals organized democratic clubs, instituted committees of correspondence, and actively forwarded the new leveling principles. The attack on ceremonial and titles of address in Congress, of which Maclay has left record in his *Journal*, was only a skirmish in the general war levied upon social distinctions.[2] It was to these democratic societies that Citizen Genêt made appeal; they rallied about him, toasted the French principles, and assured him of the warm support of the American people. The recall of Genêt was a blow to the American Jacobins, and they retaliated by direct appeals to the people to repudiate the act of the administration. Stung by their criticism of his policy of neutrality, Washington denounced them as "certain self-created societies" that offensively "assumed the tone of condemnation" of governmental policies; and went so far as to imply that such criticism was seditious. It was ill-advised for it was like a torch to dry leaves. The Federalists fell upon the democrats with gusto. They denounced the infidel French mobocracy and its American offspring. They declaimed against "secret organizations," imputing to them every evil known to Satan: the democratic clubs were called "demoniacal clubs," "nurseries of sedition," "hotbeds of atheism," "spawn of faction"; and common decency required that they be put down with a strong hand. In short the most eminent Federalists joined heartily in the silly work of turning the country into a bedlam.

A characteristic *odium theologicum* quickly gathered about the movement and extended to the whole democratic philosophy. Well-meaning but ignorant gentlemen saw in Jacobinism only atheism and immorality. John Adams professed not to know "what to make of a republic of thirty million atheists," and he attributed the unhappy result to the "encyclopedists and econo-

[2] For an amusing account see Hazen, *ibid.*, pp. 209-219.

mists, Diderot and D'Alembert, Voltaire and Rousseau," with their mad doctrines of the "equality of persons and property." But the more violently such men protested, the more insidiously "the infidel and irreligious spirit" spread through the land. It found its way into such strongholds of orthodoxy as Harvard College, to the scandal of the respectable; and as a counterblast to Paine's *Age of Reason*, a copy of Watson's *Apology for the Bible* was presented to every Harvard undergraduate, with what results in godliness no record remains to tell. On both sides there was more heat than light, more passion than reason, and in consequence such a tremendous hue and cry was worked up that the noise carried to the farthest outposts of settlement, and brought home to the most sluggish some realization of the significance of the world-wide movement of democracy then under way, and left few quite indifferent to the import of the tricolor cockade. It was the first great popularization of democratic ideals in America and when the hubbub finally subsided it was apparent to all that democracy had made a definite and stable advance, from which it must move forward to still other vantage points. Only a few unregenerate aristocrats shared with Gouverneur Morris his reasons for joy at the final overthrow of Napoleon: "'Tis done, the long agony is over. The Bourbons are restored. France reposes in the arms of her legitimate prince"; or who agreed with Robert Treat Paine in calling the democratic movement of the nineties "the melancholy record of our national degradation." The Federalists still hated Jefferson and his "revolution of 1800," but a triumphant agrarianism had broken them and their power for the time being.

So tremendous a movement naturally developed its literature of propaganda in America as elsewhere. In the main this was little more than an echo of the old-world debate, and, in particular, of the controversy between Burke and Paine which deeply stirred the entire English reading-public. Among the innumerable pamphlets, four works may be regarded as representative: Paine's *Rights of Man*, Barlow's *Advice to the Privileged Orders*, John Adams's *Discourses on Davila*, and John Quincy Adams's *Publicola;* and of these we need here concern ourselves only with *The Rights of Man* and *Publicola*, which clearly reveal the divergent political philosophies of the two parties. The chief point of difference is the familiar issue, so acrimoniously dealt with during the debate

over the Constitution, the question of minority rights as opposed
to the majority will.   Paine had made wide appeal with his argument of social expediency against Burke's doctrine of pre-contract.
His celebrated dictum, "That which a whole nation chuses to do,
it has a right to do," if granted, must destroy the reasoning not
of Burke alone, but of American Federalism, for it rested on an
interpretation of sovereignty that was vital to the question.   To
Paine sovereignty was necessarily inherent in the present majority
will; to assume that it rested elsewhere, whether in crown or
judiciary or past generations, was to deny the fundamental tenet
of democracy.   There can be no trusteeship superior to the sovereign people, he asserted—no constitution beyond their rightful
power to alter or destroy.

It was against this doctrine of the present sovereignty of the
majority will that eleven articles signed *Publicola*, and appearing
in the *Columbian Centinel* of Boston from June 8 to July 27, 1791,
were directed.   They were from the pen of John Quincy Adams,
then in his early twenties and lately admitted to practice at the
Boston bar.   Written with considerable skill, they were at once
accepted as the most effective reply offered to Paine's argument;
but they have lost their appeal today and seem rather slight and
tenuous essays in Federalistic legalism.   The outstanding note is
concern for minority rights.   To permit the majority will to function unchecked seemed to this young lawyer to open wide the
door to tyranny.   It is justified by no political philosophy, he
argued, certainly not by the doctrine of natural rights.   If all men
are endowed by their creator with certain inalienable rights, it
follows that such rights must suffer abridgment from no power,
whether monarchical or democratic.   Power may override those
rights temporarily, but power and rights are not synonymous terms.
The gist of Adams's argument is thus set down:

This principle, that a whole nation has a right to do whatever it pleases,
cannot in any sense whatever be admitted as true.   The eternal and
immutable laws of justice and of morality are paramount to all human
legislation.   The violation of those laws is certainly within the power, but
it is not among the rights of nations.   The power of a nation is the collected
power of all the individuals which compose it. . . . If, therefore, a
majority . . . are bound by no law human or divine, and have no other
rule but their sovereign will and pleasure to direct them, what possible
security can any citizen of the nation have for the protection of his unalienable rights?   The principles of liberty must still be the sport of ar-

bitrary power, and the hideous form of despotism must lay aside the diadem and the scepter, only to assume the party-colored garments of democracy.[3]

Concerning the repository of the "eternal and immutable laws of justice and morality," which are paramount to all human legislation, Adams is as vague as other Federalists; but he seems to imply that it is the body of English Common law, and that abstract justice is somehow interwoven with the British constitution. In other words, his argument conducts straight to the familiar doctrine of *vox justiciae, vox dei*, with its implied sovereignty of the judiciary. In this, with other thinkers of the abstract justice school, Adams was upholding the principle of judicial trusteeship in opposition to the democratic principle of the majority will. The distinction reveals exactly the different positions of the two parties: the democrats accepted the principle of utilitarian expediency; the Federalists espoused the doctrine of the ethical absolute as the final law. To a generation still strict in religious professions, the doctrine of the ethical absolute made strong appeal; but the democrats attacked it so sharply that it survived only by skillfully metamorphosing itself into judicial sanctions.

The final outcome of the long acrimonious discussion of fundamental principles was a curious reversal of positions: whereas the democrats were charged with being political and social romantics, appealing to a false psychology and following abstract theory, they were in fact idealists who pointed to the sordid facts of economic and social reality, in justification of new programs. No change could make things worse. The Federalists, on the other hand, finding the appeal to realism making against them, and fearful of the majority that was discontented with the *status quo*, took their stand upon abstract principle that was cousin german to a rigid legalism. It was a significant impasse to which they were brought by the exigencies of the political struggle.

[3] *The Writings of John Quincy Adams*, edited by W. C. Ford, Vol. I, pp. 70–71.

CHAPTER II

POLITICAL THINKERS

The French Group

THE change which came over political thought in America in consequence of the rise of French Jacobin philosophy is not inadequately revealed in the writings of two men, quite dissimilar in antecedents and training, but alike in fundamental purpose— Thomas Paine and Thomas Jefferson. Both were speculative thinkers, profoundly in sympathy with French revolutionary ideals: but the former was detached from local patriotisms and national interests, a delegate at large in the cause of human rights, concerned with spreading the gospel of freedom in all lands; the latter remained wholly American, and while a keenly interested spectator of the French upheaval, he was primarily concerned to discover principles that would apply to native conditions and further the cause of American democracy. Paine therefore became the popular disseminator of the philosophy of republicanism, and Jefferson, the practical statesman embodying it in political programs. Warm friends, their influence became closely interwoven during the years when agrarian democracy was gathering its strength to strike down the rule of Federalism.

I

TOM PAINE

Republican Pamphleteer

No more striking figure emerges from the times than the figure of the Thetford Quaker. English in birth and rearing, in middle life Paine came to embody the republican spirit of the American revolution; and that spirit he made it his after business to carry overseas and spread among the discontented of all lands. He was the first modern internationalist, at home wherever rights were to be won or wrongs corrected. "My country is the world," he asserted proudly, "to do good, my religion." Throughout his later life he was a fearless skirmisher on the outposts of democracy

—another "Free born John" Lilburne, seeking to complete the great work begun and thwarted in an earlier century; and his career remains a stirring record of a time when revolution threatened to sweep away the power and privilege of all kings and aristocracies. Naturally his zeal cost him dear in reputation. The passions of all who feared the loss of sinecures gathered about his head, and he became the victim of an *odium theologicum et politicum*, without parallel in our history. The Tories hunted him in packs, and their execration and vituperation outran all decency. In London clubs it became the fashion for gentlemen to wear TP nails in their boot-heels to witness how they trampled on his base principles. He was proscribed and banished, and his books burnt by the hangman. He was regarded as worse than a common felon and outlaw, because more dangerous. In America gentlemen echoed the common detestation—to be a Paine-hater was a badge of respectability. "The filthy Tom Paine," John Adams called him, and the phrase stuck like a burr to his reputation. But "reason, like time," as Paine remarked "will make its own way," and the years are bringing a larger measure of justice to him.

Like Hamilton, Paine was an alien, but endowed with a heritage quite unlike that of the brilliant boy from the West Indies. When he landed in Philadelphia in the second week in December, 1774,[1] he was in his thirty-seventh year, and had seemingly made shipwreck of his life. He had been schooled in misfortune and was marked as a social inefficient. A broken staymaker and tobacconist, he had twice been removed from the office of petty exciseman for what today would be called unionizing activity. He had separated from his wife, and his mean and petty environment seemed to offer no hope of a decent living. One stroke of good fortune had come to him, when as a delegate from his union on some business with Parliament, he made the acquaintance of Franklin, who was taken with "those wonderful eyes of his," and advised America as a likely place for getting on. So provided with little more than Franklin's letter of introduction, he set sail for new worlds, cherishing the unmilitant plan of setting up in Philadelphia a seminary of polite learning for young ladies. But the times proved unpropitious for such a venture. He found himself in a world hesitating fearfully on the brink of revolution, the elec-

---

[1] For the date of his arrival, see *Massachusetts Historical Society Proceedings*, Vol. XLIII, p. 246.

tric atmosphere of which he found strangely congenial. He at once threw himself whole-heartedly into the colonial dispute, quickly seized the main points, mastered the arguments, and thirteen months after his arrival published *Common Sense*, a pamphlet that was to spread his name and fame throughout America.

The amazing influence of *Common Sense* on a public opinion long befogged by legal quibble flowed from its direct and skillful appeal to material interests. For the first time in a tedious, inconsequential debate, it was openly asserted that governmental policies rest on economic foundations; that the question of American independence was only a question of expediency, and must be determined in the light of economic advantage. Government is no more than a utility, and that policy which was most likely to secure freedom and security "with the least expense and greatest benefit," must be preferred. The point at issue before the American people, therefore, was whether a more useful arrangement would result from continuing the old connection with England, or from setting up for themselves; and it must be decided, not in the court room or council chambers, but in the countinghouse and market place, in the field and shop, wherever plain Americans were making a living. Let the common people consult their own needs, and determine the case without regard to legal or constitutional precedents. It was a simple matter to be judged in the light of common sense and their particular interests.

To further clear thinking on this fundamental matter Paine commented on the economic consequences to America of the English connection. Throughout colonial history, he asserted with some disregard to fact, dependence had resulted in disadvantage to America; England had systematically exploited the colonies and hampered development. Whatever prosperity had been won heretofore, had been won in spite of English hostility and interference; the peculiar economic position of the colonies had proved their best reliance in the past, and would prove still more advantageous in the future, if America were free from jealous, paternal restrictions. What reason was there to expect generous treatment from a power that had never shown generosity in past dealings? How skillful was the appeal to colonial self-interest is revealed in such passages as these:

We are already greater than the King wishes us to be, and will he not hereafter endeavour to make us less? To bring the matter to one point,

Is the power who is jealous of our prosperity, a proper power to govern us? Whoever says *No*, to this question, is an Independent, for independency means no more than this, whether we shall make our own laws, or, whether the King, the greatest enemy this continent hath, or can have, shall tell us *there shall be no laws but such as I like*.

America would have flourished as much, and probably much more, had no European power taken any notice of her. The commerce by which she hath enriched herself are the necessaries of life, and will always have a market while eating is the custom of Europe. As Europe is our market for trade we ought to form no partial connection with any part of it. It is the true interest of America to steer clear of European contentions, which she never can do while by her dependence on Britain she is made the makeweight in the scale of British politics.

Our corn will fetch its price in any market in Europe, and our imported goods must be paid for buy them where we will. . . . 'Tis as great folly to pay a Bunker-hill price for law as for land.

But Paine well knew that self-interest may be so clouded by prejudice as not to see the way its nose is pointing. Though the colonial talked of his grievances, he remained colonial in psychology, held in unconscious subjection to English traditions. He was in the clutch of outworn loyalties—loyalty to the crown and loyalty to the British constitution; and to this difficult problem Paine addressed himself with great skill. To a republican, as Paine seems to have been from his landing in America, the odium which George III had incurred was a heaven-sent opportunity. In order to strike at the monarchical principle, it was only necessary to point out that the folly of the King was the best commentary upon the foolishness of hereditary monarchy. The boldness and audacity of Paine's attack on the king-principle must have added greatly to the popularity of *Common Sense* along the frontier. It was the first clear, far-carrying appeal for republicanism addressed to American ears. How successful it was, how ruthlessly it stripped away the divinity that doth hedge a king, laying bare the stupidity of the king-cult, is suggested by the remarkable change in the American attitude towards monarchy that a few months brought about. After the appearance of *Common Sense*, middle and lower class Americans shed their colonial loyalties like a last year's garment, and thenceforth they regarded the pretentions of kings as little better than flummery. King George's disgraced exciseman had his revenge; he had thrust his royal master out of the colonial affection and destroyed the monarchical principle in America.

A more difficult task remained, that of instituting "an inquiry into the *constitutional errors* of the English form of government," in order to prove what gains would result if America took herself out of the English system. Here Paine faced, single-handed, a solid phalanx of lawyers. He was the first pamphleteer to question the excellence of a constitution that was proclaimed by American Tories as the wonder of the world and the envy of other nations. In the acrimonious disputes between 1765 and 1775, this was the single point on which all professed to agree. A vast deal of laudation had been uttered; innumerable legal pamphlets had been written; and no colonial had had the temerity to question the adequacy of the British constitution to colonial needs. And now came this republican, with penetrating comment on its origin and working, to disturb the common complacency by pointing out how ill fitted it was to answer the needs of America. It was a telling attack, made with skill and shrewd insight; and it had a great part in arousing a bitter antagonism to the English system in the minds of the American yeomanry.

Paine was not a constitutional historian, but he had a keen eye for realities. The fundamental fallacy of the English system, he asserted, lay in the so-called "mixt aristocracy," which was presumed to gather the wisdom of the realm in council with the king, but which was no more than a convenient arrangement for dividing the spoils. The House of Commons had grown out of the struggles of feudal barons against the king. It presumed to speak for the common people, but the rights of the people were thus recognized only to be thwarted by the old tyrannies. The "Republican materials, in the persons of the Commons, on whose virtue depends the freedom of England," were held in check by the "remains of aristocratical tyranny in the person of the Peers," and further restrained by the "remains of Monarchical tyranny in the person of the King." From the play of these elements arose the system of checks and balances which placed control in the hands of landed property. It was based on the assumption that "the King is not to be trusted without being looked after," and that "the Commons, by being appointed for that purpose, are either wiser or more worthy of confidence than the Crown." But in spite of the supposed balance "the provision is unequal to the task," for the Crown, as the dispenser of places and pensions, is more than a match for Commons in the game of politics.

The will of the king is as much the law of the land in Britain as in France, with this difference, that instead of proceeding directly from his mouth, it is handed to the people under the formidable shape of an act of parliament. For the fate of Charles the First hath only made kings more subtle—not more just.

This was but the beginning of a long assault on the British constitution which was to engage him much in after life. *Common Sense* was a pronouncement of the new philosophy of republicanism that was taking firm hold of the American mind, and which the French Revolution was to spread so widely. It was a notable contribution, of which Paine to the end of his life was justly proud.

As he came to America almost casually, with no conscious revolutionary intent, so in the critical year 1787 he returned to Europe with the peaceful intention of perfecting an iron bridge on which he was engaged. True to his Quaker breeding he was more interested in the arts of peace than of war, but again circumstance was too much for him. Before he had completed his bridge, delegates from France came to invite him to a seat in the National Assembly. A new day was rising there; the constitution of a freer order was being constructed, and so competent a workman could not be spared. In the thick of that eager world of constitution-making, Paine finally clarified his political philosophy and gave it wide currency. He became the pamphleteer of revolution to the English-speaking world, to Philadelphia and New York equally with London. Yet he was never an extremist; he was a Girondist rather than a Jacobin, and when the Girondists were overthrown and a dictatorship set up, he remained a constitutionalist. By the Jacobin radicals he came to be regarded as a reactionary from his willingness to retain monarchy in France; but Paine was a practical Englishman with a shrewd judgment of what was politically possible, and he refused to outrun reasonable expectations of accomplishment.

It was the simplicity and clarity of his political philosophy that made its appeal so widely effective. His thinking turned on the two fundamental questions, the source of government and the purpose for which it is instituted among men; and the major premise on which he reared his logic was the thesis that sovereignty inheres in the majority will. At the basis of his philosophy was the natural-rights theory, but given a fresh significance and vitality by the assertion of the doctrine of continuous reaffirmation of the social compact. Instead of deriving the sovereign state from a fictitious compact, presumably entered into in a remote past, he derived it—as Roger Williams had done a century and half before—from a continuous compact reaffirmed by each generation. With the birth of each individual appear fresh rights which no pre-contract can justly circumscribe or nullify; ancestral arrangements are valid only to the extent that they are acceptable to the living. Hence it follows, first, that the general body of the people may at any time remake the fundamental law, and bring it into accord with present desire; and second, that there can be no law superior to this popular will expressed through the majority. His most celebrated dictum—"That which a nation chuses to do it has a right to do"—a dictum that aroused a bitterer hostility than any other of his pronouncements—was the logical expression of his republicanism that differentiated between the sovereign people and their agency, the government; and this in turn he justified by a celebrated saying out of Swift, "Government is a plain thing, and fitted to the capacity of many heads." Like Jefferson, he would not have government kept from the people, the agent domineer over the principal.

The purpose of government Paine discovered in the Benthamite principle of expediency. If a diffused well-being results from the policies of government, such government is justified; but if the tax-levies are wasted in unsocial ways, if unjust impositions are levied, if exploitation or tyranny results, such government is not justified. The agent has cheated the principal, and must be called to account. The final test of every government Paine found in its concern for the "*res publica*, the public affairs, or the public good"; any government that "does not make the *res publica* its whole and sole object, is not a good government." In its most obvious phase, concern for the *res publica* means concern for the national economy, and this in turn conditions the taxes that shall be levied and the ends for which they shall be spent—whether upon the arts of peace or war. A beneficent government has no need of standing armies and navies, or an inquisitorial police; it is established in the hearts of the people and rests securely on the common good will. It is the injustice of government that creates armies to defend the earnings of injustice. But every wise government will respect its limitations. As a child of the eighteenth century, Paine hated the leviathan state as a monster created by a minority to serve the ends of tyranny. The political state he accepted as a present necessity, but he would not have its prestige magnified and the temptation to tyranny increased by the cult of nationalism. "Government is no farther necessary," he believed, "than to supply the few cases to which society and civilization are not conveniently competent." At best it is an artificial thing.

Formal government makes but a small part of civilized life; and when even the best that human wisdom can devise is established, it is a thing more in name and idea than in fact. . . . The more perfect civilization is, the less occasion has it for government, because the more does it regulate its own affairs, and govern itself. . . . All the great laws of society are laws of nature.[2]

The maturest elaboration of Paine's political philosophy is found in *The Rights of Man.* This extraordinary work, the most influential English contribution to the revolutionary movement, was an examination of the English constitution in the light of what Paine held were the true source and ends of government. It is a brilliant reply to Burke, who rested his interpretation of the English constitution on the legal ground of the common law of contract. Following the Revolution of 1688, Burke had argued, the English people through their legal representatives, entered into a solemn contract, binding "themselves, their heirs, and posterities forever," to certain express terms; and neither in law nor in equity were they, of whatever generation, free to change those terms except by the consent of both parties to the contract. This was an elaboration of the theory of government tacitly held by the Old Whigs, which derived government from a perpetual civil contract as opposed to the radical doctrine of a revocable social contract; and in attacking it Paine allied himself with such thinkers as Price, Priestley, Franklin and Rousseau.[3] He pointed out the absurdity of carrying over the law of private property into the high realm of political principle—to seek to impose the dead past upon the living sovereignty. If sovereignty inhered in the English people in 1688, it must inhere in the English people in 1793, unless it had been violently wrested from them; no parchment terms of another age can bind that sovereignty other than voluntarily. Over against Burke's theory of a single, static contract, Paine set

[2] *Rights of Man*, Part II, pp. 407, 408.
[3] For an excellent discussion of this, see C. M. Walsh, *The Political Science of John Adams*, pp. 203–226.

the doctrine of the reaffirmation of natural rights. Any generation—as the generation of 1688—is competent to deal with its
affairs as it sees fit, but it cannot barter away the rights of those
unborn; such a contract on the face of it is null and void.

Every age and generation must be free to act for itself *in all cases* as
the ages and generations which preceded it. The vanity and presumption
of governing beyond the grave is the most ridiculous and insolent of all
tyrannies. . . . Every generation is, and must be, competent to all the
purposes which its occasions require. It is the living, and not the dead,
that are to be accommodated.[4]

Burke's defense fares even worse when the argument is examined
in the light of expediency. Illogical as the English system must
appear to the political philosopher, can it plead the justification
that it works; that it does well the things it is paid to do; that it
makes the *res publica* its main concern? The reply to such questions, Paine believed, should be sought in the condition of the
national economy; more particularly by an examination of the
account-books of the exchequer. The English people paid annually
seventeen millions sterling for the maintenance of government,
and what did they get in return? Nine millions of the total went
to pay interest on old wars, which in the budget was known as the
funded debt; of the remaining eight millions the larger part was
spent in new wars and sinecure pensions; whereas the real needs
of England—the true *res publica*—were shamelessly neglected.
The English people got little for their money except new debts to
justify new taxes. The poor were even taxed for the benefit of the
great. Thus my Lord Onslow, who was particularly zealous in
the business of proscribing Paine as "the common enemy of us
all," drew four thousand pounds from the royal chest in sinecures,
which made him "the principal pauper of the neighbourhood, and
occasioning a greater expense than the poor, the aged, and the
infirm, for ten miles around."[5] Government on the hereditary
principle of Burke did not appear to advantage in the light of such
facts.

The injustice of aristocratic government, Paine believed, was
fast bringing it to its "rotting time" in England. "The opinions
of men with respect to government are changing fast in all countries; the enormous expense of governments has provoked the

[4] *The Rights of Man*, Part I, p. 278.
[5] "Letter to Lord Onslow," in *Works*, Vol. III, p. 36.

people to think, by making them feel." Englishmen must soon throw aside the outworn monarchical system and set up a republic. Economics was on the side of revolution. The great work of revising fundamental laws was the pressing business of the time. If this could be done peacefully, by means of a national convention, it were well; if not, it would come by means of an uprising of the people. It was no lawyer's business to be determined by the law of private property, but a practical matter of determining the real will of the nation and putting it into execution. The judgment of the people must be recorded, and the judgment of the people could be had only through an adequate system of representation based on free publicity. "I do not believe that the people of England have ever been fairly and candidly dealt by," Paine declared. Henceforth they must be taken into full confidence. There must be no more *arcana imperii*—"Nations can have no secrets; and the secrets of courts, like those of individuals, are always their defects."[6]

One of the great advantages of the American Revolution has been, that it has led to a discovery of the principles, and laid open the imposition of governments. All the revolutions till then had worked within the atmosphere of a court, and never on the grand floor of a nation. The parties were always of the class of courtiers. . . . In all cases they took care to represent government as a thing made up of mysteries, which only themselves understood; and they hid from the understanding of the nation the only thing that was beneficial to know, namely, *That government is nothing more than a national association acting on the principles of a society.*[7]

For the follies of government the people pay the bill—it was this elementary lesson in public economics that Paine sought to impress upon the popular mind; and they would still be cheated and plundered by gentlemen who prospered in cozening, until they took matters into their own hands. He had no fear of popular government. He believed in the essential fairness of men and their capacity to deal wisely with the problems of society if the necessary information were set before them. "As far as my experience in public life extends, I have ever observed that the great mass of people are always just, both in their intentions and their object; but the true method of attaining such purpose does not always appear at once," [8] he argued before the French Assembly; and the

[6] *Rights of Man*, Part II, p. 428.
[7] *Ibid.*, pp. 410–411.
[8] Conway, *Life of Paine*, Vol. II, p. 4.

words express his settled conviction. Those who fear the people usually have very good reasons. Heretofore politics had been jealously guarded from free discussion; but now that the common people were coming to understand that government is justified only by its measure of service, the beginning of a new age was at hand.

The ripest product of Paine's speculations on the relation of government to the individual, is *Agrarian Justice*, a work too little known to modern readers. It is a slender tract, written in the winter of 1795–96, although not published till a year later; and it was an answer to a sermon by Watson, Bishop of Llandaff,[9] entitled *The Wisdom and Goodness of God in having made both Rich and Poor*. In this remarkable essay, Paine advanced from political to social theory, pushing his thought into the unexplored realm of economic justice. The prime impulse of his speculation is found in the contrast between the augmenting poverty of Europe and the ideal of equality; a contrast which in France had lately produced a proletarian revolt under Babeuf, and which in England was harshly aggravated by the brutal inclosure movement of the last forty years of the eighteenth century. The question which he considers lies at the heart of our social problem, namely, whether civilization is competent to cure the disease of poverty which everywhere it disseminates?

The question emerged naturally from the development of Paine's thinking. It was implied in his major principle of the *res publica*, and the solution must lie in the problem of the relation of government to social well-being. But in prescribing means to end, he parted company from Babeuf.[10] The latter was a Communist who approached the problem from the point of view of the proletarian who had been disappointed of the promised equality; whereas Paine, like Jefferson, was essentially a Physiocratic agrarian. His long residence in America had confirmed him in the belief that land monopoly was the root of economic inequality; and his observations of the evictions then going on in England, uprooting the peasants and sending them to industrial centers to become wage-workers, strengthened his conviction. The land problem must be solved if civilization were to be worth its cost,

---

[9] Author of *An Apology for the Bible* (a reply to Paine's *Age of Reason*), which was distributed among Harvard undergraduates. See above, page 324.

[10] For the program of Babeuf, see R. W. Postgate, *Revolution from 1789 to 1906*, pp. 24, 54–60.

and the technique of the solution, he believed, must be worked out by the state. With his usual directness Paine went to the heart of the problem:

The first principle of civilization ought to have been, and ought still to be, that the condition of every person born into the world, after a state of civilization commences, ought not to be worse than if he had been born before that period. But the fact is, that the condition of millions, in every country in Europe, is far worse than if they had been born before civilization began, or had been born among the Indians of North-America at the present day.[11]

It is not charity but a right, not bounty but justice, that I am pleading for. The present state of civilization is as odious as it is unjust. It is absolutely the opposite of what it should be.[12] . . . . The contrast of affluence and wretchedness . . . is like dead and living bodies chained together.[13]

It is the practice of what has unjustly obtained the name of civilization . . . to make some provision for persons becoming poor and wretched only at the time they become so. Would it not, even as a matter of economy, be far better to adopt means to prevent their becoming poor? [14]

The crux of the problem, Paine proceeds to point out, lies in the principle of private property; whether property rights are sacredly individual—as Locke had asserted—or are limited by social needs. In reply to this searching question Paine laid down the principle of social values, a theory curiously modern and profoundly suggestive, which makes *Agrarian Justice* read like a chapter out of *Progress and Poverty*. The principle is so broad, as Paine states it, that it applies equally to a capitalistic and an agrarian order.

Personal property is the *effect of society;* and it is as impossible for an individual to acquire personal property without the aid of society, as it is for him to make land originally. . . . All accumulation, therefore, of personal property, beyond what a man's own hands produce, is derived to him by living in society; and he owes on every principle of justice, of gratitude, and of civilization, a part of that accumulation back again to society from whence the whole came . . . if we examine the case minutely it will be found that the accumulation of personal property is, in many instances, the effect of paying too little for the labor that produced it; and the consequence of which is, that the working hand perishes in old age, and the employer abounds in affluence. It is, perhaps, impossible to proportion exactly the price of labor to the profits it produces; and it

[11] *Works*, Vol. III, p. 329.
[12] This and the preceding sentence were expunged from all early editions by the censor.
[13] *Ibid.*, p. 337.   [14] *Ibid.*, p. 338.

will also be said, as an apology for the injustice, that were a workman to receive an increase of wages daily he would not save it against old age, nor be much better for it in the interim. Make, then, society the treasurer to guard it for him in a common fund; for it is no reason, that because he might not make a good use of it for himself, another should take it.[15]

It is the value of the improvement only, and not of the earth itself, that is individual property. Every proprietor, therefore, of cultivated land, owes to the community a *ground-rent* . . . for the land which he holds; and it is from this ground-rent that the fund proposed in this plan is to issue.[16]

Having thus pointed out an equitable source of social income— the returning to society what society has created—Paine proposed to deal with the problem of poverty by means of a ten per cent inheritance tax to provide a fund for the endowment of the young and the pensioning of the old. It was an early form of the state insurance idea. In his own thinking Paine doubtless went much farther than this, but the practical difficulty of separating the social moiety from the private right inclined him to favor an inheritance tax as the simplest and best plan; that it would lead to greater things as the social intelligence quickened, he very likely believed. To bring men to realize that society is responsible for poverty, and that its total eradication must be regarded as the first object of civilization, was his prime purpose. He was seeking to awaken the social conscience of his generation—a generation sorely in need of idealism to offset its love of profits. *Agrarian Justice* was a contribution to the slowly developing humanitarian sentiment, and it made appeal to minds already aroused by the revolutionary movement. The republican clubs that were springing up in England and America reflected the new social thought, and the most radical became the most humanitarian. As early as 1791, in an address signed by Horne Tooke, one of Paine's English lieutenants, it was declared:

We are oppressed with a heavy national debt, a burthen of taxes, an expensive administration of government, beyond those of any people in the world. We have also a very numerous poor; and we hold that the moral obligation of providing for old age, helpless infancy, and poverty, is far superior to that of supplying the invented wants of courtly extravagance, ambition, and intrigue.[17]

[15] *Ibid.*, p. 340.   [16] *Ibid.*, p. 329.
[17] *Address and Declaration of the Friends of Universal Peace and Liberty*, quoted in Conway, *Life of Paine*, Vol. I, p. 316.

The more critically one follows the thought of Paine the more evident it becomes that the master passion of his later years was concern for a new social economy. The well-being of society became an engrossing interest with him; and his zeal for political revolution was predicated on the belief that popular control of the political state was a necessary preliminary to a juster social economy. Nothing was to be expected from the old aristocratic order. His main attack, therefore, was directed against the monarchical system, but now and then he paused to level a thrust at the rising system of capitalism. If he hated King George and the Tories, he hated the younger Pitt and the imperialists even more. Over against *Agrarian Justice* should be set his pamphlet entitled *The Decline and Fall of the English System of Finance*, written in 1796, a skillful attack upon the new funding system. Paine could not foresee, of course, the enormous expansion of credit that was to accompany the industrial revolution, but in his commentary on the quantitative theory of money, and the social consequences of inflation, he unconsciously foretold later conditions. War he regarded as the great waster, the fruitful mother of social misery. With his Quaker training he was dedicated to pacifism, and he spent his life warring against war, and disease, and poverty, and injustice, and ignorance, and unreason; but no other war would he sanction. For those futile wars bred of the ambitions of courts and monarchs, and which for all their cost in blood and money served no social purpose, he would substitute arbitration. "War is the Pharo-table of governments, and nations the dupes of the game," he declared [18]—whereas arbitration is an appeal to reason which alone should adjudicate and determine between nations.

It would be idle to attempt to trace to their sources the major ideas of his philosophy. Probably Paine did not know where he got them. He was not a student like John Adams, familiar with all the political philosophers; rather he was an epitome of a world in revolution. He absorbed ideas like a sponge. He was so wholly a child of his age that the intellectual processes of the age were no other than his own. But he was very much more than an echo; he possessed that rarest of gifts, an original mind. He looked at the world through no eyes than his own. There is a curious remark in an early pamphlet which admirably expresses his method:

[18] *Rights of Man*, Part II, p. 413.

"When precedents fail to assist us, we must return to the first
principles of things for information, and *think*, as if we were the
first men that thought." [19] It was his remarkable ability to think
from first principles that gave such freshness and vigor to his pen.
He drew largely from French thought, but at bottom he remained
English. If he was Gallic in his psychology of human nature and
his passionate humanitarianism, he was English in his practical
political sense and insistence on the economic sources of political
action. In his political theory he was curiously like Roger Williams.
A thoroughgoing idealist in aim, generous and unsparing in
service to humanity, he was a confirmed realist in the handling
of facts. He refused to be duped by imposing appearances or
great reputations, but spoke out unpleasant truths which gentlemen wished to keep hidden. Clear and direct in expression, he
seasoned his writings with homely figures and a frequent audacity
of phrase that made wide appeal. He was probably the greatest
pamphleteer that the English race has produced, and one of its
great idealists.

During his residence abroad Paine habitually thought and spoke
of himself as an American. He conceived it to be his mission to
disseminate throughout Europe the beneficent principles of the
American Revolution; yet nowhere was he hated more virulently
than in America. To the animosity which his political principles
excited among Federalists was added the detestation of the orthodox for the deism of the *Age of Reason*. The ministers outdid the
politicians in virulent attack upon his reputation, until the generous
Quaker, the friend of humanity and citizen of the world, was
shrunk and distorted into "the infidel Tom Paine." It was a
strange reward for a life spent in the service of mankind. Like all
idealists he made the mistake of underestimating the defensive
strength of vested interests, and their skill in arousing the mob
prejudice. His thousands of followers among the disfranchised
poor could not protect his reputation against the attacks of the
rich and powerful. Although reason may "make its own way,"
it makes its way with wearisome slowness and at unreasonable
cost. How tremendous were the obstacles that liberalism confronted in post-revolutionary America is revealed with sufficient
clearness in the odium visited upon our great republican pamphleteer.

[19] *Works*, Vol. I, p. 155.

II
THOMAS JEFFERSON
Agrarian Democrat

The years following the great defeat were disastrous to the party of agrarian democracy. Under the brilliant leadership of Hamilton the Federalists went forward confidently, gaining daily a firmer grip on the machinery of government, and establishing their principles in far-reaching legislative enactments. Their appeal to the wealthy classes, to those who made themselves audible above the clamor, was electrical. Hamilton was the hero of the hour, and the effusive approval that augmented with every added profit to the money brokers, seemed to indicate that the country was enthusiastically behind the Federalist policy. To what despondency the democrats were reduced is revealed in Maclay's *Journal*, with its caustic comment on political measures and motives. But the tide was already at the turn. The ideas let loose by the French Revolution were running swiftly through America, awakening a militant spirit in the democracy. Antagonism to the aristocratic arrogance of Federalism, and disgust at its coercive measures, were mounting fast. If that inchoate discontent were organized and directed by a skillful leader, it might prove strong enough to thrust the Hamiltonian party from power. To that work Thomas Jefferson devoted himself with immense tact and untiring patience. A master of political strategy, he spun his webs far and wide, quietly awaiting the time when the bumbling Federalist bees should range too carelessly in search of their honey. Accepted at once as the leader of agrarian America, he was to prove in the course of a long life the most original and native of the political leaders of the time.

Despite the mass of comment that has gathered about Jefferson, the full reach and significance of his political philosophy remains too little understood. Uncritical praise and censure have obscured or distorted his purpose, and allied his principles with narrow and temporary ends. Detraction will not let him alone. The hostility of his enemies, as a recent biographer has remarked, has frequently taken "the peculiar form of editing his works or writing his life." [20] For this distortion there is, perhaps, more than usual excuse. Certainly Jefferson is the most elusive of our great political leaders.

[20] Francis W. Hirst, *Life and Letters of Thomas Jefferson*, p. 266.

Apparently inconsistent, changing his program with the changing times, he seemed to his enemies devoid of principle, a shallow demagogue who incited the mob in order to dupe the people. One of the most bitterly hated and greatly loved men in the day when love and hate were intense, he was the spokesman of the new order at a time of transition from a dependent monarchical state, to an independent republican state. Back of the figure of Jefferson, with his aristocratic head set on a plebeian frame, was the philosophy of a new age and a new people—an age and a people not yet come to the consistency of maturity, but feeling a way through experiment to solid achievement. Far more completely than any other American of his generation he embodied the idealisms of the great revolution—its faith in human nature, its economic individualism, its conviction that here in America, through the instrumentality of political democracy, the lot of the common man should somehow be made better.

From the distinguished group of contemporary political thinkers Jefferson emerges as the preëminent intellectual, widely read, familiar with ideas, at home in the field of speculation, a critical observer of men and manners. All his life he was a student, and his devotion to his books, running often to fifteen hours a day, recalls the heroic zeal of Puritan scholars. He was trained in the law, but he was too much the intellectual, too curious about all sorts of things, to remain a lawyer. For such a man the appeal of political speculation was irresistible, and early in life he began a wide reading in the political classics that far outweighed Coke and Blackstone in creative influence on his mind. He was equally at home with the English liberals of the seventeenth century and the French liberals of the eighteenth; and if he came eventually to set the French school above the English, it was because he found in the back-to-nature philosophy, with its corollary of an agrarian economics and its emphasis on social well-being, a philosophy more consonant with Virginian experience and his own temperament than Locke's philosophy of property. But he was very far from being a narrow French partisan, as has been often charged; rather he judged old-world theory in the light of its applicability to existing American conditions, and restrained his love of speculation by immediate practical considerations. The man of affairs kept a watchful eye on the philosopher in his study.

In the major doctrines of his political philosophy Jefferson was an amalgam of English and French liberalisms, supplemented by the conscious influence of the American frontier. That fusion early took place in his mind. The first bill that he introduced into the Virginia Assembly, at the age of twenty-six, was a bill to permit slave-owners to manumit their slaves; and his first published pamphlet, issued in 1774,[21] rejected the legal reasoning of John Dickinson and Daniel Dulaney—supporting the parliamentary right to impose external taxation—and took its stand on the doctrine of natural right to local self-government and freedom of trade. When two years later he drafted the Declaration of Independence the fusion was complete. The strong influence of French humanitarianism is revealed in the passage on slavery that was stricken out on the floor of Congress, and more significantly in the change in the familiar phrasing of the several natural rights. Samuel Adams and other followers of Locke had been content with the classical enumeration of life, liberty, and property; but in Jefferson's hands the English doctrine was given a revolutionary shift. The substitution of "pursuit of happiness" for "property" marks a complete break with the Whiggish doctrine of property rights that Locke had bequeathed to the English middle class, and the substitution of a broader sociological conception; and it was this substitution that gave to the document the note of idealism which was to make its appeal so perennially human and vital. The words were far more than a political gesture to draw popular support; they were an embodiment of Jefferson's deepest convictions, and his total life thenceforward was given over to the work of providing such political machinery for America as should guarantee for all the enjoyment of those inalienable rights. If the fact that he set the pursuit of happiness above abstract property rights is to be taken as proof that Jefferson was an impractical French theorist, the critic may take what comfort he can from his deduction.

That Jefferson was an idealist was singularly fortunate for America; there was need of idealism to leaven the materialistic realism of the times. It was a critical period and he came at the turn of a long running tide. He watched the beginnings of the political shift in America from isolated colonial commonwealths to a unitary sovereign state; and his wide reading and close observation had convinced him that the impending change was fraught

[21] *A Summary View of the Rights of British America*, Williamsburg.

with momentous issues for the common man. He had meditated much on the social results of the slow oscillations in western civilization between social decentralization and centralization, with their contrasting political and economic structures; and he understood how the movement from simplicity to complexity—from freedom to regimentation—creates a psychology and an institutionalism that conducts straight to the leviathan state, controlled by a ruling caste, serving the demands of exploitation, heedless of the well-being of the regimented mass. This great lesson in social drifts he brought home to America. There had been created here the psychology and institutions of a decentralized society, with a corresponding exaltation of the individual and the breakdown of caste. In the broad spaces of America the old-world coercive state had dwindled to a mere police arrangement for parochial duties; the free citizen refused to be regimented; the several communities insisted on managing their affairs by their own agents. Such was the natural consequence of free economics; but with the turning of the tide would not the drift towards centralization nullify the results of earlier American experience and repeat here the unhappy history of European peoples?

To the philosophic mind of Jefferson, such a question was not academic, but urgent and vital. He had been bred in that older world, he believed passionately in the excellence of its virtues, and his political and social philosophy was determined by that experience. He sprang from a society deep-rooted in an agrarian economy, and he wished to preserve that society. Born on the Virginia frontier, he had never seen a hamlet so large as twenty houses before his eighteenth year; his neighbors and associates were capable and vigorous frontier democrats, who managed the affairs of local government with the same homespun skill that went to their farming. "It is not difficult," remarks an acute critic, "to see how the great principle of Jefferson's life—absolute faith in democracy—came to him. He was the product of the first West in American history; he grew up with men who ruled their country well, who fought the Indians valiantly . . . . Jefferson loved his backwoods neighbors, and he, in turn, was loved by them." [22] This early conviction of the excellence of a freehold order was confirmed by later experience; wide observation and much travel convinced him that no other people was so favored

[22] Dodd, *Statesmen of the Old South*, p. 23.

by circumstance as the American, or so vigorously self-reliant. That such well-being resulted from a plastic economics, he regarded as self-evident; and from this economic freedom came political freedom. In his European travels he saw everywhere want and wretchedness dwelling in the shadow of the aristocratic state, and he could not dissociate the two. Political tyranny was the outward and visible sign of greater tyrannies that ran down to the very roots of society; the leviathan state was the convenient instrument through which those tyrannies took their heavy toll of the common well-being. America was a land of free men; it was exploited neither by an aristocracy nor a plutocracy. Surely there could be no greater or nobler ambition for an American than to assist in preserving his country from the misery that must attend a change from the present happy condition of democratic industry, to the serfdom of the European wage-taker and peasant.

To a mind imbued with such conceptions the appeal of the Physiocratic theory of social economics would be irresistible. The ground was prepared for the sowing of the seeds of the liberal French thought. With its emphasis laid upon agriculture, its doctrine of the *produit net*, its principle of *laissez faire*, and its social concern, the Physiocratic theory accorded exactly with his familiar experience, and it must have seemed to Jefferson that it was little other than a deduction from the open facts of American life. He had read much in the works of the Physiocratic group, and was intimately acquainted with DuPont de Nemours; and the major principles of the school sank deep into his mind and creatively determined his thinking, with the result that Jeffersonian democracy as it spread through Virginia and west along the frontier assumed a pronounced Physiocratic bias. The sharp struggle between Jefferson and Hamilton must be reckoned, in part at least, a conflict between the rival principles of Quesnay and Adam Smith, between an agrarian and a capitalistic economy. Much as Jefferson feared the ambitions of an aristocracy, he feared quite as much the creation of a proletariat. As he looked into the future he saw great cities rising to breed their Roman mobs, duped and exploited by demagogues, the convenient tools of autocracy; and counting the cost in social well-being, he set his face like flint against the rising capitalism. A free yeomanry he regarded as the backbone of every great people, the producers of the real wealth, the guardians of manly independence; and the number of factory workers measured for him the extent of social disease. It is this Physiocratic conception that explains his bitter hostility to protective tariffs, national banks, funding manipulations, the machinery of credit, and all the agencies of capitalism which Hamilton was skillfully erecting in America. Not to have hated such things Jefferson must first have emptied his mind of the teachings of experience and the lessons of the social philosophers.

In the *Notes on Virginia* there is a well-known passage that amplifies his favorite thesis that a sound American economy was an agrarian economy:

The political economists of Europe have established it as a principle, that every State should endeavor to manufacture for itself; and this principle, like many others, we transfer to America. . . . But we have an immensity of land courting the industry of the husbandman. Is it best then that all our citizens should be employed in its improvement, or that one half should be called off from that to exercise manufactures and handicraft arts for the other? Those who labor in the earth are the chosen people of God, if ever he had a chosen people, whose breasts he has made his peculiar deposit for substantial and genuine virtue. It is the focus in which he keeps alive that sacred fire, which otherwise might escape from the face of the earth. Corruption of morals in the mass of cultivators is a phenomenon of which no age nor nation has furnished an example. It is the mark set on those, who not looking up to heaven, to their own soil and industry, as does the husbandman, for their subsistence, depend for it on casualties and caprice of customers. Dependence begets subservience and venality, suffocates the germ of virtue, and prepares fit tools for the designs of ambition. . . . Generally speaking the proportion which the aggregate of the other classes of citizens bears in any state to that of its husbandmen, is the proportion of its unsound to its healthy parts, and is a good enough barometer whereby to measure its degree of corruption. While we have land to labor then, let us never wish to see our citizens occupied at a work-bench, or twirling a distaff . . . for the general operations of manufacture, let our work-shops remain in Europe. It is better to carry provisions and materials to work-men there, than bring them to the provisions and materials, and with them their manners and principles. . . . The mobs of great cities add just so much to the support of pure government, as sores do to the strength of the human body. It is the manners and spirit of a people which preserve a republic in vigor. A degeneracy in these is a canker which soon eats to the heart of its laws and constitution.[23]

Such was his attitude in 1782, an attitude identical with Franklin's. Thirty-four years later he had modified his views of industrialism. The bitter experience of the Napoleonic wars, with the

[23] *Writings*, Vol. III, pp. 268–269.

hardships and losses visited upon neutral shipping, had convinced
him of the need of domestic manufactures, and he was then deeply
interested in improved machinery, new methods, original ventures. "We must now place the manufacturer by the side of the
agriculturist," he conceded, or remain in economic dependence.
But how much further the country should be industrialized,
whether it "shall be proposed to go beyond our own supply" to
compete in foreign markets, was not yet clear to him; the problem
remained still to be determined whether "the *surplus* labor"
would be "most beneficially employed in the culture of the earth,
or in the fabrications of art."[24] In such commentary Jefferson
failed to measure the thrust of economic determinism that drives
every people to go through with the industrial revolution, once it
is begun; but if we recall the primary principle of his political
philosophy, that the "care of human life and happiness, and not
their destruction, is the first and only legitimate object of good
government," we may perhaps judge what would have been his
attitude towards a centralized industrialism. He would have
judged its desirability, not by the balance sheet of corporate business, but by the social ledger. As a social economist he could not
think in terms of the economic man, nor simplify human beings to
labor commodity, nor reduce the social tie to the cash nexus. It
is inconceivable that he should have shared Hamilton's satisfaction
at the contemplation of women and children—and many of the
latter "of tender age"—wasting away in the mills; he was too
social-minded for that, too much an idealist, too human in short.
Though necessity might force him away from a simple agrarian
economy, it does not follow that he would become partisan to a
centralizing industrialism, with control vested in banking credit.

It is a common charge that Jefferson was consumed with suspicion, and it is set down against him as the mark of a mean and
ungenerous nature. That in later years he was suspicious of fair-
spoken advocates and plausible programs was as true of Jefferson as of Sam Adams; he had learned like the Boston democrat
the virtue of the saying, *felix qui cautus*, and with so much at stake
he would practice caution. He feared many things, for he was
acutely aware of the incapacity of the heedless majority to defend
itself against an able and instructed minority. As a child of an
aristocratic age he fell into the mistake of visualizing that minority

[24] *Ibid.*, Vol. X, p. 8.

in the guise of a landed gentry, rather than in the guise of plutocracy; but in his quick fear of a minority he had all history as
counselor. When he took his seat in Washington's cabinet his
suspicions of the Hamiltonian program were quickly aroused.
He believed that a monarchy was aimed at, and if that proved
unattainable, then a highly centralized state designed to hold in
check the democratic tendencies. His line of reasoning may be
summarized thus: In consequence of the republican enthusiasm
of the early years of the Revolution, democratic reorganization
of the several state governments had been successfully achieved.
Very great progress towards democracy had been made. Certain
legislative acts of agrarian assemblies were now being turned
against democracy, to invalidate it as a working system of government. But if agrarian majorities had used their power to enact
laws beneficial to their interests, they were only applying a lesson
learned from long experience with aristocratic legislatures. Such
acts were no serious indictment of the democratic principle, and
to make partisan use of them to justify curtailing the powers of
the majority, was a betrayal of popular rights. And this, Jefferson
believed, was the deliberate purpose of the Federalist leaders.
Unable to stem the popular tide in the several commonwealths,
the wealthy minority had devised a plan to superimpose upon the
sovereign commonwealths a centralized federal government, so
hedged about as to lie beyond the reach of local majorities, and
hence able to override and nullify the democratic will. Once
safely established, this federal government would gather fresh
powers into its hands, until there emerged a rigorous machine,
modeled after the British system, and as little regardful of the common interests. If this were not the Federalist purpose, why all
the praise of the British system as the ripe product of experience,
exactly adapted to the political genius of the English race?
    In the matter of appeal to past experience, which provided the
staple of Federalist argument, Jefferson discovered fresh grounds
of fear. The past he looked upon as evil, and the record of experience was a tale of injustice and bitter wrong. He would not have
America follow the trodden paths, for whither they led he knew
too well. He would countenance no entangling alliances with
old-world upper-class systems of statecraft, for such systems would
reproduce in America the evils it should be the chief business of
America to prevent. There must be erected here no counterpart

of the European state; there must be no king, no aristocracy, no plutocracy; but a new democratic organization of government, in which the welfare of the whole people should be the sole concern.

When I left Congress in '76 [he wrote as an old man] it was in the persuasion that our whole code must be revised, adapted to our republican form of government, and now that we had no negatives of Councils, Governors and Kings to restrain us from doing right, that it should be corrected in all its parts with a single eye to reason and the good of those for whose government it was planned.[25]

Not past experience but present need should instruct America in drawing the plans of a new system of government and a new code of law. In analyzing the evils of European systems Jefferson came to certain conclusions that dominated all his later thinking, and that may be phrased thus: The political state tends inevitably to self-aggrandizement, the logical outcome of which is a political leviathan, too big and too complex for popular control. With sovereign powers vested in the hands of governmental agents, those agents lie under a constant temptation to corruption and tyranny, and in the end they align the powers of the state on the side of the most ambitious and capable. The greater the power of government, the ampler its revenues, the more energetic its administration, the more dangerous it may become to the rights of men; for where the prize is greatest, men struggle most ruthlessly, and what prize could be greater than the privilege of exploiting society in the name of the state? History knows no objective more tempting to the will to power, than the control of the absolute state. A government adequately socialized, intent solely upon furthering the common well-being, Jefferson would have been unanxious about. But such governments existed only in the dreams of Sir Thomas More and the Utopians; he could discover none such either in the past or present. Everywhere strong governments were little more than efficient tax-machines to support armies and provide subsidies and places for the minority. Against such forces of corruption the people struggle in vain.

If such was the common testimony of old-world experience—and no man who knew the inner workings of government there would deny it—what reason was there to expect that like causes would work unlike results in America? To what purpose was the talk of strong government encouraged amongst the holders of the public

[25] "Autobiography," in *Writings*, Vol. I, p. 57.

debt? To what end had lobbyists for the funding bill invaded the floor of Congress? It was idle to expect in America a nullification of the law, that where power sits within, corruption waits without. The love of power is universal. Most men are potential autocrats, the strong and capable may become actual autocrats. No man is good enough, no group of men, to be trusted with unrestrained powers—in America any more than in Europe. A centralized government in control of the tax-machine, and secure from popular restraint, would undo the results of the Revolutionary War. The movement to consolidate power, Jefferson asserted, was "but Toryism in disguise." "The generalizing and concentrating all cares and powers into one body . . . has destroyed the liberty and the rights of men in every government which has ever existed under the sun."

Our country is too large to have all its affairs directed by a single government. Public servants at such a distance, and from under the eye of their constituents, must, from the circumstance of distance, be unable to administer and overlook all the details necessary for the good government of the citizens; and the same circumstance, by rendering detection impossible to their constituents, will invite the public agents to corruption, plunder and waste.[23]

The practice of local home rule had grown up in America in response to native conditions; it had resulted from democratic needs; and Jefferson was too thoroughly American, too instinctively democratic, to overlook the significance of local sovereignties in a democratic philosophy. From the sharp contrast between American and European practice he deduced a cardinal principle, namely, that good government springs from a common interest in public affairs, and that such common interest is possible only when the field of activities is circumscribed. Set government apart from the people, or above them, and public interest is lost in a sense of futility. The danger of an encroaching tyranny by a superimposed sovereignty, is made easy by the public lethargy in respect to distant and unfamiliar things, and establishes itself through the psychology of custom. Jefferson was never greatly concerned about stable government; he was very much more concerned about responsive government—that it should faithfully serve the majority will. He made no god of the political state. He had no conventional reverence for established law and order; he inquired rather what sort of law and order he was asked to accept, was it just or unjust. Changing conditions make ancient good uncouth, and established institutions tend to fall into dry-rot, or to become tyrannical. Men are more important than constitutions, and the public well-being is more sacred than statutes. An occasional revolution, he commented grimly apropos of the hue and cry over Shays's Rebellion, is salutary; if it does not come of itself it might well be brought about. Progress in government results from experiment; and it is easier and safer to experiment on a small scale than on a great. Inertia increases with size, and the more consolidated the government, the more unyielding it becomes. The longest delayed revolutions are the gravest.

In asserting the principle of the majority will, Jefferson like other democratic thinkers of the time, found himself countered by the argument of abstract justice. Vehement denunciation had greeted Paine's doctrine that what a nation chooses to do, it has a right to do. There can be no rights, it was confidently asserted, superior to the right. The people may legislate, but it remains to determine the validity of statutes in the light of justice; that which is unjust is *ipso facto* null and void. It was Coke's doctrine of judicial review, set up in America after its repudiation in England, and Jefferson's hostility to it was bitter. As an intellectual he had none of the lawyer's complacency with legal principles, or conceit of the law's sufficiency; and as a democrat he would not yield sovereignty into the hands of the judiciary. He had no veneration for the Common Law of England: it had grown up by slow accretions during centuries of absolutism; how should it be expected to answer the needs of a freer age? It must be purged of outworn elements, imbued with democratic sympathies. The Revolution had been fought in defense of rights that are broader and more human than legal principles; and to hand over those rights to be interpreted away by lawyers, seemed to him moonstruck madness. It was the law of Blackstone rather than of Coke that he feared most—that "elegant" canonization of the malign influences of Tory reaction, and that was so cried up by the smatterers and "ephemeral insects of the law" in America; whereas Coke "was as good a Whig as ever wrote":

Blackstone and Hume have made tories of all England, and are making tories of those young Americans whose native feelings of independence do not place them above the wily sophistries of a Hume or a Blackstone. These two books, and especially the former [Blackstone], have done more towards the suppression of the liberties of man, than all the million of men in arms of Bonaparte, and the millions of human lives with the sacrifice of which he will stand loaded before the judgment seat of his Maker.[27]

As Jefferson grew older his fear of judicial encroachment on the popular will became acute, but it shifted from distrust of the Common Law to concern over the Supreme Court. A strong and outspoken hatred of the Federal judiciary runs through all his later writings, and he lost no opportunity to popularize the thesis—"It is a misnomer to call a government republican, in which a branch of the supreme power is independent of the nation."

The great object of my fear is the Federal Judiciary. That body, like gravity, ever acting, with noiseless foot, and unalarming advance, gaining ground step by step, and holding what it gains, is engulfing insidiously the special governments into the jaws of that which feeds them.[28]

It is a very dangerous doctrine to consider the judges as the ultimate arbiters of all constitutional questions. It is one which would place us under the despotism of an oligarchy. . . . The Constitution has erected no such single tribunal, knowing that to whatever hands confided, with the corruptions of time and party, its members would become despots.[29]

As Jefferson watched Chief Justice John Marshall gathering all things within the purview of the Federal judiciary, preparing future strongholds by the skillful use of *obiter dicta*, legislating by means of judicial interpretation, nullifying the will of the majority, and with the power of repeal made nugatory by the complexity of the process, he saw clearly what the outcome would be. Surely that was no democracy where judge-made laws were enforced by bench warrants, and where the sovereign power lay beyond the immediate reach of the popular will. The government that he desired would not rest on the legal fiction of an abstract justice above statutes and constitutions, whereof a group of judicial gentlemen were the repositories and guardians. It would be like Paine's, "a plain thing, and fitted to the capacity of many heads"; for "where the law of the majority ceases to be acknowledged, there government ends; the law of the strongest takes its place."

Granted the truth of Jefferson's premises that power tends to contract to the hands of a few, and that all government of the few

[27] *Ibid.*, Vol. VI, p. 335.   [28] *Ibid.*, Vol. X, p. 189.   [29] *Ibid.*, Vol. X, p. 160.

is vicious, then democracy is the only form of government under which an approximation to justice can be realized. A class will serve class interests. Government by an aristocracy is government in the interest of the aristocracy. For the staple argument of the Federalists, that gentlemen of principle and property alone may be intrusted with affairs of state, Jefferson had a quiet contempt. "I have never observed men's honesty to increase with their riches," he remarked. On the contrary, he regarded the "better sort of people" as a chief hindrance to the spread of social justice. The past had been evil because the past had been exploited by gentlemen of principle and property. They had kept government away from the people, and with their secret councils and secret diplomacy they had plundered the taxpayers and drenched nations in blood. Their selfish rivalries everywhere exacted a heavy toll of society and left behind a trail of poverty and wretchedness. The future would be better in the degree that mastery passed into common hands.

From the conclusions of his democratic premise he did not shrink. If it were indeed true that the people were beasts, then the democratic government of the future would be a bestial government—and even that might be better than the old arrangement of masters and slaves. But the American people whom Jefferson trusted were very far from beasts; he was convinced that they were honest and well-meaning; and if government were brought close to them, kept responsive to their will, a new and beneficent chapter in human history would open. The populistic laws passed by the legislatures of Rhode Island and New Hampshire, about which such an uproar was raised by fearful creditors, and which were urged as an argument against popular government, gave him no concern. He understood the ways of propaganda, and he never accepted judgment of the American people from the mouths of their enemies. The cure for the evils of democracy, he believed, was more democracy. The whole are far less likely to be unjust than the few; and if sovereignty does not rest in the majority will, where shall it lodge?

Hume, the great apostle of toryism, says "the Commons established a principle, which is noble in itself, and seems specious [*i. e.* pleasing], but is belied by all history and experience, *that the people are the origin of all just power.*" And where else will this degenerate son of science, this traitor to his fellow men, find the origin of *just* power, if not in the majority of the society? Will it be in the minority? Or in the individual of that minority? [30]

The America of Jefferson's day was a simple world, with a simple domestic economy. More than ninety per cent were plain country folk, farmers and villagers, largely freeholders, managing their local affairs in the traditional way. There were no great extremes of poverty and wealth, no closely organized class groups. With its sharp restrictions on suffrage and the prestige accorded the gentry, it was still far from a political de- mocracy; but it was hastening towards a more democratic order. Remote from the cesspools of European diplomacy, and not yet acquainted with imperialism, it had no need for a leviathan state. Economic conditions sanctioned a *laissez-faire* government, simple and unambitious. In such a world the well-known words of Jefferson's first inaugural address, justified themselves to all who did not seek to use the state for personal advantage.

A wise and frugal government, which shall restrain men from injuring one another, which shall leave them otherwise free to regulate their own pursuits of industry and improvement, and shall not take from the mouth of labor the bread it has earned. This is the sum of good government, and this is necessary to close the circle of our felicities.

In one significant direction he would extend the scope of govern- ment—the encouragement of education. An intelligent people is necessary to a democracy; free schools are a sign of a free society. Tyranny thrives on ignorance and superstition, and every ex- ploiting group fears popular education. Free himself in thought and action, believing in the unshackled commerce of ideas, hating all censorships, Jefferson accounted the founding of the University of Virginia his largest contribution to the well-being of his native commonwealth.

To all who profess faith in the democratic ideal Jefferson is a perennial inspiration. A free soul, he loved freedom enough to deny it to none; an idealist, he believed that the welfare of the whole, and not the prosperity of any group, is the single end of government. He was our first great leader to erect a political philosophy native to the economics and experience of America, as he was the first to break consciously with the past. His life was dedicated to the service of freedom, and later generations may well recall his words, "I have sworn upon the altar of God eternal

[30] *Ibid.*, Vol. VII, p. 356.

hostility against every form of tyranny over the mind of man."
Europe made Jefferson wholly American. From his studies in
France he came to see that where men enjoy free access to the
sources of subsistence, government is likely to be simple and
honest, and society free and content; but where a policy of
preëmption has run its course, the function of government is
seduced from its social purpose to perpetuate the inequalities
which spring from the progressive monopolization of natural
resources, with augmenting corruption and injustice. To preserve
government in America from such degradation, to keep the natural
resources open to all, were the prime desire and object of his life.
That such an effort was foredoomed to failure, in presence of
imperious forces that shape society beyond the capacity of political
means to change or prevent, cannot detract from the nobility of
his ideal, or the inspiration of his life. Among the greater thinkers
of the constitutional period Jefferson remains by far the most
vital and suggestive, the one to whom later generations may return
most hopefully.

CHAPTER III

THE WAR OF BELLES LETTRES

To turn from the field of political theory to the realm of polite literature is not to quit the partisan battle-ground. The long struggle between Federalist and Democrat was too bitter and absorbing, too sharp in its alignment, not to conscript gentlemen of culture equally with politicians. Every available quill was called to the colors, and a civil war of *belles lettres* broke out, that exceeded in animosity any other known to our literary history. Attack and counter-attack were slashing and acrimonious. Gentlemen forgot their manners and indulged fiercely in tall language. Satire ran about the streets seeking new victims to impale; slander lay in wait for every passer-by. The crudest lies found willing listeners and sober ministers turned from writing sermons to enshrine pothouse tales in heroic couplets. In this virulent battle the Federalists, on the whole, had the better of it, for they were greater masters of invective and flayed their victims less clumsily; but the Democrats made up in ardor what they lacked in skill, and the blows that fell on carefully tied wigs must have hurt cruelly. As poetry those old satires may seem to us feeble enough, but as historical documents they are eloquent. The passion of a world in revolution, the hopes and fears of our forefathers as they watched the great fires consuming the world in which they had grown up, still survive in those stinging lines, as a reminder to later generations of the rough and inhospitable way that democratic America has traveled in its onward course.

I

THE FEDERALIST GROUP

1. THE HARTFORD WITS

What Federalism was capable of in the way of polite letters is sufficiently revealed in the work of a coterie of poetasters who are known in our literary histories as the Hartford Wits. The title of the group suggests their literary antecedents. They were the

357

representatives of a literary mode that had slowly percolated through the crust of Puritan provincialism and imparted a certain sprightliness to a dour temper. They were the literary old-guard of the expiring eighteenth century, suspicious of all innovation, contemptuous of every idealistic program. They stood stoutly by the customary and familiar. The nineteenth century was knocking at their door, but they would not open to it. And as they saw that new century coming in the guise of revolution, exciting to unheard-of innovations in the fields of politics and economics and religion and letters, giving rise to Jacobin Clubs and Jeffersonian democracy, they set themselves seriously to the work of barring its progress through their own little world. They conveniently associated the economic unrest of post-war days, that gave birth to a strange progeny in Rhode Island and New Hampshire and Massachusetts, with the contamination of French atheism, charged all unrest to the account of democracy, and hastened to put it down in the name of law and righteousness. They hated new ways with the virtuous hatred of the well-to-do, and dreamed of a future America as like the past as one generation of oysters is like another.

There is a certain historical fitness in the fact that the Wits should have arisen in Connecticut and been the intellectual children of Yale. For generations the snug little commonwealth had been the home of a tenacious conservatism, that clung to old ways and guarded the institutions of the fathers with pious zeal. Nowhere else in New England did the ruling hierarchy maintain so glacial a grip on society. The Revolution of '76 had only ruffled the surface on Connecticut life; it left the social structure quite unchanged. The church retained its unquestioned control of the machinery of the commonwealth; and the church was dominated by a clerical aristocracy, hand in glove with a mercantile aristocracy. Fresh currents of thought that were stirring the pulpits of eastern Massachusetts—suggestions of an Arianism that was to lead to the Unitarian schism—did not reach so far as New Haven, and Yale was content to remain the bulwark of an obsolete Calvinism. In such a soil Federalism would flourish like Jonah's gourd; and it exuded a special odor of sanctity from the Calvinism in which it was rooted. To stout Federalists like Timothy Dwight, the current dogma of total depravity sufficed to disprove the validity of all democratic aspiration. It was a presumption little short of blasphemous to assert that sinners are competent to manage the temporal affairs of society. The doctrine of equalitarianism was a particular stench in the nostrils of the aristocratic clergy, who disliked all leveling. The Irish immigrants seem to have been the most offensive equalitarians. A New England gentleman, traveling in Pennsylvania in the nineties, wrote home: "I have seen many, very many Irishmen, and with a few exceptions, they are . . . the most God-provoking Democrats on this side of Hell." And in 1798 Harrison Gray Otis wrote: "If some means are not adopted to prevent the indiscriminate admission of wild Irishmen and others to the right of suffrage, there will soon be an end to liberty & property." [1] To prevent, if possible, such an unhappy outcome, the upper classes of New England fell to organizing and drilling all the elements of conservatism for a vigorous defense. They wrote and spoke and preached, till the mind of respectable New England was saturated with prejudice. The democratic principle was converted into a bogey to frighten the simple. Such a hideous misshapen imp of darkness, such a vile hag of anarchy had never before been painted for the imagination of honest Yankees to shudder at; and if democracy seemed to them a wild and fearsome thing making ready to destroy their venerated social order, they only believed what the minister preached on the Sabbath and the squire asserted on week days. The plebeian democrat, very likely in debt, was quite overwhelmed by the organized forces of village respectability.

In this great work of saving the commonwealth of Connecticut from the pollutions of democracy the Hartford Wits were competent laborers. The more important members of the group were John Trumbull, Timothy Dwight, Joel Barlow, Lemuel Hopkins, David Humphreys, Richard Alsop, and Theodore Dwight. To these may be added the names of Dr. Elihu Hubbard Smith and Dr. Mason F. Cogswell, who were friends and occasional collaborators. Nearly all were Yale men with a pronounced Yale predilection for Calvinism and Federalism, admirable representatives of the oligarchical upper class of the provincial Connecticut society. Timothy Dwight, grandson of Jonathan Edwards, was a minister and president of Yale; Hopkins, Smith and Cogswell were physicians of high professional standing; Trumbull and Theodore Dwight were lawyers; Barlow and Humphreys found

[1] Quoted by Samuel Eliot Morison in *Harrison Gray Otis*, Vol. I, p. 107.

their way into the diplomatic field, and Alsop was a merchant. They were all comfortably well off and several were wealthy. Alsop was one of the few millionaires of the time; Barlow acquired a fortune in France; and Humphreys late in life established a textile industry incorporated for half a million. Hot Federalists, they found in Washington, Governor Trumbull, and Fisher Ames, their political mentors and guides. The most active of the group politically, was Theodore Dwight, who with his cousin Timothy was a director of the Eagle Bank, a Federalist institution, and bitterly opposed to the chartering of Republican banks. When one of the latter applied to the legislature for a charter he denounced it as a "child of intrigue and the mother of Discord." He was deep in the Hartford Convention, serving as its secretary and later as its historian. He denounced Jeffersonian republicanism as seeking to "discredit the ministry, decry religion, and destroy public worship," and as he saw it spreading through New England he attributed to it the certain decay of morality and the impending break-up of family ties, exclaiming with somewhat extreme vivacity: "The outlaws of Europe, the fugitives from the pillory and the gallows, have undertaken to assist our own abandoned citizens, in the pleasing work of destroying Connecticut. . . . Can imagination paint anything more dreadful on this side of hell!"

Later generations remember best the massive character of Timothy Dwight, a man endowed with all the Connecticut virtues and walking amongst his fellows with magnificent confidence in his powers. A great preacher, an authoritative theologian, a distinguished administrator—"every inch a college president"— a ready counselor on any knotty point be it in law or politics or finance or agriculture or *belles lettres*, a born leader of men, and by way of recreation an inditer of Hebraic epics and huge didactic poems and ample Connecticut pastorals, a confirmed traveler observing the manner of life in many commonwealths and preserving his observations in solid volumes—he was a man to compel the admiration of his fellows and put his stamp upon his age. So vast was the contemporary reputation of Timothy Dwight, and so many-sided, it may seem ironical that time should have shrunk him to the narrow compass of a paragraph in our literary history. And yet the more curiously one considers the work of the great president of Yale, the more insistent become one's doubts concerning the fineness of this nugget of Connecticut gold. It shows very suspicious signs of tarnish. His commanding presence and authoritative manner, his sonorous eloquence, his forwardness in defense of what few doubted, his vehement threshing of straw long since reduced to chaff, his prodigious labors, his abundant printing, no longer seem so authentic a seal of greatness as they seemed to his open-mouthed contemporaries; and one suspects that he impressed his fellow citizens by the completeness with which he measured up to every Connecticut ideal, rather than by the creative vigor of his mind. The great Timothy, in short, seems to a later generation to have been little more than a walking repository of the venerable Connecticut *status quo*.

The intellectual inquisitiveness that gave birth to disintegrating theory in the mind of his grandfather Jonathan Edwards, and made him a profoundly revolutionary influence in his time, was wholly lacking in the grandson. The latter refused to follow the questioning intellect into unsurveyed fields. He would not meddle with change. His mind was closed as tight as his study windows in January. He read widely in the fields of rationalism, but he read only to refute. Now and then to be sure, certain generous promptings visited him: he spoke out against slavery; he encouraged the higher education of women. But from such temptations to become a living voice he turned away to follow the main-traveled road of Connecticut prejudice. His eyes were fixed lovingly upon the past, and his fondest dreams for his native commonwealth hovered about the ideal of a church-state which John Cotton had labored to establish and Increase Mather to preserve. It is with those capable theocrats of Massachusetts Bay, rather than with Thomas Hooker of Hartford, that he is to be associated. Two men could scarcely be more alike than Timothy Dwight and Increase Mather; their careers ran in similar lines; each was the unmitered pope of his generation, and each owed his extraordinary influence to the same sterling qualities. As ecclesiastical politicians they drew no line between religious and secular affairs, but were prompt with a hand in every affair of the commonwealth. They spoke and wrote with unquestioned authority. They regarded the minister as the responsible leader of society who must not suffer his flock to be led astray. The church was the guardian of morality, and the state was its secular arm. The true faith must not be put in jeopardy by unfaith. To Timothy Dwight infidelity and democracy went hand in hand, and to suffer the commonwealth to fall under the control of the godless meant the end of all morality and religion. To uphold the established order—of which he was a distinguished member—was for him the first of Christian duties. A stalwart Federalist, he was a good hater of all Jacobins. His detestation of Jefferson was virulent and he swallowed the nastiest tales about the great Virginian without a qualm, never doubting their authenticity. It was sometimes hinted that he was too much the aristocrat to feel the warmest sympathy for the unprosperous, and there seems to have been ground for the suspicion. The unprosperous were likely to be infected with Jeffersonian heresies, and as he watched them being drawn off to the York-state frontier, he rejoiced that their voting power was no longer to be feared. Such restless spirits, he pointed out, "are impatient of the restraints of law, religion, and morality; grumble about the taxes, by which Rulers, Ministers, and Schoolmasters are supported. . . . We have many troubles even now; but we should have many more, if this body of foresters had remained at home." [2] If the disaffected did not like the way the Congregational-Federalist party managed the good state of Connecticut, it were a godsend if they should remove beyond its boundaries.

But it is with the literary work of Timothy Dwight that we are more immediately concerned, and in all his abundant output, totaling fourteen volumes and perhaps as much more in manuscript, the same solid qualities are revealed. It is the occasional work of a man wanting humor, playfulness, grace, lacking subtlety and creative suggestiveness, but with a shrewd common sense, a great vigor, and a certain grandiose imagination. A sonorous declaimer, he dearly loved combat and the shock of marshaled argument. He went out of his way to invite majestic effects. In *The Conquest of Canaan* he described so many thunderstorms that Trumbull suggested he ought to furnish a lightning rod with the poem. Such a man could not move easily in narrow spaces. An epic was none too slight to contain his exuberant rhetoric. His ready versification, one often feels, runs like a water pipe with the faucet off; the words flow in an unbroken stream with never a pause to pick or choose. Yet even in his amazing copiousness there is vigor; a well-stocked mind is pouring out the gatherings of years. When he pauses to give advice—as he was fond of doing— his abundant sense is worth listening to; the homely wisdom of

[2] *Travels*, Vol. II, p. 458.

his talk to the farmers in the sixth part of *Greenfield Hill* is not unlike Franklin. As a satirist he belongs to the Churchill school; he is downright, abusive, often violent, quite lacking the lightness of touch and the easy gayety that runs so pleasantly through *M'Fingal*. His *Triumph of Infidelity* is solid old-fashioned pulpit-thumping. The spirit of toleration was withheld from him by his fairy godmother, and he knew no other way of dealing with those who persisted in disagreement after their mistakes had been pointed out, than the cudgel. In this tremendous poem he lays about him vigorously. On Hume and Voltaire and Priestley, and all their followers, his blows fall smartly. Bloody crowns ought to be plentiful, but—though he does not seem to know it—the blows fall on straw men and none proves mortal. On the whole one prefers him in the pastoral mood when he lays aside his ministerial gown, and *Greenfield Hill*, unless one excepts the *Travels in New England and New York*, remains his most attractive work. Yet even that is sadly in need of winnowing. A great college president Timothy Dwight may very well have been; he was worshiped by his admirers only this side idolatry; but a great thinker, a steadfast friend of truth in whatever garb it might appear, a generous kindly soul loving even publicans and sinners, regardful of others and forgetful of self, he assuredly was not.

2. "The Anarchiad"

Most of the political satire of the Wits was done in collaboration, and consists of occasional sketches contributed to newspapers—with explanatory comments and notes—dealing with matters of current interest. Of the major works thus produced, *The Anarchiad*, *The Echo*, and *The Political Greenhouse*, the first will suffice to reveal the political sympathies of the Hartford group. *The Anarchiad* is a mock epic designed to counteract the populistic tendencies of post-war times. It was published in *The New Haven Gazette* between October 26, 1786, and September 13, 1787. In 1861 it was resurrected from a long sleep by Luther G. Riggs, and re-issued with an introduction and notes. "This fearless satire," according to the editor, "is supposed to have exerted great and beneficial influence upon the public mind, and to have tended in no small degree to check the leaders of insubordination and infidel philosophy"; and it must be regarded as " a *national Poem*, battling nobly for the right universal, for the majesty of law, and for the

Federal government." The idea was got from a contemporary English screed entitled *The Rolliad*, one of the numerous political satires of which the late eighteenth century was so fond. Probably most of the members of the group had a hand in it, but the acrid quality of its comment owes more to Hopkins than to the others.

For such work the angular Connecticut physician was admirably fitted. The son of a Waterbury farmer, Dr. Lemuel Hopkins was the most picturesque member of the Hartford Wits, the most characteristically Yankee. Brought up at the plow-tail, he received nevertheless an excellent education, and because of a hereditary predisposition to consumption turned to the medical profession. After serving his apprenticeship at Wallingford he entered upon his practice at Litchfield in 1776. During the Revolution he served for a short time as a volunteer, but soon returned to his lancet and medicine case. In 1784 he removed to Hartford where he spent the remainder of his life. In person he was tall, lean, stooping, rawboned, with coarse features and large brilliant eyes. His uncouth appearance and eccentricity of manner made him a striking figure, and his caustic wit rendered him a redoubtable antagonist. As a physician he stood at the head of the Connecticut profession. He was one of the founders of the Medical Society of Connecticut, and as a frequent contributor to professional literature he exerted a wide influence on the current practice.

The eccentric doctor seems to have been as honest as he was outspoken. He was uncompromising in his warfare on all quacks, both medical and political. For a time as a young man he was a disciple of French infidel philosophy, but he cured his mental indisposition by a severe Biblical regimen, and having restored himself to the robust health of Calvinistic Christianity, he devoted himself to the work of curing others. He became in consequence a specialist in the treatment of the ravages caused by the *bacillus gallicus*. For every sort of humbug he had a hearty contempt, and any political nostrum not listed in the Federalistic materia medica he regarded as arrant quackery. He thought no better of old wives' remedies in government than in medicine, and when the Rhode Island legislature passed its paper-money act in 1785, and six months later Shays's Rebellion broke out, and mobs were besieging the legislature of New Hampshire, he proposed to speak plainly to the good people of Connecticut on the follies of popular delusions. This would seem to have been the origin of *The Anar-chiad*. It sprang from the indignation of Dr. Hopkins, when, to quote from the poem,

> In visions fair, the scenes of fate unroll,
> And Massachusetts opens on my soul.
> There Chaos, Anarch old, asserts his sway,
> And mobs in myriads blacken all the way.

The sardonic temper of Dr. Hopkins fitted him for virulent satire, and in this bitterest of the productions of the Wits, the reins were on the neck of the muse. Scarcely another New England satire reflects so sharply the class consciousness that underlay the bitter struggle between agrarianism and capitalism. It is a slash-ing attack upon agrarian economics and democratic liberalism, a versified echo of the anger of creditors who were fighting the measures of populistic legislatures. The staple of the satire is the wickedness of all paper-money issues, with the State of Rhode Island as the chief of agrarian sinners. About this main theme is gathered a miscellany of Federalist shibboleths—the godlessness of Shays and his crew, the seditious spirit of all who oppose the new Constitution, the demagoguery of democratic politicians—and the satire rises to a patriotic crescendo in declaiming against the folly of the democratic ideal. So tremendous a work, however, cannot be adequately described; the lines must speak for them-selves. The following bits may serve in lieu of the whole, the first of which is a comment on Rhode Island, the pariah of States:

> Hail! realm of rogues, renown'd for fraud and guile,
> All hail! ye knav'ries of yon little isle.
> There prowls the rascal, cloth'd with legal pow'r,
> To snare the orphan, and the poor devour;
> The crafty knave his creditor besets
> And advertising paper pays his debts; .
> Bankrupts their creditors with rage pursue,
> No stop, no mercy from the debtor crew.
> Arm'd with new tests, the licens'd villain bold,
> Presents his bills, and robs them of their gold;
> Their ears, though rogues and counterfeiters lose,
> No legal robber fears the gallows noose.
> Look through the State, the unhallow'd ground appears
> A pen of dragons, and a cave of bears;
> A nest of vipers, mix'd with adders foul;
> The screeching night-bird, and the greater owl:
> For now, unrighteousness, a deluge wide,

Pours round the land an overwhelming tide;
And dark injustice, wrapp'd in paper sheets,
Rolls a dread torrent through the wasted streets;
While net of law th' unwary fry draws in
To damning deeds, and scarce they know they sin.
New paper struck, new tests, new tenders made,
Insult mankind, and help the thriving trade.
Each weekly print new lists of cheats proclaims,
Proud to enroll their knav'ries and their names;
The wiser race, the snares of law to shun,
Like Lot from Sodom, from Rhode Island run. . . .[3]

Nor less abhorr'd, the certain woe that waits
The giddy rage of democratic States,
Whose pop'lar breath, high-blown in restless tide,
No laws can temper, and no reason guide:
An equal sway, their mind indignant spurns;
To wanton sway, the bliss of freedom turns;
Led by wild demagogues, the factious crowd,
Mean, fierce, imperious, insolent and loud,
Nor fame, nor wealth, nor power, nor system draws—
They see no object, and perceive no cause;
But feel, by turns, in one disastrous hour,
Th' extremes of license, and th' extremes of power. . . .[(]

Will this vain scheme bid restless factions cease,
Check foreign wars, or fix internal peace?
Call public credit from her grave to rise,
Or gain in grandeur what they lose in size? . . .
But know, ye favor'd race, one potent head
Must rule your States, and strike your foes with dread.
The finance regulate, the trade control,
Live through the empire, and accord the whole.
Ere death invades, the night's deep curtain falls,
Through ruin'd realms the voice of UNION calls; . . .
On you she calls! attend the warning cry;
YE LIVE UNITED, OR DIVIDED DIE! [4]

But chief the race allured by fleeting fame,
Who seek on earth the politicians name;
Auspicious race! whom folly joys to bless,
And wealth and honor crown with glad success;
Formed, like balloons, by emptiness to rise
On pop'lar gales, to waft them through the skies . . .
See, from the shades, on tiny pinions swell
And rise, the young DEMOCRACY of *hell!*
Before their face the *powers of Congress* fade,
And *public credit* sinks, an empty shade;

[3] Number III.   [4] Number X.